Cancún & the Yucatán
For Dummies, 2nd

D0595215

0 _____ 1/8 mi
0 ___ .125 km   (N)

Well of Sacrifice
Snack bar and toilets *(Sacrificial Cenote)*

Sacred Way
(Sacbé)

Main Ball Court

NORTH TEMPLE   **"NEW" CHICHÉN**

Parking
Visitor Center   Temple of Jaguars
Main Tourist   Temple of the Skulls
Entrance   *(Tzompantli)*
Platform of the Eagles   Platform of Venus   Temple of the Warriors

Pyramid of Kukulkán   Ball Court
(El Castillo)

Councillor's House   Group of the
Thousand Columns

Tomb of the High Priest   Northeast
(Tumba del Gran Sacerdote)   Colonnade
Ball Court   Ball Court
Secondary
Temple of the   Tourist
Grinding Stones   Entrance   Steambath 2

Temple of the Deer

Little Holes   Ball Court   The Market   180
(Chichan-Chob)   Cenote   Hotel Mayaland
Xtoloc

The Observatory   **"OLD" CHICHÉN**
(El Caracol)

Steambath 1   Temple of Obscure Writing
Temple of the Sculptured Panels   *(Akab Dzib)*

Edifice of the Nuns   Hacienda
(Edificio de las Monjas)   Chichén

Church

Mileage Chart: Distances in the Yucatán[1]

	Akumal	Cancún	Chichén-Itzá	Cobá	Cozumel[2]	Isla Mujeres[2]	Playa del Carmen	Puerto Morelos	Puerto Aventuras	Tulum	Xcaret	Xel-ha	Xpu-ha
Akumal	*												
Cancún	105km/65mi	*											
Chichén-Itzá	175km/109mi (via Cobá)	178km/110mi	*										
Cobá	70km/44mi	143km/89mi (via Nuevo Xcán)	110km/68mi	*									
Cozumel[2]	55km/34mi	72km/45mi	238km/148mi	123km/76mi	*								
Isla Mujeres[2]	115km/71mi	5km/3mi	188km/117mi	153km/95mi (via Nuevo Xcán)	58km/36mi	*							
Playa del Carmen	37km/23mi	68km/42mi	220km/136mi	105km/65mi	18km/11mi	78km/48mi	*						
Puerto Morelos	69km/43mi	36km/22mi	194km/120mi	137km/85mi	30km/19mi	46km/29mi	32km/20mi	*					
Puerto Aventuras	7km/4mi	87km/54mi	245km/152mi	88km/55mi	37km/23mi	97km/60mi	25km/16mi	58km/36mi	*				
Tulum	26km/16mi	131km/81mi	154km/95mi (via Cobá)	44km/27mi	81km/50mi	141km/87mi	63km/39mi	95km/59mi	44km/27mi	*			
Xcaret	33km/21mi	74km/46mi	225km/140mi	101km/63mi	24km/15mi	84km/52mi	6km/3.7mi	38km/24mi	22km/14mi	59km/37mi	*		
Xel-ha	17km/11mi	122km/76mi (via Cobá)	162km/100mi (via Cobá)	51km/32mi	72km/45mi	132km/82mi	54km/33mi	87km/54mi	35km/22mi	9km/5.6mi	50km/31mi	*	
Xpu-ha	4km/2.5mi	101km/63mi	179km/111mi (via Cobá)	72km/45mi	51km/32mi	106km/66mi	33km/21mi	65km/40mi	3km/1.9mi	30km/19mi	18km/11mi	21km/13mi	*

[1] Distances given in kilometers/miles
[2] Both Cozumel and Isla Mujeres are islands; travel by boat is required.

Plan your trip
with
For Dummies

Covering the most popular destinations in North America and Europe, *For Dummies* travel guides are the ultimate user-friendly trip planners. Available wherever books are sold or go to www.dummies.com

And book it with
our online partner,
Frommers.com

- ✔ Book airfare, hotels and packages
- ✔ Find the hottest deals
- ✔ Get breaking travel news
- ✔ Enter to win vacations
- ✔ Share trip photos and stories
- ✔ And much more

Frommers.com, rated the
#1 Travel Web Site by PC Magazine

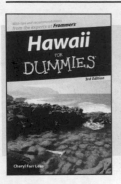

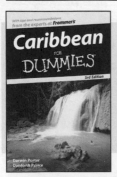

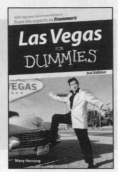
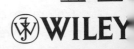

Cancún & the Yucatán

FOR

DUMMIES®

2ND EDITION

by Lynne Bairstow and David Baird

WILEY

Wiley Publishing, Inc.

Cancún & the Yucatán For Dummies® 2nd Edition
Published by
Wiley Publishing, Inc.
111 River St.
Hoboken, NJ 07030-5774
www.wiley.com

WILEY

About the Authors

For **Lynne Bairstow** (who wrote Chapters 1 through 12, 16 through 18, and the Appendix), Mexico has become more home to her than her native United States. After exploring the country and living in Puerto Vallarta for most of the past 15 years, she has developed a true love of Mexico and its complex, colorful culture. Her local friends now claim she has *patas saladas* — a term translated as "salty feet," meaning she has become a true Vallarta local. Her travel articles on Mexico have been published in *The New York Times, San Francisco Chronicle, Los Angeles Times, Private Air, Luxury Living,* and *Alaska Airlines Magazine.* In 2000, Lynne was awarded the Pluma de Plata, an honor granted by the Mexican Government to foreign writers, for her work with the Frommer's guide to Mexico.

David Baird (who wrote Chapters 13, 14, and 15) is a writer, editor, and translator who feels uncomfortable writing about himself in the third person (too much like writing his own obituary). Now based in Austin, Texas, he spent years living in various parts of Mexico, Brazil, Peru, and Puerto Rico. But, whenever possible, he manages to get back to the turquoise-blue waters of the Yucatán because he thinks he looks good in that color, and because he's excessively fond of the local cooking.

Dedication

This book is dedicated to my many friends in Mexico who, through sharing their insights, anecdotes, knowledge, and explorations of Mexico, have shared their love of this country. In particular, Ricardo, Carlos, Claudia, and Alejandra have shared with me and have shown me what a magical place Mexico is, and how much more I have to discover and enjoy.

— *Lynne Bairstow*

To my brother John, whose sheer willpower overcame my objections and forced me to take that vacation many, many years ago that first brought me to these shores.

— *David Baird*

Authors' Acknowledgments

Many thanks to the people who helped me gather the information, tips, and treasures that have made their way into this book. I am especially grateful for the assistance of Alejandra Macedo, my friend and research assistant whose tireless work ensured that the information in this book is correct, and that no grain of sand was left unturned in seeking out the fun there is to have in Cancún and Isla Mujeres.

— *Lynne Bairstow*

I would like to acknowledge my indebtedness to the irrepressible Desiré Sanromán, a Cozumeleña who knows her island and befriended me for reasons that are not quite clear (sympathy? pity? concern for the readers I might mislead?). I would also thank that most capable of guides, Claudia Hurtado Valenzuela, who opened the doors of the Riviera Maya to me, and whose views on all matters touristic were well worth hearing.

— *David Baird*

Publisher's Acknowledgments

We're proud of this book; please send us your comments through our Dummies online registration form located at www.dummies.com/register/.

Some of the people who helped bring this book to market include the following:

Editorial

Editors: Tere Stouffer, Marc Nadeau

(Previous edition: Kelly Ewing, Kelly Regan)

Cartographers: Roberta Stockwell, Tim Lohnes

Editorial Manager: Michelle Hacker

Editorial Supervisor: Michelle Hacker

Editorial Assistant: Melissa Bennett

Senior Photo Editor: Richard Fox

Cover Photos: © Cosmo Condina/ Getty Images (front cover), © AGE Fotostock/SuperStock, Inc. (back cover)

Cartoons: Rich Tennant (www.the5thwave.com)

Composition Services

Project Coordinator: Michael Kruzil

Layout and Graphics: Carl Byers, Denny Hager, Joyce Haughey, Barry Offringa, Lynsey Osborn, Heather Ryan

Proofreaders: Laura Albert, David Faust, Leeann Harney, Jessica Kramer, Carl William Pierce, TECHBOOKS Production Services

Indexer: TECHBOOKS Production Services

Publishing and Editorial for Consumer Dummies

Diane Graves Steele, Vice President and Publisher, Consumer Dummies

Joyce Pepple, Acquisitions Director, Consumer Dummies

Kristin A. Cocks, Product Development Director, Consumer Dummies

Michael Spring, Vice President and Publisher, Travel

Kelly Regan, Editorial Director, Travel

Publishing for Technology Dummies

Andy Cummings, Vice President and Publisher, Dummies Technology/General User

Composition Services

Gerry Fahey, Vice President of Production Services

Debbie Stailey, Director of Composition Services

Contents at a Glance

Maps at a Glance

Table of Contents

Part IV: Traveling Around Isla Mujeres and Cozumel 163

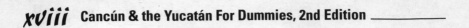

Introduction

*M*exico's Yucatán peninsula not only offers travelers some of the best beaches in the world, but also presents a rich, 1,000-year-old culture and amazing natural wonders to explore. Whether it's the ancient Mayan pyramids or the Caribbean reef off Cancún and Cozumel, this spectacular coastline is a virtual playground for travelers. In addition to the many natural attractions, the Yucatán's beach resorts have added golf, tennis, diving, and abundant watersports to their many lures. But can the rest of your knowledge about this area fit inside a mango seed? For many people, Mexico is simultaneously familiar and mysterious, and some opinions of this land are influenced by inaccurate or outdated stereotypes.

How do you sift through the destination choices — and then all the hotel options — without throwing in the beach towel in a daze of confusion? How do you plan a vacation that's perfect for you — not one that simply follows the recommendations of a friend or travel agent? You've come to the right place. This guide rescues you from both information overload and detail deficit — those annoying syndromes that afflict far too many would-be travelers. We give you enough specifics to help you figure out and plan the type of trip you want and steer clear of the type of trip you don't want.

Sure, plenty of other guidebooks cover Mexico and the beach resorts of its popular Yucatán peninsula, but many of them may as well be encyclopedias: They include practically everything you can possibly see and do. When the time comes to decide upon accommodations, attractions, activities, and meals, you have a tough time finding the best options because they're buried in with other mediocre to not-so-hot suggestions.

Cancún & the Yucatán For Dummies, 2nd Edition, is a whole new enchilada. In the following pages, we streamline the options, focusing on the high points (and warning you about the low points) of each vacation spot. Because this book covers a specific area and the most traveled-to region among Mexico's beach resorts, it's able to focus on the most popular (and most exciting) destinations. With the straightforward tips we offer — how to get there, what to expect when you arrive, where to stay, where to eat, and where to have big fun — arranging your dream vacation couldn't be easier.

About This Book

You can use this book in three ways:

- ✔ **As a trip planner:** Whether you've already decided on Cancún or are still considering your options along the Riviera Maya, this book helps you zero in on the ideal beach resort for you. It guides you through all the necessary steps of making your travel arrangements, from finding the cheapest airfare and considering travel insurance to figuring out a budget and packing like a pro. Chapters are self-contained, so you don't have to read them in order. Just flip to the chapters as you need them.

- ✔ **As a beach-resort guide:** Pack this book along with your sunscreen — it will come in just as handy while you're away. Turn to the appropriate destination chapters whenever you need to find the best beaches, a good place to eat, a worthwhile boat cruise, a challenging golf course, the lowdown on a hot nightspot, or tips on any other diversions.

- ✔ **For an enjoyable overview:** If you want a feel for Cancún and the other popular beach resorts on Mexico's Yucatán peninsula, read this book from start to finish to get a taste of all the highlights.

 Travel information is subject to change at any time — call ahead for confirmation when making your travel plans. Your safety is important to us (and to the publisher), so we encourage you to stay alert and be aware of your surroundings. Keep a close eye on cameras, purses, and wallets — all favorite targets of thieves and pickpockets.

Conventions Used in This Book

Two of us collaborated on this book, but we each cover different destinations in the Yucatán. That's why although we call ourselves "we" in this introduction, in each chapter the "we" turns into "I" — so you get the benefit of our individual opinions. (To find out who wrote which chapters, see our "About the Author" information at the front of the book.)

In this book, we use the Mexican method for providing street addresses. Using this style, the building number comes after the street name, not before it. For example, if a hotel has a building number of 22 and is located on *Calle Atocha* (Atocha Street), the address is written as Calle Atocha 22. Likewise, in many towns, you often come across an address in which the building has no number. In these cases, the address is written Calle Atocha s/n, where s/n stands for *sin número* (without number).

In this book, we include reviews of our favorite hotels and restaurants, as well as information about the best attractions within the Yucatán. As we describe each listing, we use abbreviations for commonly accepted credit cards. Here's what those abbreviations stand for:

AE (American Express)

DC (Diners Club)

DISC (Discover Card)

MC (MasterCard)

V (Visa)

We also include some general pricing information to help you as you decide where to unpack your bags or where to dine on the local cuisine. We use a system of dollar signs (in U.S. dollars) to show a range of costs so that you can make quick comparisons.

Prices in this book are quoted only in U.S. dollars, because most hotels in Mexico quote prices in U.S. dollars. So, although the value of the peso continues to fluctuate, such currency fluctuations are unlikely to affect the hotel rates.

Unless we say otherwise, the lodging rates given are for two people spending one night in a standard double room. At the end of each listing, we give prices for both high season — the most popular travel time that runs roughly from Christmas to Easter — and the generally lower-priced summer season (or low season). At the top of the listing, the dollar sign pricing system indicates the high-season rates. Some hotel rates are much higher than others no matter what time of year it is. Don't be too quick to skip an accommodation that seems out of your price range, though. Some rates include breakfast, both breakfast and dinner, or even three meals per day. Other resorts are *all-inclusive,* which means that after you pay for your room, you never have to dip into your pocket again for meals, beverages, tips, taxes, most activities, or transportation to and from the airport. So, although a price tag may seem sky-high at first, you may actually find it affordable upon second glance. The dining rates are for main courses only.

Check out the following table to decipher the dollar signs:

Cost	Hotel	Restaurant
$	Less than $75	Less than $15
$$	$76–$125	$16–$30
$$$	$126–$175	$31–$50
$$$$	$176–$250	$51 and up
$$$$$	More than $250 per night	

Foolish Assumptions

As we wrote this book, we made some assumptions about you and what your needs may be as a traveler. Here's what we assumed about you:

✔ You may be an inexperienced traveler looking for guidance when determining whether to take a trip to Cancún (or one of the other beach resorts of the Yucatán) and how to plan for it.

✔ You may be an experienced traveler who hasn't had much time to explore the Yucatán or its beaches and wants expert advice when you finally do get a chance to enjoy some time in the sun.

✔ You're not looking for a book that provides all the information available about Mexico or that lists every hotel, restaurant, or attraction available to you. Instead, you're looking for a book that focuses on the places that offer the best or most unique experiences in the beach resorts of the Yucatán.

How This Book Is Organized

We have divided this book into six parts. The chapters within each part cover specific subjects in detail. Skip around as much as you like. You don't have to read this book in any particular order. In fact, think of these pages as a buffet: You can consume whatever you want — and no one cares if you eat the flan for dessert before you have the enchiladas.

For each beach resort, we include a section at the end of each chapter called "Fast Facts." These sections give you handy information that you may need when traveling in Mexico, including phone numbers and addresses to use in an emergency, area hospitals and pharmacies, names of local newspapers and magazines, locations for maps, and more.

Part 1: Introducing Cancún and the Yucatán

In this part, we compare and contrast the Yucatán's most popular beach resorts so that you can decide which place best suits your tastes and needs. Sure, they all have gorgeous beaches, but that's where the similarities end. To help you plan a vacation that's tailored to your preferences, this part guides you through the process of figuring out which resort or resorts are best for you.

We also give you a brief overview of the area's history, local customs, cuisines, language, and fiestas and celebrations. We take you through the best — and worst — times of year to travel and explain the differences between high season and low season. We also tell you about special holidays that may help you decide when to visit this part of Mexico.

Part II: Planning Your Trip to Cancún and the Yucatán

This part is where we lay out everything you need to make all the arrangements for your trip. We start by helping you manage your money, explaining how to estimate the total cost of your vacation and how to stay within your budget. We help you decide whether to use a travel agent, a packager, or the Internet. We offer advice on finding the best airfare — and airline — for your destination. We also offer special trip-planning advice for families, singles, gay and lesbian travelers, seniors, and travelers who are physically challenged. Finally, we take you through all the ins and outs of other vacation essentials, from getting a passport and considering travel insurance to staying safe and packing like a pro.

Part III: Discovering Cancún

Welcome to Mexico's most popular beach resort. This area is a great destination for first-time travelers to Mexico. Why? Because it has all the comforts of home (familiar restaurant and hotel chains along with great shopping), plus easy access to diverse cultural and geographical activities (excursions to the ancient ruins of Tulum, covered in Chapter 15), world-class scuba diving, and plenty of Mexican fiestas. We provide all the details for getting to, eating at, staying in, and playing at all of Cancún's hot spots.

Part IV: Traveling Around Isla Mujeres and Cozumel

Staying on a tropical island is a dream for many, and these two island getaways, not far from Cancún, offer a distinctive, relaxed vacation experience. Although Isla Mujeres is actually an older tourist town than its sister across the channel, it's a decidedly laid-back anecdote to the nonstop activity of Cancún. Cozumel's calling card has always been its myriad water activities, mostly centered around the famous reef that outlines the southwest coast. If you're looking for a diver's paradise, you can stop and get off the boat at Cozumel! Cozumel is increasingly becoming one of cruisings' most popular ports-of-call.

Part V: Exploring the Yucatán

This region has more to it than the well-known names of Cancún and Cozumel. Further south along the mainland from Cancún, the Riviera Maya provides a stunning stretch of pristine beaches, unique towns, and mega-resorts down to Tulum, in the south. Check out the sizzling hot (as in popular!) town of Playa del Carmen, visit one of the regions' ecoparks, or see some nearby ancient ruins. The area offers plenty for everyone. In this part, we cover all the information you need to travel to and around these areas.

Part VI: The Part of Tens

Every *For Dummies* book has a Part of Tens. In this part, we tell you how to avoid looking like a tourist, take a look at the ten most common myths about Mexico, and describe ten of our favorite regional dishes.

Quick Concierge appendix

We also include a Quick Concierge appendix, which contains lots of handy information you may need when traveling in Mexico's Yucatán, like phone numbers and addresses of emergency personnel or area hospitals and pharmacies, contact information for baby sitters, lists of local newspapers and magazines, protocol for sending mail or finding taxis, and more. Also included in this appendix is a list of useful toll-free numbers and Web sites, as well as a guide to other sources of information. It's printed on yellow paper near the back of this book; check it out when searching for answers to lots of little questions that may come up as you travel.

Icons Used in This Book

Throughout this book, helpful icons highlight particularly useful information. Here's a look at what each symbol means:

 Keep an eye out for the Bargain Alert icon as you look for money-saving tips and great deals.

 Watch for the Heads Up icon to identify annoying or potentially dangerous situations such as tourist traps, unsafe neighborhoods, budgetary rip-offs, and other things to avoid.

 Look to the Kid Friendly icon for attractions, hotels, restaurants, and activities that are particularly hospitable to children or people traveling with kids.

 The Tip icon alerts you to practical advice and hints to make your trip run more smoothly.

 Note the Viva Mexico icon for food, places, or experiences that offer a true taste of the spirit of Mexico.

Where to Go from Here

Nothing quite compares to a beach vacation — whether you spend it lazing in the sun or pursuing active, water-bound activities — and it's even better when planned with the right advice and insider tips. Whether you're a veteran traveler or new to the game, *Cancún & the Yucatán For Dummies,* 2nd Edition, helps you put together just the kind of trip you have in mind. So, start turning these pages, and before you know it, you'll feel those balmy beach breezes on your face!

Part I
Introducing Cancún and the Yucatán

The 5th Wave   By Rich Tennant

"Of all the stuff we came back from Mexico with,
I think these adobe bathrobes were the least
well thought out."

In this part . . .

*P*lanning a trip can be daunting — so we're here to give you a sense of the place you're visiting. Mexico's Yucatán is a vast part of a varied country with a bevy of unique beach resorts — plus some amazing archeological sites. In Chapter 1, we introduce you to the highlights of the most popular resorts, restaurants, beaches, shopping areas, and other hot spots. In Chapter 2, we dig a little deeper into the area, giving you the lowdown on the rich history and architecture of Cancún and the Yucatán, plus information about local cuisine, folklore, and language. Chapter 3 helps you choose the destination that best matches your idea of the perfect seaside getaway, while Chapter 4 helps you decide when to go, with special information on local festivals that you shouldn't miss.

Chapter 1

Discovering the Best of Cancún and the Yucatán

In This Chapter

▶ Scoping out Cancún and the Yucatán's stellar beaches

▶ Discovering the top places to stay

▶ Uncovering the best restaurants and nightlife

▶ Exploring the Yucatán's most unforgettable places and experiences

The Yucatán may very well be the beach vacation destination of your dreams. All those glossy images of long stretches of pure, powdery, white-sand beaches and tranquil turquoise waters do exist — and they're found along the eastern coast of Mexico's Yucatán Peninsula.

The Yucatán Peninsula welcomes more visitors than any other part of Mexico. Its tremendous variety attracts every kind of traveler with an unequaled mix of sophisticated resorts, rustic inns, ancient Maya culture, exquisite beaches, and exhilarating adventures.

Between the two of us, we've logged thousands of miles crisscrossing the peninsula, and these are our personal favorites — the best places to go, the best restaurants, the best hotels, and must-see, one-of-a-kind experiences.

The Best Beach Vacations

Cancún and the Yucatán have a multitude of stunning beaches — considered the best in Mexico. Known for powdery white sand and crystal-clear turquoise waters, these settings are what make great vacations. The following are our favorite beach getaways:

✔ **Cancún:** Essentially one long ribbon of white sand bordering aquamarine water, Cancún has one of Mexico's most beautifully situated beaches. If you want tropical drinks brought to you while you lounge in the sand, this is the place for you. Although Cancún has a reputation as a bustling, modern megaresort, it's also a great place for exploring Caribbean reefs, tranquil lagoons, and the surrounding jungle. The most tranquil waters and beaches on Cancún Island are those at the northern tip, facing the Bahía de Mujeres. See Chapter 11.

✔ **Isla Mujeres:** If laid-back is what you're after, this idyllic island offers peaceful, small-town beach life at its best. Most accommodations are smaller, inexpensive inns, with a few unique, luxurious places tossed in. Bike — or take a golf cart — around the island to explore rocky coves and sandy beaches, or focus your tanning efforts on the wide beachfront of Playa Norte. Here you'll find calm waters and *palapa* (thatched roof) restaurants, where you can have fresh-caught fish for lunch. You're close to great diving and snorkeling just offshore, as well as to Isla Contoy National Park, which features great bird life and its own dramatic, uninhabited beach. If all that tranquillity starts to get to you, you're only a ferry ride away from the action in Cancún. See Chapter 12.

✔ **Cozumel:** It may not have lots of big, sandy beaches, but Cozumel has something the mainland doesn't: the calm, waveless waters of the sheltered western shore. The sea is so calm and full of marine life that it's like swimming in an aquarium. See Chapter 13.

✔ **Playa del Carmen:** This is one of our absolute favorite Mexican beach vacations. Stylish and hip, Playa del Carmen offers a beautiful beach and an eclectic assortment of small hotels, inns, and cabañas. The social scene is focused on the beach by day and the pedestrian-only Quinta Avenida (5th Avenue) by night, with its fun assortment of restaurants, clubs, sidewalk cafes, and shops. You're also close to the coast's major attractions, including nature parks, ruins, and *cenotes* (sinkholes or natural wells). Cozumel Island is just a quick ferry trip away. Enjoy it while it's a manageable size. See Chapter 14.

✔ **Tulum:** Fronting some of the best beaches on the entire coast, Tulum's small *palapa* hotels offer guests a little slice of paradise far from crowds and megaresorts. The bustling town lies inland; at the coast, things are quiet and will remain so because all these hotels are small and must generate their own electricity. If you can pull yourself away from the beach, ruins and a vast nature preserve are nearby. See Chapter 15.

The Best Luxury Resorts

If money is no object, Cancún and the southern coast of the Yucatán have no shortage of places to park yourself in style. There's a string of terrific upscale hotels in Cancún's hotel zone, with a growing array of luxury resorts as you head south along the Yucatán's Riviera Maya.

As an added bonus, most of the Yucatán's resorts have recently added brand-new spas that raise the art of relaxation and pampering to a new level. What could be better than a massage on the beach? (Maybe a massage on the beach with a margarita, too?)

The following are a few of our favorite luxury resorts:

- **Le Méridien Cancún Resort & Spa:** Although there are grander hotels in Cancún, we prefer this resort, as it's the most intimate of the luxury hotels, with an understated sense of highly personalized service. Most notable is its 4,546 square-meter (15,000 square-foot) Spa del Mar. See Chapter 10.

- **Fiesta Americana Grand Aqua:** Because this resort was just opening at press time, we can't say we've had the experience of staying here, but the exquisite design and detailed amenities blew us away — it's certain to become our top pick for luxury that indulges the senses without overwhelming them. Clean design and a color scheme that mirrors the aquamarine and white beach landscape are inherently relaxing. Add a superb spa, dazzling selection of restaurants, and a chill music scene in the evenings around the pool, and the mood is set for a more modern take on luxury. See Chapter 10.

- **Ikal del Mar:** Small, secluded, and private, Ikal del Mar offers extraordinary personal service and spa treatments. Rooms spread out through the jungle, and there's a beautiful seaside pool and restaurant. See Chapter 14.

- **Maroma:** You can't ask for a better setting for a resort than this beautiful stretch of Caribbean coast with palm trees and manicured gardens. You begin to relax before you even take the first sip of your welcome cocktail. Service is very attentive, and the rooms are large and luxurious. See Chapter 14.

- **Paraíso de la Bonita:** Operated by InterContinental Hotels, this resort has a super-equipped spa based on the elaborate system of thalassotherapy. The guest rooms are elaborate creations, and the hotel provides all kinds of service. It has three pools and an immaculately kept beach. See Chapter 14.

The Best Good-Value Accommodations

Being on a budget in the Yucatán doesn't mean you have to sacrifice style — or the perfect beach vacation. There are plenty of well-priced options, and here are our favorites:

- **Cancún INN Suites El Patio:** This European-style inn welcomes many guests for repeat or long-term stays. Each room is tastefully decorated, and all surround a plant-filled courtyard. Special packages combine Spanish lessons and accommodations. It's an oasis of cultured hospitality in one of Mexico's most commercial beach resorts. See Chapter 10.

- **Rey del Caribe Hotel:** Not only will you find exceptional value here, but you'll also support a true ecological hotel, which uses environmentally sensitive practices from collecting rainwater to composting. Sunny rooms are surrounded by lush jungle landscaping — and all in the heart of downtown Cancún! See Chapter 10.

✔ **Treetops:** An economical, quiet hotel steps from both the beach and Avenida 5, Treetops could easily get by on its location alone. But the owners have gone out of their way to create a distinctive lodging with plenty of amenities. The hotel has its very own *cenote* (natural well) and piece of shady jungle, making it a lovely place to relax after a trying day of strolling the beach and wandering the village streets. See Chapter 14.

✔ **Villa Catarina Rooms & Cabañas:** These stylishly rustic rooms nestle in a garden of tall palms, flowering trees, and singing birds. Just a block from the wide beach and tranquil Caribbean, it's a short walk from the action of Avenida 5. See Chapter 14.

The Most Unique Places to Get Away from It All

The Yucatán offers a multitude of unique places to escape the world and relax in seaside splendor. While some of the specific hotels in this section offer more activity than others, all transport you to a truly "away" state of mind:

✔ **Isla Mujeres:** If there's one island in Mexico that guarantees a respite from stress, it's Isla Mujeres. You'll find an ample selection of hotels and restaurants, and they're as laid-back as their patrons. Here life moves along in pure *mañana* mode. Visitors stretch out and doze beneath shady palms or languidly stroll about. For many, the best part about this getaway is that it's comfortably close to Cancún's international airport, as well as shopping and dining, should you choose to reconnect. See Chapter 12.

✔ **Casa de los Sueños Resort & Spa Zenter:** This intimate inn combines the sense of being at a private villa with the ideal complements of a holistic spa, daily yoga classes, and delectable fusion cuisine served from the onsite restaurant. The resort's private pier is an ideal launch for snorkeling, with Garrafon Reef just offshore. See Chapter 12.

✔ **Na Balam:** One of Isla's older hotels, it has made a name for itself as a favored center of yoga retreats and workshops. Set on a broad stretch of beach, this unique inn allows you to indulge in a daily offering of yoga, Tai Chi, or meditation, making it an ideal place for a change in attitude. Its recommended restaurant offers healthful cuisine with many vegetarian options. See Chapter 12.

✔ **The Yucatán's Riviera Maya:** Away from the busy resort of Cancún, a string of quiet getaways, including Capitán Lafitte, KaiLuum, Paamul, Punta Bete, and a portion of Xpu-ha, offer tranquillity on beautiful beaches at low prices. See Chapter 14.

✔ **Hotel Jungla Caribe:** In a town filled with exceptional inns, this one's a standout. The eclectic décor combines neoclassical details with a decidedly tropical touch. The rooms and suites surround a stylish courtyard, restaurant, and pool. You couldn't be better located — 1 block from the beach, with an entrance on happening Avenida 5. See Chapter 14.

✔ **Deseo Hotel + Lounge:** Perhaps it should be Hotel = Lounge. That may be an overstatement, but the lounge is at the center of everything, making Deseo the perfect fit if you're an outgoing type who is into an alternative lodging experience. Although it may be too lively for some looking to truly get away from it all, for others, the scene here is an ideal departure from everyday life. See Chapter 14.

✔ **Tulum:** Near the Tulum ruins, about two dozen beachside *palapa* inns offer some of the most peaceful getaways in the country. This stretch just may offer the best sandy beaches on the entire coast. Life here among the birds and coconut palms is decidedly unhurried. See Chapter 15.

The Best Restaurants

Best doesn't necessarily mean most luxurious. Although some of the restaurants listed in this section are fancy affairs, others are simple places to get fine, authentic Yucatecan cuisine:

✔ **Aïoli:** Simply exquisite French and Mediterranean gourmet specialties served in a warm and cozy country French setting, at the hotel Le Méridien. For quality and exceptional service, it's Cancún's best value in fine dining. See Chapter 10.

✔ **La Dolce Vita:** A longtime favorite, La Dolce Vita remains untouched by newer arrivals. It continues to draw diners with such blissful dishes as green tagliolini with lobster medallions, veal with morels, and fresh salmon with cream sauce, all served (at night) to the sound of live jazz music. See Chapter 10.

✔ **Labná:** A showcase of authentic Yucatecan cuisine and music, in downtown Cancún, this is the place to sample regional specialties such as pork *pibil, papadzules,* and *poc chuc.* See Chapter 10.

✔ **Zazil Ha:** It doesn't get more relaxed and casual than Zazil Ha, with its sandy floor beneath thatched *palapas* and palms. This is the place for island atmosphere and well-prepared food. Along with its signature seafood and Caribbean cuisine, this restaurant continues to prove that vegetarian cuisine can be both artfully and tastefully prepared. It also offers special menus for those participating in yoga retreats on the island. See Chapter 12.

✔ **Cabaña del Pescador (Lobster House):** If you want an ideally seasoned, succulent lobster dinner, Cabaña del Pescador (Lobster House) is the place. If you want anything else, you're out of luck — lobster dinner, expertly prepared, is all it serves. When you've achieved perfection, why bother with anything else? See Chapter 13.

✔ **Prima:** The Italian food here is fresh, fresh, fresh — from the hydroponically grown vegetables to the pasta and garlic bread. And it's all prepared after you walk in, most of it by owner Albert Domínguez, who concocts unforgettable shrimp fettuccine with pesto, crab ravioli with cream sauce, and crisp house salad in a chilled bowl. See Chapter 13.

✔ **Media Luna:** The inviting atmosphere of this sidewalk cafe on Avenida 5 is enough to lure you in. The expertly executed and innovative menu, together with great prices, makes it one of the top choices on the Caribbean coast. See Chapter 14.

✔ **Yaxché:** No restaurant in the Yucatán explores the region's culinary traditions and use of local ingredients more than this one. Its menu presents several pleasant surprises and is a welcome relief from the standard offerings of most Yucatecan restaurants. See Chapter 14.

The Best Activities and Attractions

With the ocean as tempting as it is off the Yucatán coast, you're certain to find multiple ways to enjoy it above and below the surface. On dry land, you can also find plenty of ways to fill your days. Here are our favorite things to do:

✔ **Scuba diving in Cozumel and along the Yucatán's Caribbean coast:** The coral reefs off the island are among the top five dive spots in the world and constitute Mexico's premier diving destination. The Yucatán's coastal reef, part of the second-largest reef system in the world, affords excellent diving all along the coast. Especially beautiful is the Chinchorro Reef, lying 20 miles offshore from Majahual or Xcalak. Diving from Isla Mujeres is also quite spectacular. See Chapters 12 and 13.

✔ **Snorkeling:** Even if you're not usually the sporting type, you don't want to miss the chance to try snorkeling the same reef system so highly acclaimed by divers. The waters offshore are so clear that snorkelers are guaranteed to see clouds of tropical fish in every color of the rainbow, and possibly even a turtle or two. You can see a stunningly beautiful underwater world. One of the best places is El Garrafon Park in Isla Mujeres. See Chapters 11, 12, and 13.

✔ *Cenote* **diving on the Yucatán Mainland:** Dive into the clear depths of the Yucatán's *cenotes* (natural wells) for an interesting twist on underwater exploration. The Maya considered the *cenotes* sacred — and their vivid colors seem otherworldly indeed. Most are located between Playa del Carmen and Tulum, and dive shops in these areas regularly run trips for experienced divers. For recommended dive shops, see Chapters 13 and 14.

✔ **Fly-fishing off the Punta Allen and Majahual Peninsulas:** Serious anglers enjoy the challenge of fly-fishing the saltwater flats and lagoons on the protected sides of these peninsulas. See Chapter 14.

✔ **Birding:** The Yucatán Peninsula is an ornithological paradise, with hundreds of species awaiting the birder's gaze and list. One very special place is Isla Contoy, with more than 70 species of birds as well as a host of marine and animal life. See Chapter 12.

✔ **Getting a bird's-eye view:** The new Panoramic Tower is the best way to get the lay of the island and Cancún. The gentle ride rotates at the top to give you the perfect 360-degee perspective. See Chapter 12.

The Best Archaeological Sites

In addition to beautiful beaches, the Yucatán also offers a spectacular glance into this region's rich history through its various architectural sites and ruins. These are our top picks for a day-trip in the Yucatán:

✔ **Tulum:** Some dismiss Tulum as less important than other ruins in the Yucatán Peninsula, but this seaside Maya fortress is still inspiring. The sight of its crumbling stone walls against the stark contrast of the clear turquoise ocean just beyond is extraordinary. See Chapter 15.

✔ **Chichén Itzá:** Stand beside the giant serpent head at the foot of the El Castillo pyramid and marvel at the architects and astronomers who positioned the building so precisely that shadow and sunlight form a serpent's body slithering from peak to the earth at each equinox (Mar 21 and Sept 21). See Chapter 15.

✔ **Ek Balam:** In recent years, this has been the site of the most astounding archeological discoveries in Mexico. Ek Balam's main pyramid is taller than Chichén Itzá's, and it holds a sacred doorway bordered with elaborate stucco figures of priests and kings and rich iconography. See Chapter 15.

The Best Shopping

Beyond the ubiquitous T-shirts and glass pyramids, you'll find captivating treasures to take home from your trip to the Yucatán. Here are our favorite shopping experiences:

✔ **Resort wear in Cancún:** Resort clothing — especially if you can find a sale — can be a bargain here. And the selection may be wider than what's available at home. Almost every mall on the island contains trendy boutiques that specialize in locally designed and imported clothing. See Chapter 11.

✔ **Duty free in Cancún:** If you're looking for European perfume, fine watches, or other imported goods, you'll find the prices in Cancún's duty-free shops (at the major malls on the island and in downtown Cancún) hard to beat. See Chapter 11.

✔ **Precious gemstones in Isla Mujeres:** Isla Mujeres, also a duty-free zone, offers an impressive selection of both precious stones and superb craftsmen who can make jewelry designs to order. See Chapter 12.

✔ **Quinta Avenida, Playa del Carmen:** This pedestrian-only street offers leisurely shopping at its best. No cars, no hassle; simply stroll down the street and let your eye pick out objects of interest. Expect a good bit of counterculture merchandise, such as batik clothing and fabric, Guatemalan textiles, and inventive jewelry and artwork. But you'll also find quality Mexican handcrafts, premium tequilas, and Cuban cigars. See Chapter 14.

The Best Nightlife

Although, as expected, Cancún is home to much of the Yucatán's nightlife, that resort city isn't the only place to have a good time after dark. Along the Caribbean coast, beachside dance floors with live bands and extended happy hours in seaside bars dominate the nightlife. Here are some favorite hot spots, from live music in hotel lobby bars to hip techno dance clubs:

✔ **Coco Bongo, Nulldog Café, Glazz, and Mango Tango:** These Cancún bars all offer good drinks, hot music, and great dance floors. **Mango Tango** is a top spot for live Cuban and Caribbean rhythms in Cancún. See Chapter 11.

✔ **The City:** Here's one place that has it all: Currently Cancún's hottest club, The City revels 24-hours a day. The City Beach Club is the spot for revelry in the sun, with pools and a wave machine to simulate surfing. At night, choose from the Terrace Bar, The Lounge, or The Club — there's a spot for everyone here! See Chapter 11.

✔ **The Lobby Lounge:** Located in Cancún's luxurious Ritz-Carlton Hotel, this is the most elegant evening spot on the island. Romantic live music, a selection of fine cigars, and more than 120 premium tequilas (plus tastings) allow you to savor the spirit of Mexico. See Chapter 11.

✔ **Quinta Avenida, Playa del Carmen:** Stroll along the lively, pedestrian-only Fifth Avenue to find the bar that's right for you. With live music venues, tequila bars, sports bars, and cafes, you're sure to find something to fit your mood. See Chapter 14.

Chapter 2

Digging Deeper into the Yucatán

*T*he resorts of Mexico's Yucatán are known for glorious white-sand beaches bordering tranquil, translucent waters. It would be easy to let that be the sole draw to this destination, but there's so much more here to enjoy. The Yucatán's rich history has left mysteries still be discovered and ruins that make for popular explorations. So, what's the story behind them?

In this chapter, we relay a brief history of the area and its cultural highpoints. We also sample the unusual and memorable culinary specialties of the region, and I even provide some tips for the local lingo. Finally, we recommend reading and films that can help you enjoy this place much more than you would if you limit your perspective to a beach blanket in the sand.

Introducing the Yucatán

A quick look at the geography of the Yucatán Peninsula belies the uniqueness of this area — although the entire peninsula is a flat slab of limestone, it is a land unlike anywhere else on Earth. Millions of years ago, this area absorbed the force of a giant meteor. The impact sent shock waves through the brittle limestone, fracturing it throughout, creating an immense network of fissures that drain all rainwater away from the surface.

When driving through northern and central Yucatán, you don't see any rivers, lakes, or watercourses. The vast subterranean basin, which stretches for miles across the peninsula, is invisible but for the area's many *cenotes* — sinkholes or natural wells that exist nowhere else. Many are perfectly round vertical shafts that look like nothing else in nature (such as the Grand Cenote at Chichén Itzá); others retain a partial roof, often perforated by tree roots — quiet, dark, and cool, they are the opposite of the warm, brightly lit outside world. To the Maya, they were sacred passageways to the underworld.

Those curious people, **the Maya,** are another fascinating part of this land. The ancients left behind elegant and mysterious ruins that, despite all that we now know, seem to defy interpretation. Almost every year, archaeological excavation leads to the discovery of more ruins, adding to a growing picture of an urban civilization that thrived in an area where only scantily populated jungle now exists. What can we make of such a civilization? What value do we accord the Maya among the other lost civilizations of the ancient world? Even this is unclear, but the art and architecture they left behind are stunning expressions of a rich and complex cosmological view.

Then there was the arrival of the Spaniards, in the early 1500s — an event that in hindsight seems almost apocalyptic. Military conquest and old-world diseases decimated the native population. A new social order predicated on a starkly different religion rose in place of the old one. Through all of this, the Maya held on to their language but lost most of the living memory of their pre-Hispanic ways. What they retained they cloaked in the language of myth and legend that was worked into a rough synthesis of old and new. They selectively appropriated elements of the new religion that could help make sense of the world, and this process continues today in the many Maya communities that have native churches.

For these reasons and more, the Yucatán is a curious place; it may beckon you with its turquoise-blue waters and tropical Caribbean climate, but what will ultimately hold your attention is the unique character of the land and its people. There is no other place like it.

The Land

The Yucatán is edged by the dull aquamarine Gulf of Mexico on the west and north, and the clear cerulean blue Caribbean Sea on the east, where the resorts covered in this book are found. The peninsula covers almost 134,400 square kilometers (84,000 square miles), with nearly 1,600 kilometers (1,000 miles) of shoreline. Most of the land is porous limestone, with thin soil supporting a primarily low, scrubby jungle. In most of the Yucatán there is no surface water; instead, rainwater filters through the limestone into underground rivers.

In the state of Quintana Roo, where Cancún and most of the areas explored in this book are located, there are several protected areas which are among the region's most beautiful, wild, and important. In 1986, the state ambitiously set aside the 1.3 million–acre **Sian Ka'an Biosphere Reserve,** conserving a significant part of the coast in the face of development south of Tulum. **Isla Contoy,** off the coast of Isla

Mujeres and Cancún, is a beautiful island refuge for hundreds of birds, turtles, plants, and other wildlife. And in 1990, the 150-acre **Jardín Botánico,** south of Puerto Morelos, opened to the public. Along with the Botanical Garden at Cozumel's Chankanaab Lagoon, it gives visitors an idea of the biological importance of Yucatán's lengthy shoreline: Four of Mexico's eight marine turtle species — loggerhead, green, hawksbill, and leatherback — nest on Quintana Roo's shores, and more than 600 species of birds, reptiles, and mammals have been counted.

History 101: The Main Events

Mexico's history extends much longer that that of her neighbor to the north. Once the center of civilization in the Western Hemisphere, Mexico's ancient inhabitants were sophisticated and cultured. The Yucatán was home to the Maya, and remnants of their advanced, mysterious civilization are still being found, unlocking clues to their fascinating culture. Modern-day Mexicans are proud of their deep, rich history, and within many aspects of daily life, you find a nod to the mysticism and sacred traditions of ancient times.

Pre-Hispanic civilizations

The earliest "Mexicans" were perhaps Stone Age hunter-gatherers coming from the north, descendants of a race that had crossed the Bering Strait and reached North America around 12,000 B.C. This is the prevailing theory, but there is a growing body of evidence that points to an earlier crossing of peoples from Asia to the New World. What we know for certain is that Mexico was populated by 10,000 B.C. Sometime between 5200 and 1500 B.C. they began practicing agriculture and domesticating animals.

The Pre-Classic Period (1500 B.C.–A.D. 300)

Eventually, agriculture improved to the point that it could provide enough food to support large communities and enough surplus to free some of the population from agricultural work. A civilization emerged that we call the **Olmec** — an enigmatic people who settled the lower Gulf Coast in what is now Tabasco and Veracruz. Anthropologists regard them as the mother culture of Mesoamerica, because they established a pattern for later civilizations in a wide area stretching from northern Mexico into Central America. The Olmec developed the basic calendar used throughout the region, established principles of urban layout and architecture, and originated the cult of the jaguar and the sacredness of jade. They may also have bequeathed the sacred ritual of *the ball game* — a universal element of Mesoamerican culture. In this popular game that was part ritual, part sport, players on two teams tried to knock a hard rubber ball through one of the two stone rings placed high on either wall of a ball court, using only their elbows, knees, and hips (no hands). According to legend, the losing players paid for defeat with their lives.

The Maya civilization began developing in the pre-Classic period, around 500 B.C. Our understanding of this period is only sketchy, but Olmec influences are apparent everywhere. The Maya perfected the Olmec calendar and, somewhere along the way, developed their ornate system of hieroglyphic writing and their early architecture. Two other civilizations also began their rise to prominence around this time: the people of Teotihuacán, just north of present-day Mexico City, and the Zapotec of Monte Albán, in the valley of Oaxaca.

The Classic Period (A.D. 300–900)

The flourishing of these three civilizations marks the boundaries of this period — the heyday of pre-Columbian Mesoamerican artistic and cultural achievements. These include the pyramids and palaces in Teotihuacán; the ceremonial center of Monte Albán; and the stelae and temples of Palenque, Bonampak, and the Tikal site in Guatemala. Beyond their achievements in art and architecture, the Maya made significant discoveries in science, including the use of the zero in mathematics and a complex calendar with which the priests could predict eclipses and the movements of the stars for centuries to come.

The inhabitants of **Teotihuacán** (100 B.C.–A.D. 700, near present-day Mexico City) built a city that, at its zenith, is thought to have had 100,000 or more inhabitants covering 14 square kilometers (9 square miles). It was a well-organized city, built on a grid with streams channeled to follow the city's plan. Different social classes, such as artisans and merchants, were assigned to specific neighborhoods. Teotihuacán exerted tremendous influence as far away as Guatemala and the Yucatán Peninsula. Its feathered serpent god, later known as **Quetzalcoatl,** became part of the pantheon of many succeeding cultures, including the Toltecs, who brought the cult to the Yucatán where the god became known as Kukulkán. The ruling classes were industrious, literate, and cosmopolitan. The beautiful sculpture and ceramics of Teotihuacán display a highly stylized and refined aesthetic whose influences can be seen clearly in objects of Maya and Zapotec origin. Around the 7th century, the city was abandoned for unknown reasons. Who these people were and where they went remain mysteries.

The Post-Classic Period (A.D. 900–1521)

Warfare became a more conspicuous activity of the civilizations that flourished in this period. Social development was impressive but not as cosmopolitan as the Maya, Teotihuacán, and Zapotec societies. In central Mexico, a people known as the **Toltec** established their capital at Tula in the 10th century. They were originally one of the barbarous hordes of Indians that periodically migrated from the north. At some stage in their development, the Toltec were influenced by remnants of Teotihuacán culture and adopted the feathered serpent Quetzalcoatl as their god. They also revered a god known as **Tezcatlipoca,** or "smoking mirror," who later became a god of the Aztecs.

During this period, the Maya built beautiful cities near the Yucatán's Puuc hills. The regional architecture, called **Puuc style,** is characterized by elaborate exterior stonework appearing above door frames and extending to the roofline. Examples of this architecture, such as the Codz Poop at Kabah and the palaces at Uxmal, Sayil, and Labná, are beautiful and quite impressive. Associated with the cities of the Puuc region was Chichén Itzá, ruled by the Itzáes. This metropolis evidences strong Toltec influences in its architectural style as well as the cult of the plumed-serpent god, Kukulkán.

The precise nature of this Toltec influence is a subject of debate. But there is an intriguing myth in central Mexico that tells how Quetzalcoatl quarrels with Tezcatlipoca and through trickery is shamed by his rival into leaving Tula, the capital of the Toltec empire. He leaves heading eastward toward the morning star, vowing someday to return. In the language of myth, this could be a shorthand telling of an actual civil war between two factions in Tula, each led by the priesthood of a particular god. Could the losing faction have migrated to the Yucatán and formed the ruling class of Chichén Itzá? Perhaps. What we do know for certain is that this myth of the eventual return of Quetzalcoatl became, in the hands of the Spanish, a powerful weapon of conquest.

The Conquest

In 1517, the first Spaniards arrived in Mexico and skirmished with Maya Indians off the coast of the Yucatán Peninsula. One of the fledgling expeditions ended in a shipwreck, leaving several Spaniards stranded as prisoners of the Maya. The Spanish sent out another expedition, under the command of **Hernán Cortez,** which landed on Cozumel in February 1519. Cortez inquired about the gold and riches of the interior, and the coastal Maya were happy to describe the wealth and splendor of the Aztec empire in central Mexico. Cortez promptly disobeyed all orders from his superior, the governor of Cuba, and sailed to the mainland.

He and his army arrived when the Aztec empire was at the height of its wealth and power. **Moctezuma II** ruled over the central and southern highlands and extracted tribute from lowland peoples. His greatest temples were literally plated with gold and encrusted with the blood of sacrificial captives. Moctezuma was a fool, a mystic, and something of a coward. Despite his wealth and military power, he dithered in his capital at Tenochtitlán, sending messengers with gifts and suggestions that Cortez leave. Meanwhile, Cortez negotiated his way into the highlands, always cloaking his real intentions. Moctezuma, terrified, convinced himself that Cortez was in fact the god Quetzalcoatl making his long-awaited return. By the time the Spaniards arrived in the Aztec capital, Cortez had gained some ascendancy over the lesser Indian states that were resentful tributaries to the Aztec. In November 1519, Cortez confronted Moctezuma and took him hostage in an effort to leverage control of the empire.

In the middle of Cortez's dangerous game of manipulation, another Spanish expedition arrived with orders to end Cortez's authority over the mission. Cortez hastened to meet the rival's force and persuade them to join his own. In the meantime, the Aztec chased the garrison out of Tenochtitlán, and either they or the Spaniards killed Moctezuma. For the next year and a half, Cortez laid siege to Tenochtitlán, with the help of rival Indians and a decimating epidemic of smallpox, to which the Indians had no resistance. In the end, the Aztec capital fell, and, when it did, all of central Mexico lay at the feet of the conquistadors.

Having begun as a pirate expedition by Cortez and his men without the authority of the Spanish crown or its governor in Cuba, the conquest of Mexico resulted in a vast expansion of the Spanish empire. The king legitimized Cortez following his victory over the Aztec and ordered the forced conversion to Christianity of this new colony, to be called **New Spain.** In the two centuries that followed, Franciscan and Augustinian friars converted millions of Indians to Christianity, and the Spanish lords built huge feudal estates on which the Indian farmers were little more than serfs. The silver and gold that Cortez looted made Spain the richest country in Europe.

The Colonial Period

Hernán Cortez set about building a new city upon the ruins of the old Aztec capital. Over the 3 centuries of the colonial period, Spain became rich from New World gold and silver, chiseled out by Indian labor. A new class system developed. Those born in Spain considered themselves superior to the *criollos* (Spaniards born in Mexico). Those of other races and the *castas* (mixtures of Spanish and Indian, Spanish and African, or Indian and African) occupied the bottom rungs of society. It took great cunning to stay a step ahead of the avaricious Crown, which demanded increasing taxes and contributions from its fabled foreign conquests. Still, wealthy colonists prospered enough to develop an extravagant society.

However, discontent with the mother country simmered for years. In 1808, Napoléon invaded Spain and crowned his brother Joseph king in place of Charles IV. To many in Mexico, allegiance to France was out of the question; discontent reached the level of revolt.

Independence

The rebellion began in 1810, when **Father Miguel Hidalgo** gave the *grito,* a cry for independence, from his church in the town of Dolores, Guanajuato. The uprising soon became a full-fledged revolution, as Hidalgo and Ignacio Allende gathered an "army" of citizens and threatened Mexico City. Although Hidalgo ultimately failed and was executed, he is honored as "the Father of Mexican Independence."

Political instability engulfed the young republic, which ran through a dizzying succession of presidents and dictators as struggles between federalists and centralists, and conservatives and liberals, divided the country. Moreover, Mexico waged a disastrous war with the United States, which resulted in the loss of half its territory.

Political instability persisted and included a brief period where the control of the country was assumed by Archduke Maximilian of Austria, who accepted the position of Mexican emperor with the support of French troops, until he was captured and executed by a firing squad in 1867. His adversary and successor (as president of Mexico) was **Benito Juárez,** a Zapotec Indian lawyer and one of the great heroes of Mexican history. Juárez did his best to unify and strengthen his country before dying of a heart attack in 1872; his impact on Mexico's future was profound, and his plans and visions bore fruit for decades.

The Porfiriato and the Revolution

A few years after Juárez's death, one of his generals, **Porfirio Díaz,** assumed power in a coup. He ruled Mexico from 1877 to 1911, a period now called the *Porfiriato*. He stayed in power through repressive measures and by courting the favor of powerful nations. With foreign investment came the concentration of great wealth in few hands, and social conditions worsened.

In 1910, Francisco Madero called for an armed rebellion that became the **Mexican Revolution** (*La Revolución* in Mexico; the revolution against Spain is the *Guerra de Independencia*). Díaz was sent into exile. Madero became president, but was promptly betrayed and executed. For the next few years, the revolutionaries fought among themselves, until **Lázaro Cárdenas** was elected in 1934, instituting reforms that solidified the outcome of the Revolution. He implemented a massive redistribution of land, nationalized the oil industry, and gave shape to the ruling political party (now the **Partido Revolucionario Institucional,** or **PRI**) by bringing a broad representation of Mexican society under its banner and establishing mechanisms for consensus building. Most Mexicans practically canonize Cárdenas.

Modern Mexico

The presidents who followed were noted more for graft than for leadership. The party's base narrowed as many of the reform-minded elements were marginalized. Economic progress, a lot of it in the form of large development projects, became the PRI's main basis for legitimacy. Although the PRI maintained its grip on power, it lost all semblance of being a progressive party.

In the years that followed, opposition political parties grew in power and legitimacy. Facing pressure and scrutiny from national and international organizations, and widespread public discontent, the PRI had to concede defeat in state and congressional elections throughout the '90s. Elements of the PRI pushed for, and achieved, reforms from within and greater political openness. This led to deep divisions between party activists, rancorous campaigns for party leadership, and even political assassination. The party began choosing its candidates through primaries instead of by appointment.

But in the presidential elections of 2000, Vicente Fox of the opposition party **Partido Acción Nacional (PAN)** won by a landslide. In hindsight, there was no way that the PRI could have won in a fair election. For most Mexicans, a government under the PRI was all that they had ever known. Many voted for Fox just to see whether the PRI would let go of power. It did, and the transition ran smoothly, thanks in large part to the outgoing president, Ernesto Zedillo, who was one of the PRI reformers.

Since then, Mexico has sailed into the uncharted waters of coalition politics, with three main parties, PRI, PAN, and **Partido de la Revolución Democrática (PRD).** To their credit, the sailing has been much smoother than many observers predicted. But the real test will be weathering the economic slowdown that accompanied the downturn in the U.S. economy, and in carrying out the next presidential elections in 2006.

Building Blocks: Local Architecture

Mexico's artistic and architectural legacy reaches back more than 3,000 years. Until the conquest of Mexico in A.D. 1521, art, architecture, politics, and religion were intertwined. Although the European conquest influenced the style and subject of Mexican art, this continuity remained throughout the colonial period.

Pre-Hispanic forms

Mexico's **pyramids** were truncated platforms crowned with a temple. Many sites have circular buildings, such as El Caracol at **Chichén Itzá,** usually called the observatory and dedicated to the god of the wind. El Castillo at Chichén Itzá has 365 steps — one for every day of the year. The Temple of the Magicians at **Uxmal** has beautifully rounded and sloping sides. Evidence of building one pyramidal structure on top of another, a widely accepted practice, has been found throughout Mesoamerica.

Architects of many Toltec, Aztec, and Teotihuacán edifices alternated sloping panels (*talud*) with vertical panels (*tablero*). Elements of this style occasionally show up in the Yucatán. **Dzibanché,** a newly excavated site near Lago Bacalar, in southern Quintana Roo state, has at least one temple with this characteristic. The true arch was unknown in Mesoamerica, but the Maya made use of the corbelled arch — a method of stacking stones that allows each successive stone to be cantilevered out a little farther than the one below it, until the two sides meet at the top, forming an inverted V.

Throughout Mexico, carved stone and mural art on pyramids served a religious and historic function rather than an ornamental one. **Hieroglyphs,** picture symbols etched on stone or painted on walls or pottery, functioned as the written language of the ancient peoples, particularly the Maya. By deciphering the glyphs, scholars allow the ancients to speak again, providing us with specific names to attach to rulers and their families, and demystifying the great dynastic histories of the Maya. For more on this, read *A Forest of Kings,* by Linda Schele and David Freidel (Morrow), and *Blood of Kings,* by Linda Schele and Mary Ellen Miller (George Braziller).

Carving important historic figures on freestanding stone slabs, or **stelae,** was a common Maya commemorative device. Several are in place at Cobá; Calakmul has the most, and good examples are on display in the Museum of Anthropology in Mexico City and the archaeology museum in Villahermosa. **Pottery** played an important role, and different indigenous groups are distinguished by their different uses of color and style. The Maya painted pottery with scenes from daily and historic life.

Pre-Hispanic cultures left a number of fantastic painted **murals,** some of which are remarkably preserved, such as those at Bonampak and Cacaxtla. Amazing stone murals or mosaics, using thousands of pieces of fitted stone to form figures of warriors, snakes, or geometric designs, decorate the pyramid facades at Uxmal and Chichén Itzá.

Spanish influence

With the arrival of the Spaniards, new forms of architecture came to Mexico. Many sites that were occupied by indigenous groups at the time of the conquest were razed, and in their place appeared Catholic churches, public buildings, and palaces for conquerors and the king's bureaucrats. In the Yucatán, churches at Izamal, Tecoh, Santa Elena, and Muná rest atop former pyramidal structures. Indian artisans, who formerly worked on pyramidal structures, were recruited to build the new buildings, often guided by drawings of European buildings. Frequently left on their own, the indigenous artisans implanted traditional symbolism in the new buildings: a plaster angel swaddled in feathers, reminiscent of the god Quetzalcoatl, and the face of an ancient god surrounded by corn leaves. They used pre-Hispanic calendar counts — the 13 steps to heaven or the nine levels of the underworld — to determine how many florets to carve around the church doorway.

To convert the native populations, New World Spanish priests and architects altered their normal ways of teaching and building. Often before the church was built, an open-air atrium was constructed to accommodate large numbers of parishioners for services. *Posas* (shelters) at the four corners of churchyards were another architectural technique unique to Mexico, again to accommodate crowds. Because of the language barrier between the Spanish and the natives, church adornment became more explicit. Biblical tales came to life in frescoes splashed across church walls. Christian symbolism in stone supplanted that of pre-Hispanic ideas as the natives tried to make sense of it all. Baroque became even more ornate in Mexico and was dubbed **churrigueresque** or **ultrabaroque.** Exuberant and complicated, it combines Gothic, baroque, and plateresque elements.

Almost every village in the Yucatán Peninsula has the remains of **missions, monasteries, convents,** and **parish churches.** Many were built in the 16th century following the early arrival of Franciscan friars. Examples include the Mission of San Bernardino de Sisal in Valladolid; the fine altarpiece at Teabo; the folk-art *retablo* (altarpiece) at Tecoh; the large church and convent at Mani with its *retablos* and limestone crucifix; the facade, altar, and central *retablo* of the church at Oxkutzcab; the 16-bell belfry at Ytholin; the baroque facade and altarpiece at Maxcanu; the cathedral at Mérida; the vast atrium and church at Izamal; and the baroque *retablo* and murals at Tabi.

Religion, Myth, and Folklore

Mexico is predominantly Roman Catholic, a religion introduced by the Spaniards during the Conquest of Mexico. Despite its preponderance, the Catholic faith in many places in Mexico has pre-Hispanic undercurrents. You need only visit the *curandero* section of a Mexican market (where you can purchase *copal,* an incense agreeable to the gods; rustic beeswax candles, a traditional offering; the native species of tobacco used to ward off evil; and so on), or attend a village festivity featuring pre-Hispanic-influenced dancers, to understand that these beliefs often run parallel with Christian ones.

Mexico's complicated mythological heritage from pre-Hispanic religion is full of images derived from nature — the wind, jaguars, eagles, snakes, flowers, and more — all intertwined with elaborate mythological stories to explain the universe, climate, seasons, and geography. Most groups believed in an underworld (not a hell), usually containing 9 levels, and a heaven of 13 levels — which is why the numbers 9 and 13 are so mythologically significant. The solar calendar count of 365 days and the ceremonial calendar of 260 days are significant as well. How one died determined one's resting place after death: in the underworld (*Xibalba* to the Maya), in heaven, or at one of the four cardinal points. For example, men who died in battle or women who died in childbirth went straight to the sun. Everyone else first had to make a journey through the underworld.

Gods and goddesses

Each of the ancient cultures had its gods and goddesses, and while the names may not have crossed cultures, their characteristics or purposes often did. Chaac, the hook-nosed rain god of the Maya, was Tlaloc, the squat rain god of the Aztecs; Quetzalcoatl, the plumed-serpent god/man of the Toltecs, became Kukulkán of the Maya. The tales of the powers and creation of these deities make up Mexico's rich mythology. Sorting out the pre-Hispanic pantheon and beliefs in ancient Mexico can become an all-consuming study (the Maya alone had 166 deities), so here's a list of some of the most important gods:

Chaac: Maya rain god

Ehécatl: Wind god whose temple is usually round; another aspect of Quetzalcoatl

Itzamná: Maya god above all, who invented corn, cacao (chocolate), and writing and reading

Ixchel: Maya goddess of water, weaving, and childbirth

Kinich Ahau: Maya sun god

Kukulkán: Quetzalcoatl's name in the Yucatán

Ometeotl: God/goddess, all-powerful creator of the universe, and ruler of heaven, earth, and the underworld

Quetzalcoatl: A mortal who took on legendary characteristics as a god (or vice versa). When he left Tula in shame after a night of succumbing to temptations, he promised to return. He reappeared in the Yucatán. He is also symbolized as Venus, the moving star, and Ehécatl, the wind god. Quetzalcoatl is credited with giving the Maya cacao and teaching them how to grow it, harvest it, roast it, and turn it into a drink with ceremonial and magical properties.

Tlaloc: Aztec rain god

Taste of the Yucatán: Local Cuisine

Authentic Mexican food differs dramatically from what is frequently served in the United States under that name. For many, Mexico will be new and exciting culinary territory. Even grizzled veterans will be pleasantly surprised by the wide variation in specialties and traditions offered from region to region.

Despite regional differences, some generalizations can be made. Mexican food usually isn't pepper-hot when it arrives at the table (though many dishes must have a certain amount of piquancy, and some home cooking can be very spicy, depending on a family's or chef's tastes). Chiles and sauces add piquant flavor after the food is served; you'll never see a table in Mexico without one or both of these condiments. Mexicans don't drown their cooking in cheese and sour cream, à la Tex-Mex, and they use a great variety of ingredients. But the basis of Mexican food is simple — tortillas, beans, chiles, and tomatoes — the same as it was centuries ago, before the Europeans arrived.

In the Yucatán, as throughout Mexico, you'll frequently encounter these basic foods. Traditional **tortillas** are of the corn variety — they are actually made from a paste of ground corn, water, and lime, called *masa.* This grainy dough is patted and pressed into flat round cakes, tortillas, or take on a variety of other shapes that hold meat or other fillings.

A **taco** is anything folded or rolled into a tortilla, and sometimes a double tortilla. The tortilla can be served either soft or fried. *Flautas* and *quesadillas* are species of tacos. For Mexicans, the taco is the quintessential fast food, and the taco stand *(taquería)* — a ubiquitous sight — is a great place to get a filling meal.

Chiles are also a staple in the Yucatán, and in Mexico. Many kinds of chile peppers exist, and Mexicans call each of them by one name when they're fresh and another when they're dried. Some are blazing hot with only a mild flavor; some are mild but have a rich, complex flavor. They can be pickled, smoked, stuffed, stewed, chopped, and used in an endless variety of dishes.

Yucatecan cooking is the most distinct of the many kinds of regional cooking, probably because the Maya and Caribbean cultural traditions influenced it. Yucatecans are great fans of **achiote** (or *annatto,* a red seed pod from a tree that grows in the Caribbean area), which is the basic ingredient for perhaps its most famous dish, *cochinita pibil* (pork wrapped in banana leaves and baked in a pit with a *pibil* sauce of achiote, sour orange, and spices). Good **seafood** is readily available. Many of the most common Mexican dishes are given a different name and a different twist here. Waiters are happy to explain what's what. With a couple of meals under your belt, you'll feel like a native.

As distinctive as the food itself is the meal system in Mexico. The morning meal, known as *el desayuno,* can be something light, such as coffee and sweet bread, or something more substantial: eggs, beans, tortillas, bread, fruit, and juice. It can be eaten early or late and is always a sure bet in Mexico. The variety and sweetness of the fruits is remarkable, and you can't go wrong with Mexican egg dishes.

In Mexico, the main meal of the day, known as *la comida* (or *almuerzo*), is eaten between 2 and 4 p.m. Stores and businesses close, and most people go home to eat and perhaps take a short afternoon *siesta* (nap) before going about their business. The first course is the *sopa,* which can be either soup *(caldo)* or rice *(sopa de arroz)* or both; then comes the main course, which ideally is a meat or fish dish prepared in some kind of sauce and served with beans, followed by dessert.

Between 8 and 10 p.m., most Mexicans have a light meal called *la cena*. If eaten at home, it is something like a sandwich, bread and jam, or perhaps a couple of tacos made from some of the day's leftovers. At restaurants, the most common thing to eat is *antojitos* (literally, "little cravings"), a general label for light fare. Antojitos include tostadas, tamales, tacos, and simple enchiladas, and are big hits with travelers. Large restaurants offer complete meals as well. In the Yucatán, antojitos include *papadzules* (a species of enchilada filled with hard-boiled egg), *sincronizadas* (small tostadas), and *panuchos* (fried tortillas filled with bean paste and topped with *cochinita pibil* and marinated onions).

There are also some unique attributes to beverages in Mexico. All over the country, you'll find shops selling *jugos* (juices) and *licuados* (smoothies) made from several kinds of tropical fruit. They're excellent and refreshing; while traveling, we take full advantage of them. You'll also come across *aguas frescas* — water flavored with hibiscus, melon, tamarind, or lime. Soft drinks come in more flavors than in any other country we know. Pepsi and Coca-Cola taste the way they did in the United States years ago, before the makers started adding corn syrup. The coffee is generally good, and **hot chocolate** is a traditional drink, as is *atole* — a hot, corn-based beverage that can be sweet or bitter.

Of course, Mexico has a proud and lucrative **beer**-brewing tradition. **Mezcal** and **tequila** come from the agave plant, which is not a type of cactus, but is actually a distant cousin of the lily. Tequila is a variety of mezcal produced from the *A. tequilana* species of agave in and around the area of Tequila, in the state of Jalisco. Mezcal comes from various parts of Mexico and from different varieties of agave. The distilling process is usually much less sophisticated than that of tequila, and, with its stronger smell and taste, mezcal is much more easily detected on the drinker's breath. In some places, it comes with a worm in the bottle; you are supposed to eat the worm after polishing off the mezcal. *¡Salud!*

Word to the Wise: The Local Lingo

Most Mexicans are very patient with foreigners who try to speak their language; it helps a lot to know a few basic phrases. Table 2-1 gives you simple phrases for expressing basic needs.

Table 2-1	English-Spanish Phrases	
English	*Spanish*	*Pronunciation*
Good day	**Buen día**	bwehn *dee*-ah
Good morning	**Buenos días**	*bweh*-nohss *dee*-ahss
How are you?	**¿Cómo está?**	*koh*-moh ehss-*tah?*

(continued)

Table 2-1 *(continued)*

English	Spanish	Pronunciation
Very well	**Muy bien**	mwee byehn
Thank you	**Gracias**	*grah*-syahss
You're welcome	**De nada**	deh *nah*-dah
Good-bye	**Adiós**	ah-*dyohss*
Please	**Por favor**	pohr fah-*vohr*
Yes	**Sí**	see
No	**No**	noh
Excuse me	**Perdóneme**	pehr-*doh*-neh-meh
Give me	**Déme**	*deh*-meh
Where is . . . ?	**¿Dónde está . . . ?**	*dohn*-deh ehss-*tah?*
the station	**la estación**	lah ehss-tah-*syohn*
a hotel	**un hotel**	oon oh-*tehl*
a gas station	**una gasolinera**	*oo*-nah gah-soh-lee-*neh*-rah
a restaurant	**un restaurante**	oon res-tow-*rahn*-teh
the toilet	**el baño**	el *bah*-nyoh
a good doctor	**un buen médico**	oon bwehn *meh*-dee-coh
the road to . . .	**el camino a/hacia . . .**	el cah-*mee*-noh ah/*ah*-syah
To the right	**A la derecha**	ah lah deh-*reh*-chah
To the left	**A la izquierda**	ah lah ees-*kyehr*-dah
Straight ahead	**Derecho**	deh-*reh*-choh
I would like	**Quisiera**	key-*syeh*-rah
I want	**Quiero**	*kyeh*-roh
to eat	**comer**	koh-*mehr*
a room	**una habitación**	*oo*-nah ah-bee-tah-*syohn*
Do you have . . . ?	**¿Tiene usted . . . ?**	tyeh-neh oo-*sted?*
a book	**un libro**	oon *lee*-broh
a dictionary	**un diccionario**	oon deek-syow-*nah*-ryo

English	Spanish	Pronunciation
How much is it?	¿Cuánto cuesta?	*kwahn*-toh *kwehss*-tah?
When?	¿Cuándo?	*kwahn*-doh?
What?	¿Qué?	keh?
There is (Is there . . . ?)	¿Hay (. . . ?)	eye?
What is there?	¿Qué hay?	keh eye?
Yesterday	Ayer	ah-*yer*
Today	Hoy	oy
Tomorrow	Mañana	mah-*nyah*-nah
Good	Bueno	*bweh*-noh
Bad	Malo	*mah*-loh
Better (best)	(Lo) Mejor	(loh) meh-*hohr*
More	Más	mahs
Less	Menos	*meh*-nohss
No smoking	Se prohibe fumar	seh proh-*ee*-beh foo-*mahr*
Postcard	Tarjeta postal	tar-*heh*-ta pohs-*tahl*
Insect repellent	Repelente contra insectos	reh-peh-*lehn*-te *cohn*-trah een-*sehk*-tos
Do you speak English?	¿Habla usted inglés?	*ah*-blah oo-*sted* een-*glehs*?
Is there anyone here who speaks English?	¿Hay alguien aquí que hable inglés?	eye *ahl*-gyehn ah-*kee* keh ah-*bleh* een-*glehs*?
I speak a little Spanish.	Hablo un poco de español.	ah-*bloh* oon *poh*-koh deh ehss-pah-*nyohl*
I don't understand Spanish very well.	No (lo) entiendo muy bien el español.	noh (loh) ehn-*tyehn*-doh mwee byehn el ehss-pah-*nyohl*
The meal is good.	Me gusta la comida.	meh *goo*-stah lah koh-*mee*-dah
What time is it?	¿Qué hora es?	keh *oh*-rah ehss?
May I see your menu?	¿Puedo ver el menú (la carta)?	*pueh*-do vehr el meh-*noo* (lah *car*-tah)?
The check, please.	La cuenta, por favor.	lah *quehn*-tah pohr fa-*vorh*

(continued)

Table 2-1 *(continued)*

English	Spanish	Pronunciation
What do I owe you?	¿Cuánto le debo?	*kwahn*-toh leh *deh*-boh?
What did you say?	¿Mande? (formal)	*mahn*-deh?
	¿Cómo? (informal)	*koh*-moh?
I want (to see) . . .	Quiero (ver) . . .	*kyeh*-roh (vehr)
a room	un cuarto or una habitación	oon *kwar*-toh, *oo*-nah ah-bee-tah-*syohn*
for two persons	para dos personas	*pah*-rah dohss pehr-*soh*-nahs
with (without) bathroom	con (sin) baño	kohn (seen) *bah*-nyoh
We are staying here only . . .	Nos quedamos aquí solamente . . .	nohs keh-*dah*-mohss ah-*kee* soh-lah-*mehn*-teh
one night	una noche	*oo*-nah *noh*-cheh
one week	una semana	*oo*-nah seh-*mah*-nah
We are leaving . . .	Partimos (Salimos) . . .	pahr-*tee*-mohss (sah-*lee*-mohss)
tomorrow	mañana	mah-*nya*-nah
Do you accept . . . ?	¿Acepta usted . . . ?	ah-*sehp*-tah oo-*sted*
traveler's checks?	cheques de viajero?	*cheh*-kehss deh byah-*heh*-roh?
Is there a Laundromat . . . ?	¿Hay una lavandería . . . ?	eye *oo*-nah lah-*vahn*-deh-*ree*-ah
near here?	cerca de aquí?	*sehr*-kah deh ah-*kee*
Please send these clothes to the laundry.	Hágame el favor de mandar esta ropa a la lavandería.	ah-gah-meh el fah-*vohr* deh mahn-*dahr* ehss-tah *roh*-pah a lah lah-*vahn*-deh-*ree*-ah

Table 2-2 helps you with Spanish numbers.

Table 2-2	Spanish Numbers
1	uno (*ooh*-noh)
2	dos (dohss)
3	tres (trehss)

4	cuatro (*kwah*-troh)
5	cinco (*seen*-koh)
6	seis (sayss)
7	siete (*syeh*-teh)
8	ocho (*oh*-choh)
9	nueve (*nweh*-beh)
10	diez (dyess)
11	once (*ohn*-seh)
12	doce (*doh*-seh)
13	trece (*treh*-seh)
14	catorce (kah-*tohr*-seh)
15	quince (*keen*-seh)
16	dieciseis (dyess-ee-*sayss*)
17	diecisiete (dyess-ee-*syeh*-teh)
18	dieciocho (dyess-ee-*oh*-choh)
19	diecinueve (dyess-ee-*nweh*-beh)
20	veinte (*bayn*-teh)
30	treinta (*trayn*-tah)
40	cuarenta (kwah-*ren*-tah)
50	cincuenta (seen-*kwen*-tah)
60	sesenta (seh-*sehn*-tah)
70	setenta (seh-*tehn*-tah)
80	ochenta (oh-*chehn*-tah)
90	noventa (noh-*behn*-tah)
100	cien (syehn)
200	doscientos (do-*syehn*-tohs)
500	quinientos (kee-*nyehn*-tohs)
1,000	mil (meel)

Table 2-3 helps you nail down basic transportation terminology.

Table 2-3	Transportation Terms	
English	**Spanish**	**Pronunciation**
Airport	**Aeropuerto**	ah-eh-roh-*pwehr*-toh
Flight	**Vuelo**	*bweh*-loh
Rental car	**Arrendadora de autos**	ah-rehn-da-doh-rah deh ow-tohs
Bus	**Autobús**	ow-toh-*boos*
Bus or truck	**Camión**	ka-*myohn*
Lane	**Carril**	kah-*reel*
Nonstop	**Directo**	dee-*rehk*-toh
Baggage (claim area)	**Equipajes**	eh-kee-*pah*-hehss
Luggage storage area	**Guarda equipaje**	gwar-dah eh-kee-*pah*-heh
Arrival gates	**Llegadas**	yeh-*gah*-dahss
First class	**Primera**	pree-*meh*-rah
Second class	**Segunda**	seh-*goon*-dah
Nonstop	**Sin escala**	seen ess-*kah*-lah
Baggage claim area	**Recibo de equipajes**	reh-see-boh deh eh-kee-*pah*-hehss
Waiting room	**Sala de espera**	*sah*-lah deh ehss-*peh*-rah
Toilets	**Sanitarios**	sah-nee-*tah*-ryohss
Ticket window	**Taquilla**	tah-*kee*-yah

Table 2-4 helps you order food in restaurants.

Table 2-4	Menu Glossary
Menu Item	**Meaning**
Achiote	Small red seed of the *annatto* tree.
Achiote preparado	A Yucatecan prepared paste made of ground *achiote*, wheat and corn flour, cumin, cinnamon, salt, onion, garlic, and oregano.

Menu Item	Meaning
Agua fresca	Fruit-flavored water, usually watermelon, cantaloupe, chia seed with lemon, hibiscus flower, rice, or ground melon-seed mixture.
Antojito	Typical Mexican supper foods, usually made with *masa* or tortillas, have a filling or topping such as sausage, cheese, beans, and onions; includes such things as *tacos, tostadas, sopes,* and *garnachas.*
Atole	A thick, lightly sweet, hot drink made with finely ground corn and usually flavored with vanilla, pecan, strawberry, pineapple, or chocolate.
Botana	An appetizer.
Buñuelos	Round, thin, deep-fried crispy fritters dipped in sugar.
Carnitas	Pork deep-cooked (not fried) in lard, and then simmered and served with corn tortillas for tacos.
Ceviche	Fresh raw seafood marinated in fresh lime juice and garnished with chopped tomatoes, onions, chiles, and sometimes cilantro.
Chayote	A vegetable pear or mirliton, a type of spiny squash boiled and served as an accompaniment to meat dishes.
Chiles en nogada	Poblano peppers stuffed with a mixture of ground pork and beef, spices, fruits, raisins, and almonds. Can be served either warm — fried in a light batter — or cold, sans batter. Either way it is covered in walnut-and-cream sauce.
Chiles rellenos	Usually poblano peppers stuffed with cheese or spicy ground meat with raisins, rolled in a batter, and fried.
Churro	Tube-shaped, breadlike fritter, dipped in sugar and sometimes filled with *cajeta* (milk-based caramel) or chocolate.
Cochinita pibil	Pork wrapped in banana leaves, pit-baked in a *pibil* sauce of *achiote,* sour orange, and spices; common in the Yucatán.
Enchilada	A tortilla dipped in sauce, usually filled with chicken or white cheese, and sometimes topped with *mole* (*enchiladas rojas* or *de mole*), or with tomato sauce and sour cream (*enchiladas suizas* — Swiss enchiladas), or covered in a green sauce (*enchiladas verdes),* or topped with onions, sour cream, and guacamole (*enchiladas potosinas).*

(continued)

Table 2-4 *(continued)*

Menu Item	Meaning
Escabeche	A lightly pickled sauce used in Yucatecan chicken stew.
Frijoles refritos	Pinto beans mashed and cooked with lard.
Garnachas	A thickish small circle of fried *masa* with pinched sides, topped with pork or chicken, onions, and avocado, or sometimes chopped potatoes and tomatoes; typical as a *botana* in Veracruz and the Yucatán.
Gorditas	Thick, fried corn tortillas, slit and stuffed with choice of cheese, beans, beef, chicken, with or without lettuce, tomato, and onion garnish.
Horchata	Refreshing drink made of ground rice or melon seeds, ground almonds, cinnamon, and lightly sweetened.
Huevos mexicanos	Scrambled eggs with chopped onions, hot green peppers, and tomatoes.
Huitlacoche	Sometimes spelled "cuitlacoche." A mushroom-flavored black fungus that appears on corn in the rainy season; considered a delicacy.
Masa	Ground corn soaked in lime; the basis for tamales, corn tortillas, and soups.
Mixiote	Rabbit, lamb, or chicken cooked in a mild chile sauce (usually chile *ancho* or *pasilla*), and then wrapped like a tamal and steamed. It is generally served with tortillas for tacos, with traditional garnishes of pickled onions, hot sauce, chopped cilantro, and lime wedges.
Pan de muerto	Sweet bread made around the Days of the Dead (Nov 1–2), in the form of mummies or dolls, or round with bone designs.
Pan dulce	Lightly sweetened bread in many configurations, usually served at breakfast or bought in any bakery.
Papadzules	Tortillas stuffed with hard-boiled eggs and seeds (pumpkin or sunflower) in a tomato sauce.
Pibil	Pit-baked pork or chicken in a sauce of tomato, onion, mild red pepper, cilantro, and vinegar.
Pipián	A sauce made with ground pumpkin seeds, nuts, and mild peppers.

Menu Item	Meaning
Poc chuc	Slices of pork with onion marinated in a tangy sour orange sauce and charcoal-broiled; a Yucatecan specialty.
Pulque	A drink made of fermented juice of the maguey plant; best in the state of Hidalgo and around Mexico City.
Quesadilla	Corn or flour tortillas stuffed with melted white cheese and lightly fried.
Queso relleno	Literally "stuffed cheese," a mild yellow cheese stuffed with minced meat and spices; a Yucatecan specialty.
Salsa verde	An uncooked sauce using the green tomatillo and puréed with spicy or mild hot peppers, onions, garlic, and cilantro; on tables countrywide.
Sopa de flor de calabaza	A soup made of chopped squash or pumpkin blossoms.
Sopa de lima	A tangy soup made with chicken broth and accented with fresh lime; popular in Yucatán.
Sopa de tortilla	A traditional chicken broth–based soup, seasoned with chiles, tomatoes, onion, and garlic, served with crispy fried strips of corn tortillas.
Sope	Pronounced *soh*-peh. An *antojito* similar to a *garnacha*, except spread with refried beans and topped with crumbled cheese and onions.
Tacos al pastor	Thin slices of flavored pork roasted on a revolving cylinder dripping with onion slices and juice of fresh pineapple slices. Served in small corn tortillas, topped with chopped onion and cilantro.
Tamal	Incorrectly called a tamale (*tamal* singular, *tamales* plural). A meat or sweet filling rolled with fresh *masa*, wrapped in a corn husk or banana leaf, and steamed.
Tikin xic	Also seen on menus as "tik-n-xic" and "tikik chick." Charbroiled fish brushed with *achiote* sauce.
Torta	A sandwich, usually on *bolillo* bread, typically with sliced avocado, onions, tomatoes, with a choice of meat and often cheese.
Xtabentun	Pronounced shtah-behn-*toon*."A Yucatecan liquor made of fermented honey and flavored with anise. It comes *seco* (dry) or *crema* (sweet).

Background Check: Recommended Books and Movies

Studying up on Mexico can be one of the most fun bits of "research" you'll ever do. If you'd like to learn a bit more about this fascinating country before you go — which we encourage — these books and movies are an enjoyable way to do it.

Books

For an overview of pre-Hispanic cultures, pick up a copy of Michael D. Coe's *Mexico: From the Olmecs to the Aztecs* (Thames & Hudson) or Nigel Davies's *Ancient Kingdoms of Mexico* (Penguin). For the Maya, Michael Coe's *The Maya* (Thames & Hudson) is probably the best general account. For a survey of Mexican history through modern times, *A Short History of Mexico* by J. Patrick McHenry (Doubleday) provides a complete, yet concise account.

John L. Stephens' *Incidents of Travel in the Yucatán, Vols. I and II* (Dover Publications) are considered among the great books of archeological discovery, as well as being travel classics. The two volumes chart the course of Stephens' discoveries of the Yucatán, beginning in 1841. Before his expeditions, little was known of the region, and the Mayan culture had not been discovered. During his travels, Stephens found and described 44 Mayan sites, and his account of these remains the most authoritative in existence.

For a more modern exploration of the region's archeology, Peter Tompkins' *Mysteries of the Mexican Pyramids* (Harper & Row) is a visually rich book, which explores not only the ruins of the Maya in the Yucatán, but the whole of Mexico's archeological treasures.

For contemporary culture, start with Octavio Paz's classic, *The Labyrinth of Solitude* (Grove Press), which still generates controversy among Mexicans. Lesley Byrd Simpson's *Many Mexicos* (University of California Press) provides comprehensive account of Mexican history with a cultural context. A classic on understanding the culture of this country is *Distant Neighbors,* by Alan Riding (Vintage).

To read up on the art and architecture of Mexico, start with *Art and Time in Mexico: From the Conquest to the Revolution,* by Elizabeth Wilder Weismann (Harper & Row), which covers religious, public, and private architecture. *Casa Mexicana,* by Tim Street-Porter (Stewart, Tabori, and Chang), takes readers through the interiors of some of Mexico's finest homes-turned-museums, public buildings, and private homes.

Maya Art and Architecture, by Mary Ellen Miller (Thames and Hudson) showcases the best of the artistic expression of this culture, with interpretations into its meanings.

For a wonderful read on the food of the Yucatán and Mexico, pick up *Mexico, One Plate at a Time,* by celebrity chef and Mexico aficionado Rick Bayless (Scribner).

Naturalist's Mexico, by Roland H. Wauer (Texas A&M University Press), is a fabulous guide to birding. *Mexico: A Hiker's Guide to Mexico's Natural History,* by Jim Conrad (The Mountaineers Books), covers flora and fauna and tells how to find the easy-to-reach as well as out-of-the-way spots he describes. *Peterson Field Guides: Mexican Birds,* by Roger Tory Peterson and Edward L. Chalif (Houghton Mifflin), is an excellent guide.

Movies

Mexico has served as a backdrop for countless movies. Here are just a few of our favorites, all available on DVD.

The 2003 blockbuster *Frida* starring Selma Hayak and Alfred Molina is not only an entertaining way to learn about two of Mexico's most famous personalities, but also of its history. The exquisite cinematography perfectly captures Mexico's inherent spirit of Magic Realism.

Que Viva Mexico is a little-known masterpiece by Russian filmmaker Sergei Eisenstein, who created a documentary of Mexican history, politics and culture, out of a series of short *novellas,* which ultimately tie together. Although Eisenstein's budget ran out before he could complete the project, in 1979 this film was completed by Grigory Alexandrov, the film's original producer. It's an absolute must for anyone interested in Mexico or Mexican cinema.

Mexico's contemporary filmmakers are creating a sensation lately, and none more so than director Alfonso Cuarón. One of his early and highly acclaimed movies is the 2001 classic *Y Tu Mama Tambien (And Your Mother Too),* featuring heartthrobs Gael Garcia Bernal and Diego Luna. This sexy, yet compelling, coming of age movie not only showcases both the grit and beauty of Mexico, but the universality of love and life lessons.

Like Water for Chocolate is the 1993 film based on the book of the same name by Laura Esquivel, filmed by the author's husband, acclaimed contemporary Mexican director Alfonso Arau. Expect to be very hungry after watching this lushly visual film, which tells the story of a young woman who suppresses her passions under the watchful eye of a stern mother, and channels them into her cooking. In the process, we learn of the traditional norms of Mexican culture, and a great deal of the country's culinary treasures.

Chapter 3

Choosing Where to Go

*T*he Yucatán may be the beach vacation of your dreams. All those glossy images of long stretches of pure, powdery, white-sand beaches and tranquil turquoise waters do exist — and they're found along the eastern coast of Mexico's Yucatán Peninsula.

Not only does this vacation destination boast possibly the most perfect beaches in the world, but it also has the added attraction of nearby ruins of ancient cultures, nature-oriented diversions that make avid adventurers drool, and enough shopping, dining, spa services, and nightlife to entertain the most demanding of consumers. This chapter helps you plan your ideal escape to the magical shores of Mexico's Yucatán.

The Yucatán has a lot going for it in terms of attracting travelers — warm weather, miles and miles of coastline, and a location so close to the United States that sometimes it almost seems like a part of it. Although the official language is Spanish, the use of English is almost as common as Spanish in all the resort areas covered in this book. A visit to Mexico's Yucatán can offer the experience of visiting a foreign country accompanied by many of the familiarities of home.

Introducing the Yucatán

The beaches of Cancún and the Yucatán are, in a word, spectacular — and the main reason most people travel here. But the two areas also have differences. Whereas Cancún is a full-blown resort, known as much for its sizzling nightlife as its tropical tanning opportunities, the resorts further south along the coast are custom-made for pure relaxation and lazy days of napping under a palm tree.

You can also explore a couple of laid-back islands, along with unique, ecologically oriented enclaves. Deciding which one is right for you depends a lot on what you're looking for in a vacation. As you read this chapter, think about what you really want in a destination. Romance? Family fun? Lively singles scene? And consider how you want to travel. Budget? Luxury? Somewhere in between? These considerations can help narrow down your planning. One thing's for certain — no matter what you're seeking, at least one Yucatán beach resort fits the bill perfectly.

If you don't know where to begin in choosing between Cancún or a rustic costal retreat, don't worry. In this book, we tell you everything you need to know about each of the destinations that we cover in order to help decide which one is right for you. In this chapter, we give you a rundown of the highlights and drawbacks of each of the region's most popular beach resorts. Because the type of accommodations you want may determine where you go — or don't go — we also explain the different types of lodging available at each destination.

Picking the Right Beach Resort

The resorts along Mexico's Yucatán Peninsula are known for their crystalline waters, which border the coral reefs of the Caribbean, and flat, scrubby landscapes. This area was the land of the ancient Maya, and the remains of their impressive civilization are close enough to the popular beach destinations to explore easily.

More than 26,000 hotel rooms to choose from and a full complement of attractions make Cancún the most popular choice for travelers to Mexico today — more than 7 million visitors come here each year. But Cancún's popularity has also given rise to a whole range of more relaxed options further down the coast to the south, appealing to those who love many aspects of Cancún, but who want a heavier dose of the natural. Cozumel Island, actually an older and more traditional vacation destination, offers a laid-back retreat beneath palm fronds and sunny skies — with the added allure of world-class diving. And, all along the Yucatán coast — now known as the *Riviera Maya* — you can find everything from *palapa*-topped huts to extravagant, luxury hotels or sprawling all-inclusive resorts — all of which border stunning beaches and a tropical jungle. In a nutshell, each resort has its own look, character, and special something. The following sections are snapshots to help you focus on the resort that's right for you.

Also see the "Exploring the Riviera Maya" section later in this chapter for a concise rating of each aspect of the resort areas covered in this book.

Choosing Cancún

Cancún is Mexico's most popular beach resort — and the reason most people travel to Mexico. Simply stated, it perfectly showcases both the country's breathtaking natural beauty and the depth of its 1,000-year history. Cancún is also especially comforting for first-time visitors to Mexico, because it offers a familiarity of life back home that makes foreigners feel instantly at ease in the beach resort.

Cancún offers an unrivaled combination of high-quality accommodations, dreamy beaches, and diverse, nearby shopping, dining, and nightlife. The added lure of ancient culture is also abundant in all directions. And the best part? Cancún is also a modern mega-resort. Even if you're a bit apprehensive about visiting foreign soil, you'll feel completely at home and at ease in Cancún. English is spoken, dollars are accepted, roads are well paved, and lawns are manicured. Malls are the place for shopping and dining, and you'll quickly spot recognizable names for dining, shopping, nightclubbing, and sleeping.

Two principal parts comprise Cancún: **Isla Cancún** (Cancún Island), with a 14-mile-long strip of beachfront hotels reminiscent of Miami Beach, and **Ciudad Cancún** (Cancún City), on the mainland, with smaller hotels, as well as the functional elements of any community.

Cancún, located on the Yucatán Peninsula, is also the departure point for wonderful day-trips to the nearby islands of Cozumel and Isla Mujeres (meaning Island of Women), where you can enjoy first-class diving, as well as the inland remains of ancient cultures.

If you're looking for an incredible introduction to Mexico's beaches and want to experience a Mexican-lite vacation while enjoying world-class shopping in a pampered environment, Cancún is your beach. (Check out the chapters in Part III for more detailed information on this area.)

Top aspects of a vacation in Cancún include

- ✔ Great beaches of powdery, white sand and turquoise-blue water

- ✔ First-class facilities, modern accommodations, and tons of shopping and dining options

- ✔ Numerous outdoor activities including jungle tours, visits to Mayan ruins, and eco-oriented theme parks

- ✔ No need to worry about communication — an English language-friendly destination

But also consider the following:

- ✔ You can easily forget that you're in Mexico and may miss the Mexican experience altogether.

- ✔ Built for tourism, the prices in Cancún are higher than in most other Mexican beach resorts.

- ✔ Cancún's popularity means you'll have lots of company here!

Contemplating Isla Mujeres

Isla Mujeres is a perfect island escape, offering you an idyllic Mexican beach experience complete with a wide stretch of palm-fringed beach, abundant opportunities for diving, snorkeling, and fishing, a tiny but lively town, intriguing guesthouses and small hotels, and an ample dose of culture that's *muy Mexicana*. Where Mexico's only other true island — Cozumel — has become a bustling cruise ship port of call, Isla Mujeres remains a laid-back island, the kind where you can string a hammock between two palms and simply doze away a week in perfect sea breezes and sunshine.

Isla's proximity to Cancún and its active international airport (just 3 miles off Cancún's shore) makes the island easily accessible. When you're there, you'll feel a million miles away from the bustle of civilization. Restaurants are of the family-owned variety, and accommodations are in small, independently owned hotels and guesthouses, with a few deluxe options in the mix.

If you're looking for a true laid-back vacation, and you prefer the simplistic to the superlative, Isla Mujeres is your spot. (Check out Chapter 12 for more detailed information.)

Top aspects of a vacation in Isla Mujeres include

✔ Excellent value for money, with numerous inexpensive hotel and dining options

✔ A relaxed pace and simple lifestyle

✔ Abundant options to enjoy the surrounding Caribbean waters — snorkeling, diving, deep-sea fishing, and explorations of nearby ecological preserves and a small Mayan ruin

But also consider the following:

✔ The island may be *too* small and relaxed for those who prefer constant activity.

✔ During the day, the island crowds up with day-trippers from Cancún.

✔ Nightlife is quiet and the dining scene simple — this isn't the place for those who prefer a little glitz.

Diving into Cozumel

If underwater beauty is your most important criteria for choosing a beach, then Cozumel will dazzle you. Considered by many to be one of the top-five diving spots in the world, few places can top the aquatic splendor of the waters surrounding this island, about 45 miles south of Cancún.

And when you come up for air or if you're a nondiver, Cozumel has several inland attractions, a variety of watersports, a new golf course, and ample choices for dining and libations. As Mexico's most important port of call for cruise ships, Cozumel also has the best duty-free shopping and one of the largest selections of fine-jewelry shops in the country. The island's one town, San Miguel, has a charming old-Mexico feel to it.

Mexico's Yucatán Peninsula

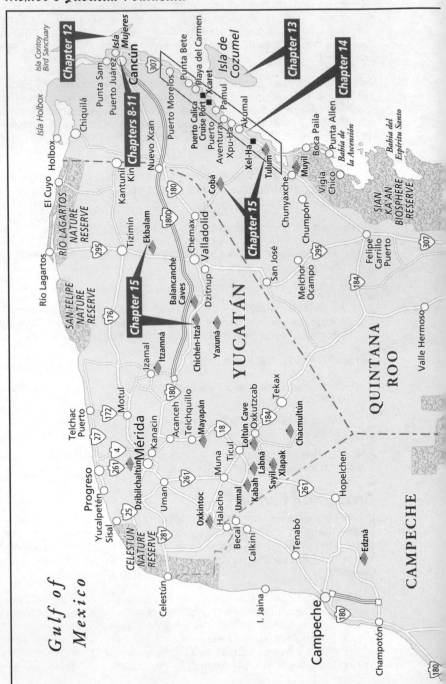

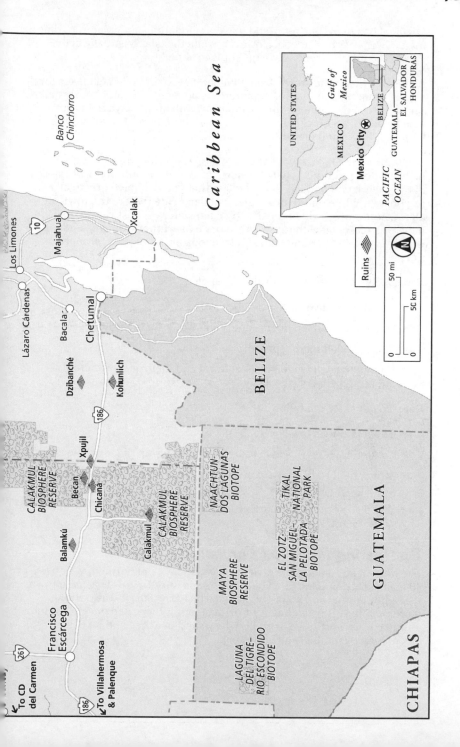

Cozumel has more budget-friendly accommodations and places to dine than newer, nearby Cancún. However, while the island is really active during the day, it's generally a quiet place at night.

Just a short ferry ride away from mainland Mexico, Cozumel makes for a great jumping-off point for explorations along the Yucatán's coastline. Just across the channel from Cozumel is captivating Playa del Carmen, which has grown quickly in recent years due to its central location and funky-sophisticated charms.

In addition to being a diver's dream destination, staying in Cozumel can be like enjoying multiple beach resorts in one vacation! On the oceanside of the island, you find a deserted coast that you can have practically all to yourself. While on the protected mainland side (where the town and all the hotels are), you find perfectly calm waters — just right for swimming or snorkeling without seagrass or any surf that can wreak havoc with those string bathing suits. (Take a look at Chapter 13 for more on Cozumel.)

Top aspects of a vacation in Cozumel include

- World-class diving
- Secluded beaches on one side, calm water on the other
- Relaxed island atmosphere
- Proximity to the mainland's cultural and historical attractions — only a short ferry ride away

But also consider the following:

- The nightlife is low-key.
- Cozumel is super-casual; there's not a dress-up place on the island.
- Stores tend to be more expensive than elsewhere because they cater to cruise-ship visitors.
- When the cruise ships arrive, crowds descend on the town and nature park.

Considering Playa del Carmen

The hottest spot along the Riviera Maya is Playa del Carmen, which lies 40 miles south of Cancún. Playa — as locals refer to it — is a small town that's both funky and sophisticated. In the early '80s, it was nothing more than the ferry landing for Cozumel, but it has since developed into an engaging resort town, with powdery-sand beaches and an eclectic mix of lodging, dining, and shopping.

Playa attracts visitors who are looking for a combination of simplicity and variety. Recently, though, Playa has also attracted developers. As they rapidly change the beachscape to the north and south with the addition of mega-resorts, they're also changing Playa's previously playful, laid-back vibe. But Playa still has enough of its original flavor to make it different from any other resort in the area.

Top aspects of a vacation in Playa include

- ✔ Great beaches and great water
- ✔ Friendly crowds (emphasis on the friendly)
- ✔ Good dining scene and an active street life
- ✔ Excellent location for day-trippers

But also consider the following:

- ✔ The boomtown feel that impinges on the zen of total relaxation
- ✔ Friendly crowds (emphasis on the *crowds*)
- ✔ A rental car is necessary if you want to snorkel or dive
- ✔ Parking problems

Exploring the Riviera Maya

Cancún's popularity has given rise to a growing curiosity and desire to explore other parts of the Yucatán's Caribbean coastline. The 81-mile stretch of coast called the Riviera Maya is now a mix of small resort towns, nature parks, all-inclusive resorts, and roadside attractions extending all the way from Cancún south to the town and ruins of Tulum. This area is ideal for either more adventurous travelers or those who simply want to get to their all-inclusive hotel and stay there.

If you love getting away from it all, the Riviera Maya is a natural choice for exploration and relaxation. (See the chapters in Part V for more details.)

Top aspects of a vacation in the Riviera Maya include

- ✔ Beautiful beaches and an array of ecoparks ideal for nature lovers
- ✔ Favored by more adventurous travelers, some of whom have settled here to offer eclectic accommodations, shopping, and dining options
- ✔ Smaller crowds and lower prices
- ✔ All-inclusive heaven with great savings for travelers with children

But also consider the following:

- ✔ Limited shopping and dining exist outside of Playa del Carmen.
- ✔ Unless you consider stargazing an aspect of nightlife, you won't find much to do here.
- ✔ Without a rental car, you'll be stuck where you stay.

Table 3-1　The Yucatán's Resorts: The Score Card (3 points indicate the highest rating)

Points for:	Cancún Riviera	Cozumel	Isla Mujeres	Playa del Carmen	Maya
Luxury	3	2	2	2	2
Nightlife	3	2	1	3	1
Great food	2	2	1	3	1
Beaches	3	2	2	3	3
Bargain	1	2	3	2	2
Local color	1	2	3	2	2
Mexican culture	2	2	1	1	2
Golf	1	2	0	2	1
Senior appeal	2	1	2	1	1
Hiking	1	1	1	1	2
Natural beauty	2	3	3	2	3
Sightseeing	3	1	1	2	3
Diving/ snorkeling	3	3	3	2	3
Watersports	3	2	2	2	2
Peace and quiet	1	2	3	1	3

Visiting More Than One Resort

Although most people who travel to the Yucatán are headed for a beach chair or hammock slung between palm trees — and then simply want to stay put — it's easy to combine several destinations in one trip. Start in Cancún to revel away a few days before heading down the coast for some serious relaxation. Or reverse that, rest up on a silken beach for a few days, and then head back to Cancún's hotel zone to shop and dine away your last days. With most destinations in this book within a few hours — or less — of one another, combining destinations is easy. A few favorite combinations are Cancún and Isla Mujeres, or Playa del Carmen and Cozumel. However, if the thought of packing and unpacking isn't your idea of a vacation, it's easy to make day-trips to other destinations from wherever you decide to settle in — and, it's a great way to plan *next year's* vacation!

Chapter 4

Deciding When to Go

● ●

In This Chapter

▶ Figuring out the Yucatán's weather patterns
▶ Understanding the secret of the seasons
▶ Planning your trip around festivals and special events

● ●

*M*exico's Yucatán beach resorts enjoy sun-drenched and moderate
winters, and they logically attract the most visitors when the
weather at home is cold and dreary. However, almost any time of the
year has its pros and cons for travel. In this chapter, we review what you
can expect from the weather during different months of the year. We also
highlight some of the Yucatán's most festive celebrations that you may
want to plan your trip around.

Forecasting the Weather

Mexico's Yucatán Peninsula has two main climatic seasons: a **rainy
season** (May to mid-October), and a **dry season** (mid-October through
April). The rainy season can be of little consequence in the dry, interior
part of this region, but the coastal region typically receives regular tropical showers, which begin around 4 or 5 p.m. and last a few hours, as well
as an occasional tropical storm that passes up the coast. Although the
daily rains can come on suddenly and be quite strong, they usually end
just as quickly as they began, and they cool the air for the evening.
During peak hurricane season (September and October), take a look at
the weather reports just before traveling to see whether you may run
into any particularly foul weather and pack an umbrella just in case.

Hurricane season runs from June through October and particularly
affects the Yucatán Peninsula.

June, July, and August are very hot and humid on the Yucatán Peninsula,
with temperatures rising into the mid-80s (30°C) and 90s (33°C). Most of
the coastal part of this region experiences temperatures in the 80s in the
hottest months. During winter months, temperatures average 70 to 75
(22°–25°C) during the days, and about 55 to 65 (12°–18°C) in the evenings.

Unlocking the Secret of the Seasons

Mexico — and its Yucatán Peninsula — have two principal travel seasons: high and low. The **high season** begins around December 20 and continues through Easter, although in some places the high season can begin as early as mid-November. The **low season** begins the day after Easter and continues to mid-December; during the low season, prices may drop between 20 and 50%. At beach destinations popular with Mexican travelers, such as Cancún, the prices jump up to high-season levels during July and August, the traditional, national summer vacation period. Prices may rise dramatically during the weeks of **Easter** and **Christmas,** which are the two peak travel weeks in Mexico. In Isla Mujeres and Playa del Carmen, both on the Yucatán coast, the high season starts in mid-November as well, but a "second" high season occurs in August, when many European visitors arrive. We mention all these exceptions and others in the relevant chapters later in this book.

 We find **November** to be the best month to travel to Mexico: The scenery is still green from the recently ended rainy season, and temperatures are just beginning to turn a bit cooler, which can produce crystal-clear skies. Crowds are also at a minimum, and you're likely to find some good deals.

 One time you may want to avoid is **spring break** (usually from March through early April). The highest concentration of high-octane party crowds is found in Cancún. Frankly, why travel to see college kids behaving badly? Other times you may want to avoid are the weeks of Christmas and Easter. During these traditional Mexican holiday periods, both crowds and prices are at their highest, although the crowds consist more of families and couples than young and rowdy revelers.

Yucatán's Calendar of Events

 Mexicans are known for throwing a great party — *fiesta!* — and their love of fireworks is legendary. You may choose to plan your visit around a colorful national or religious celebration. Watersports enthusiasts may consider visiting during one of the numerous regattas and sport-fishing festivals held at many of the resorts. Remember, however, that during national holidays, Mexican banks and government offices — including immigration — are closed.

Christmas and Easter are celebrated similarly to the way they're celebrated in the United States, but Christmas is much more religiously oriented, and less emphasis is placed on Santa and the exchange of gifts.

January, February, and March

Día de Reyes (Three Kings Day) commemorates the three kings bringing gifts to the Christ child. On this day, children receive gifts, much like the traditional exchange of gifts that accompanies Christmas in the United

States. Friends and families gather to share the *Rosca de Reyes,* a special cake. A small doll representing the Christ child is placed within the cake; whoever receives the doll in his or her piece must host a party the next month that features *tamales* (meat or sweet filling wrapped in a corn husk) and *atole* (a thick, slightly sweet hot drink). January 6.

Music, dances, processions, food, and other festivities are features of **Día de la Candelaria (Candlemass)** and lead up to a blessing of seed and candles in a celebration that mixes pre-Hispanic and European traditions marking the end of winter. All those who attended the Three Kings celebration reunite to share *atole* and *tamales* at a party hosted by the recipient of the doll found in the *rosca.* February 2.

Día de la Constitución (Constitution Day) is a celebration in honor of the current Mexican constitution that was signed in 1917 as a result of the Mexican Revolution of 1910. If you're in Mexico on this day, you'll see a parade wherever you are. February 5.

Carnaval (Carnival) is the last celebration before Lent, and it's celebrated with special gusto in Cozumel. Here, the celebration resembles New Orleans's Mardi Gras with a festive atmosphere and parades. You're best off making reservations in advance and arriving a couple of days before the beginning of celebrations. Three days preceding Ash Wednesday and the beginning of Lent.

Benito Juárez was a reformist leader and president of Mexico who became a national hero. The national holiday honoring **Benito Juárez's Birthday** is the same date of the **spring equinox,** an important celebration of the ancient Mexicans. In Chichén-Itzá (chee-*chin* eat-*zah*), the ancient Mayan city located 112 miles (179 kilometers) from Cancún, the celebration of the first day of spring is particularly interesting. The Temple of Kukulkán — Chichén-Itzá's main pyramid — aligns with the sun, and the shadow of the body of its plumed serpent moves slowly from the top of the building downward. When the shadow reaches the bottom, the body joins the carved-stone snake's head at the base of the pyramid. According to ancient legend, at the moment that the serpent is whole, the earth is fertilized to assure a bountiful growing season. Visitors come from around the world to marvel at this sight, so advance arrangements are advisable. In the custom of the ancient Mexicans, dances are performed, and prayers to the elements and the four cardinal points (north, south, east, and west) are said in order to renew their energy for the upcoming year. It's customary to wear white with a red ribbon. March 21. (You can see the serpent's shadow at Chichén-Itzá from March 19 to 23.)

April, May, and June

Semana Santa (Holy Week) celebrates the last week in the life of Christ from Palm Sunday through Easter Sunday with somber religious processions, spoofs of Judas, and reenactments of specific biblical events, plus food and craft fairs. Businesses close during this traditional week of

Mexican national vacations. If you plan on traveling to Mexico or around the Yucatán during Holy Week, make your reservations early. Airline seats on flights into and out of the country are reserved months in advance. Buses to almost anywhere in Mexico are always full, so try arriving on the Wednesday or Thursday prior to the start of Holy Week. Easter Sunday is quiet. The following week is a traditional vacation period. Week before Easter.

Labor Day is a national holiday celebrating workers. It features country-wide parades and fiestas. May 1.

Cinco de Mayo is a national holiday that celebrates the defeat of the French at the Battle of Puebla in 1862. May 5.

The month long **Fiestas de Mayo (May Festivities)** is celebrated in Chetumal, at the Mayan Kohunlich ruins. During the first week of this cultural celebration, visitors can witness the ritual of the sacred copal of Kihunlich, the pyramid of masks. Other festivities include fireworks, dances, and theatre reenactments of centuries-old wars. For more information, visit the state's official events Web site, www.quintanaroo.gob.mx/nuestroestado/eventos/eventos2000/eventos_2000.htm.

July, August, and September

Mexico begins **Día de Independencia (Independence Day)** — the holiday that marks Mexico's independence from Spain — at 11 p.m. on September 15, with the president of Mexico's famous independence *grito* (shout) from the National Palace in Mexico City. The rest of the country watches the event on TV or participates in local celebrations, which mirror the festivities at the national level. September 16 is actually Independence Day and is celebrated with parades, picnics, and family reunions throughout the country. September 15 and 16.

During the **fall equinox,** Chichén-Itzá once again takes center stage as the same shadow play that occurs during the spring equinox repeats itself for the fall equinox. September 21 and 22.

October, November, and December

What's commonly called the **Día de los Muertos (Day of the Dead)** is actually two days: All Saints Day, honoring saints and deceased children, and All Souls Day, honoring deceased adults. Relatives gather at cemeteries countrywide, carrying candles and food and often spending the night beside the graves of loved ones. Weeks before, bakers begin producing bread formed in the shape of mummies and round loaves decorated with bread "bones." Decorated sugar skulls emblazoned with glittery names are sold everywhere. Many days ahead, homes and churches erect special altars laden with bread, fruit, flowers, candles, photographs of saints and of the deceased, and favorite foods. On these two nights, children walk through the streets dressed in costumes and masks, often carrying mock coffins and pumpkin lanterns, into which they expect money to be dropped. November 1 and 2.

The **Annual Mexico-Caribbean Food Festival (Festival Gastronomico del Caribe Mexicano)** in Cancún features a broad range of culinary creations from the finest restaurants in this popular resort and a number of others from the Mayan Riviera and Isla Mujeres. Generally held the first two weeks of November, visit http://festivalgastronomico.qroo.gob.mx or www.cancun.info for details and schedules.

Día de Revolución (Revolution Day) is a national holiday commemorating the start of the Mexican Revolution in 1910 with parades, speeches, rodeos, and patriotic events. November 20.

During the **Día de Nuestra Señora de Guadalupe (Feast of the Virgin of Guadalupe)**, the patroness of Mexico is honored throughout the country with religious processions, street fairs, dancing, fireworks, and masses. It's one of Mexico's most moving and beautiful displays of traditional culture. In December 1531, the Virgin of Guadalupe appeared to a young man, Juan Diego, on a hill near Mexico City. He convinced the bishop that he had seen the apparition by revealing his cloak, upon which the Virgin was emblazoned. December 12.

Christmas Posadas celebrates the Holy Family's trek to Bethlehem. On each of the nine nights before Christmas, door-to-door candlelit processions in cities and villages nationwide reenact the Holy Family's search for an inn. December 15 to 24.

Part II
Planning Your Trip to Cancún and the Yucatán

The 5th Wave   By Rich Tennant

In this part . . .

Ready to travel to Mexico's Yucatán? Well then, it's probably time to do a little planning. In this part, we help you with all the things you need to consider when booking your ideal trip to one of Mexico's Yucatán beach destinations. Nothing will take away the pleasure of lazy days faster than worries about spending too much money, so spend some time reading through Chapter 5 to ward away those stressful thoughts and stay in the green. Chapters 6 and 7 help you get to the area and book your accommodations; we also help you decide whether to use a travel agent or take care of the arrangements on your own and cover the pros and cons of package deals. In Chapter 8, we offer some tips for travelers with special needs — whether you're a solo traveler or a family — in order to help ensure that you pick exactly the right place that fulfills both your personal requirements and your expectations. Finally, Chapter 9 covers all the final details — from getting your passport to packing your bags — you need to enjoy a hassle-free vacation.

Chapter 5

Managing Your Money

In This Chapter

▶ Figuring out the expenses of your trip

▶ Discovering budget-saving tips

▶ Understanding Mexican currency

▶ Dealing with a stolen wallet

he brochures are in front of you, and visions of lazy, sunny days fill your thoughts — so who wants to think about money? Trust me — take a few minutes to figure out your expected expenses now, so you can enjoy a worry-free vacation later.

Your budget is greatly affected by your choice of beach resort. An all-inclusive resort on the Riviera Maya costs more than a modest beach-side hotel in Cozumel. Within Cancún itself, a room on the beach of Isla Cancún is considerably more expensive than one in Ciudad Cancún (Cancún City), and ditto for all the other expenses down the line. After you decide where you want to go, and you have your hotel and airfare down, it's a good idea to calculate the other estimated costs associated with your trip to plan a proper budget.

Most people save all year to be able to enjoy a wonderful vacation, so in this chapter, we share with you the finer points of stretching your dollars into pesos. We tell you about the nuances of changing currency to get more for your money and present the pros and cons of traveler's checks, credit cards, and cash. Finally, we tell you how to regroup after your wallet is lost or stolen.

Planning Your Budget

To make certain you don't forget any expenses, try taking a mental stroll through your entire trip. Start with the costs of transportation from your home to the airport, your airline tickets, and transfers to your hotel. Add your daily hotel rate (don't forget taxes!), meals, activities, entertainment, taxis, tips, your return to the airport, and finally, your return trip home from the airport and any parking fees you may have incurred. Just to be safe, add an extra 15 to 20% for extra, unexpected costs that may pop up.

Calculating your hotel cost

The biggest part of your vacation budget will go toward your hotel and airfare, so we suggest keeping those expenses as low as possible. In the various destination chapters in Parts III, IV, and V of this book, we use dollar signs ($–$$$$$) to indicate the price category of each hotel. (Check out Chapter 7 for a rundown on the price categories and their corresponding dollar signs.) You can get a room for $30 a night, or you can get a room for $700 a night!

Keep in mind that some room rates include breakfast — or may even include all meals, beverages, and entertainment — so be sure to compare mangos with mangos. Also, when finalizing your reservations, check whether the total cost includes taxes and tips. Even within a resort, the price of rooms can vary widely.

Room location — oceanfront versus a view of a dumpster — is one differential. Ask yourself how much your room location matters. Do you view your room as simply a place to sleep, shower, and dress? Or will you not feel officially "on vacation" unless you can fall asleep to the sound of the surf? If so, a pricier room may well be worth it. However, remember that many "garden view" rooms in our recommendations are only steps away from the beach and possibly even more tranquil than their oceanfront counterparts.

 Feeling romantic? Special packages for **honeymooners** are really popular in Mexican beach resorts. Even if you've been hitched for a while, it could be a second honeymoon, right? If you ask, you may end up with a complimentary bottle of champagne and flower petals on your bed.

 Mexico couldn't be more accommodating to travelers with children. Many of the larger chains don't charge extra for children staying in the same room as their parents, and some offer special meal programs and other amenities for younger travelers. Although rollaway beds are common, you may have a challenge finding a crib. Ask about this contingency when making your reservation.

Totaling transportation costs

After taking care of your airfare (for tips on keeping airfare costs down see Chapter 6), your transportation costs vary depending upon your choice of Yucatán beach resorts. Although some areas — like Cancún — offer economical shuttles and great public transportation options, others along the Riviera Maya are more expensive to get to and have little in the way of local transportation once you've arrived at your resort, making a rental car desirable if you're the type of traveler who likes to explore. These extra charges, however, can make getting around cost even more than getting there.

One advantage of a **package** tour (when you make one payment that covers airfare, hotel, round-trip transportation to and from your accommodations, and occasionally meals or tours) is that the round-trip ground transportation between the airport and your hotel is usually included. If you're not sure whether your package covers ground transportation, ask. Note that the taxi union inside Mexico is strong, so you're unlikely to find any shuttle transportation provided by your hotel.

 Generally, renting a car doesn't make sense, unless you're planning to explore the Yucatán on your own (and possibly Cozumel, if you're looking to explore the far side of the island there). Renting a small car runs about $70 a day on average, including insurance, so you may want to squeeze your car-dependent explorations into a day or two at the most. Also try to time your rental-car excursions to coincide with your arrival or departure so that you can use your wheels for either leg of your airport-hotel transportation needs.

As a rule, taxis tend to be the most economical and efficient transportation for getting around Cancún, Cozumel, and Isla. In each of the chapters detailing these resorts in Parts III, IV, and V, we provide taxi rates for getting around town.

Estimating dining dollars

In each resort's dining section, we describe our favorite restaurants, all of which include dollar signs ($–$$$$$) to give you an idea of the prices you can expect to pay. Refer to the Introduction of this book for a detailed explanation of these price categories.

The prices quoted refer to main courses at dinner, unless otherwise specified. We eliminated the most expensive shrimp and lobster dishes from our estimates to avoid pre-trip sticker shock. In most cases, you can find additional entrees above and below the quoted price range. To estimate your total dining expenses, add in estimated costs for beverages, appetizers, desserts, and tips as well.

Hotels increasingly are offering dining plans. To help you wade through the terminology, here's a review of the basics:

- ✓ **Continental plan (CP):** Includes a light breakfast — usually juices, fruits, pastries or breads, and coffee.

- ✓ **Breakfast plan (BP):** Includes a full, traditional American-style breakfast of eggs, bacon, French toast, hash browns, and so on.

- ✓ **Modified American plan (MAP):** Includes breakfast (usually a full one) and dinner.

- ✓ **Full American plan (FAP):** Includes three meals a day.

- ✓ **All-inclusive:** Includes three all-you-can-eat meals a day, plus snacks, soft drinks, alcoholic beverages, and entertainment, including special theme parties. Sometimes, additional charges apply for premium liquors or wines.

- ✓ **European plan (EP):** No meals are included.

Mexican beach-resort hotels are known for their expansive breakfast buffets. But the buffets can also be expensive, averaging about $20, even for small children. If breakfast is your main meal or only meal of the day, these all-you-can-eat extravaganzas may be worthwhile; otherwise, you're probably better off sleeping in or finding breakfast elsewhere.

Be sure to explore restaurants away from your hotel. You're likely to get a much better dining value, and you can truly savor the diverse flavors of Mexico. For eateries that best represent the flavorful (and we don't mean spicy) cuisine of Mexico, look for the Viva Mexico icon that accompanies some of the restaurant reviews throughout this book.

While you're in Mexico, be sure to try the local beers. Corona is the best-known brew, but other excellent choices are Bohemia, Modelo Especial, Pacifico, Indio, and Dos Equis Negro. Beer in Mexico is often cheaper than soft drinks! Your vacation is looking better and better, isn't it?

Getting tipping tips

Many travelers skimp on tips in Mexico, but please don't. Most of the employees in this country's hospitality industry receive the majority of their income from tips. For bellmen or porters, the equivalent of $1 per bag is appropriate. For hotel housekeeping, tip between $1 and $2 per night, depending upon the type of hotel you're staying in. For restaurant service, 15% is standard, but consider 20% if the service is particularly noteworthy. Oddly enough, the one area you don't need to consider tips for is taxis — it's not customary to tip taxi drivers here unless they help with baggage, or you've hired them on an hourly basis, and they double as a tour guide.

You'll no doubt run into all sorts of enterprising young boys looking for a tip to point you in the direction of your restaurant, help you into a parking spot, or do some other sort of unnecessary favor. In cases like these, tip as you see fit or as the spirit moves you.

Sightseeing

You're going to a beach resort, so regardless of your budget, you always have the option of simply soaking up the tropical sun during the day and then taking in the moonlit nights. It's the most economical plan and a relaxing and enjoyable option for many. Still, with so much to do and see, you're likely to want to spend some time and money getting out and enjoying the many treasures of Mexico.

Pricing for **sightseeing tours** varies by the destination, the length of time of the excursion, whether a meal and beverages are included, and other extras. However, here are some pretty typical ranges that you can use as a guideline: A city tour generally runs from $12 to $20; half-day boat cruises that include lunch can cost between $40 and $60; and full-day excursions to neighboring ruins run between $60 and $150.

If you plan to take part in any **sports-related activities** like golf, diving, or sport fishing, you may find the prices to be higher than back home. Dives range from around $50 to $70 for a two-tank dive, but here, you tend to really get what you pay for in terms of quality of equipment and dive guides, so it's best to pay up. Cozumel has the greatest selection of expert dive shops, and the competition makes Cozumel's prices the most reasonable for the quality of experience. Going fishing? You have to decide on variables beyond your point of departure, including size of boat, charter options, and type of gear and refreshments, but count on between $50 and $75 per person for a half-day charter.

Shopping

If **shopping** is your calling, you can plan to spend or save here. Besides silver jewelry and other souvenirs, the best excuse for shopping in Mexico is the great price of duty-free perfumes, watches, and other goods in Cancún and along the Riviera Maya. We discuss shopping specialties in greater detail within the respective destination chapters.

Catching the nightlife

As for **nightlife,** the cost depends more on your personal tastes. The hot nightlife is concentrated in Cancún, so if that's important to you, this is *the* spot in the Yucatán, although Playa del Carmen has some notable options as well. In Cancún, $20 cover charges are common during busier times. When you're out on the town, beer is the best bargain and costs about $1 to $3 per beer. National-branded drinks can run you around $3 to $5 each. Ladies can easily find bargains like two-for-one or all-you-can-drink specials.

Cutting Costs — But Not the Fun

While planning your trip, you need to keep in mind certain things that may help you save some money. Before you leave for vacation, don't forget to consider the incidentals that can really add up — hotel taxes, tips, and telephone surcharges.

Here are a few other suggestions to help keep a lid on expenses so that they don't run amuck and blow your vacation budget:

- ✔ **Travel in the off-season.** If you can travel at nonpeak times (September through November, for example), you can usually find better hotel bargains.

- ✔ **Travel on off days of the week.** If you can travel on a Tuesday, Wednesday, or Thursday, you may find cheaper flights to your destination. When you inquire about airfares, ask whether flying on a different day is cheaper.

- ✔ **Try a package tour.** With one call to a travel agent or packager, you can book airfare, hotel, ground transportation, and even some sightseeing for many of these destinations for a lot less than if you tried to put the trip together yourself. (See Chapter 5 for specific suggestions of package tour companies to contact.)

✔ **Always ask for discount rates.** Membership in AAA, frequent-flier plans, AARP, or other groups may qualify you for a discount on plane tickets and hotel rooms if you book them in the United States. In Mexico, you can generally get a discount based on how full the hotel is at the time you show up; however, you're also taking a chance on a vacancy not being available.

✔ **Get a room off the beach.** Accommodations within walking distance of the shore can be much cheaper than those right on the beach. Beaches in Mexico are public, so you don't need to stay in a hotel that's on the sand to spend most of your vacation at the beach.

✔ **Share your room with your kids.** In Mexico, this setup is usually the norm rather than the exception, so book a room with two double beds. Most hotels won't charge extra for up to two children staying in their parent's room.

✔ **Use public transportation whenever practical.** Not only will you save taxi fare, but simply getting to where you're going can be like a mini-excursion as you enjoy the local scene. In Cancún, you're apt to run into mostly tourists on the clean, public buses of the hotel zone.

✔ **Cut down on the souvenirs.** We don't expect you to return home without any local treasures, but think hard about whether that oversized sombrero will be as charming back home. Your photographs and memories are likely to be your best momentos.

✔ **Use public phones and prepaid phone cards to call home.** Avoid using the phone in your hotel room to call outside the hotel. Charges can be astronomical, even for local calls. Rather than placing the call yourself, ask the concierge to make a reservation for you — they do it as a service.

 You'll even be charged a surcharge for using your own calling card and its 800 number. *Remember:* Most 800 numbers are not toll-free when dialed from Mexico.

Also avoid using the public phones that urge you, in English, to call home using their 800 number. This ploy is the absolute most expensive way to call home, and the service charges the call to your home phone. The best option? Buy a Ladatel (brand name for Mexico's public phones) phone card, available at most pharmacies, and dial direct using the instructions in the appendix of this book.

✔ **Steer clear of the minibar and room service.** Those little bottles can really add up! Consider buying your own supplies and bringing them to your room, and you'll save a bundle. Likewise, room service is the most expensive way to dine — a service charge and tip are added on top of generally inflated prices. Also, some hotels provide complimentary bottled water, but others can charge as much as $5 per bottle, so be sure you know what you're drinking.

✔ **Drink local.** Imported labels can be twice the price as the locally popular brands, which often are also imported but just different brands than the ones you may be accustomed to seeing. At least ask what's being served as the house brand — you may be pleasantly surprised.

✔ **Follow Mexican custom and have lunch as your main meal.** If the restaurant of your dreams is open only for dinner, save that one for a "splurge" evening and try the others for your midday meal. Lunch tabs are usually a fraction of their dinner counterparts, and they frequently feature many of the same specialties.

✔ **Skimp on shrimp and lobster.** Sure, we know — you're sitting seaside and dreaming of that tasty lobster. Just understand that they're the priciest items on the menu, and the less expensive, local, fresh fish is often just as good or better.

✔ **Buy Mexican bottled water.** Forget the water labels that you know — Mexico's bottled waters are just as good as the imports and about half the price. Look for such brands as Santa María, Ciel, and Bonafont.

Making Sense of the Peso

The currency in Mexico is the **Mexican peso,** and in recent years, economists have been talking about its amazing recovery and resiliency against the U.S. dollar. At press time, each peso was worth close to 11 U.S. cents, which means that an item costing 11 pesos would be equivalent to US$1. Like most things in Mexico, the paper currency is colorful, and it comes in denominations of 20 (blue), 50 (pink), 100 (red), 200 (green), and 500 (burgundy) pesos. Coins come in denominations of 1, 2, 5, 10, and 20 pesos and 50 **centavos** (100 centavos equals 1 peso).

 New 50- and 500-peso bills look very similar, but 50-peso bills have a slightly pinkish hue and are smaller in size. However, always double-check how much you're paying and your change to avoid unpleasant surprises. The same applies to 10- and 20-peso coins. Twenty-peso coins are slightly larger than the 10-peso coins, but they look very similar.

Getting change continues to be a problem in Mexico. Small-denomination bills and coins are hard to come by, so start collecting them early in your trip and continue as you travel. Shopkeepers — and especially taxi drivers — always seem to be out of change and small bills; that's doubly true in a market. In other words, don't try to pay with a 500-peso bill when buying a 20-peso trinket.

Before you leave your hotel, it's a good idea to get a hundred pesos —
about US$9 — in change so that you're sure to have change for cab and
bus fares.

In this book, we use the universal currency sign ($) to indicate both U.S.
dollars and pesos in Mexico. When you're in Mexico, you'll notice the
common use of the currency symbol ($), generally indicating the price
in pesos. Go ahead and ask if you're not sure because some higher-end
places do tend to price their goods in U.S. dollars. Often, if a price is
quoted in U.S. dollars, the letters "USD" follow the price.

The rate of exchange fluctuates a tiny bit daily, so you're probably better
off not exchanging too much currency at once. Don't forget, however,
to have enough pesos to carry you over a weekend or Mexican holiday,
when banks are closed. In general, avoid carrying the U.S. $100 bill, the
bill most commonly counterfeited in Mexico, and therefore, the most dif-
ficult to exchange, especially in smaller towns. Because small bills and
coins in pesos are hard to come by in Mexico, the U.S. $1 bill is very
useful for tipping. A tip of U.S. coins is of no value to the service
provider because they can't be exchanged into Mexican currency.

To make your dollars go further, remember that ATMs offer the best
exchange rate; however, you need to consider any service fees. Mexican
banks offer the next-best fare, and they don't charge commission, unless
you're cashing traveler's checks, in which case they usually charge a
small commission. After banks, *casas de cambio* (houses of exchange)
are your next best option, and they usually charge a commission. You
can almost always get a lower exchange rate than when you exchange
your money at a hotel front desk.

Choosing Traveler's Checks, Credit Cards, or Cash

You need to think about *what kind* of money you're going to spend on
your vacation before you leave home.

ATMs and cash

These days, all the Mexico beach resorts detailed in this book have 24-
hour ATMs linked to a national network that almost always includes your
bank at home. **Cirrus** (☎ 800-424-7787; Internet: www.mastercard.com/
cardholderservices/atm/) and **Plus** (☎ 800-843-7587; Internet: www.
visa.com/atms) are the two most popular networks; check the back of
your ATM card to see which network your bank belongs to. The 800-
numbers and Web sites will give you specific locations of ATMs where
you can withdraw money while on vacation. Using ATMs permits you to
withdraw only as much cash as you need for a few days, which eliminates

the insecurity (and the pick-pocketing threat) of carrying around a wad of cash. Note, however, that a daily withdrawal maximum of about US $1,000 is common, though this amount does depend on your particular bank and type of account.

One important reminder: Many banks now charge a fee ranging from 50 cents to $3 when a non-account-holder uses their ATMs. Your own bank may also assess a fee for using an ATM that's not one of its branch locations. These fees mean that, in some cases, you get charged *twice* just for using your bankcard when you're on vacation. Although an ATM card can be an amazing convenience when traveling in another country (put your card in the machine and out comes foreign currency at an extremely advantageous exchange rate), banks are also likely to slap you with a "foreign currency transaction fee" just for making them do the pesos-to-dollars-to-pesos conversion math.

 As in many places worldwide, ATMs in Mexico are often targets for criminals looking to capture your bankcard information for fraudulent card-copying purposes. To be on the safe side, only use bank-sponsored ATMs, and even then, check the ATM carefully for any small cameras or other recording devices that can be used to copy your card. Shield the touch-pad when entering your PIN, for further protection against fraud.

Credit cards

Credit cards are invaluable when traveling. They're a safe way to carry "money," and they provide a convenient record of all your travel expenses when you arrive home.

 Travel with at least two different credit cards if you can. Depending on where you go, you may find MasterCard accepted more frequently than Visa (or vice versa), American Express honored or refused, and so on.

You can get **cash advances** from your credit card at any bank, and you don't even need to go to a teller — you can get a cash advance at the ATM if you know your **PIN number.** If you've forgotten your PIN number or didn't even know you had one, call the phone number on the back of your credit card and ask the bank to send it to you. It usually takes five to seven business days, though some banks will do it over the phone if you tell them your mother's maiden name or some other piece of personal information.

 Remember the hidden expense to contend with when borrowing cash from a credit card: Interest rates for cash advances are often significantly higher than rates for credit-card purchases. More importantly, you start paying interest on the advance *the moment you receive the cash.* On an airline-affiliated credit card, a cash advance does not earn frequent-flier miles.

Traveler's checks

Traveler's checks are something of an anachronism from the days when people wrote personal checks instead of going to an ATM. Because you can replace traveler's checks if lost or stolen, they were a sound alternative to filling your wallet with cash at the beginning of a trip.

Still, if you prefer the security of traveler's checks, you can get them at almost any bank. **American Express** offers checks in denominations of $20, $50, $100, $500, and $1,000. You pay a service charge ranging from 1 to 4%, though AAA members can obtain checks without a fee at most AAA offices. You can also get American Express traveler's checks over the phone by calling ☎ **800-221-7282.**

Visa (☎ **800-227-6811**) also offers traveler's checks, available at Citibank locations across the country and at several other banks. The service charge ranges between 1.5 and 2%; checks come in denominations of $50, $100, $500, and $1,000. **MasterCard** also offers traveler's checks; call ☎ **800-223-9920** for a location near you.

Although traveler's checks are very safe, consider that:

✔ You usually get charged a commission to cash your traveler's checks, and when you add that to the exchange-rate loss, you end up getting fewer pesos for your money.

✔ Many smaller shops don't take traveler's checks, so if you plan to shop, cash the traveler's checks before you embark on your shopping expedition.

Taxing Matters

There's a 15% **value-added tax (IVA)** on goods and services in most of Mexico, and it's supposed to be included in the posted price. This tax is 10% in Cancún and Cozumel. Unlike other countries (Canada and Spain, for example), Mexico doesn't refund this tax when visitors leave the country, so you don't need to hang on to those receipts for tax purposes.

All published prices you encounter in your travels around Mexico's beaches are likely to include all applicable taxes, except for hotel rates, which are usually published without the 15% IVA and the 2% lodging tax.

An **exit tax** of approximately $18 is imposed on every foreigner leaving Mexico. This tax is usually — but not always — included in the price of airline tickets. Be sure to reserve at least this amount in cash for your departure day if you're not certain that it's included in your ticket price.

Dealing with a Lost or Stolen Wallet

Odds are that if your wallet is gone, you've seen the last of it, and the police aren't likely to recover it for you. However, after you realize it's gone and you cancel your credit cards, you need to inform the police. You may need the police-report number for credit-card or insurance purposes later. After you've covered all the formalities and before you head to the nearest bar to drown your sorrows, retrace your steps — you may be surprised at how many honest people are in Mexico, and you may discover someone trying to find you to return your wallet.

Almost every credit-card company has an emergency toll-free number you can call if your wallet or purse is stolen. They may be able to wire you a cash advance off your credit card immediately; in many places, they can get you an emergency credit card within a day or two. The issuing bank's toll-free number is usually on the back of the credit card, but that doesn't help you much if the card was stolen. Write down the number on the back of your card before you leave and keep it in a safe place just in case.

If your credit card is stolen, major credit-card companies have emergency 800 numbers. Here's a list of numbers to call in the United States as well as internationally:

- ✔ **American Express** cardholders and traveler's check holders call ☎ 800-327-2177 (U.S. toll free); ☎ 336-393-1111 (international direct-dial) for gold and green cards.

- ✔ The toll-free, U.S. emergency number for **Visa** is ☎ 800-336-8472; from other countries, call ☎ 410-902-8012. Your card issuer can also provide you with the toll-free, lost/stolen-card number for the country or countries you plan to visit.

- ✔ **MasterCard** holders need to dial ☎ 800-826-2181 in the United States or 800-307-7309 from anywhere in the world; or ☎ 314-542-7111. Also check with your card issuer for the toll-free, lost/stolen-card number for the country or countries you want to visit.

For other credit cards, call the toll-free number directory at ☎ 800-555-1212.

To dial a U.S. toll-free number from inside Mexico, you must dial 001-880 and then the last seven digits of the toll-free number.

If you opt to carry **traveler's checks,** be sure to keep a record of their serial numbers so that you can handle this type of emergency. If you need emergency cash over the weekend when all banks and American

Express offices are closed, you can have money wired to you via **Western Union** (☎ 800-325-6000; www.westernunion.com).

Identity theft and fraud are potential complications of losing your wallet, especially if you've lost your driver's license along with your cash and credit cards. Notify the major credit-reporting bureaus immediately; placing a fraud alert on your records may protect you against liability for criminal activity. The three major U.S. credit-reporting agencies are **Equifax** (☎ 800-766-0008; www.equifax.com), **Experian** (☎ 888-397-3742; www.experian.com), and **TransUnion** (☎ 800-680-7289; www.transunion.com). Finally, if you've lost all forms of photo ID, call your airline and explain the situation; it may allow you to board the plane if you have a photocopy of your passport or birth certificate and a copy of the police report you've filed.

Chapter 6

Getting to the Yucatán

●●

In This Chapter
▶ Taking a look at airlines and airfares
▶ Understanding package tours

●●

*T*he obvious first step in enjoying your Mexican beach vacation is getting there. It's easy to do, but the options available can make a big
difference in the price you'll pay. To help minimize both the cost and the
time it will take to arrive, in this chapter, we point you in the direction of
available planning tools — including the Internet — and explain the benefits and limitations of traveling on a package tour. We offer tips on getting
the best airfares and choosing the best airline to whisk you away to your
dreamy beach along the Yucatán Peninsula.

Flying to Cancún and the Yucatán

The first step for the independent travel planner is finding the airlines
that fly to Cancún or Cozumel, the two major airport gateways for the
Yucatán's beach resorts In addition to regularly scheduled service,
direct charter services from U.S. cities to Cancún and Cozumel are
making it possible to fly direct from the largest airports in the United
States. However, if you find that no direct flights are available, you can
always reach your destination through a connection in Mexico City.

If you're booked on a flight through Mexico City, make sure your luggage
is checked through to your final destination. This arrangement is possible
if you're flying with affiliated or code-share airlines — separate airlines
that work closely together to help travelers reach final destinations via
connecting flights. This way, you don't have to lug your bags through
the Mexico City airport, and it saves a lot of time during the connecting
process.

For information about saving money on airfares using the Internet, see
the "Researching and Booking Your Trip Online" section later in this
chapter.

The main airlines operating direct or nonstop flights to Cancún and the Yucatán Peninsula include

✓ **Aeromexico** (☎ 800-237-6639; Internet: www.aeromexico.com). Flights to Cancún and Cozumel.

✓ **American Airlines** (☎ 800-433-7300; Internet: www.aa.com). Flights to Cancún and Cozumel.

✓ **ATA** (☎ 800-225-2995; Internet: www.ata.com). Flights to Cancún.

✓ **British Airways** (☎ 800-247-9297, 0345-222-111 or 0845-77-333-77 in Britain; Internet: www.british-airways.com). Flights from London to Cancún.

✓ **Continental Airlines** (☎ 800-525-0280; Internet: www.continental.com). Flights to Cancún and Cozumel.

✓ **Delta** (☎ 800-221-1212; Internet: www.delta.com). Flights to Cancún and Cozumel (serviced through Aeromexico).

✓ **Mexicana** (☎ 800-531-7921; Internet: www.mexicana.com). Flights to Cancún and Cozumel.

✓ **Northwest Airlines** (☎ 800-225-2525; Internet: www.nwa.com). Seasonal flights to Cancún and Cozumel.

✓ **US Airways** (☎ 800-428-4322; Internet: www.usairways.com). Flights to Cancún and Cozumel.

Getting the Best Deal on Your Airfare

Competition among the major U.S. airlines is unlike that of any other industry. A coach seat is virtually the same from one carrier to another, yet the difference in price may run as high as $1,000.

Business travelers, who need flexibility to purchase their tickets at the last minute, change their itinerary at a moment's notice, or want to get home before the weekend, pay the premium rate, known as the *full fare.* Passengers who can book their ticket long in advance, who don't mind staying over Saturday night, or who are willing to travel on a Tuesday, Wednesday, or Thursday pay the least.

Consolidators, also known as bucket shops, are great sources for international tickets, although they usually can't beat the Internet on fares within North America. Start by looking in Sunday newspaper travel sections; if you're a U.S. traveler, focus on the *New York Times, Los Angeles Times,* and *Miami Herald.* For less-developed destinations, small travel agents who cater to immigrant communities in large cities often have the best deals.

 Bucket shop tickets are usually nonrefundable or rigged with stiff cancellation penalties, often as high as 50 to 75% of the ticket price, and some put you on charter airlines with questionable safety records.

Several reliable consolidators are worldwide and available on the Net. **STA Travel** (☎ 800-781-4040; www.statravel.com), the world's leader in student travel, offers good fares for travelers of all ages. **Flights.com** (☎ 800-TRAV-800; www.flights.com) has excellent fares worldwide and local Web sites in 12 countries. **FlyCheap** (☎ 800-FLY-CHEAP; www.1800flycheap.com) is owned by package-holiday megalith MyTravel and so has especially good access to fares for sunny destinations. **Air Tickets Direct** (☎ 800-778-3447; www.airticketsdirect.com) is based in Montreal and leverages the currently weak Canadian dollar for low fares; it'll also book trips to places that U.S. travel agents won't touch, such as Cuba.

Here are some travel tips — tested and true — for getting the lowest possible fare:

✔ **Timing is everything.** If you can, avoid peak travel times. In Mexico, the weeks surrounding the Christmas/New Year holidays and Easter are so jam-packed that we find it unenjoyable to be at a beach resort anyway. Airfares are relatively expensive anytime between January and May, with September through mid-November offering the best deals. Specials pop up throughout the year, however, based on current demand, and last-minute specials on package tours are an increasingly popular way to travel.

✔ **Book in advance for great deals.** Forgetting what we said in the previous sentence, you can also save big by booking early — with excellent fares available for 30-, 60-, or even 90-day advance bookings. Note that if you need to change your schedule, a penalty charge of $75 to $150 is common.

✔ **Choose an off-peak travel day.** Traveling on a Tuesday, Wednesday, or even Thursday can also save you money. Even if you can't travel both ways on these lower-fare days, you can still save by flying off-peak at least one way.

✔ **Book travel during the midnight hour.** In the middle of the week, just after midnight, many airlines download cancelled low-priced airfares into their computers, so shortly after midnight is a great time to buy newly discounted seats. Midnight is the cutoff time for holding reservations. You may benefit by snagging cheap tickets that were just released by those who reserved — but never purchased — their tickets.

Researching and Booking Your Trip Online

The "big three" online travel agencies, **Expedia** (www.expedia.com), **Travelocity** (www.travelocity.com), and **Orbitz** (www.orbitz.com), sell most of the air tickets bought on the Internet. (If you're a Canadian traveler, try www.expedia.ca and www.travelocity.ca; U.K. residents can go for expedia.co.uk and opodo.co.uk.) Each has different business deals with the airlines and may offer different fares on the same flights, so shopping around is wise. Expedia and Travelocity will also send you an **e-mail notification** when a cheap fare becomes available to your favorite destination. Of the smaller travel agency Web sites, **SideStep** (www.sidestep.com) receives good reviews from users. It's a browser add-on that purports to "search 140 sites at once," but in reality beats competitors' fares only as often as other sites do.

Great **last-minute deals** are available through free weekly e-mail services provided directly by the airlines. Most of these deals are announced on Tuesday or Wednesday and must be purchased online. Most are only valid for travel that weekend, but some (such as Southwest's) can be booked weeks or months in advance. Sign up for weekly e-mail alerts at airline Web sites or check mega-sites that compile comprehensive lists of last-minute specials, such as **Smarter Living** (www.smarterliving.com). For last-minute trips, www.site59.com in the United States and www.lastminute.com in Europe often have better deals than the major-label sites.

If you're willing to give up some control over your flight details, use an *opaque fare service* like **Priceline** (www.priceline.com) or **Hotwire** (www.hotwire.com). Both offer rock-bottom prices in exchange for travel on a "mystery airline" at a mysterious time of day, often with a mysterious change of planes en route. The mystery airlines are all major, well-known carriers — and the possibility of being sent from Philadelphia to Chicago via Tampa is remote. But your chances of getting a 6 a.m. or 11 p.m. flight are pretty high. Hotwire tells you flight prices before you buy; Priceline usually has better deals than Hotwire, but you have to play its "name our price" game. *Note:* In 2004 Priceline added non-opaque service to its roster. You now have the option to choose exact flights, times, and airlines from a list of offers — or opt to bid on opaque fares as before.

Understanding Escorted and Package Tours

First, bear in mind that there's a big difference between an escorted tour and a package tour. With an *escorted tour,* the tour company takes care of all the details and tells you what to expect at each attraction. You know your costs up front, and an escorted tour can take you to the maximum number of sights in the minimum amount of time with the least amount of hassle. However, escorted tours are rare in Cancún and elsewhere in the Yucatán; most travelers, once they arrive at their destination, simply book tours and excursions with local travel agents.

Package tours generally consist of round-trip airfare, ground transportation to and from your hotel, and your hotel room price, including taxes. Some packages also include all food and beverages and most entertainment and sports, when booked at an all-inclusive resort. You may find that a package tour can save you big bucks and is an ideal vacation option.

For popular destinations like Cancún, package tours are the smart way to go. In many cases, a package that includes airfare, hotel, and transportation to and from the airport costs less than just the hotel alone if you booked it yourself.

Some package tours offer a better class of hotels than others, and some offer the same hotels for lower prices. Some offer flights on scheduled airlines; others book charter planes (which are known for having miniscule amounts of legroom). In some packages, your choice of accommodations and travel days may be limited. Some tours let you choose between escorted vacations and independent vacations; others allow you to add on just a few excursions or escorted day-trips (also at discounted prices) without booking an entirely escorted tour.

To find package tours, check out the travel section of your local Sunday newspaper or the ads in the back of national travel magazines such as *Travel & Leisure, National Geographic Traveler,* and *Condé Nast Traveler.* **Liberty Travel** (call ☎ **888-271-1584** to find the store nearest you; www.libertytravel.com) is one of the biggest packagers in the Northeast and usually boasts a full-page ad in Sunday papers.

Another good source of package deals is the airlines themselves. Most major airlines offer air/land packages, including **Aeromexico Vacations** (☎ 800-245-8585; www.aeromexico.com), **American Airlines Vacations** (☎ 800-321-2121; www.aavacations.com), **Delta Vacations** (☎ 800-221-6666; www.deltavacations.com), **Continental Airlines Vacations** (☎ 800-301-3800; www.covacations.com), **Mexicana Vacations** (☎ 800-531-9321; www.mexicana.com) and **United Vacations** (☎ 888-854-3899; www.unitedvacations.com). Several big **online travel agencies** — Expedia, Travelocity, Orbitz, Site59, and Lastminute.com — also do a brisk business in packages. If you're unsure about the pedigree of a smaller packager, check with the Better Business Bureau in the city where the company is based, or go online at www.bbb.org. If a packager won't tell you where it's based, don't fly with it.

You can even shop for these packages online — try these sites for a start:

✔ One specialist in Mexico vacation packages is www.mexicotravel net.com, an agency that offers most of the well-known travel packages to Mexico beach resorts, plus offers last-minute specials.

✔ Check out www.2travel.com and find a page with links to a number of the big-name Mexico packagers, including several of the ones listed in this chapter.

✔ For last-minute, air-only packages or package bargains, check out **Vacation Hotline** at www.vacationhotline.net. After you find your deal, you need to call the number to make final booking arrangements, but it offers packages from both the popular Apple and Funjet vacation wholesalers.

Several companies specialize in packages to Mexico's beaches; they usually fly in their own, chartered airplanes, so they can offer greatly discounted rates. Here are some of the packagers we prefer:

- ✔ **Apple Vacations** (☎ 800-365-2775; Internet: www.applevacations. com) offers inclusive packages to all the beach resorts and has the largest selection of hotels in Cancún, Cozumel, and the Riviera Maya. Apple perks include special baggage handling (company representatives take your bags from the airport directly to the hotel room, saving you the hassle) and the services of an Apple representative at the major hotels. Apple vacations must be booked through a travel agent, but both its Web site and toll-free number easily connect you with one close to you.

- ✔ **Classic Custom Vacations** (☎ 800-635-1333; www.classiccustom vacations.com) specializes in package vacations to Mexico's finest luxury resorts. It combines discounted first-class and economy airfare with stays at the most exclusive hotels in Cancún and the Riviera Maya, as well as other destinations in Mexico. In many cases, packages also include meals, airport transfers, and upgrades. The prices are not for bargain hunters but for those who seek luxury.

- ✔ **Funjet Vacations** (bookable through any travel agent, with general information available on its Web site at www.funjet.com) is one of the largest vacation packagers in the United States. Funjet has packages to Cancún, Cozumel, and the Riviera Maya.

- ✔ **GOGO Worldwide Vacations** (☎ 888-636-3942; Internet: www.gogo wwv.com) has trips to all the major beach destinations, including Cancún, offering several exclusive deals from higher-end hotels. These trips are bookable through any travel agent.

- ✔ **Pleasant Mexico Holidays** (☎ 800-448-3333; Internet: www.pleasant holidays.com) is another of the largest vacation packagers in the United States with hotels in Cancún and Cozumel.

The biggest hotel chains and resorts also offer packages. If you already know where you want to stay, call the hotel or resort and ask whether it offers land/air packages.

Chapter 7

Booking Your Accommodations

● ●

In This Chapter

▶ Choosing a room that's right for you
▶ Surfing for hotel rooms
▶ Getting the best room at the best rate

● ●

*W*hether you've chosen a package deal or you're planning your trip on your own, getting a room is a crucial part of your vacation planning. In this chapter, we help you decipher the various rates and provide some tips on how to get the best one, including searching the Internet for your ideal place to stay. We also compare the pros and cons of different types of places to stay.

Getting to Know Your Options

From small inns to large all-inclusives, the beach resorts along Mexico's Yucatán Peninsula offer every type of vacation accommodation. And the prices can vary even more! Recommendations for specific places to stay are in the chapters devoted to the individual beach towns. We try to provide the widest range of options — both in types of hotels as well as budgets — but we always keep comfort in mind. What you find in this book is what we believe to be the best value for your money. Here are the major types of accommodations:

▱ **Resorts:** These accommodations tend to be the most popular option — especially with package tours — because they offer the most modern amenities, including cable TV, hair dryers, in-room safes, and generally, a selection of places to dine or have a drink. Large by definition, they may also boast various types of sporting facilities, spa services, shopping arcades, and tour-desk services. These places also tend to be the most expensive type of accommodation, but can be heavily discounted if your timing is right.

▱ **Hotels:** These quarters tend to be smaller than resorts, with fewer facilities. In terms of style, look for anything from hacienda-style villas to all-suite hotels or sleek, modern structures. Most hotels at Mexican beach resorts have at least a small swimming pool, and if they're not located directly on a beach, hotels frequently offer shuttle service to a beach club or an affiliate beachfront hotel.

✔ **All-inclusives:** In Mexico, all-inclusives are gaining rapidly in popularity, and they seem to be getting larger and larger in size. As the name implies, all-inclusives tie everything together in one price — your room, meals, libations, entertainment, sports activities, and sometimes, off-site excursions. The advantage that many travelers find with this option is an expected fixed price for their vacation — helpful if you need to stay within a strict budget. Many all-inclusives have their own nightclubs or, at least, offer evening shows and entertainment, such as theme nights, talent contests, or costume parties. As for the food, you may never go hungry, but you're unlikely to go gourmet either. Food quality can be an important variable, about which it helps to have talked to someone who's recently been to the particular all-inclusive, or check online message boards for up-to-date commentaries on the buffets.

✔ **Condos, apartments, and villas:** One of these accommodations can be a good option, especially if you're considering a stay longer than a week, and the reach of the Internet has made these lodging options extremely viable. Many condos, apartments, and villas come with housekeepers or even cooks. It's hard to know exactly what you're getting — and often it's futile to complain after you arrive — so again, word of mouth can be helpful here. At the very least, ask for references or search on the Internet to see whether anyone can offer an experience. In addition to the Internet, select options are always advertised in the major metropolitan newspapers, such as the *Los Angeles Times,* the *Chicago Tribune,* and *The New York Times.* Our recommendation? Save this option for your second visit when you have a better idea about the various parts of town and the area in general.

In Mexico, where smoking is still the norm, expect that your room will be smoker-friendly. However having said that, an increasing number of hotels — especially the larger resorts — now offer non-smoking rooms. And, many of the holistic-oriented retreats along the Riviera Maya are smoke-free. Be sure to ask when booking a room to ensure you get your preference.

Mexico's system of rating hotels and resorts is more generous on its handing out of "stars." Here, the top-of-the-line resorts are known as "Grand Turismo," and from there, it ranges from five stars down. So, booking a four-star resort will generally result in much more modest accommodations than the equivalent ranking in the United States.

Table 7-1 shows how you how we've categorized hotel prices in each of the remaining chapters. Our rankings consider prices for a room based on double occupancy for one night during high season.

Table 7-1	Key to Hotel Dollar Signs	
Dollar Sign(s)	*Price Range*	*What to Expect*
$	Less than $75	These accommodations are simple and simply inexpensive. Rooms will likely be small, and televisions are not necessarily provided. Parking is not provided but rather catch-as-you-can on the street. These may include basic rooms with hammocks for sleeping in.
$$	$76–$125	A bit classier, these mid-range accommodations offer more room, more extras (such as irons, hair dryers, or a microwave), and a more convenient location than the preceding category.
$$$	$126–$175	Rooms in this category are generally beachfront, and come with plenty of extras to make your stay comfortable — such as restaurants, a large pool, and tour services, but may not be as modern as other choices. Or, in some of the more remote parts of the Yucatán, this category may be the top-of-the-line.
$$$$	$176–$250	Higher-class still, these accommodations are plush, and with ocean views and direct beach access. Think chocolates on your pillow, a classy restaurant, underground parking garages, and often on-site spas. Many all-inclusives fall into this category, so your meals and drinks will also be part of the price you pay for the room.
$$$$$	$251 and up	These top-rated accommodations come with luxury amenities such as valet parking, on-premise spas, and in-room hot tubs, plasma-screen TVs and CD players — but you pay through the nose for 'em.

Finding the Best Room at the Best Rate

Finding the best hotel room your money can buy isn't rocket science. With our advice in this section, you may very well find a terrific deal on your room.

Finding the best rate

When it comes to rates, the most common term is **rack rate.** The rack rate is the maximum rate that a resort or hotel charges for a room. It's the rate you get if you walk in off the street and ask for a room on a night that the place is close to being full.

The rack rate is the first rate a hotel offers, but you usually don't have to pay it. Always ask whether a lower rate or special package is available — it can't hurt, and you may at least end up with a free breakfast or spa service.

In this book, we use rack rates as a guidepost, not expecting that you'll have to pay them. Minimum night stays, special promotions, and seasonal discounts can all go a long way in bringing the rack rate down. Also, be sure to mention your frequent-flier or corporate-rewards programs if you book with one of the larger hotel chains. Please note that rates change very often, so the prices quoted in this book may be different from the prices you're quoted when you make your reservation.

Room rates also rise and fall with occupancy rates. If your choice of hotels is close to empty, it pays to negotiate. Resorts tend to be much more crowded during weekends. If you're traveling off-season (see Chapter 4 for peak and low occupancy times), you can almost certainly negotiate a bargain.

Our experience is you'll get the best rate by booking your hotel as part of an air-hotel package (see Chapter 6), but in lieu of that, try contacting the local number for your best chance of negotiating the best rate. Just note — it may help if you speak Spanish.

Surfing the Web for hotel deals

Shopping online for hotels is generally done one of two ways: by booking through the hotel's own Web site or through an independent booking agency (or a fare-service agency like Priceline). These Internet hotel agencies have multiplied in mind-boggling numbers of late, competing for the business of millions of consumers surfing for accommodations around the world. This competitiveness can be a boon if you have the patience and time to shop and compare the online sites for good deals — but shop they must, for prices can vary considerably from site to site. And keep in mind that hotels at the top of a site's listing may be there for no other reason than that they paid to get the placement.

Of the "big three" sites, **Expedia** offers a long list of special deals and *virtual tours* or photos of available rooms so you can see what you're paying for (a feature that helps counter the claims that the best rooms are often held back from bargain booking Web sites). **Travelocity** posts unvarnished customer reviews and ranks its properties according to the AAA rating system. Also reliable are **Hotels.com** and **Quikbook.com.** An excellent free program, **TravelAxe** (www.travelaxe.net), can help you search multiple hotel sites at once, even ones you may never have heard of — and conveniently lists the total price of the room, including the taxes and service charges. Another booking site, **Travelweb** (www.travelweb. com), is partly owned by the hotels it represents (including the Hilton, Hyatt, and Starwood chains) and is therefore plugged directly into the hotels' reservations systems — unlike independent online agencies, which have to fax or e-mail reservation requests to the hotel, a good portion of which get misplaced in the shuffle. More than once, travelers have arrived at the hotel, only to be told that they have no reservation. To be fair, many of the major sites are undergoing improvements in service and ease of use, and Expedia will soon be able to plug directly into the reservations systems of many hotel chains — none of which can be bad news for consumers. In the meantime, it's a good idea to get a confirmation number and make a printout of any online booking transaction.

In the opaque Web site category, **Priceline** and **Hotwire** are even better for hotels than for airfares; with both, you're allowed to choose the neighborhood and quality level of your hotel before offering up your money. Priceline's hotel product even covers Europe and Asia, although it's much better at getting five-star lodging for three-star prices than at finding anything at the bottom of the scale. On the down side, many hotels stick Priceline guests in their least desirable rooms. Be sure to go to the BiddingforTravel Web site (www.biddingfortravel.com) before bidding on a hotel room on Priceline; it features a fairly up-to-date list of hotels that Priceline uses in major cities. For both Priceline and Hotwire, you pay upfront, and the fee is nonrefundable. *Note:* Some hotels do not provide loyalty program credits or points or other frequent-stay amenities when you book a room through opaque online services.

✔ Although the name **All Hotels on the Web** (www.all-hotels.com) is something of a misnomer, the site *does* have tens of thousands of listings throughout the world. Bear in mind that each hotel has paid a small fee ($25 and up) to be listed, so it's less of an objective list and more like a book of online brochures.

✔ **hoteldiscount!com** (www.hoteldiscount.com) lists bargain room rates at hotels in more than 50 U.S. and international cities. The cool thing is that hoteldiscount!com prebooks blocks of rooms in advance, so sometimes it has rooms — at discount rates — at hotels that are "sold out." Select a city and input your dates, and you get a list of the best prices for a selection of hotels. This site is notable for delivering deep discounts in cities where hotel rooms are expensive. The toll-free number is printed all over the site (☎ 800-96-HOTEL); call it if you want more options than are listed online.

✔ **InnSite** (www.innsite.com) has B&B listings in all 50 states and more than 50 countries around the globe. Find an inn at your destination, see pictures of the rooms, and check prices and availability. This extensive directory of bed-and-breakfasts includes listings only if the proprietor submitted one. (It's free to get an inn listed.)

Innkeepers write the descriptions, and many listings link to the inns' own Web sites. Also check out the **Bed and Breakfast Channel** (www.bedandbreakfast.com).

✔ **TravelWeb** (www.travelweb.com) lists more than 26,000 hotels in 170 countries, focusing on chains such as Hyatt and Hilton, and you can book almost 90% of these listings online. The site's Click-It Weekends, updated each Monday, offers weekend deals at many leading hotel chains.

✔ Specific to Mexico, **Mexico Boutique Hotels** (http://mexico boutiquehotels.com) has listings of small, unique properties that are unlikely to show up on the radar screens of most travel agents or large Web travel sites. In addition to very complete descriptions, the site also offers an online booking service.

✔ Check the Web sites of Mexico's top hotel chains for special deals. These include www.caminoreal.com, www.hyatt.com, www.starwoodhotels.com, and www.fiestaamericana.com.

Reserving the best room

After you make your reservation, asking one or two more pointed questions can go a long way toward making sure you get the best room in the house. Always ask for a corner room. They're usually larger, quieter, and have more windows and light than standard rooms, and they don't always cost more. Also ask whether the hotel is renovating; if it is, request a room away from the renovation work. Inquire, too, about the location of the restaurants, bars, and discos in the hotel — all sources of annoying noise. And if you aren't happy with your room when you arrive, talk to the front desk. If they have another room, they should be happy to accommodate you, within reason.

Mention you are honeymooners, and ask for the best available room — Mexico beach resorts are especially accommodating to newlyweds.

Most beachfront hotels offer either ground-floor rooms with terraces, or upper-level rooms with balconies. If you have a preference, be sure to request it at the time of booking.

Chapter 8

Catering to Special Needs or Interests

● ●

In This Chapter

▶ Bringing the kids along

▶ Traveling tips for those with special needs

▶ Getting hitched in Mexico

● ●

*M*ost individuals consider themselves unique and as having special needs, but some types of travelers really do warrant a little extra advice. In this chapter, we cover information that's helpful to know if you're traveling with children. If you're a senior traveler or you're traveling solo, we have plenty of tips for you, too. Individuals with disabilities can also mine this chapter for useful info. Gay and lesbian travelers can find a section devoted to them as well. And for those of you planning a wedding, we include a section on tying the knot in Mexico. Throughout the chapter, we clue you in on what to expect, offer useful tips, and whenever possible, steer you to experts concerning your particular circumstances.

Traveling with the Brood: Advice for Families

Children are considered the national treasure of Mexico, and Mexicans warmly welcome and cater to your children. Although many parents were reluctant to bring young children to Mexico in the past, primarily due to health concerns, we can't think of a better place to introduce children to the exciting adventure of exploring a different culture. One of the best destinations for children in Mexico is Cancún. Hotels can often arrange for a baby sitter. Some hotels in the moderate-to-luxury range have small playgrounds and pools for children and hire caretakers who offer special-activity programs during the day, but few budget hotels offer these amenities. All-inclusive resorts make great options for family travel.

Before leaving for your trip, check with your pediatrician or family doctor to get advice on medications to take along. Mexican-brand disposable diapers cost about the same as diapers in the United States, but the quality is poorer. You can purchase U.S.-brand diapers, but you'll pay a higher price. Familiar, brand-name baby foods are sold in many stores. Dry cereals, powdered formulas, baby bottles, and purified water are all easily available in midsize and large cities or resorts.

Cribs, however, may present a problem; only the largest and most luxurious hotels provide them. However, rollaway beds to accommodate children staying in a room with their parents are often available. Child seats or highchairs at restaurants are common, and most restaurants go out of their way to accommodate your children. You may want to seriously consider bringing your own car seat along because they're not readily available to rent in Mexico.

We recommend you take coloring books, puzzles, and small games with you to keep your children entertained during the flight or whenever you're traveling from one destination to the next. Another good idea is to take a blank notebook, in which you and your children can paste souvenirs from your trip — perhaps the label from the beer daddy drank on the beach, or small shells and flowers that they collect. And don't forget to carry small scissors and a glue stick with you, or the blank notebook may remain blank.

You can find good family-oriented vacation advice on the Internet from sites like the (www.familytravelforum.com), a comprehensive site that offers customized trip planning; **Family Travel Network** (www.family travelnetwork.com), an award-winning site that offers travel features, deals, and tips; **Traveling Internationally with Your Kids** (www.travel withyourkids.com), a comprehensive site that offers customized trip planning; and **Family Travel Files** (www.thefamilytravelfiles.com), which offers an online magazine and a directory of off-the-beaten-path tours and tour operators for families.

Throughout this book, you'll notice the KidFriendly icon, which will alert you to those hotels, restaurants, and activities that are especially suitable for family travelers. If parents are looking for a little alone-time, we also list local babysitting resources in the Fast Facts section of the appendix.

For children under 18 traveling without parents or with only one parent, they must travel with a notarized letter from the absent parent or parents authorizing the travel. We go over this in detail in Chapter 9, in the discussion on entry requirements into Mexico. Don't arrive at the airport without it, or your trip to those powdery white beaches of the Yucatán will be delayed!

Making Age Work for You: Tips for Seniors

People over the age of 60 are traveling more than ever before. And why not? Being a senior citizen entitles you to some terrific travel bargains.

Mention the fact that you're a senior citizen when you make your travel reservations. Although all of the major U.S. airlines except America West have cancelled their senior discount and coupon book programs, many hotels still offer discounts for seniors. In most cities, people over the age of 60 qualify for reduced admission to theaters, museums, and other attractions, as well as discounted fares on public transportation.

Members of **AARP** (formerly known as the American Association of Retired Persons), 601 E St. NW, Washington, DC 20049 (☎ 888-687-2277 or 202-434-2277; www.aarp.org), get discounts on hotels, airfares, and car rentals. AARP offers members a wide range of benefits, including *AARP: The Magazine* and a monthly newsletter. Anyone over 50 can join.

Many reliable agencies and organizations target the 50-plus market. **Elderhostel** (☎ 877-426-8056; www.elderhostel.org) arranges study programs for those aged 55 and over (and a spouse or companion of any age) in the United States and in more than 80 countries around the world. Most courses last five to seven days in the United States (2–4 weeks abroad), and many include airfare, accommodations in university dormitories or modest inns, meals, and tuition. **ElderTreks** (☎ 800-741-7956; www.eldertreks.com) offers small-group tours to off-the-beaten-path or adventure-travel locations, restricted to travelers 50 and older. **INTRAV** (☎ 800-456-8100; www.intrav.com) is a high-end tour operator that caters to the mature, discerning traveler, not specifically seniors, with trips around the world that include guided safaris, polar expeditions, private-jet adventures, and small-boat cruises down jungle rivers.

Recommended publications offering travel resources and discounts for seniors include: the quarterly magazine *Travel 50 & Beyond* (www.travel50andbeyond.com); *Travel Unlimited: Uncommon Adventures for the Mature Traveler* (Avalon); *101 Tips for Mature Travelers,* available from Grand Circle Travel (☎ 800-221-2610 or 617-350-7500; www.gct.com); *The 50+ Traveler's Guidebook* (St. Martin's Press); and *Unbelievably Good Deals and Great Adventures That You Absolutely Can't Get Unless You're Over 50* (McGraw-Hill) by Joann Rattner Heilman.

Mature Outlook (☎ 800-267-3277) is a similar organization, sponsored by Sears, which offers discounts on car rentals and hotel stays. The $19.95 annual membership fee also gets you $200 in Sears coupons and a bimonthly magazine, *New Outlook,* plus access to its online version, at www.newoutlook.ca. Membership is open to all Sears customers 18 and over, but the organization's primary focus is on the 50-and-over market.

Mexico is a popular country for retirees and for senior travelers. For decades, North Americans have been living indefinitely in Mexico by returning to the border and re-crossing with a new tourist permit every six months. Mexican immigration officials have caught on, and they now limit the maximum time you can spend in the country to six months in any given year. This measure is meant to encourage even partial residents to comply with the proper documentation procedures.

AIM (Apdo. Postal 31–70, 45050 Guadalajara, Jalisco, Mexico) is a well-written, candid, and very informative newsletter for prospective retirees. Subscriptions are $18 to the United States and $21 to Canada. Back issues are three for $5.

Sanborn Tours (2015 S. 10th St., Post Office Drawer 519, McAllen, TX 78505-0519; ☎ 800-395-8482) offers a "Retire in Mexico" orientation tour.

Accessing the Yucatán: Advice for Travelers with Disabilities

Many travel agencies offer customized tours and itineraries for travelers with disabilities. **Flying Wheels Travel** (☎ 507-451-5005; www.flying wheelstravel.com) offers escorted tours and cruises that emphasize sports and private tours in minivans with lifts. **Access-Able Travel Source** (☎ 303-232-2979; www.access-able.com) offers extensive access information and advice for traveling around the world with disabilities. **Accessible Journeys** (☎ 800-846-4537 or 610-521-0339) offers tours for wheelchair travelers and their families and friends.

Organizations that offer assistance to disabled travelers include **MossRehab** (www.mossresourcenet.org), which provides a library of accessible-travel resources online; **SATH (Society for Accessible Travel and Hospitality)** (☎ 212-447-7284; www.sath.org; annual membership fees: $45 adults, $30 seniors and students), which offers a wealth of travel resources for all types of disabilities and informed recommendations on destinations, access guides, travel agents, tour operators, vehicle rentals, and companion services; and the **American Foundation for the Blind** (AFB) (☎ 800-232-5463; www.afb.org), a referral resource for the blind or visually impaired that includes that includes information on traveling with Seeing Eye dogs.

For more information specifically targeted to travelers with disabilities, the community Web site **iCan** (www.icanonline.net/channels/travel/index.cfm) has destination guides and several regular columns on accessible travel. Also check out the quarterly magazine *Emerging Horizons* ($14.95 per year, $19.95 outside the United States; www.emerginghorizons.com); **Twin Peaks Press** (☎ 360-694-2462; http://disabilitybookshop.virtualave.net/blist84.htm), offering travel-related books for travelers with special needs; and *Open World Magazine,* published by SATH (subscription: $13 per year, $21 outside the United States).

A World of Options, a 658-page book of resources for travelers with disabilities, covers everything from biking trips to scuba outfitters. It costs $35 and is available from **Mobility International USA** (P.O. Box 10767, Eugene, OR 97440; ☎ 541-343-1284 voice and TTY; Internet: www.miusa.org).

We need to say that Mexico does fall far behind other countries when it comes to accessible travel. In fact, the area may seem like one giant obstacle course to travelers in wheelchairs or on crutches. At airports, you may encounter steep stairs before finding a well-hidden elevator or escalator — if one exists at all. Airlines often arrange wheelchair assistance for passengers to the baggage area. Porters are generally available to help with luggage at airports and large bus stations after you clear baggage claim.

In addition, escalators (and you won't find many in the beach resorts) are often non-operational. Stairs without handrails abound. Few restrooms are equipped for travelers with disabilities, and when one is available, access to it may be via a narrow passage that won't accommodate a wheelchair or a person on crutches. Many deluxe hotels (the most expensive) now have rooms with baths for people with disabilities. Budget travelers may be best off looking for single-story motels, although accessing showers and bathrooms may still pose a problem outside of specially equipped deluxe hotels. Generally speaking, no matter where you are, someone will lend a hand, although you may have to ask for it.

Although Cancún's international airport has become increasingly modernized in recent years, in other parts of Mexico few airports offer the luxury of boarding an airplane from the waiting room. You either descend stairs to a bus that ferries you to a waiting plane that you board by climbing stairs, or you walk across the airport tarmac to your plane and climb up the stairs. Deplaning presents the same problems in reverse.

In our opinion, the wide, modern streets and sidewalks of Cancún make it the most "accessible" resort. In addition to the superior public facilities, you can find numerous accommodation options for travelers with disabilities.

Following the Rainbow: Resources for Gay and Lesbian Travelers

Mexico is a conservative country with deeply rooted Catholic religious traditions. Public displays of same-sex affection are rare, and two men displaying such behavior is still considered shocking, especially outside the major resort areas. Women in Mexico frequently walk hand in hand, but anything more would cross the boundary of acceptability. However, gay and lesbian travelers are generally treated with respect and shouldn't experience any harassment, assuming that the appropriate regard is given to local culture and customs. Cancún is the most gay-friendly of the resorts in the Yucatán, with Playa del Rey (also known as Playa Delfines) a popular meeting spot for boys and girls.

Many agencies offer tours and travel itineraries specifically for gay and lesbian travelers. **Above and Beyond Tours** (☎ **800-397-2681;** www.above

beyondtours.com) is the exclusive gay and lesbian tour operator for United Airlines. **Now, Voyager** (☎ 800-255-6951; www.nowvoyager.com) is a well-known San Francisco–based gay-owned and operated travel service. **Olivia Cruises & Resorts** (☎ 800-631-6277 or 510-655-0364; www.olivia.com) charters entire resorts and ships for exclusive lesbian vacations and offers smaller group experiences for both gay and lesbian travelers.

The following travel guides are available at most travel bookstores and gay and lesbian bookstores, or you can order them from **Giovanni's Room** bookstore, 1145 Pine St., Philadelphia, PA 19107 (☎ 215-923-2960; www.giovannisroom.com): *Frommer's Gay & Lesbian Europe,* an excellent travel resource (www.frommers.com); *Out and About* (☎ 800-929-2268 or 415-644-8044; www.outandabout.com), which offers guidebooks and a newsletter ($20/yr; 10 issues) packed with solid information on the global gay and lesbian scene; *Spartacus International Gay Guide* (Bruno Gmünder Verlag; www.spartacusworld.com/gayguide/) and *Odysseus,* both good, annual English-language guidebooks focused on gay men; the *Damron* guides (www.damron.com), with separate, annual books for gay men and lesbians; and *Gay Travel A to Z: The World of Gay & Lesbian Travel Options at Your Fingertips* by Marianne Ferrari (Ferrari International; P.O. Box 35575, Phoenix, AZ 85069), a very good gay and lesbian guidebook series.

Arco Iris is a gay-owned, full-service travel agency and tour operator specializing in Mexico packages and special group travel. Contact the agency by phone (☎ 800-765-4370 or 619-297-0897; fax: 619-297-6419) or through its Web site at www.arcoiristours.com. The agency also publishes the *Cancún Pink Pages* guide, which is free with the booking of any package tour or can be ordered for $5 online on its Web site.

Traveling Solo

Mexico is a great place to travel on your own without really being or feeling alone. Although identical room rates for single and double occupancy are slowly becoming a trend in Mexico, many of the hotels mentioned in this book still offer singles at lower rates.

Mexicans are very friendly, and meeting other foreigners is easy. But if you don't like the idea of traveling alone, try **Travel Companion Exchange (TCE)** (P.O. Box 833, Amityville, NY 11701; ☎ 800-392-1256 or 631-454-0880; fax: 631-454-0170; Internet: www.whytravelalone.com), which brings prospective travelers together. Members complete a profile and then place an anonymous listing of their travel interests in the newsletter. Prospective traveling companions then make contact through the exchange. Membership costs $99 for six months or $159 for a year. TCE also offers an excellent booklet, for $3.95, on avoiding theft and scams while traveling abroad.

A female traveling alone in Mexico may actually be safer than traveling in the United States. But use the same commonsense precautions you would use when traveling anywhere else in the world and stay alert to what's going on around you.

Mexicans, in general, and men, in particular, are nosy about single travelers, especially women. If taxi drivers or anyone else with whom you don't want to become friendly ask about your marital status, family, and so on, my advice is to make up a set of answers (regardless of the truth): "I'm married, I'm traveling with friends, and I have three children."

 Saying you're single and traveling alone may send the wrong message about availability. Face it — whether you like it or not, Mexico is still a macho country with the double standards that a macho attitude implies. Movies and television shows exported from the United States have created an image of sexually aggressive North American women. If someone bothers you, don't try to be polite — just leave or head into a public place.

You may even consider wearing a ring that resembles a wedding band. Most Mexican men stay away at the sight of a ring, and it also deters many uncomfortable questions.

For specific tips and travel packages for single women traveling to Mexico, check out the following online resources:

- ✔ Gutsy Women Travel: www.gutsywomentravel.com
- ✔ Women's Travel Club: www.womenstravelclub.com

For a directory of travel clubs for women, including solo women travelers, visit Transitions Abroad, at www.transitionsabroad.com/listings/travel/women/websiteswomenclubs.shtml

Planning a Wedding in Mexico

Mexico's beaches may be old favorites for romantic honeymoons, but have you ever considered taking the plunge in Mexico? A destination wedding saves money and can be less hassle compared with marrying back home. Many hotels and attractions offer wedding packages, which can include everything from booking the officiant to hiring the videographer. Choose the package you want and, presto, your wedding planning is done! Several properties also provide the services of a wedding coordinator (either for free or at a reasonable cost) who not only scouts out sweetheart pink roses but can also handle marriage licenses and other formalities. A destination wedding can be as informal or as traditional as you like. After returning from their honeymoon, many couples hold a reception for people who couldn't join them. At these parties, couples sometimes continue the theme of their wedding locale (decorate with piñatas or hire a mariachi band, for example) and show a video of their ceremony so that everyone can share in their happiness.

If you invite guests to your destination wedding, find out about group rates for hotels and airfare, which can save 20% or more off regular prices. Plan as far ahead as possible so that people can arrange their schedules to join you.

Under a treaty between the United States and Mexico, Mexican civil marriages are automatically valid in the United States. You need certified copies of birth certificates, driver's licenses, or passports; certified proof of divorce or the death certificate of any former spouses (if applicable); tourist cards (provided when you enter Mexico); and results of blood tests performed in Mexico within 15 days before the ceremony.

 Check with a local, on-site wedding planner through your hotel to verify all the necessary requirements and obtain an application well in advance of your desired wedding date. Contact the **Mexican Tourism Board** (☎ 800-446-3942; Internet: www.visitmexico.com) for information.

For more information, see *Honeymoon Vacations For Dummies* (Wiley).

Chapter 9

Taking Care of the Remaining Details

*A*re you ready? Really ready? Before you can string that hammock between the palms, you need to take care of a few final details to get to your personal paradise. In this chapter, we cover the essentials and the requirements of getting into Mexico — and then back home again. We also review the ins and outs of dealing with travel insurance, ensuring a safe trip, deciding whether you should rent a car, and making sure that you pack everything you need for your Yucatán beach vacation.

Arriving in and Departing from Mexico

All travelers to Mexico are required to present **proof of citizenship,** such as an original birth certificate with a raised seal, a valid passport, or naturalization papers. If you're using a birth certificate, also have a current form of photo identification, such as a driver's license or an official ID car, although we highly recommend using a valid passport instead. If your last name on the birth certificate is different from your current name (women using a married name, for example), also bring a photo identification card *and* legal proof of the name change, like the original marriage license or certificate.

When reentering the United States, you must prove both your citizenship *and* your identification, so always carry a picture ID, such as a driver's license or valid passport. We strongly recommend using your passport to avoid any potential problems. *Note:* As of December 31, 2006, a passport will be required for air and sea travel to and from Mexico.

Although birth certificates enable you to enter Mexico, they don't enable you to reenter the United States. And although you can enter Mexico using a driver's license as identification, this documentation alone is not acceptable identification for reentering the United States. While in Mexico, you must also obtain a **Mexican tourist permit (FMT),** which is issued free of charge by Mexican border officials after proof of citizenship is accepted. These forms are generally provided by the airline aboard your flight into Mexico.

 The tourist permit is more important than a passport in Mexico, so guard it carefully. If you lose it, you may not be permitted to leave the country until you can replace it — a bureaucratic hassle that can take anywhere from a few hours to a week. (If you do lose your tourist permit, get a police report from local authorities indicating that your documents were stolen; having one *may* lessen the hassle of exiting the country without all your identification.) Also contact the nearest consular office to report the stolen papers so that it can issue a reentry document.

Note that children under the age of 18 traveling without parents or with only one parent must have a notarized letter from the absent parent or parents authorizing the travel. The letter must include the duration of the visit, destination, names of accompanying adults, parents' home addresses, telephone numbers, and so on. You must also attach a picture of the child to this letter.

Getting a Passport

Although you can enter Mexico without a passport, the only legal form of identification recognized around the world is a valid passport, and for that reason alone, having yours whenever you travel abroad is a good idea. In the United States, you're used to your driver's license being the all-purpose ID card. Abroad, it only proves that some American state lets you drive. Getting a passport is easy, but it takes some time to complete the process.

Applying for a U.S. passport

If you're applying for a first-time passport, follow these steps:

1. **Complete a passport application in person at a U.S. passport office; a federal, state, or probate court; or a major post office.**

   To find your regional passport office, either check the **U.S. State Department** Web site, http://travel.state.gov/passport_services.html, or call the **National Passport Information Center** (☎ 877-487-2778) for automated information.

2. **Present a certified birth certificate as proof of citizenship.**

   Bringing along your driver's license, state or military ID, or Social Security card is also a good idea.

3. **Submit two identical passport-sized photos, measuring 2 x 2 inches in size. You often find businesses that take these photos near a passport office.**

   Note: You can't use a strip from a photo-vending machine because the pictures aren't identical.

4. **Pay a fee. For people 16 and over, a passport is valid for ten years and costs $85. For those 15 and under, a passport is valid for five years and costs $70.**

 Allow plenty of time before your trip to apply for a passport; processing normally takes three weeks but can take longer during busy periods (especially spring).

If you have a passport in your current name that was issued within the past 15 years (and you were over age 16 when it was issued), you can renew the passport by mail for $55. The U.S. State Department's Bureau of Consular Affairs maintains an excellent Web site (http://travel. state.gov) that provides everything you need to know about passports (including downloadable applications and locations of passport offices). For general information, call the **National Passport Agency** (☎ 202-647-0518). To find your regional passport office, either check the U.S. State Department Web site or call the **National Passport Information Center** toll-free number (☎ 877-487-2778) for automated information.

Applying for other passports

The following list offers more information for citizens of Australia, Canada, New Zealand, and the United Kingdom.

✔ If you're **Australian,** visit a local post office or passport office, call the **Australia Passport Information Service** (☎ 131-232 toll-free from Australia), or log on to www.passports.gov.au for details on how and where to apply.

✔ If you're **Canadian,** pick up an application at passport offices throughout Canada, post offices, or from the central **Passport Office, Department of Foreign Affairs and International Trade,** Ottawa, ON K1A 0G3 (☎ 800-567-6868; www.ppt.gc.ca). Applications must be accompanied by two identical passport-sized photographs and proof of Canadian citizenship. Processing takes five to ten days if you apply in person, or about three weeks by mail.

✔ If you're a **New Zealander,** pick up a passport application at any New Zealand Passports Office or download it from its Web site. Contact the **Passports Office** at ☎ **0800-225-050** in New Zealand or 04-474-8100, or log on to www.passports.govt.nz.

✔ If you're a **United Kingdom** resident, pick up applications for a standard ten-year passport (five-year passport for children under 16) at passport offices, major post offices, or a travel agency. For information, contact the **United Kingdom Passport Service** (☎ **0870-521-0410;** www.ukpa.gov.uk).

Clearing U.S. Customs

You *can* take it with you — up to a point. Technically, no limits exist on how much loot U.S. citizens can bring back into the United States from a trip abroad, but the Customs authority *does* put limits on how much you can bring in for free. (This rule is mainly for taxation purposes, to separate tourists with souvenirs from importers.)

U.S. citizens may bring home $400 worth of goods duty-free, providing you've been out of the country at least 48 hours and haven't used the exemption in the past 30 days. This amount includes one liter of an alcoholic beverage (you must, of course, be older than 21), 200 cigarettes, and 100 cigars. Anything you mail home from abroad is exempt from the $400 limit. You may mail up to $200 worth of goods to yourself (marked "for personal use") and up to $100 to others (marked "unsolicited gift") once each day, so long as the package does not include alcohol or tobacco products. You'll have to pay an import duty on anything over these limits.

Note that buying items at a **duty-free shop** before flying home does *not* exempt them from counting toward U.S. Customs limits (monetary or otherwise). The "duty" that you're avoiding in those shops is the local tax on the item (like state sales tax in the United States), not any import duty that may be assessed by the U.S. Customs office.

If you have further questions or for a list of specific items you cannot bring into the United States, look in your phone book (under U.S. Government, Department of the Treasury, U.S. Customs Service) to find the nearest Customs office. Or check out the Customs Service Web site at www.customs.ustreas.gov/travel/travel.htm.

Playing It Safe with Travel and Medical Insurance

Three kinds of travel insurance are available: trip-cancellation insurance, medical insurance, and lost luggage insurance. The cost of travel insurance varies widely, depending on the cost and length of your trip, your age and health, and the type of trip you're taking, but expect to pay between 5 and 8% of the vacation itself. Here is our advice on all three.

✔ **Trip-cancellation insurance** helps you get your money back if you have to back out of a trip, if you have to go home early, or if your travel supplier goes bankrupt. Allowed reasons for cancellation can range from sickness to natural disasters to the State Department declaring your destination unsafe for travel. (Insurers usually won't cover vague fears, though, as many travelers discovered who tried to cancel their trips in October 2001 because they were wary of flying.)

A good resource is **"Travel Guard Alerts,"** a list of companies considered high-risk by Travel Guard International (www.travelinsured. com). Protect yourself further by paying for the insurance with a credit card — by law, consumers can get their money back on goods and services not received if they report the loss within 60 days after the charge is listed on their credit-card statement.

Note: Many tour operators, particularly those offering trips to remote or high-risk areas, include insurance in the cost of the trip or can arrange insurance policies through a partnering provider, a convenient and often cost-effective way for the traveler to obtain insurance. Make sure the tour company is a reputable one, however: Some experts suggest you avoid buying insurance from the tour or cruise company you're traveling with, saying it's better to buy from a third-party insurer than to put all your money in one place.

✔ For domestic travel, buying **medical insurance** for a trip doesn't make sense for most travelers. Most existing health policies cover you if you get sick away from home — but check before you go, particularly if you're insured by an HMO.

For travel overseas, most health plans (including Medicare and Medicaid) do not provide coverage, and the ones that do often require you to pay for services upfront and reimburse you only after you return home. Even if your plan does cover overseas treatment, most out-of-country hospitals make you pay your bills up front, and send you a refund only after you've returned home and filed the necessary paperwork with your insurance company. As a safety net, you may want to buy travel medical insurance, particularly if you're traveling to a remote or high-risk area where emergency evacuation is a possible scenario. If you require additional medical insurance, try **MEDEX Assistance** (☎ 410-453-6300; www. medexassist.com) or **Travel Assistance International** (☎ 800-821-2828; www.travelassistance.com; for general information on services, call the company's Worldwide Assistance Services, Inc., at ☎ 800-777-8710).

✔ **Lost luggage insurance** is not necessary for most travelers. On domestic flights, checked baggage is covered up to $2,500 per ticketed passenger. On international flights (including U.S. portions of international trips), baggage coverage is limited to approximately $9.07 per pound, up to approximately $635 per checked bag. If you plan to check items more valuable than the standard liability, see if your valuables are covered by your homeowner's policy, get baggage insurance as part of your comprehensive travel-insurance package or buy Travel Guard's "BagTrak" product. Don't buy insurance at the airport, because it's usually overpriced. Be sure to take any valuables or irreplaceable items with you in your carry-on luggage, because many valuables (including books, money and electronics) aren't covered by airline policies.

If your luggage is lost, immediately file a lost-luggage claim at the airport, detailing the luggage contents. For most airlines, you must report delayed, damaged, or lost baggage within 4 hours of arrival. The airlines are required to deliver luggage, once found, directly to your house or destination free of charge.

For more information, contact one of the following recommended insurers: **Access America** (☎ 866-807-3982; www.accessamerica. com); **Travel Guard International** (☎ 800-826-4919; www.travel guard.com); **Travel Insured International** (☎ 800-243-3174; www. travelinsured.com); and **Travelex Insurance Services** (☎ 888-457-4602; www.travelex-insurance.com).

Staying Healthy When You Travel

Apart from how getting sick can ruin your vacation, it also can present the problem of finding a doctor you trust when you're away from home. Bring all your medications with you, as well as a prescription for more if you run out. Bring an extra pair of contact lenses in case you lose one. And don't forget the Pepto-Bismol for common travelers' ailments like upset stomach or diarrhea.

If you have health insurance, check with your provider to find out the extent of your coverage outside of your home area. Be sure to carry your identification card in your wallet. And if you worry that your existing policy isn't sufficient, purchase medical insurance for more comprehensive coverage. (See the "Playing It Safe with Travel and Medical Insurance," section earlier in this chapter.)

Talk to your doctor before leaving on a trip if you have a serious and/ or chronic illness. For conditions such as epilepsy, diabetes, or heart problems, wear a **MedicAlert identification tag** (☎ **888-633-4298**; www. medicalert.org), which immediately alerts doctors to your condition and gives them access to your records through MedicAlert's 24-hour hotline. Contact the **International Association for Medical Assistance to Travelers (IAMAT)** (☎ 716-754-4883 or, in Canada, 416-652-0137; www. iamat.org) for tips on travel and health concerns in the countries you're visiting, and lists of local, English-speaking doctors. The United States **Centers for Disease Control and Prevention** (☎ **800-311-3435**; www.cdc.gov) provides up-to-date information on health hazards by region or country and offers tips on food safety.

If you do get sick, ask the concierge at your hotel to recommend a local doctor — even his or her own doctor, if necessary. Another good option is to call the closest consular office and ask for a referral to a doctor. Most consulates have a listing of reputable English-speaking doctors. Most beach destinations in Mexico have at least one modern facility staffed by doctors used to treating the most common ailments of tourists.

In the case of an emergency, a service from the United States can fly people to American hospitals: **Air-Evac** (☎ **888-554-9729,** www.airevac.com) is a 24-hour air ambulance. You can also contact the service in Guadalajara (☎ **01-800-305-9400,** 3-616-9616, or 3-615-2471). Several companies offer air-evac service; for a list, refer to the U.S. State Department Web site at http://travel.state.gov/medical.html.

 If you're traveling with **infants and/or children** in Mexico, be extra careful to avoid anything that's not bottled. You can purchase infant formulas, baby foods, canned milk, and other baby supplies from grocery stores. Your best bet is to carry extra baby eats when you go out. Most Mexican restaurants will cheerfully warm bottles and packaged goods for your child.

Be especially careful of sun exposure because **sunburn** can be extremely dangerous. Protect the little ones with special SPF bathing suits and cover-ups and regularly apply a strong sunscreen.

Dehydration can also make your child seriously ill. Make sure that your child drinks plenty of water and juices throughout the day. Especially when they're in the pool or at the beach having fun, they may not remember that they're thirsty, so it's up to you to remind them. Sunburn also contributes to and complicates dehydration.

From our 12 years' experience of living in and traveling throughout Mexico, we can honestly say that most health problems that foreign tourists to Mexico encounter are self-induced. If you take in too much sun, too many margaritas, and too many street tacos within hours of your arrival, don't blame the water if you get sick. You'd be surprised how many people try to make up for all the fun they've missed in the past year on their first day on vacation in Mexico.

Staying Safe

If you find yourself getting friendly with the locals — and we mean friendly to the point of a fling — don't be embarrassed to carry or insist on stopping for condoms and then use them! Too many vacationing men and women are filled with morning-after regrets because they didn't protect themselves. Don't allow your fear of being judged make you do something that's frankly stupid. Also know that Mexico's teen-to-20-something population has a rapidly escalating **AIDS** rate — especially in resort areas — due to the transient nature of the population and poor overall education about this disease.

Avoiding turista!

It's called "travelers' diarrhea" or *turista,* the Spanish word for "tourist." I'm talking about the persistent diarrhea, often accompanied by fever, nausea, and vomiting, that used to attack many travelers to Mexico. Some folks in the United States call this affliction "Montezuma's revenge," but you won't hear it referred to this way in Mexico. Widespread improvements in infrastructure, sanitation, and education have practically eliminated this ailment, especially in well-developed resort areas. Most travelers make a habit of drinking only bottled water, which also helps to protect against unfamiliar bacteria. In resort areas, and generally throughout Mexico, only purified ice is used. Doctors say this ailment isn't caused by just one "bug," but by a combination of consuming different foods and water, upsetting your schedule, being overtired, and experiencing the stresses of travel. A good high-potency (or "therapeutic") vitamin supplement and extra vitamin C can help. And yogurt is good for healthy digestion. If you do happen to come down with this ailment, nothing beats Pepto-Bismol, readily available in Mexico.

Preventing *turista:* The U.S. Public Health Service recommends the following measures for preventing travelers' diarrhea:

✔ Get enough sleep.

✔ Don't overdo the sun.

✔ Drink only purified water, which means tea, coffee, and other beverages made with boiled water; canned or bottled carbonated beverages and water; or beer and wine. Most restaurants with a large tourist clientele use only purified water and ice.

✔ Choose food carefully. In general, avoid salads, uncooked vegetables, and unpasteurized milk or milk products (including cheese). However, salads in a first-class restaurant, or in a restaurant that serves a lot of tourists, are generally safe to eat. Choose food that's freshly cooked and still hot. Peelable fruit is ideal. Don't eat undercooked meat, fish, or shellfish.

✔ In addition, something as simple as washing hands frequently can prevent the spread of germs and go a long way toward keeping *turista* at bay.

Because **dehydration** can quickly become life-threatening, be especially careful to replace fluids and electrolytes (potassium, sodium, and the like) during a bout of diarrhea. Rehydrate by drinking Pedialyte, a rehydration solution available at most Mexican pharmacies, sports drinks, or glasses of natural fruit juice (high in potassium) with a pinch of salt added. Or try a glass of boiled, pure water with a quarter teaspoon of sodium bicarbonate (baking soda) and a bit of lime juice added.

When it comes to **drugs,** many outsiders have the impression that the easygoing nature of these tropical towns means an equally laid-back attitude exists toward drug use. Not so. Marijuana, cocaine, ecstasy, and other mood-altering drugs are illegal in Mexico. In some places, police randomly search people — including obvious tourists — who are walking the streets at night.

If you do choose to indulge, don't expect any special treatment if you're caught. In fact, everything bad you've ever heard about a Mexican jail is considered to be close to the truth — if not a rose-colored version of it. Mexico employs the Napoleonic Code of law, meaning that you're guilty until proven innocent. Simply stated, time in jail isn't worth the potential high. That's what tequila's for!

Renting a Car

The first thing you should know is that car-rental costs are high in Mexico because cars are more expensive. However, the condition of rental cars has improved greatly over the years, and clean, comfortable, new cars are the norm. The basic cost for a one-day rental of a Volkswagen (VW) Beetle, with unlimited mileage (but before the 15% tax and $15 to $25 daily for insurance), is $35 in Cancún. Renting by the week gives you a lower daily rate. At press time, Avis was offering a basic seven-day weekly rate for a Ford Fiesta (before tax or insurance) of $216 in Cancún. Prices may be considerably higher if you rent around a major holiday.

Car-rental companies usually write a credit-card charge in U.S. dollars.

Be careful of deductibles, which vary greatly in Mexico. Some deductibles are as high as $2,500, which immediately comes out of your pocket in case of car damage. Hertz has a $1,000 deductible on a VW Beetle; the deductible at Avis is $500 for the same car.

 Always get the insurance. Insurance is offered in two parts. Collision and damage insurance covers your car and others if the accident is your fault, and personal accident insurance covers you and anyone in your car. Read the fine print on the back of your rental agreement and note that insurance may be invalid if you have an accident while driving on an unpaved road.

Finding the best car-rental deal

 Car-rental rates vary even more than airline fares. The price depends on the size of the car, the length of time you keep it, where and when you pick it up and drop it off, where you take it, and a host of other factors.

Asking a few key questions can save you hundreds of dollars. For example, weekend rates may be lower than weekday rates. Ask whether the rate is the same for Friday morning pickup as it is for Thursday night. If you're keeping the car five or more days, a weekly rate may be cheaper than the daily rate. Some companies may assess a drop-off charge if you don't return the car to the same renting location; others, notably National, do not. Ask whether the rate is cheaper if you pick up the car at the airport or a location in town. Don't forget to mention membership in AAA, AARP, frequent-flier programs, and trade unions. These memberships usually entitle you to discounts ranging from 5 to 30%. Ask your travel agent to check any and all of these rates. And most car rentals are worth at least 500 miles on your frequent-flier account!

As with other aspects of planning your trip, using the Internet can make comparison shopping for a car rental much easier. All the major booking Web sites — **Travelocity** (www.travelocity.com), **Expedia** (www.expedia.com), **Orbitz** (www.orbitz.com), **Yahoo! Travel** (www.travel.yahoo.com), and **Cheap Tickets** (www.cheaptickets.com), for example — have search engines that can dig up discounted car-rental rates. Just enter the size of the car you want, the pickup and return dates, and the city where you want to rent, and the server returns a price. You can even make the reservation through these sites.

In addition to the standard coverage, car-rental companies also offer additional liability insurance (if you harm others in an accident), personal accident insurance (if you harm yourself or your passengers), and personal effects insurance (if your luggage is stolen from your car). If you have insurance on your car at home, you're probably covered for most of these unlikelihoods. If your own insurance doesn't cover you for rentals or if you don't have auto insurance, consider the additional coverage. But weigh the likelihood of getting into an accident or losing your luggage against the cost of these insurance options (as much as $20 per day combined), which can significantly add to the price of your rental.

Some companies also offer refueling packages, in which you pay for an entire tank of gas up front. The price is usually fairly competitive with local gas prices, but you don't get credit for any gas remaining in the tank. If you reject this option, you pay only for the gas you use, but you have to return the car with a full tank or face charges of $3 to $4 a gallon for any shortfall. If a stop at a gas station on the way to the airport will make you miss your plane, by all means take advantage of the fuel purchase option. Otherwise, skip it.

Remembering that safety comes first

If you decide to rent a car and drive in Mexico, you need to keep a few things in mind:

- ✔ Most Mexican roads are not up to U.S. standards of smoothness, hardness, width of curve, grade of hill, or safety markings. The roads in and around Cancún are a notable exception, but elsewhere in the Yucatán, this observation generally holds true.

- ✔ Driving at night is dangerous — the roads aren't good, and they're rarely lit; trucks, carts, pedestrians, and bicycles usually have no lights; and you can hit potholes, animals, rocks, dead ends, or uncrossable bridges without warning.

- ✔ Never turn left by stopping in the middle of a highway with your left signal on. Instead, pull off the highway onto the right shoulder, wait for traffic to clear, and then proceed across the road.

✔ Credit cards are generally not accepted for gas purchases.

✔ Places called *vulcanizadora* or *llantera* repair flat tires. Such places are commonly open 24 hours a day on the most traveled highways. Even if the place looks empty, chances are you'll find someone who can help you fix a flat.

✔ When possible, many Mexicans drive away from minor accidents, or try to make an immediate settlement, to avoid involving the police.

✔ If the police arrive while the involved persons are still at the scene, everyone may be locked up until responsibility is determined and damages are settled. If you were in a rental car, notify the rental company immediately and ask how to contact the nearest adjuster. (You did buy insurance with the rental, right?)

Packing for the Yucatán

Start packing by taking out everything you think you need and laying it out on the bed. Then get rid of half of it.

It's not that the airlines won't let you take it all — they will, with some limits — but why would you want to get a hernia from lugging half your house around with you? Suitcase straps can be particularly painful when hanging from sunburned shoulders.

So what are the bare essentials? Comfortable walking shoes, a camera, a versatile sweater and/or jacket, a belt, a swimsuit, toiletries and medications (pack these in your carry-on bag so you have them if the airline loses your luggage), and something to sleep in. Unless you're attending a board meeting, a funeral, or one of the city's finest restaurants, you probably don't need a suit or a fancy dress. Even the nicest restaurants tend to be casual when it comes to dress, especially for men. Women, on the other hand, tend to enjoy those sexy resort dresses, and they're definitely appropriate in any of the resorts covered in this book. When it comes to essentials, you get the most use out of a pair of jeans or khakis and a comfortable sweater.

Electricity runs on the same current in Mexico as in the United States and Canada, so feel free to bring a hair dryer, personal stereo, or whatever else you'd like to plug in. Don't bother to bring a travel iron — most hotels offer irons and ironing boards, or they offer the service at a very reasonable rate.

When choosing your suitcase, think about the kind of traveling you're doing. If you'll be walking with your luggage on hard floors, a bag with wheels makes sense. If you'll be carrying your luggage over uneven roads or up and down stairs, wheels don't help much. A fold-over garment bag helps keep dressy clothes wrinkle-free, but it can be a nuisance if you'll be packing and unpacking a lot. Hard-sided luggage protects breakable items better, but it weighs more than soft-sided bags.

When packing, start with the biggest, hardest items (usually shoes) and then fit smaller items in and around them. Pack breakable items in between several layers of clothes or keep them in your carry-on bag. Put items that may leak, like shampoos or suntan lotions, in resealable plastic bags. Lock your suitcase with a small padlock (available at most luggage stores if your bag doesn't already have one) and put a distinctive identification tag on the outside so that your bag is easy to spot on the carousel.

Stricter security measures now dictate that each passenger is only allowed to bring one carry-on bag and one personal item (a purse, backpack, or briefcase) on the plane, and the items you do bring onboard are subject to strict size limitations. Both must fit in the overhead compartment or under the seat in front of you.

Among the items you may consider carrying on are a book; any breakable items you don't want to put in your suitcase; a personal stereo with headphones; a snack (in the likely event you don't like the airline food); a bottle of water; any vital documents you don't want to lose in your luggage (your return ticket, passport, wallet, and so on); and some empty space for the sweater or jacket that you won't be wearing while you're waiting for your luggage in an overheated terminal. Also carry aboard any prescription medications, your glasses or spare contact lenses, and your camera. We always carry a change of clothes (shorts, T-shirt, and swimsuit) — just in case our checked baggage is lost. If the airline loses your luggage, you're likely to have it again within 24 hours, but having these essentials allows you to jump right into vacation fun anyway.

Here's a quick checklist of items you don't want to forget:

- ✔ At least two swimsuits
- ✔ Sunglasses
- ✔ Comfortable walking shoes
- ✔ Sandals
- ✔ Hat or cap
- ✔ Sunscreen
- ✔ Driver's license (if you plan to rent a car)
- ✔ Scuba certification (if you plan to dive)
- ✔ Casual slacks other than jeans (for men, especially if you plan on hitting the trendiest discos, some of which don't allow shorts or jeans)
- ✔ A *pareo* (sarong) that can double as a long or short skirt, or a wrap (for women)

Staying Connected by Cellphone or E-Mail

The three letters that define much of the world's **wireless capabilities** are GSM (Global System for Mobiles), a big, seamless network that makes for easy cross-border cellphone use throughout Europe and dozens of other countries worldwide. In the United States, T-Mobile, and Cingular use this quasi-universal system; in Mexico, USACell and Telcel are the predominant mobile carriers, and both use GSM.

If your cellphone is on a GSM system and you have a world-capable multiband phone such as many Sony Ericsson, Motorola, or Samsung models, you can make and receive calls across civilized areas on much of the globe, from Andorra to Uganda. Just call your wireless operator and ask for *international roaming* to be activated on your account. Unfortunately, per-minute charges can be high — usually $1 to $1.50.

 That's why it's important to buy an *unlocked* world phone from the get-go. Many cellphone operators sell *locked* phones that restrict you from using any other removable computer memory phone chip (called a *SIM card*) other than the ones they supply. Having an unlocked phone allows you to install a cheap, prepaid SIM card (found at a local retailer) in your destination country. (Show your phone to the salesperson; not all phones work on all networks.) You'll get a local phone number — and much, much lower calling rates. Getting an already locked phone unlocked can be a complicated process, but it can be done; just call your cellular operator and say you'll be going abroad for several months and want to use the phone with a local provider.

For many, **renting** a phone is a good idea. (Even worldphone owners will have to rent new phones if they're traveling to non-GSM regions, such as Japan or Korea.) Although you can rent a phone from any number of overseas sites, including kiosks at airports and at car-rental agencies, we suggest renting the phone before you leave home. That way you can give loved ones and business associates your new number, make sure the phone works, and take the phone wherever you go — especially helpful for overseas trips through several countries, where local phone-rental agencies often bill in local currency and may not let you take the phone to another country.

Phone rental isn't cheap. You'll usually pay $40 to $50 per week, plus airtime fees of at least a dollar a minute. The bottom line: Shop around.

Phone rentals in Mexico are still rare, so it's best to rent before your arrival. One option is to purchase an inexpensive phone that takes pre-paid cards, which you can purchase at any Telcel service provider in Mexico, for just the amount of service you feel you'll need during your trip.

Two good wireless rental companies are **InTouch USA** (☎ 800-872-7626; www.intouchglobal.com) and **RoadPost** (☎ 888-290-1606 or 905-272-5665; www.roadpost.com). Give them your itinerary, and they'll tell you what wireless products you need. InTouch will also, for free, advise you on whether your existing phone will work overseas; simply call ☎ 703-222-7161 between 9 a.m. and 4 p.m. EST, or go to http://intouch global.com/travel.htm.

Accessing the Internet Away from Home

You have any number of ways to check your e-mail and access the Internet on the road. Of course, using your own laptop — or even a PDA (personal digital assistant) or electronic organizer with a modem — gives you the most flexibility. But even if you don't have a computer, you can still access your e-mail and even your office computer from cybercafes.

It's hard nowadays to find a city that doesn't have a few cybercafes. Although there's no definitive directory for cybercafes — these are independent businesses, after all — three places to start looking are at www.cybercaptive.com and www.cybercafe.com.

Within Mexico's popular tourism destinations, cybercafes are very common, catering to traveler's increasing need — or desire — to stay connected while away. In each of the different locations in Mexico's Yucatán, we list several recommended cybercafes, along with rates and hours.

If you're bringing your own computer, the buzzword in computer access to familiarize yourself with is **Wi-Fi** (wireless fidelity), and more and more hotels, cafes, and retailers are signing on as wireless hotspots from where you can get high-speed connection without cable wires, networking hardware, or a phone line. You can get Wi-Fi connection one of several ways. Many laptops sold in the last year have built-in Wi-Fi capability (an 802.11b wireless Ethernet connection). Mac owners have their own networking technology, Apple AirPort. For those with older computers, an 802.11b/**Wi-Fi card** (around $50) can be plugged in to your laptop. You sign up for wireless access service much as you do cellphone service, through a plan offered by one of several commercial companies that have made wireless service available in airports, hotel lobbies, and coffee shops, primarily in the United States (followed by the U.K. and Japan). **T-Mobile Hotspot** (www.t-mobile.com/hotspot) serves up wireless connections at more than 1,000 Starbucks coffee shops nationwide. **Boingo** (www.boingo.com) and **Wayport** (www.wayport.com) have set up networks in airports and high-class hotel lobbies. IPass providers also give you access to a few hundred wireless hotel lobby setups. Best of all, you don't need to be staying at the Four Seasons to use the hotel's network; just set yourself up on a nice couch in the lobby. The companies' pricing policies can be byzantine, with a variety of monthly, per-connection, and per-minute plans, but in general you pay around $30 a month for limited access — and as more and more companies jump on the wireless bandwagon, prices are likely to get even more competitive.

There are also places that provide **free wireless networks** in cities around the world. To locate these free hotspots, go to www.personal telco.net/index.cgi/WirelessCommunities.

 If Wi-Fi isn't available at your destination, most business-class hotels throughout the world offer dataports for laptop modems, and a few thousand hotels in the United States and Europe now offer free high-speed Internet access using an Ethernet network cable. You can bring your own cables, but most hotels rent them for around $10. Call your hotel in advance to see what your options are.

In addition, major Internet Service Providers (ISP) have **local access numbers** around the world, allowing you to go online by simply placing a local call. Check your ISP's Web site or call its toll-free number and ask how you can use your current account away from home, and how much it will cost. If you're traveling outside the reach of your ISP, the **iPass** network has dial-up numbers in most of the world's countries. You'll have to sign up with an iPass provider, who will then tell you how to set up your computer for your destination(s). For a list of iPass providers, go to www.ipass.com and click on "Individual Purchase." One solid provider is **i2roam** (www.i2roam.com; ☎ **866-811-6209** or 920-235-0475).

Wherever you go, bring a **connection kit** of the right power and phone adapters, a spare phone cord, and a spare Ethernet network cable — or find out whether your hotel supplies them to guests. Because Mexico shares the same electric current as the United States, you won't need any special adaptors or equipment other than what you'd use at home.

Keeping Up with Airline Security Measures

With the federalization of airport security, security procedures at U.S. airports are more stable and consistent than ever. Generally, you'll be fine if you arrive at the airport **1 hour** before a domestic flight and **2 hours** before an international flight; if you show up late, tell an airline employee and she'll probably whisk you to the front of the line.

Bring a **current, government-issued photo ID** such as a driver's license or passport. Keep your ID at the ready to show at check-in, the security checkpoint, and sometimes even the gate. (Children under 18 do not need government-issued photo IDs for domestic flights, but they do for international flights to most countries.)

In 2003, the TSA phased out **gate check-in** at all U.S. airports. And **e-tickets** have made paper tickets nearly obsolete. Passengers with e-tickets can beat the ticket-counter lines by using airport **electronic kiosks** or even **online check-in** from your home computer. Online check-in involves logging on to your airlines' Web site, accessing your reservation, and printing out your boarding pass — and the airline may even offer you bonus miles to do so! If you're using a kiosk at the airport, bring the credit card you used to book the ticket or your frequent-flier card. Print out your boarding pass from the kiosk and simply proceed to the security checkpoint with your pass and a photo ID. If you're checking bags or looking to snag an exit-row seat, you will be able to do so using most airline kiosks. Even the smaller airlines are employing the kiosk system, but always call your airline to make sure these alternatives are available. **Curbside check-in** is also a good way to avoid lines, although a few airlines still ban curbside check-in; call before you go.

Security checkpoint lines are getting shorter than they were during late 2001 and 2002, but some doozies remain. If you have trouble standing for long periods of time, tell an airline employee; the airline will provide a wheelchair. Speed up security by **not wearing metal objects** such as big belt buckles. If you've got metallic body parts, a note from your doctor can prevent a long chat with security screeners. Keep in mind that only **ticketed passengers** are allowed past security, except for folks escorting disabled passengers or children.

Federalization has stabilized **what you can carry on** and **what you can't.** The general rule is that sharp things are out, nail clippers are okay, and food and beverages must be passed through the X-ray machine — but that security screeners can't make you drink from your coffee cup. Bring food in your carry-on rather than checking it, because explosive-detection machines used on checked luggage have been known to mistake food (especially chocolate, for some reason) for bombs. Travelers in the United States are allowed one carry-on bag, plus a personal item, such as a purse, briefcase, or laptop bag. Carry-on hoarders can stuff all sorts of things into a laptop bag; as long as it has a laptop in it, it's still considered a personal item. The Transportation Security Administration (TSA) has issued a list of restricted items; check its Web site (www.tsa.gov/public/index.jsp) for details.

Airport screeners may decide that your checked luggage needs to be searched by hand. You can now purchase luggage locks that allow screeners to open and re-lock a checked bag with a special code or key if hand-searching is necessary. For more information on the locks, visit www.travelsentry.org. You can also look for Travel Sentry certified locks at luggage or travel shops and Brookstone stores (you can buy them online at www.brookstone.com). If you use something other than TSA-approved locks, your lock will be cut off your suitcase if a TSA agent needs to hand-search your luggage.

Part III
Discovering Cancún

The 5th Wave   By Rich Tennant

"All I know is what the swim-up bartender told me. Wearing these should improve our game by 25 percent."

In this part . . .

The most popular of Mexico's beach resorts, Cancún perfectly showcases the country's breathtaking natural beauty and the depth of its 1,000-year-old history. Cancún is both the peak of Caribbean splendor and a modern mega-resort. It boasts translucent turquoise waters, powdery white sand beaches, and a wide array of nearby shopping, dining, and nightlife choices, in addition to a ton of other activities. Stays at most resorts are offered at exceptional value, and Cancún is easily accessible by air.

Many travelers who are apprehensive about visiting foreign soil feel completely at home and at ease in Cancún: English is spoken, dollars are accepted, roads are well paved, and lawns are manicured. A lot of the shopping and dining takes place in malls, and we swear that some hotels seem larger than a small town. In the following chapters, we introduce you to this Caribbean-coast jewel and offer lots of tips for making the most of your stay on this nonstop island.

Chapter 10

Settling into Cancún

In This Chapter

▶ Knowing what to expect when you arrive
▶ Finding your way around
▶ Sizing up the hotel locations
▶ Evaluating Cancún's top hotel choices
▶ Discovering Cancún's best restaurants
▶ Discovering helpful information and resources

*I*n 1974, a team of Mexican-government computer analysts selected Cancún as an area for tourism development because of its ideal combination of features to attract travelers — a reliable climate; beautiful, untouched white-sand beaches; clear, shallow water; and proximity to historic ruins. Cancún is actually an island, a 14-mile-long sliver of land shaped roughly like the number "7." Two bridges, spanning the expansive Nichupté Lagoon, connect Cancún to the mainland. (Cancún means "Golden Snake" in the Mayan language.)

With more than 25,000 hotel rooms in the area to choose from, Cancún can no longer claim to be "untouched." But this resort town has an accommodation for every taste and every budget. Here, I review the two main areas — **Cancún Island (Isla Cancún)** and **Cancún City (Ciudad Cancún),** located inland, to the west of the island.

Cancún is definitely the destination to try out an air-hotel package. Although the rack rates at Cancún's hotels are among the highest in Mexico, the package deals are among the best because of the large number of charter companies operating here. If you do arrive without a hotel reservation — not recommended during peak weeks surrounding the Christmas and Easter holidays — you're likely to be able to bargain your way into a great rate. For more information on air-hotel packages, see Chapter 7.

Although you do need a passport or other appropriate credentials (see Chapter 9) to enter Cancún, after that, you couldn't be in a more American-friendly destination if you tried. If this trip is your first to Mexico — or to a foreign country — you'll probably find that any sense of culture shock is practically nonexistent. But you'll be more comfortable knowing a few details before you arrive. In this chapter, I take you from the plane, through the airport, and to your hotel, helping you quickly get your bearings in this easy-to-navigate resort. I continue with tips on everything from taxis to taxes.

Arriving in Cancún

Cancún has one of Mexico's busiest and most modern airports, which seems to be in a constant state of construction to improve and expand its services. Still, it's easy to navigate. After checking in with immigration, collecting your bags, and passing through the Customs checkpoint, you're ready to enjoy your holiday!

Navigating passport control and Customs

Immigration check-in can be a lengthy wait, depending on the number of planes arriving at the same time, but it's generally an easy and unremarkable process in which officials ask you to show your passport and complete a tourist card, known as the **FMT**. (See Chapter 9 for more information.)

 Your FMT is an important document, so take good care of it. You're supposed to keep the FMT with you at all times, because you may be required to show it if you run into any sort of trouble. You also need to turn in the FMT upon departure; you may even be unable to leave without returning it.

Next is the baggage claim area. Here, porters stand by to help with your bags, and they're well worth the price of the tip — about a dollar a bag. After you collect your luggage, you pass through another checkpoint. Something that looks like a traffic light awaits you here — otherwise known as Mexico's random search procedure for Customs. You press a button, and if the light turns green, you're free to go. If it turns red, you need to open each of your bags for a quick search. If you have an unusually large bag or an excessive amount of luggage, you may be searched regardless of the traffic-light outcome.

Getting to your hotel

Just past the traffic light, you'll be offered a package of tourist information — take it! Included in this welcome kit, presented by the Visitor's Bureau, is a wealth of discount coupons as well as handy maps. Next, you pass through what appears to be an information booth area, with big glossy photos of the treasures that await you out the door. Don't stop here — unless you want to subject yourself to a timeshare pitch. This pitch may reward you with free transportation to your hotel, but there will be a cost in time spent listening to the sales presentation at a later time. Just move on through and exit to the street, where you'll find transportation to your hotel. Choose between a *colectivo* (shared minivan) or a private taxi. If three or more of you are traveling together,

Where to Stay in Isla Cancún (Hotel Zone)

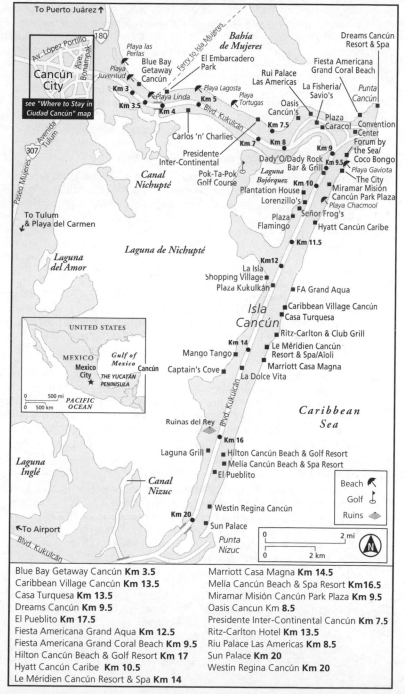

Blue Bay Getaway Cancún **Km 3.5**
Caribbean Village Cancún **Km 13.5**
Casa Turquesa **Km 13.5**
Dreams Cancún **Km 9.5**
El Pueblito **Km 17.5**
Fiesta Americana Grand Aqua **Km 12.5**
Fiesta Americana Grand Coral Beach **Km 9.5**
Hilton Cancún Beach & Golf Resort **Km 17**
Hyatt Cancún Caribe **Km 10.5**
Le Méridien Cancún Resort & Spa **Km 14**

Marriott Casa Magna **Km 14.5**
Melía Cancún Beach & Spa Resort **Km16.5**
Miramar Misión Cancún Park Plaza **Km 9.5**
Oasis Cancun Km **8.5**
Presidente Inter-Continental Cancún **Km 7.5**
Ritz-Carlton Hotel **Km 13.5**
Riu Palace Las Americas **Km 8.5**
Sun Palace **Km 20**
Westin Regina Cancún **Km 20**

you're probably better off opting for the private cab service. With so many hotels for the collective van to stop at, it can easily take an hour to get to your room, and believe me, the drivers wait until the vans are fully packed before departing! Check out the Cancún Orientation Map in this chapter to see where your hotel is positioned relative to the airport.

The airport is on the mainland, close to the southern end of the Cancún area. It's about 9 miles to downtown **Ciudad Cancún** (Cancún City), which is also on the mainland. The start of the **Zona Hotelera (Hotel Zone),** located on **Isla Cancún** (Cancún Island), is 6½ miles from the airport — about a 20-minute drive east from the airport along wide, well-paved roads.

Riding with a colectivo or hiring a taxi

If you do choose the *colectivo* service, which consists of air-conditioned vans, buy your ticket at the booth that's located to the far right as you exit the baggage claim area. You can purchase tickets for private cab service at a booth inside the airport terminal. Tickets for both the *colectivo* vans and the private taxis are based on a fixed rate depending on the distance to your destination. A taxi ticket is good for up to four passengers. The *colectivos* run from Cancún's international airport into town and the Hotel Zone and cost about $9 per person.

Rates for a **private taxi** from the airport are around $20 to downtown Cancún or $28 to $40 to the Hotel Zone, depending on your destination. There's minibus transportation (for $9.50) from the airport to the Puerto Juárez passenger ferry that takes you to Isla Mujeres. You can also hire a private taxi for this trip for about $40.

No colectivo service returns to the airport from Ciudad Cancún or the Hotel Zone, so you must hire a taxi, but the rate should be much less than the trip from the airport. The reason? Only federally chartered taxis may take fares *from* the airport, but any local taxi may bring passengers *to* the airport. Ask for a fare estimate at your hotel, but expect to pay about half what you were charged to get from the airport to your hotel.

Renting a car

Most major car-rental firms have outlets at the airport, so if you're renting a car, consider picking it up and dropping it off at the airport to save on airport-transportation costs. Another way to save money is to arrange for the rental before you leave home. If you wait until you arrive, the daily cost of a rental car may be around $50 to $75 for a compact car, where by pre-booking, the same Ford Fiesta or similar will rent for $35 to $40 per day.

Although you certainly don't have to rent a car here — taxis and buses are plentiful — this destination is one where having a car may make sense for a day or two. First, it can be a convenience, although it's not likely to save you bundles on transportation costs, based on the low relative prices of transportation around Cancún. The roads in and around Cancún are excellent, and parking is readily available in most of the shopping/entertainment malls. The second — and main — reason for renting a car, however, is the flexibility that it provides in exploring the surrounding areas — a day-trip down the coast or to nearby sights is definitely recommended. But if you're not comfortable driving, you can easily cover this ground in one of the many sightseeing tours available.

 If you do rent a car, keep any valuables out of plain site. Although Cancún's crime rate is very low, the only real problem tends to be rental-car break-ins.

Major car rental services include:

- ✔ **Avis** (☎ **800-331-1212** in the U.S., or 998-886-0221; www.avis.com)

- ✔ **Budget** (☎ **800-527-0700** in the U.S., or 998-884-5011; fax: 998-884-4812; www.budget.com or https://rent.drive budget.com/)

- ✔ **Dollar** (☎ **800-800-4000** in the U.S., or 998-886-2300; www.dollar.com)

- ✔ **Hertz** (☎ **800-654-3131** in the U.S. and Canada, or 998-886-0045; www.hertz.com)

- ✔ **National** (☎ **800-328-4567** in the U.S., or 998-886-0655; www.nationalcar.com)

Getting Around Cancún

As I discuss a bit in the "Getting to your hotel" section earlier in this chapter, there are really two Cancúns: **Isla Cancún** (Cancún Island) and **Ciudad Cancún** (Cancún City). The latter, on the mainland, has restaurants, shops, and less expensive hotels, as well as all the other establishments that make life function — pharmacies, dentists, automotive shops, banks, travel and airline agencies, car-rental firms, and so on — which are all located within an approximately nine-square-block area. The city's main thoroughfare is **Avenida Tulum.** Heading south, Avenida Tulum becomes the highway to the airport, Playa del Carmen, and Tulum. (It actually runs all the way down to Belize.) Heading north, Avenida Tulum intersects the highway to Mérida and the road to Puerto Juárez and the Isla Mujeres ferries.

The famed **Zona Hotelera** (Hotel Zone, also called the **Zona Turística,** or Tourist Zone) stretches out along Isla Cancún, which is a sandy strip of land 14 miles long and shaped like a "7." The Playa Linda Bridge, at the north end of the island, and the Punta Nizuc Bridge, at the southern end, connect Isla Cancún to the mainland. Between these two bridges lies **Laguna Nichupté.** Avenida Cobá, coming from Cancún City, becomes Blvd. Kukulcán, the island's main traffic artery. Actually, Blvd. Kukulcán is the only main road on the island, so getting lost here would really take some effort! To get the hang of pronouncing it quickly enough, say koo-cool-*can*

Looking for more information?

Here's a list of the best Web sites for additional information about Cancún:

✔ **All About Cancún** (www.cancunmx.com): Before taking off on a vacation, every traveler has a few questions, and this site is a good place to start. It contains a database of answers to the most commonly asked questions. Just look for "The Online Experts" section. The site can be slow, but it has input from lots of recent travelers to the region.

✔ **Cancún Convention and Visitors Bureau** (www.cancun.info): The official site of the Cancún Convention and Visitors Bureau provides excellent information on events and area attractions.

✔ **Cancún Online** (www.cancun.com): Cancún Online is a comprehensive guide that has lots of information about things to do and see in Cancún. Just remember that advertisers pay to be included and provide most of the details. Highlights include forums, live chats, property-swaps, and bulletin boards, plus information on local Internet access, news, and events. You can even reserve a golf tee time or plan your wedding online.

✔ **Cancún Travel Guide** (www.go2cancun.com): This group specializing in online information about Mexico has put together an excellent resource for Cancún rentals, hotels, and area attractions. Note that only paying advertisers are listed, but you can find most of the major players here.

✔ **Mexico Web Cancún Chat** (www.mexicoweb.com/travel/chat.html): This site features one of the more active online chats specifically about Cancún, with several different topics to select from. The users share inside information on everything from the cheapest beers to the quality of food at various all-inclusive resorts.

(as in, *Cancún is sooo cool!*). Cancún's international airport is located just inland from the south end of the island.

Ciudad Cancún's street-numbering system is a holdover from its early days. Addresses in the city are still expressed by the number of the building lot and the *manzana* (block) or *supermanzana* (group of city blocks). The city is still relatively compact, and you can easily cover the downtown commercial section on foot. Streets here are named after famous Mayan cities. Chichén-Itzá, Tulum, and Uxmal are the names of the boulevards in downtown Cancún, as well as nearby archeological sites.

On the island, addresses are given by their kilometer (km) number on Blvd. Kukulcán or by reference to some well-known location. The point on the island closest to Ciudad Cancún is km 1; km 20 is found at the very bottom of the "7" at Punta Nizuc, where the Club Med is located.

Taking a taxi

Taxi prices in Cancún are clearly set by zone, although keeping track of what's in which zone can take some work. Taxi rates within the Hotel Zone are a minimum fare of $5 per ride, making it one of the most expensive taxi areas in Mexico.

In addition, taxis operating in the Hotel Zone feel perfectly justified in having a discriminatory pricing structure: Local residents pay about half of what tourists pay, and guests at higher-priced hotels pay about twice the fare that guests in budget hotels are charged. You can thank the taxi union for this discrepancy — it establishes the rate schedule. Rates should be posted outside your hotel; however, if you have a question, all taxi drivers are required to have an official rate card in their taxis, although it's generally in Spanish.

Within the downtown area, the cost is about $1.50 per cab ride (not per person); within any other zone, it's $5. Traveling between two zones also costs $5. If you cross two zones, the cost is $7.50. Settle on a price in advance or check at your hotel where destinations and prices are generally posted. Trips to the airport from most zones cost $14. Taxis also have a rate of $18 per hour for travel around the city and Hotel Zone, but you can generally negotiate this rate down to $10 to $12. If you want to hire a taxi to take you to Chichén-Itzá or along the Riviera Maya, expect to pay about $30 per hour — many taxi drivers feel that they're also providing guide services.

Catching a bus

Bus travel within Cancún continues to improve and is increasingly the most popular way of getting around for both residents and tourists. Air-conditioned and rarely crowded, the Hotel Zone buses run 24 hours a day. You can easily spot the bus stops using the signs posted along the road that have a bus on them. Bus stops are in front of most of the main hotels and shopping centers. In town, almost everything is within walking distance. The city buses marked Ruta 1 and Ruta 2 (also marked "Hoteles") travel frequently from the mainland to the beaches along Avenida Tulum (the main street) and all the way to Punta Nizuc at the far end of the Hotel Zone on Isla Cancún.

Ruta 8 buses go to Puerto Juárez/Punta Sam, where you can catch ferries to Isla Mujeres. The buses stop on the east side of Avenida Tulum. These buses operate between 6 a.m. and 10 p.m. daily. Beware of private buses along the same route; they charge far more than the public ones. The public buses have the fare amount painted on the front; at the time of publication, the fare was 6 pesos (60 cents).

Zipping around on a moped

Mopeds are a convenient and popular way to cruise around through the very congested traffic, but they can be dangerous. Rentals start at $25 for a day, and the shops require a credit-card voucher as security for the moped.

When you rent a moped, you should receive a crash helmet (it's the law) and instructions on how to lock the wheels when you park. Be sure to read the fine print on the back of the rental agreement regarding liability for repairs or replacement in case of accident, theft, or vandalism.

Choosing Your Location

Island hotels are stacked along the beach like dominoes; almost all of them offer clean, modern facilities. Extravagance reigns in the more recently built hotels, many of which are awash in a sea of marble and glass. However, some hotels, although they are exclusive, adopt a more relaxed attitude.

The water is placid on the upper end of the island facing Bahía de Mujeres (Bay of the Women), while beaches lining the long side of the island facing the Caribbean are subject to choppier water and crashing waves on windy days. Be aware that the farther south you go on the island, the longer it takes (20 to 30 minutes in traffic) to get back to the "action spots," which are primarily located between the Plaza Flamingo and Punta Cancún on the island — close to the point that connects the two parts of the 7 — and along Avenida Tulum on the mainland. (To get an idea of Cancún's different neighborhoods, see the "Cancún Orientation Map" earlier in this chapter.)

Almost all major hotel chains are represented along **Isla Cancún,** also known as the **Hotel Zone,** so you can view my selections as a representative summary, with a select number of notable places to stay. The reality is that Cancún is such a popular package destination from the United States that prices and special deals are often the deciding factors for vacationers traveling here.

Ciudad Cancún is the more authentic Mexican town of the two locations, where the workers in the hotels live and day-to-day business is conducted for those not on vacation. The area offers independently owned, smaller, and much less expensive stays — the difference in prices between these

---

Living la vida local

For condo, home, and villa rentals as an alternative to hotel stays, check with **Cancún Hideaways,** a company specializing in luxury properties, downtown apartments, and condos — many offered at prices much lower than comparable hotel accommodations. Owner Maggie Rodriguez, a former resident of Cancún, has made this niche market her specialty. You can preview her offerings at **www.cancun-hideaways.com.**

accommodations and their island counterparts is truly remarkable. Many hotels in Ciudad Cancún offer a shuttle service to sister-properties in Isla Cancún, meaning you can still access the beach for a fraction of the price in return for a little extra travel time. Many of the best restaurants are located here, especially if you're looking for a meal in a type of restaurant other than those you can find back home. It also goes without saying that you get the best value for your meal dollar or peso in Ciudad Cancún.

Staying in Style

Each hotel listing includes specific rack rates for two people spending one night in a standard room, double occupancy during high season (Christmas to Easter), unless otherwise indicated. Rack rates simply mean published rates and tend to be the highest rate paid — you can do better, especially if you're purchasing a package that includes airfare. (See Chapter 7 for tips on avoiding paying rack rates.) The rack rate prices quoted here include the 12% room tax — note that this tax is 5% lower than in most other resorts in Mexico, where the standard tax is 17%. Please refer to the Introduction of this book for an explanation of the price categories.

Hotels often double the normal rates during Christmas and Easter weeks, but low-season rates can be anywhere from 20 to 60% below high-season rates. Some rates may seem much higher than others, but many of these higher rates are *all-inclusive* — meaning that your meals and beverages are included in the price of your stay. All tips and taxes and most activities and entertainment are also included in all-inclusive rates.

All hotels listed here have air-conditioning, unless otherwise indicated. Parking is available at all island hotels.

Antillano
$ **Ciudad Cancún**

A quiet and very clean choice, the Antillano is close to the Ciudad Cancún bus terminal. Rooms overlook either the main downtown street, Avenida Tulum, the side streets, or the interior lawn and pool. Rooms facing the lawn and pool are the most desirable because they are the quietest. Each room has coordinated furnishings, one or two double beds, a sink area separate from the bathroom, and red-tile floors. A bonus: This inexpensive hotel provides guests the use of its beach club on the island. To find Antillano from Avenida Tulum, walk west on Claveles a half block; it's opposite the restaurant Rosa Mexicana. Parking is on the street.

See map p. 117. Av. Claveles 1 (corner of Av. Tulum). ☎ *998-884-1532; Fax: 998-884-1878.* www.hotelantillano.com. *48 units. Street parking. Rack rates: High season $75 double; low season $60 double. AE, MC, V.*

Blue Bay Getaway Cancún
$$$ Isla Cancún

Blue Bay is a spirited yet relaxing all-inclusive adults-only resort — no kids under 16 are allowed — that's favored by young adults in particular. One of its best features is its prime location — right at the northern end of the Hotel Zone, close to the major shopping plazas, restaurants, and nightlife, with a terrific beach with calm waters for swimming. Surrounded by acres of tropical gardens, the comfortable, clean, guest rooms are located in two sections: the central building, where rooms are decorated in rustic wood, and the remaining nine buildings, which feature rooms in a colorful Mexican décor. The main lobby, administrative offices, restaurants, and Tequila Sunrise bar are all located in the central building, meaning you're close to all the action — and more noise — if your room is in this section. Included are all your meals, served at any of the four restaurants, and libations, which you can find in the four bars. During the evenings, guests may enjoy a variety of theme-night dinners, nightly shows, and live entertainment in an outdoor theater with capacity for 150 guests. Activities and facilities include three swimming pools, a tennis court, an exercise room, windsurfing, kayaks, catamarans, boogie boards, complimentary snorkeling and scuba lessons, and a marina. Safes are available for an extra charge, as is dry-cleaning and laundry service. Note that clothing is optional on the beaches of this Blue Bay resort.

See map p. 109. Blvd. Kukulcán, km 3.5. ☎ *800-BLUE-BAY in the U.S or 800-211-1000, or 998-848-7900. Fax: 998-848-7994.* www.bluebayresorts.com. *385 units. Free parking. Rack rates: High season $280 double; low season $180 double. Rates are all-inclusive (room, food, beverages, and activities). AE, MC, V.*

Cancún INN Suites El Patio
$ Ciudad Cancún

A European-style guesthouse, Cancún INN Suites El Patio caters to travelers looking for more of the area's culture. Many guests at this small hotel stay for up to a month and enjoy its combination of excellent value and warm hospitality. You won't find any bars, pools, or loud parties in this place; what you do find is excellent service and impeccable accommodations. Rooms face the plant-filled interior courtyard, dotted with groupings of wrought-iron chairs and tables. Each room has a slightly different décor and set of amenities, but all have white-tile floors and rustic wood furnishings in their various configurations. Some rooms have light kitchenette facilities, and the guesthouse also offers a common kitchen area with purified water and a cooler for stocking your own supplies. A small restaurant — actually closer to a dining room — serves breakfast and dinner. Although a public phone is located in the entranceway, the staff can also arrange for a cellular phone in your room. The game and TV room has a large-screen cable TV, a library stocked with books on Mexican culture, backgammon, cards, and board games. The hotel offers special packages for lodging and Spanish lessons and discounts for longer stays.

Where to Stay in Ciudad Cancún (Cancún City)

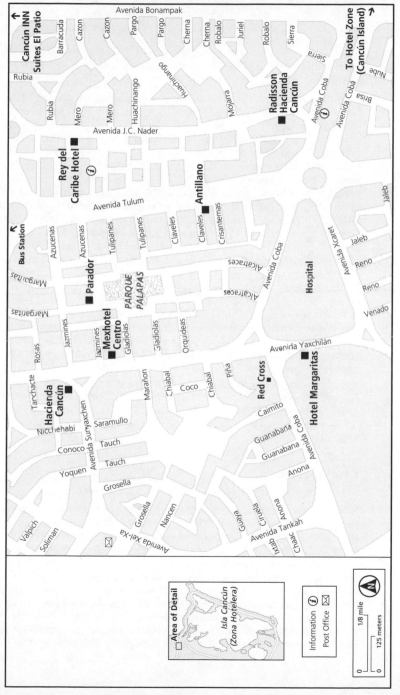

See map p. 117. Av. Bonampak 51 and Cereza, SM2A, Centro. ☎ *998-884-3500. Fax: 998-884-3540.* www.cancuninn.com. *18 units. Rack rates: $40–$55 double, includes morning coffee and bread. Ask for discounts for longer stays. AE, MC, V.*

Caribbean Village Cancún
$$$ Isla Cancún

Considered one of the best all-inclusive values on Cancún Island, this resort's most notable feature is its location, on one of the island's widest stretches of beach. It's also a convenient 20 minutes from the airport and within walking distance of the island's more popular dining and shopping venues. Included in the price of your room are all meals, drinks, and a range of activities and sporting options that include tennis, sailing, wind-surfing, boogie boarding, kayaking, and canoeing. This resort attracts a younger, fun-loving, active crowd — the pool area seems to be the scene of one constant party! In addition to the two interconnected beachfront swimming pools, a popular spot is the oversized Jacuzzi — with room enough for a party of 12. Rooms here are standard resort — not remark-able, and smallish in size, with carpeting and rattan furnishings. All rooms are located in a six-story building that surrounds the pool area and have a view of either the ocean or Nichupte Lagoon. If you can, reserve one of the 17 higher-priced Junior or Master suites — they're well worth the extra charge, giving you more room as well as your own private terrace over-looking the ocean. Four restaurants are available for dining, plus four bars and a disco that jams until 2 a.m. The resort receives consistently high praise (especially for its friendly service) and welcomes many return guests. For those *very* young travelers, a Little Village kids' club offers supervised activities.

See map p. 109. Blvd. Kukulcán, km 13.5. ☎ *800-858-2258 in the U.S., or 998-848-8000. Fax: 998-848-0002.* www.occidentalhotels.com. *300 units. Free parking. Rack rates: High season $266 double; low season $214 double. Rates are all-inclusive. Children under 2 are complimentary, for children ages 2–12, add $46 per night, per child. AE, MC, V.*

Casa Turquesa
$$$$$ Isla Cancún

Romantic, tranquil, and elegant, Casa Turquesa is an oasis of relaxation in the midst of this playful island. If the Mediterranean-style ambience weren't appealing enough, its exceptional stretch of beach (fronting bril-liant turquoise waters) is sure to inspire a positive attitude adjustment. Casa Turquesa is a true boutique hotel, one that caters to couples and is noted for its exceptional service. All suites feature queen- or king-size beds, plus balconies with Jacuzzis. In-room extras include CD players and bathrobes; bathrooms themselves are extra-large, with double sinks and a separate tub and shower. Blue-and-white canopy shade tents dot the area surrounding the attractive pool area and beach; the adjacent Turquesa Pool Bar is open from 10 a.m. to 5 p.m. daily. For dining, the Belle-Vue

Cancún Orientation Map

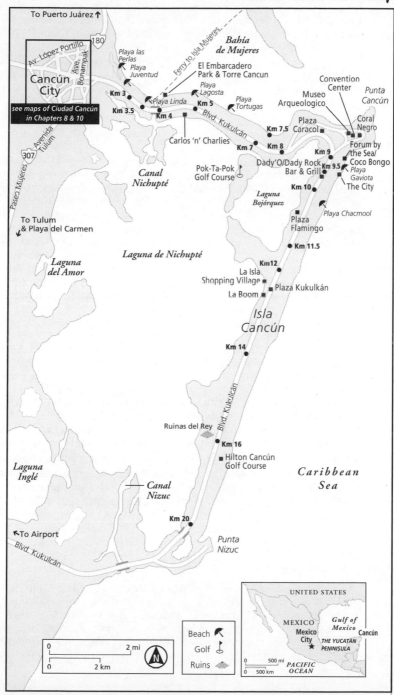

restaurant, serving international gourmet fare, is open 24 hours, and the formal Celebrity restaurant serves seafood and angus beef from 6 p.m. to midnight. If you prefer not to leave the comfort of your room, 24-hour room service is also available.

See map p. 109. Blvd. Kukulcán, km 13.5. ☎ *888-528-8300 in the U.S., or 998-885-2925. Fax: 998-885-2922.* www.casaturquesa.com. *33 suites. Free parking. Rack rates: $286–$357. AE, DC, MC, V.*

Dreams Cancún Resort & Spa
$$$$ Isla Cancún

Formerly the Camino Real Cancún, the all-inclusive Dreams Resort is among the island's most appealing places to stay, located on four acres right at the tip of Punta Cancún. The setting is sophisticated, but the hotel is very welcoming to children. The architecture of the hotel is contemporary and sleek, with bright colors and strategic angles. Rooms in the newer 18-story Club Section have extra services and amenities, including a private lounge area, evening cocktails and hors d'ouvres, and a private concierge. All rooms have ocean views, as well as either a balcony or terrace, and marble and mosaic tile detailing in the rooms. In addition to the oceanfront pool, Dreams has a private saltwater lagoon with sea turtles and tropical fish. Dreams all-inclusive concept is more oriented to quality experiences than unlimited buffets — your room price here includes gourmet meals, 24-hour room service, premium brand drinks, as well as the use of all resort amenities, watersports, evening entertainment, airport transfers and tips. The fitness center and spa is the focal point of the resort's amenities, but it also has three lighted tennis courts, beach volleyball, a sailing pier, and a watersports center keep things active; extra charges apply to some of these activities, such as diving, jet skis, and sport fishing. For those with trouble disconnecting, there's also a 24-hour business center with Internet access. The hotel's three restaurants — including the popular María Bonita Mexican theme restaurant — and the lively Azucar Cuban dance club are all on-site.

See map p. 109. Blvd. Kukulcán, Punta Cancún. ☎ *866-237-3267 in the U.S., or 998-848-7000. Fax: 998-848-7001 or 998-848-7009.* www.dreamscancun.com. *381 units. Guarded parking adjacent to hotel. Rack rates: High season $275 standard double, $320 Club room, double; low season $195 standard double; $230 Club double. AE, DC, MC, V.*

El Pueblito
$$$ Isla Cancún

The El Pueblito looks like a traditional Mexican hacienda and has the gracious, hospitable service to match. Several three-story buildings (no elevators) are terraced in a V-shape down a gentle hillside toward the sea, with a meandering swimming pool with waterfalls running between them, to a beachside, thatched-roof restaurant. Consistent renovations and upgrades and a changeover to an all-inclusive concept have made this hotel more appealing than ever and another exceptional all-inclusive value. Rooms are very large and have rattan furnishings, travertine marble floors, large bathrooms, and either a balcony or terrace facing the pool or sea. In addition to a constant flow of buffet-style meals and snacks, a nightly theme party, complete with entertainment, also awaits guests. Miniature golf and a water slide, plus a full program of kid's activities, make this place an ideal choice for families with children. Baby-sitting services are available for $10 per hour. The hotel is located toward the southern end of the island past the Hilton Resort.

See map p. 109. Blvd. Kukulcán, km 17.5, past the Hilton Resort. ☎ *998-885-0422, 998-881-8800. Fax: 998-885-0731.* www.pueblitohotels.com. *349 units. Free parking. Rack rates: High season $300 double, low season $240 double. Rates are all-inclusive. AE, MC, V.*

Fiesta Americana Grand Aqua
$$$$$ Isla Cancún

Stunning, stylish, and sensual, Aqua is certain to emerge as Cancún's most coveted place to stay. The resort was on the brink of opening at press time, so I can't comment on service or the actual details of a stay, however I was so enthused at its opening, I couldn't wait to share the news. The entire hotel seems to mirror the predominant colors of Cancún — turquoise and white — in a sublimely chic manner. This hotel was built for sophisticated travelers, and those who appreciate hip style, and look for the cutting edge in places to stay. Aqua aims to stimulate your five senses, and upon arrival — under a crystal cube fountain — you're offered a fusion tea, and a blend of relaxing and stimulating aromatherapy. The oasis of eight oceanfront pools is surrounded by chaise longues, queen-size recliners or private cabanas. All rooms and common areas emphasize the views to the pool and ocean beyond. Rooms are generous in size, and all face the ocean and have balconies. A very large bathroom features a large soaking tub and organic bath products. Guests can tailor their turndown service by selecting from a pillow menu and choice of aromatherapy oils and candles. Mini Zen gardens or a fishbowl add unique touches to room décor, and high-speed Internet access, flat screen TVs, and CD/DVD players are standard, while suites offer extras like a Bose surround-sound system. Twenty-nine rooms are "Grand Club," which include continental breakfast and a club room with butler service, snacks, bar service, and private check-in. The 1,500 sq. meter spa here is among the hotel's most notable attractions, with 12 treatment rooms offering a blend Eastern, pre-Hispanic and Western treatments. Outdoor Pilates, Tai Chi, and yoga classes are offered daily, and massage cabanas are also available on the beach. Another hallmark of this hotel is certain to be its collection of restaurants, chief among them **SIETE,** under the direction of premier Mexican chef and cookbook author, Patricia Quintana, featuring her sophisticated take on traditional Mexican cuisine. Chef Michelle Bernstein, formerly a rising culinary star in Miami, presides over **MB,** serving healthy comfort food. There's also an Italian restaurant, deli, chill-out lounge and 24-hour room service. After dark, the hotel shifts moods, with fire pits, torch-lights, and ambient music.

See map p. 109. Blvd. Kukulcán, km 12.5, Zona Hotelera. ☎ *800-343-7821 or 800-fiesta-1 in the U.S., or 998-881-7600. Fax: 998-881-7601.* www.fiestaamericana. com. *371 rooms and suites. Free parking. Rack rates: High season $393–$466 standard; $516 Grand Club rooms; $750 suite; low season $215–$313 standard; $363 Grand Club rooms; $600 suite. Ask about Fiesta Break packages. AE, DC, MC, V. Small pets allowed with prior reservation.*

Fiesta Americana Grand Coral Beach
$$$$$ Isla Cancún

A spectacularly grand hotel, the Fiesta Americana has one of the best locations in Cancún with its 1,000 feet of prime beachfront property and proximity to the main shopping and entertainment centers — perfect for the traveler looking to be at the heart of all that Cancún has to offer. The great Punta Cancún location (opposite the convention center) has the advantage of facing the beach to the north, meaning that the surf is calm and perfect for swimming. When it comes to the hotel itself, the operative word here is *big* — everything at the Fiesta Americana seems oversized, from the lobby to the rooms. Service is gracious, if cool, because the hotel aims for a more sophisticated ambience. The finishings of elegant dark-green granite and an abundance of marble extend from the lobby to the large guest rooms, all of which have balconies facing the ocean, and most of which were remodeled in 2004. A 660-foot-long, free-form swimming pool with swim-up bars and a casual poolside snack bar borders the beach. A full watersports equipment rental service is on the beach. Dining here is a highlight with an exquisite gourmet restaurant, Basilique, along with two other more casual dining options, plus five bars. If tennis is your game, this hotel has the best facilities in Cancún. Three indoor tennis courts with stadium seating are part of an extensive fitness center and spa.

See map p. 109. Blvd. Kukulcán, km 9.5. ☎ *800-343-7821 or 800- fiesta-1 in the U.S., or 998-881-3200. Fax: 998-881-3273.* www.fiestaamericana.com.mx. *602 units. Rack rates: High season $328–$555 double, $529–$650 Club Floors double (with Continental breakfast, afternoon snacks and cocktails, upgraded bathroom amenities); low season $222–$424 double, $381–$504 Club Floors double. Up to 2 children included in parents' room at no extra charge. AE, MC, V.*

Hacienda Cancún
$ Ciudad Cancún

An extremely pleasing little hotel — and a great value — Hacienda Cancún is perfect for travelers on a budget. The facade has been remodeled to look like a hacienda, and rooms continue the theme, with their rustic-style Mexican furnishings. Guest rooms are clean and very comfortable; all have two double beds and windows (but no views). The hotel offers a nice, small pool, and cafe under a shaded palapa in the back. To find it from

Avenida Yaxchilán, turn west on Sunyaxchen; it's on your right next to the Hotel Caribe International, opposite 100% Natural. Parking is on the street. *See map p. 117. Sunyaxchen 39–40.* ☎ **998-884-3672.** *Fax: 998-884-1208. E-mail:* hhda@cancun.com.mx. *35 units. Rack rates: High season $45 double; low season $38 double. MC, V.*

Hilton Cancún Beach & Golf Resort
$$$$ Isla Cancún

The Hilton in Cancún is especially perfect for anyone whose motto is "the bigger the better." Grand, expansive, and fully equipped, this is a true resort in every sense of the word. The Hilton Cancún is situated on 250 acres of prime Cancún beachfront property with its own 18-hole, par-72 golf course across the street and a location that gives every room a sea view. (Some have both sea and lagoon views.) Like the sprawling resort, rooms are grandly spacious and immaculately decorated in a minimalist style, all of which were renovated in 2004. Area rugs and pale furnishings soften marble floors and bathrooms. The more elegant Beach Club rooms and Villas are set off from the main hotel in two- and three-story buildings (no elevators) and have their own check-in and concierge service, plus nightly complimentary cocktails. The hotel is especially appealing to golfers because it's one of only two hotels in Cancún with an on-site course. (The other is the Mélia, which has an 18-hole executive course.) The seven interconnected pools with a swim-up bar, two lighted tennis courts, a large, fully equipped gym, and a beachfront watersports center make the Hilton Cancún a good choice for those looking for an action-packed stay. Just opened is the new Wellness Spa, highlights of which are oceanfront massage cabanas, yoga, and aromatherapy. The Kids Club program is one of the best on the island, making it great for families.

See map p. 109. Blvd. Kukulcán, km 17, Retorno Lacandones. ☎ **800-228-3000** *in the U.S., or 998-881-8000. Fax: 998-881-8080.* www.hiltoncancun.com.mx. *426 units. Rack rates: $119–$269 standard double, $179–$309 Villas. AE, DC, MC, V.*

Hotel Margaritas
$–$$ Ciudad Cancún

This four-story hotel (with elevator) in downtown Cancún is comfortable and unpretentious, offering one of the best values in Cancún. Rooms have white tile floors and a small balcony and are exceptionally clean and bright and pleasantly decorated. The attractive pool is surrounded by lounge chairs and has a wading section for children. The hotel offers complimentary safes at the front desk and more services than most budget hotels.

See map p. 117. Av. Yaxchilán 41, SM22, Centro. ☎ **998-884-9333.** *Fax: 998-884-1324. 100 units. Rack rates: $85 double, includes breakfast. AE, MC, V.*

Hyatt Cancún Caribe
$$$$$ Isla Cancún

Although this is one of Cancún's older hotels, it remains a favored choice for travelers wanting a more sophisticated place to stay at a reasonable price. Although the beach is a bit rocky, there's a precious lagoon-style pool above the beach. All rooms will be completely remodeled by mid-2005, and are located either in a seven-story curved building that backs the pool or in a collection of villas adjacent to the main building. The rooms themselves, though small, are decorated in muted colors with light wood furnishings. The combination marble tub has Mexican tile accents, and small furnished balconies overlook the pool and beach (bottom floors have terraces). Rooms are quieter and more private in the villa section; you'll also enjoy larger bathrooms and a large ground-floor terrace. These rooms are all Regency Club rooms, and so offer extra services and amenities. In addition to the pool, the hotel has three lighted tennis courts, a jogging track, and massage services, as well as three restaurants, including the recommended Blue Bayou.

Blvd. Kukulcán, km 10.5. ☎ *800-228-9000 in the U.S., or 998-848-7800. Fax: 998-883-1514. www.hyatt.com. 226 rooms and villa suites. Free parking. Rack rates: High season $279–$479 double. AE, MC, V.*

Le Méridien Cancún Resort & Spa
$$$$$ Isla Cancún

Of all the luxury properties in Cancún, I find Le Méridien the most inviting, with a polished yet welcoming sense of personal service. Although other hotels tend to overdo a sense of formality in an attempt to justify their prices, Le Méridien has an elegantly casual style that makes you comfortable enough to thoroughly relax. From the intimate lobby and reception area to the most outstanding concierge service in Cancún, guests feel immediately pampered upon arrival. The hotel itself is smaller than others and feels more like an upscale boutique hotel than an immense resort — a welcome relief to those overstressed by activity at home. The décor throughout the rooms and common areas is one of understated good taste — both classy and comforting, not overdone. Rooms are generous in size, and most have small balconies overlooking the pool with a view to the ocean. A very large marble bathroom has a separate tub and a glassed-in shower. The hotel attracts many Europeans and younger, sophisticated travelers, and is ideal for a second honeymoon or romantic break. Certainly, a highlight of — or even a reason for — staying here is time spent at the **Spa del Mar,** one of Mexico's finest and most complete European spa facilities, featuring two levels and more than 15,000 square feet of services dedicated to your body and soul. A complete fitness center with extensive cardio and weight machines is found on the upper level. The spa is located below and comprised of a healthy snack bar, a full-service salon, and 14 treatment rooms, as well as separate men's and women's steam rooms, saunas, whirlpools, cold plunge pools, inhalation rooms, tranquility rooms, lockers, and changing areas.

The health club may become a necessity if you fully enjoy the gourmet restaurant, **Aioli,** with its specialties based on Mediterranean and Provençal cuisines. (Check out Chapter 10 for a detailed listing of this restaurant.) The menu is simply delicious — not pretentious. Adjoining the spa is a large swimming pool that cascades down three levels. Above the spa is a tennis center with two championship tennis courts with lights. Watersports equipment is available for rent on the beach. A supervised children's program has its own Penguin Clubhouse, play equipment, and a wading pool. Baby-sitting services are also available for $12 per hour; after 10 p.m,. add a $10 taxi charge.

See map p. 109. Retorno del Rey, km 14, Zona Hotelera. ☎ 800-543-4300 in the U.S., or 998-881-2200. Fax: 998-881-2201. www.meridiencancun.com.mx. 213 units. Free parking. Rack rates: High season $290 standard, $450 suite; low season $220 standard, $350 suite. Ask for special spa packages. AE, DC, MC, V. Small pets accepted, with advanced reservation.

Marriott Casa Magna
$$$$ Isla Cancún

This property is quintessential Marriott. Travelers who are familiar with the chain's standards feel at home here and appreciate the hotel's attention to detailed service. In fact, if you're on your first trip to Mexico, and you're looking for a little familiarity of home, this hotel is a great choice because it feels like a slice of the United States transported to a stunning stretch of Caribbean beach. Guest rooms have contemporary furnishings, tiled floors, and ceiling fans; most have balconies. All suites occupy corners and have enormous terraces, oceanviews, and TVs in both the living room and the bedroom. The Marriott Casa Magna offers five on-site restaurants to choose from, plus a lobby bar with live music. Alongside the meandering oceanfront pool are two lighted tennis courts. The hotel caters to family travelers with specially priced packages (up to two children can stay free with parents) and the Club Amigos supervised children's program. A more deluxe offering from Marriott, the 450-room luxury **JW Cancún Resort & Spa** (☎ **998-848-9600**), is located on the beach next to the Casa Magna. Its hallmark is a 20,000-square-foot European spa and fitness center.

See map p. 109. Blvd. Kukulcán, km 14.5. ☎ 800-228-9290 in the U.S., or 998-881-2000. Fax: 998-881-2071. www.marriott.com. 452 units. Rack rates: High season $225–$254 double, $350 suite; low season $139–$160 double, $300 suite. Ask about available packages. AE, DC, MC, V.

Melía Cancún Beach & Spa Resort
$$$$ Isla Cancún

The large, ultra-modern Melía is popular for weddings, conventions, and other group events, but is also a great option for individual travelers looking for a lively place to stay. The resort is a landmark of sorts, known for its spectacular nine-story, pyramid-shaped lobby atrium, with cascading waterfalls and a bevy of palms. Guest rooms are small but adequate, with marble floors, bright décor, and balconies — about half offer ocean or lagoon view. Opt for the Royal Beach floor, and you'll enjoy larger rooms and upgraded amenities and services. Two unique pools, an executive 18-hole golf course, three tennis courts, two paddle tennis courts lit for night, and a 6,000-square-foot spa and fitness center mean it has among the broadest range of amenities on the island. Dining choices are also ample, with five restaurants to choose from, as well as three bars and 24-hour room service.

Blvd. Kukulcán, km 16.5. ☎ *800-336-3542 in the U.S., or 998-885-1114. Fax: 998-885-1963.* www.solmelia.com. *400 rooms. Free parking. Rack rates: $190–$330. AE, DC, MC, V.*

Mexhotel Centro
$$ Ciudad Cancún

One of the perennially popular hotels in downtown Cancún, Mexhotel Centro has the warmth and style of a small hacienda. Three floors (with elevator) of rooms front a lovely palm-shaded pool area with comfortable tables and chairs and a restaurant. Standard rooms are extra-clean with muted décor, two double beds framed with wrought-iron headboards, large tile bathrooms with separate sinks, desks, and over-bed reading lights. Although prices may seem high for the location, beach and pool privileges at its sister resort in the Hotel Zone, Mexhotel Resort Cancún, make it a great bargain. (Guests do have to pay an extra charge for transportation, but the hotel is close to the bus route.) The hotel is between Jazmines and Gladiolas, kitty-corner from Perico's.

See map p. 117. Yaxchilan 31, SM 22. ☎ *988-884-3078 (also fax). 81 units. Free parking. Rack rates: $50–$100. MC, V.*

Miramar Misión Cancún Park Plaza
$$$ Isla Cancún

Another good choice for travelers looking for well-priced rooms right on the beach, the ingeniously designed Miramar offers partial views of both the lagoon and ocean from all its rooms. A notable feature is the large, rectangular swimming pool that extends through the hotel and down to the beach and contains built-in, submerged sun chairs. The hotel also offers an oversized whirlpool (they claim, the largest in Cancún), a sundeck, and a snack bar on the seventh-floor roof. Rooms are on the small side but are bright and comfortable with a small balcony and bamboo furniture; bathrooms have polished limestone vanities. In addition to three restaurants, **Batacha,** a popular nightclub features live music for dancing from 9 p.m. to 4 a.m. Tuesday to Sunday.

See map p. 109. Blvd. Kukulcán, km 9.5. ☎ *998-883-1755. Fax: 998-883-1136.* www.hotelesmision.com. *300 units. Rack rates: High season $220; low season $160 double. AE, MC, V.*

Oasis Cancún
$$$ Isla Cancún

From the street, the Oasis may not be much to look at, but the location is ideal because it's set on Cancún's best beach for safe swimming. The ocean side has a small but pretty patio garden and pool. Oasis is close to all the shops and restaurants clustered near Punta Cancún and the convention center. You can choose between rooms with either a lagoon or oceanview. The rooms, all of which were remodeled in 2004, are large with a pleasing, comfortable décor. They feature marble floors and either two double beds or a king-size bed. Several studios with kitchenettes are also available upon request. In addition to a restaurant and three bars, the hotel also has two lighted tennis courts, watersports equipment rental, and a small marina with its own fishing fleet.

See map p. 109. Blvd. Kukulcán, km 8.5, next to the Playa Linda dock. ☎ *800-221-2222 in the U.S., or 998-883-0800. Fax: 998-883-2087. 216 units. Free parking. Rack rates: High season $145–$250 double; low season $138–$158 double. Price includes buffet breakfast. Children under 12 are free. AE, MC, V.*

Parador
$ Ciudad Cancún

The convenient location and rock-bottom prices make this otherwise non-descript hotel among the most popular downtown hotels. Guest rooms, located on one of three floors, are arranged around two long, narrow garden courtyards leading back to a small pool (with an even smaller, separate children's pool) and grassy sunning area. The rooms are contemporary and basic, each with two double beds and a shower. The hotel is next to Pop's restaurant, almost at the corner of Uxmal. Street parking is limited.

See map p. 117. Av. Tulum 26. ☎ *998-884-1043, 998-884-1310. Fax: 998-884-9712. 66 units. Rack rates: High season $53 double; low season $39 double. Ask about promotional rates. MC, V.*

Presidente Inter-Continental Cancún
$$$–$$$$$ Isla Cancún

On the island's best beach, facing the placid Bahía de Mujeres, the Presidente's location is reason enough to stay here, and it's just a two-minute walk to Cancún's public Pok-Ta-Pok Golf Club. Cool and spacious, the Presidente sports a postmodern design with lavish marble and wicker accents and a strong use of color. Guests have a choice of two double beds or one king-size bed. All rooms have tastefully simple unfinished pine furniture. The expansive pool has a pyramid-shaped waterfall and is surrounded by cushioned lounge chairs. In addition to lighted tennis courts and a small fitness center, the marina has watersports equipment rentals. Coming from Cancún City, the Presidente is on the left side of the street before you get to Punta Cancún. For its ambience, I feel that the Presidente

is an ideal choice for a romantic getaway or for couples who enjoy indulging in the sports of golf, tennis, or even shopping.
See map p. 109. Blvd. Kukulcán, km 7.5. ☎ *800-327-0200 in the U.S., or 998-848-8700. Fax: 998-883-2602.* www.interconti.com. *299 units. Rack rates: High season $240–$300 double; low season $150–$230 double. Ask about special promotional packages. Children under 17 are free in their parents' room. AE, MC, V.*

Radisson Hacienda Cancún
$$–$$$ Ciudad Cancún

The nicest hotel in downtown Cancún, the Hacienda Cancún is also one of the very best values in the area, managed by Radisson. It offers all the expected comforts of a chain like Radisson, yet in an atmosphere of Mexican hospitality. Resembling a Mexican hacienda, rooms are set off from a large rotunda-style lobby, lush gardens, and a pleasant pool area, which has a separate wading section for children. All rooms have brightly colored fabric accents; views of the garden, the pool, or the street; and a small sitting area and balcony. Bathrooms have a combination tub and shower. For the price, I found the extra in-room amenities of a coffeemaker, hair dryer, and iron to be nice extras. In addition to two restaurants, the hotel offers a generally lively lobby bar, as well as tennis courts and a small gym. Guests of the Hacienda may enjoy a complimentary shuttle service to Isla Cancún's beaches. The hotel is located right behind the state government building and within walking distance of downtown Cancún dining and shopping.
See map p. 117. Av. Nader 1, SM2, Centro. ☎ *800-333-3333 in the U.S., 01-800-711-1531 in Mexico, or 998-881-6500. Fax: 998-884-7954.* www.radissoncancun.com. *248 units. Rack rates: High season $100 standard, $125 Jr. suite; low season $90 standard, $115 Jr. suite. AE, MC, V.*

Refugio del Pirata Morgan
$ Ciudad Cancún

Although not actually in the town of Cancún, but on the highway leading north from Cancún to Punta Sam, this is the place for those who want a true encounter with nature in Cancún. Located on a wide, virgin stretch of beach, away from the crowd of hotels and nightlife, this "refuge" is exactly that: no phones, no television, just blissful peace and quiet. There are ten simple cabañas, with both beds and hammocks, each named for the predominate color of décor. A small restaurant offers a basic selection of dining choices featuring fresh fish — otherwise, the nearest restaurant is 2 kilometers (1¼ miles) away.
Carretera Punta Sam, Isla Blanca, km 9 ☎ *998-860-3386 (within Mexico dial 044 first, because this is a cellphone). 10 units. Free parking. Rack rates: $40 room; $5 hammock.*

Rey del Caribe Hotel

$-$$ Ciudad Cancún

This hotel, located in the center of downtown is a unique oasis — a 100% ecological hotel, where every detail has been thought out to achieve the goal of living in an organic and environmentally friendly manner. The whole atmosphere of the place is one of warmth, which derives from the on-site owners, who, caring as much as they do for Mother Earth, extend this sentiment to guests as well. You easily forget you're in the midst of downtown Cancún in the tropical jungle setting, with blooming orchids and other flowering plants. A pool, hot tub, and the restaurant are surrounded by gardens populated with statues of Mayan deities — it's a lovely, tranquil setting. There's a daily-changing schedule of yoga, Tai-Chi, and meditation sessions, as well as special classes on astrology, tarot, and other subjects. Rooms are large and sunny, and all are air-conditioned, with your choice of one king or two full-size beds, a kitchenette, and terrace. The detail of ecological sensitivity is truly impressive, ranging from the use of collected rain water to waste composting. Recycling is encouraged and solar power used wherever possible. This is a place that not only feels good to stay in, but makes you feel good to stay in.

See map p. 117. Ave. Uxmal, corner with Nadar, SM 2-A. ☎ *998-884-2028; Fax: 998-884-9857; www.*reycaribe.com. *24 units. Free parking. Rack rates: $63–$100, high season; $40-$80 low season. Rates include breakfast. MC, V.*

Ritz-Carlton Hotel

$$$$$ Isla Cancún

The grand-scale Ritz-Carlton is a fountain of formality in this casual beach resort, perfect for someone who wants a Palm Beach–style experience in Mexico. The décor — in both public areas as well as guest rooms — is sumptuous and formal with thick carpets, elaborate chandeliers, and fresh flowers throughout. The hotel fronts a 1,200-foot white-sand beach, and all rooms overlook the ocean, pool (heated during winter months), and tropical gardens. In all rooms, marble bathrooms have telephones, separate tubs and showers, and lighted makeup mirrors. Ritz-Carlton Club floors offer guests five mini-meals a day, private butler service, and premium bath products. **The Club Grill,** a fashionable English pub, is one of the best restaurants in the city, and the **Lobby Lounge** is the original home of proper tequila tastings, featuring one of the world's most extensive menus of fine tequilas, as well as Cuban cigars. I love its white-draped cabañas for two on the beach! There's a salon and very good fitness center, plus three lighted tennis courts. The recently opened Kayantá Spa offers an excellent selection of Mayan and Mexican-inspired treatments and massages. The Ritz Kids program has supervised activities for children, and baby-sitting services are also available. The hotel has won countless recognitions and accolades for service. Special packages for golfing, spa, and weekend getaways are worth exploring.

See map p. 109. Retorno del Rey 36, off Blvd. Kukulcán, km 13.5. ☎ *800-241-3333 in the U.S. and Canada, or 998-881-0808. Fax: 998-881-0815.* www.ritzcarlton.com. *365 units. Free guarded parking. Rack rates: High season $369–$475 double; $389–$850 Club floors; low season $189–$279 double; Club floors $295–$429. AE, MC, V.*

Riu Palace Las Americas
$$$ Isla Cancún

The all-inclusive Riu Palace is part of a family of Riu resorts in Cancún known for their grand, opulent style. This one is the smallest of the three in Cancún, and the most elegant, steeped in pearl-white Greco style, and my choice for a high-end all-inclusive vacation in Cancún. The location is prime — near the central shopping, dining, and nightlife centers, just a 5-minute walk to the Convention Center. All rooms are spacious junior suites with ocean or lagoon views, a separate seating area, and a balcony or terrace. Eight also feature a Jacuzzi. Two central pools overlook the ocean and a wide stretch of beach, with one heated during winter months. There's also a solarium, fitness center, Spa (extra charges apply), and a host of sports and activities ranging from windsurfing to tennis. The hotel has six restaurants and five bars, offering guests virtually 24 hours of all-inclusive snacks, meals, and beverages. And, if that's not enough, guests have exchange privileges at the Riu Cancún, next door.

Blvd. Kukulcán, Lote 4. ☎ *888-666-8816; 998-891-4300. 368 units. Free, unguarded parking. Rack rates: High season $413–$627 double; low season $287–$464 double, all-inclusive. AE, MC, V.*

Sun Palace
$$$$$ Isla Cancún

If you're looking for an all-inclusive resort on a great stretch of Caribbean beach, this member of the popular Palace Resorts is a prime pick. Here what you get is a fantastic beach, one of the widest on the island. Located toward the southern end of the island, next to the Westin Regina, it's further away from Hotel Zone action, which may be what you want, in order to revel in all of the included goodies that go with staying here. Suites feature modern Mexican décor, and all have marble floors and a combination bath with whirlpool tub. All also have either oceanview balconies or terraces, and come with premium extras like bathrobes and hair dryers. In addition to the beachside pool, the resort offers an indoor pool, plus a large Jacuzzi with a waterfall. A nicely equipped health club and tennis court complement the ample activities program. For dining, you can choose from one of three restaurants or order in from 24-hour room service. Sun Palace also has weekly theme parties. One of the best perks to staying here is that excursions to Tulum, Chichén-Itzá, or Isla Mujeres are also included in its activities program. When you stay at any of the Palace resorts, you have the option of visiting any other members of its chain — and you have two others in Cancún to choose from.

See map p. 109. Blvd. Kukulcán, km 20. ☎ *800-346-8225, 998-885-0533. Fax: 998-885-1593.* www.palaceresorts.com. *237 suites. Free parking. Rack rates: $310–$398, double. Rates are all-inclusive. AE, DC, MC, V.*

Westin Regina Cancún
$$$$$ Isla Cancún

A stunning hotel, the Westin Regina is great for anyone wanting the beauty of Cancún's beaches and a little distance between them and the more bois-terous, flashy parts of Cancún's hotel strip. The strikingly austere but grand architectural style of the Westin Regina is the stamp of leading Latin-American architect Ricardo Legorreta. A series of five swimming pools front the beach, and the Westin offers two lighted tennis counts and a small fitness center with spa services. The hotel is divided into two sec-tions, the main building and the more exclusive six-story, hot-pink, tower section. Standard rooms are unusually large and beautifully furnished with cool, contemporary furniture. The rooms on the sixth floor have balconies, and first-floor rooms have terraces. Rooms in the tower all have ocean or lagoon views and extensive use of marble, furniture with Olinalá lacquer accents, Berber-carpet area rugs, oak tables and chairs, and terraces with lounge chairs. Note that this hotel is a 15- to 20-minute ride from the lively strip that lies between the Plaza Flamingo and Punta Cancún, so it's a better choice for if you want to relish a little more seclusion than Cancún typically offers. However, you can easily join the action when you're so inclined — buses stop in front, and taxis are readily available.

See map p. 109. Blvd. Kukulcán, km 20. ☎ *800-228-3000 in the U.S., 800-902-2300 in Mexico, or 998-848-7400. Fax: 998-885-0666.* www.westin.com. *293 units. Rack rates: High season $285–$450 double; low season $160–$299 double. AE, DC, MC, V.*

Dining Out

The restaurant scene in Cancún is populated in large part by U.S.-based franchise chains, which need no introduction — Hard Rock Cafe, Planet Hollywood, Rainforest Cafe, Tony Roma's, TGI Fridays, Ruth's Chris Steak House, Outback Steakhouse, and the usual fast-food burger places. And surprisingly, contrary to the conventional travel wisdom, many of the best restaurants in Cancún are located either in hotels or shopping malls. The restaurants of the new Aqua Fiesta Americana (not yet opened at press time) appeared to be especially promising, including one called "7," which is under the direction of renowned Mexican Chef Patricia Quintana.

Most restaurants are located in the Hotel Zone in Isla Cancún, which is logical because that's where most of the tourists who dine out are stay-ing. However, don't dismiss the charms of dining in Ciudad Cancún (Cancún City). You're likely to find a great meal — at a fraction of the price of an Isla Cancún eatery — accompanied by a dose of local color.

As in many of Mexico's beach resorts, even the finest restaurants in town can be comfortably casual when it comes to dress. Men rarely wear jackets, although ladies are frequently seen in dressy resort wear — basically, everything goes, attire-wise.

For those traveling with kids, Cancún has no shortage of options. From Johnny Rockets to McDonald's, this destination has plenty of kid-friendly — and kid-familiar — places.

Prices in Cancún restaurants can cover an extended range, boosted by shrimp and lobster dishes, which can top $20 for an entree. If you're watching your budget, even the higher-priced places generally have less-expensive options — you just need to avoid the premium seafood dishes. Tips generally run about 15% of the bill, and most wait staff really depend on tips for their income, so be generous if the service warrants.

Cancún's Best Restaurants

The restaurants listed here are either locally owned, one-of-a-kind restaurants or exceptional selections at area hotels. Many feature live music as an accompaniment to the dining experience. I arrange the restaurants alphabetically and note their locations and general price categories. Refer to the Introduction of this book for an explanation of the price categories. Also see Chapter 18 for more information on Mexican cuisine.

100% Natural
$ Isla Cancún VEGETARIAN/MEXICAN

If you want a healthy reprieve from an overindulgent night — or if you just like your meals as fresh and natural as possible — this restaurant is your oasis. No matter what your dining preference, you owe it to yourself to try a true Mexican tradition, the fresh fruit *liquado* (lee-*qwa*-doe) — a blended drink that combines fresh fruit, ice, and either water or milk. (Think combos of mango and milk, or mango and watermelon, juiced in an icy tall glass.) Of course, other creative combinations mix in yogurt, granola, or other goodies. But 100% Natural has more than just drinks — the restaurant offers a bountiful selection of basic Mexican fare and terrific sandwiches served on whole-grain breads. (Look for numerous vegetarian options, too.) Breakfast here is a delight, as well as a good value. The atmosphere is abundant with plants and bright colors. The restaurant has two locations; the Plaza Terramar store is open 24 hours.

See map p. 133. Plaza Kukulcán, Blvd. Kukulcán 13, ☎ 998-885-2904. Also at Plaza Terramar, ☎ 998-883-3636. Reservations not accepted. Main courses: $2.80–$12.50. MC, V. Open: Daily 8 a.m.–11 p.m.

Where to Dine in Isla Cancún

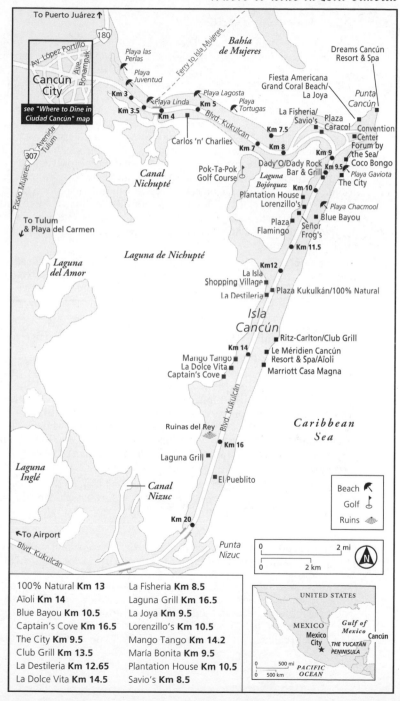

To Puerto Juárez ↑

180

Av. López Portillo
Ave. Bonampak

Cancún City

see "Where to Dine in Ciudad Cancún" map

Avenida Tulum

307

Paseo Mujeres

To Tulum
& Playa del Carmen

Ferry to Isla Mujeres

Playa las Perlas
Playa Juventud

Bahía de Mujeres

Km 3
Playa Linda
Km 3.5
Km 4
Playa Lagosta
Km 5
Playa Linda
Blvd. Kukulcán
Carlos 'n' Charlies
Playa Tortugas
Km 7.5
Km 7
Km 8

Fiesta Americana Grand Coral Beach/ La Joya
La Fisheria/ Savio's
Plaza Caracol

Dreams Cancún Resort & Spa

Punta Cancún

Convention Center
Forum by the Sea/
Coco Bongo
Km 9
Km 9.5
Playa Gaviota
The City

Canal Nichupté

Pok-Ta-Pok Golf Course
Dady'O/Dady Rock Bar & Grill
Laguna Bojórquez
Km 10
Plantation House
Lorenzillo's

Plaza Flamingo
Señor Frog's

Playa Chacmool
Blue Bayou

Km 11.5

Laguna de Nichupté

Km12
La Isla Shopping Village
La Destileria
Plaza Kukulkán/100% Natural

Laguna del Amor

Isla Cancún

Ritz-Carlton/Club Grill
Km 14
Mango Tango
La Dolce Vita
Captain's Cove

Le Méridien Cancún Resort & Spa/Aïoli
Marriott Casa Magna

Ruinas del Rey
Km 16

Caribbean Sea

Laguna Grill

Laguna Inglé

Canal Nizuc

El Pueblito

Km 20

←To Airport
Blvd. Kukulcán

Punta Nizuc

Blvd. Kukulcán

Beach	⚓
Golf	⛳
Ruins	〰

0 — 2 mi
0 — 2 km

100% Natural **Km 13**
Aïoli **Km 14**
Blue Bayou **Km 10.5**
Captain's Cove **Km 16.5**
The City **Km 9.5**
Club Grill **Km 13.5**
La Destileria **Km 12.65**
La Dolce Vita **Km 14.5**

La Fisheria **Km 8.5**
Laguna Grill **Km 16.5**
La Joya **Km 9.5**
Lorenzillo's **Km 10.5**
Mango Tango **Km 14.2**
María Bonita **Km 9.5**
Plantation House **Km 10.5**
Savio's **Km 8.5**

UNITED STATES

MEXICO
Mexico City ★
THE YUCATÁN PENINSULA
Gulf of Mexico Cancún

0 — 500 mi
0 — 500 km
PACIFIC OCEAN

Aïoli

$$$$ Isla Cancún FRENCH

Aïoli, in Le Méridien Hotel, is a Provençal — but definitely not provincial — restaurant that offers exquisite French and Mediterranean gourmet specialties in a warm and cozy country French setting. Although it offers perhaps the best breakfast buffet in Cancún (for $20), most visitors outside the hotel come only for dinner, where low lighting and superb service make for a romantic evening. Starters include traditional pâtés and delightful escargots served in the shell with a white wine and herb butter sauce. A specialty is duck breast served in a honey and lavender sauce. Equally scrumptious is the rack of lamb, prepared in a Moroccan style and served with couscous. Pan-seared grouper is topped with a paste of black olives, crushed potato, and tomato, and the bouillabaisse is laden with an exceptional array of seafood. Desserts are decadent in true French style, including the signature Fifth Element, a sinfully delicious dish rich with chocolate. For the quality and the originality of the cuisine, coupled with the excellence in service, Aïoli gets my top pick for the best fine-dining value in Cancún.

See map p. 133. Le Méridien Hotel, Retorno del Rey, km 14. ☎ *998-881-2200.* www.meridiencancun.com.mx. *Free parking. Reservations required. Main courses: $14–$30. AE, DC, MC, V. Open: Mon–Sun 6:30 a.m.–11 p.m.*

Blue Bayou

$$$$ Isla Cancún CAJUN

You may not associate Cancún with Cajun dining, but this restaurant receives plenty of raves — not to mention repeat diners. Crawfish are flown in daily from Louisiana, and the signature Maya Blackened Seafood Platter is a favorite, combining the Caribbean with the Cajun's best. The restaurant serves certified Angus beef, and the Ribeye with Green Goddess sauce is excellent. The bi-level setting is remarkable — the lower level has a lush hanging garden with waterfall. Adding to the ambience is live jazz, played nightly, as well as a special "dine and dance" every Thursday through Saturday.

See map p. 133. Blvd. Kukulcán, km 10.5, in the Hyatt Cancún Caribe Hotel. ☎ *998-883-0044, ext. 54. Reservations not necessary. Main courses: $15–$33. AE, MC, V. Open: Daily 6:30 p.m.–11 p.m.*

Captain's Cove

$$ Isla Cancún INTERNATIONAL/SEAFOOD

Captain's Cove's multilevel dining room is a draw for diners who come for the good value, heaping servings, friendly service, and the consummate tropical ambience. Diners face big, open windows overlooking the lagoon and Royal Yacht Club Marina. (Sunsets from the upper-level deck are stunning.) For breakfast, an extremely popular all-you-can-eat buffet beats the

Where to Dine in Ciudad Cancún (Cancún City)

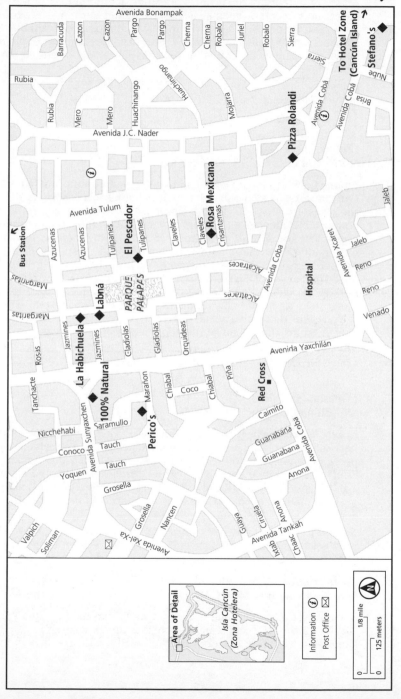

price and quality of most hotel offerings. Main courses of USDA Angus steak and seafood — such as Islander coconut shrimp — are top bets at lunch and dinner, and a menu catering to children is available. Dessert standouts include flaming coffees, crêpes, and Key lime pie. Captain's Cove sits almost at the end of Blvd. Kukulcán, on the lagoon side opposite the Omni Hotel.

See map p. 133. Blvd. Kukulcán, km 16.5 ☎ 998-885-0016. Reservations recommended. Main courses: $12–$40; breakfast buffet $10 and up. AE, MC, V. Open: Daily 7 a.m.–11 p.m.

Club Grill
$$$$ Isla Cancún   INTERNATIONAL

Among Cancún's most elegant and stylish restaurants, located in the Ritz-Carlton Hotel, is also one of its most delicious. The gracious service and the old-world charm begin the moment you enter the anteroom, with its comfortable couches and chairs and selection of fine tequilas and Cuban cigars. The scene continues into a candlelit dining room with padded side chairs and tables that shimmer with silver and crystal. Elegant plates of peppered scallops, truffles, and potatoes in tequila sauce; grilled lamb; or mixed grill arrive at a leisurely pace after the appetizer. The restaurant has both smoking and nonsmoking sections. After dinner, take a turn on the dance floor, as a band plays romantic music starting at 8 p.m. Club Grill is the place for that truly special night out. A dress code is enforced: No sandals or tennis shoes, and gentlemen must wear long pants.

See map p. 133. Ritz-Carlton Hotel, Blvd. Kukulcán, km 13.5. ☎ 998-881-0808. Reservations required. Main courses: $11–$40. AE, DC, MC, V. Open: Tues–Sun 7–11 p.m.

El Pescador
$$ Ciudad Cancún   SEAFOOD

El Pescador is the best spot for fresh seafood in Cancún. A line often forms here for the well-prepared fresh seafood served in a street-side patio and upstairs venue. Feast on shrimp cocktail, conch, octopus, *camarones à la criolla* (Creole-style shrimp), charcoal-broiled lobster, and stone crabs. Can't decide? Try a little of everything with the *Zarzuela* combination seafood plate, cooked in white wine and garlic. El Pescador also features a Mexican specialty menu as well.

See map p. 135. Tulipanes 28, off Av. Tulum. ☎ 998-884-2673. Fax: 998-884-3639. Reservations not accepted. Main courses: $5–$30. AE, MC, V. Open: Daily 11 a.m.–11 p.m.

La Destileria
$$$ Isla Cancún   MEXICAN

If you want to experience tequila in its native habitat, don't miss this place — although technically, this restaurant is across the country from the region where the beverage is produced. La Destileria is more than a tequila-inspired restaurant, it's a mini-museum that honors the "spirit" of Mexico. Over 150 brands of tequila are served here, including some true treasures that never make their way across the country's northern border — so be adventurous! The margaritas are among the best on the island as well. When you decide it's time to pair some food with your tequila, choose from dishes on the refined Mexican menu, anything from quesadillas with squash blossom flowers to shrimp in a delicate tequila-lime sauce. It even serves *escamoles* (crisp-fried ant eggs) as an appetizer for the adventurous — or for those whose squeamishness has been diminished by the tequila!

See map p. 133. Blvd. Kukulcán, km 12.65, across from Kukulcán Plaza. ☎ *998-885-1086 or 998-885-1087. Reservations not necessary. Main courses: $8–$30. AE, MC, V. Open: Daily 1 p.m. to midnight.*

La Dolce Vita
$$$ Isla Cancún   ITALIAN/SEAFOOD

The casually elegant La Dolce Vita is known as Cancún's favorite Italian restaurant. Appetizers include pâté of quail liver and carpaccio in vinaigrette or mushrooms Provençal. The chef specializes in homemade pastas combined with fresh seafood. You can order green tagliolini with lobster medallions, linguine with clams or seafood, or rigatoni Mexican-style (with *chorizo*, mushrooms, and jalapeños) as a main course, or as an appetizer for half price. Other main courses include veal with morels, fresh salmon with cream sauce, and fresh fish in a variety of sauces. Recently added choices include vegetarian lasagna and grilled whole lobster. Choose between dining in air-conditioned comfort or on an open-air terrace with a view of the lagoon. Dinner is accompanied by live jazz from 7:00 p.m. to 11:30 p.m., Monday through Saturday.

See map p. 133. Blvd. Kukulcán, km 14.5 (on the lagoon, across from the Marriott Casamagna). ☎ *998-885-0150 or 998-885-0161. Fax: 998-885-0590.* www.cancun. com/dining/dolce. *Reservations required for dinner. Main courses: $9–$29. AE, MC, V. Open: Daily noon to midnight.*

La Fisheria
$$ Isla Cancún   SEAFOOD

La Fisheria is one of the exceptions to the rule about never finding good food in a shopping mall eatery. The expansive menu at La Fisheria includes shark fingers with a jalapeño dip, grouper filet stuffed with seafood in lobster sauce, Acapulco-style *ceviche* (in tomato sauce), New England clam chowder, steamed mussels, grilled red snapper with pasta — you get the idea. The menu changes daily, but there's always *tikin xik*, that great Yucatecan grilled fish marinated in *achiote* sauce (made from the paste of the achiote chile). If seafood isn't your bag, a wood-burning, oven-made pizza may do, or perhaps one of the grilled chicken or beef dishes. If you're at the mall shopping, La Fisheria is your best bet — but even if you're not, it's also a reason to stop by. La Fisheria has a nonsmoking section.

See map p. 133. Plaza Caracol, Shopping Center, Paseo Kukulkán km 8.5, 2nd floor.
☎ *998-883-1395. Reservations not necessary. Main courses: $6.50–$21. AE, MC, V.*
Open: Daily 11 a.m.–11 p.m.

La Habichuela
$$–$$$ Ciudad Cancún   GOURMET SEAFOOD/CARIBBEAN/MEXICAN

Enjoy some of downtown Cancún's finest food as you dine alfresco in this romantic garden setting. Tables in pink-and-white linens sit on a vine-draped patio, as stars twinkle overhead and soft music plays in the background. For an all-out culinary adventure, try *habichuela* (string bean) soup; shrimp in any number of sauces, including Jamaican tamarind, tequila, and a ginger-and-mushroom combination; and the Maya coffee with *xtabentun* (a strong, sweet, anise-based liquor). The grilled seafood and steaks are excellent as well, but La Habichuela is a good place to try a Mexican specialty such as chicken mole or *tampiqueña*-style beef (thinly sliced, marinated, and grilled). A more unusual — and divine — choice is the *Cocobichuela,* lobster and shrimp in curry sauce served in a coconut shell and topped with fruit.

See map p. 135. Margaritas 25. ☎ *998-884-3158. E-mail:* habichuela@osel. net.mx. *Free parking. Reservations recommended in high season. Main courses: $10–$32. AE, MC, V. Open: Daily noon to midnight.*

La Joya
$$$$ Isla Cancún   MEXICAN/INTERNATIONAL

La Joya (the Jewel) is truly a gem of a dining experience, with a menu of gourmet Mexican cuisine in a suitably upscale atmosphere. For starters, try the lobster quesadillas, made with mellow panela cheese. Baked pumpkin flower soup or a rich, lobster-infused version of the Mexican classic *pozole* are equally tempting first courses. Main dishes range from red snapper Cozumel (grilled and topped with a rainbow of coconut-infused sauces) to beef medallions on a bed of sautéed cactus petals in a creamy chipotle sauce. Entertaining touches include a cigar show, guided Tequila tastings, and live music nightly, ranging from mariachis to classical piano. Thursdays through Saturdays, there's a special folkloric show with live mariachi music. This restaurant was Mexico's first to earn the Five Diamond Award by AAA.

See map p. 133. Blvd. Kukulcán, km 9.5, at the Fiesta Americana Grand Coral Beach hotel. ☎ *998-881-3200. Reservations receommneded on weekends. Main courses: $25–$40. AE, MC, V. Open: Daily 6:30–11 p.m.*

Labná
$$ Ciudad Cancún   YUCATECAN

To steep yourself in Yucatecan cuisine and music, head directly to this showcase of Mayan moods and regional foods. Specialties served here include a sublime lime soup, *poc chuc* (marinated, barbecue-style pork), chicken or pork *pibil* (sweet and spicy barbeque sauce served over shredded meat), and appetizers such as *papadzules* (tortillas stuffed with boiled eggs in a green pumpkin sauce). The Labná Special is a sampler of four typically Yucatecan main courses, including poc chuc, while another specialty of the house is baked suckling pig, served with guacamole. The refreshing Yucatecan beverage, *Agua de Chaya*, is also served here, a blend of sweetened water and the leaf of the Chaya plant, abundant in the area, to which D'Aristi liquor can be added for an extra kick. The large, informal dining room is decorated with fascinating photographs of the region, dating back to the 1900s.

See map p. 135. Margaritas 29, next to City Hall and the Habicula restaurant, Santa María. ☎ *998-892-3056. Reservations accepted. Main courses: $5–$18. AE, MC, V. Open: Daily noon to 10 p.m.*

Laguna Grill
$$$ Isla Cancún FUSION

Laguna Grill offers diners a contemporary culinary experience in a lush, tropical setting overlooking the lagoon. A tropical garden welcomes you at the entrance, while a small creek meanders through the restaurant set with tables made from the trunks of regional, tropical trees. As magical as the décor is, the real star here is the kitchen, with its offering of Pacific-rim cuisine fused with regional flavors. Starters include martini goyza (steamed dumplings) and shrimp tempura served on a mango mint salad, or ahi tuna and shrimp cervichi in a spicy oriental sauce. Fish and seafood dominate the menu of entrees, in a variety of preparations that combine Asian and Mexican flavors such as ginger, cilantro, garlic, and hoisen sauce. Grilled shrimp are served over a cilantro and guajillo-chile risotto. For beef-lovers, the rib-eye served over a garlic, spinach and sweet potato mash is sublime. Deserts are as creative as the main dishes with the pineapple-papaya strudel in a Malibu rum sauce a standout. If you're an early diner, request a table on the outside deck for a spectacular sunset view. An impressive selection of wines is available.

See map p. 133. Blvd. Kukulcán, km 16.5. ☎ *998-885-0267.* www.lagunagrill. com.mx. *Reservations recommended. Main courses: $15–$45. AE, MC, V. Open: Daily 2 pm to midnight.*

Lorenzillo's
$$–$$$ Isla Cancún SEAFOOD

A personal favorite; I never miss a stop here when I'm in Cancún. Live lobster is the overwhelming favorite, and part of the appeal is the chance to select your dinner out of the giant lobster tank. A dock leads down to the main dining area, overlooking the lagoon and topped by a giant *palapa*. When the place is packed (which is often), a wharf-side bar handles the overflow. In addition to the lobster — it comes grilled, steamed, or stuffed — good bets are the shrimp stuffed with cheese and wrapped in

Dining at sea

One unique way to combine dinner with sightseeing is to board the **Lobster Dinner Cruise** (☎ 998-849-4748). Cruise the tranquil, turquoise waters of the lagoon aboard the *Columbus,* a pirate-style ship, while feasting on lobster or steak dinners accompanied by wine, with romantic music serenading you. The cost is $49 per person, and the cruise departs two times daily from the Royal Mayan Marina. A sunset dinner cruise leaves at 4:30 p.m. during winter months and 5:30 p.m. during the summer. A moonlight cruise leaves at 7:30 p.m. during the winter and 8:30 p.m. during the summer. Another — albiet livelier — option is the **Captain Hook Lobster Dinner Cruise** (☎ 998-849-4451), which is similar, but with the added attraction of a pirate show, making this the choice for families. It costs $58 and departs at 7 p.m. from El Embarcadero.

bacon, the admiral's fillet coated in toasted almonds and a light mustard sauce, or the seafood-stuffed squid. Desserts include the tempting "Martinique": Belgian chocolate with hazelnuts, almonds, and pecans, served with vanilla ice cream. A new sunset pier offers a lighter menu of cold seafood, sandwiches, and salads. The atmosphere is festive and friendly, and children are very welcome.

See map p. 133. Blvd. Kukulcán, km 10.5. ☎ *998-883-1254.* www.lorenzillos.com.mx. *Free parking in lot across the street, plus valet parking. Reservations recommended. Main courses: $12–$50. AE, MC, V. Open: Daily noon to midnight.*

Mango Tango
$$–$$$ **Isla Cancún** **INTERNATIONAL**

Mango Tango has sizzling floor shows (featuring salsa, tango, and other Latin dancing) and live reggae music, but the kitchen is the real star here. Try the peel-your-own shrimp, Argentine-style grilled meat with *chimichurri* sauce (sauce with roasted vegetables and spices), and other tropical specialties. Mango Tango salad is shrimp, chicken, avocado, red onion, tomato, and mushrooms served on mango slices. Entrees include rice with seafood and fried bananas. Creole gumbo comes with lobster, shrimp, and squid, and coconut-and-mango cake is a suitable finish to the meal. The restaurant serves a fixed-price menu that includes your choice of a soup or salad, entrée, and dessert, with three hours of domestic open bar, for $40 (half-price for children ages 4 to 12). The beauty of dining here is that you can stay and enjoy one of the current hot nightspots in Cancún.

See map p. 133. Blvd. Kukulcán, km 14.2, opposite the Ritz-Carlton Hotel. ☎ *998-885-0303. Reservations recommended. Main courses: $12-$47. Three-course dinner, $40. AE, MC, V. Open: Daily 2 p.m.–2 a.m.*

Périco's
$$–$$$ Ciudad Cancún   MEXICAN/SEAFOOD/STEAKS

Perico's is arguably the most tourist-friendly spot in Ciudad Cancún. With colorful murals that almost dance off the walls, a bar area overhung with baskets (and saddles for bar stools), inviting leather tables and chairs, and waiters dressed like Pancho Villa, it's no wonder the place is always booming and festive. The extensive menu offers well-prepared steak, seafood, and traditional Mexican dishes for moderate rates (except for the lobster), but the food here is less the point than the fun. Périco's is a place not only to eat and drink, but also to let loose and join in the fun. Don't be surprised if everybody drops their forks, dons huge Mexican sombreros, and snakes around the dining room in a conga dance. You can still have fun whether or not you join in, but Périco's is definitely not the place for that romantic evening alone. There's marimba music from 7:30 to 9:30 p.m. and mariachis from 9:30 p.m. to midnight. Expect a crowd.

See map p. 135. Yaxchilán 61. ☎ *998-884-3152. Reservations recommended only in high season. Main courses: $9–$40. AE, MC, V. Open: Daily 1 p.m.–1 a.m.*

Plantation House
$$$$ Isla Cancún   CARIBBEAN/FRENCH

Elegant Caribbean fare — styled after the time when it was infused with European influences — is served up in this pale yellow-and-blue clapboard restaurant overlooking Nichupté lagoon. The décor combines island-style colonial charm with elegant touches of wood and crystal. The service is excellent, but the food is only mediocre, especially considering the price. For starters, try the signature poached shrimp with lemon juice and olive oil or a creamy crabmeat soup. Move on to the main event, which may consist of veal Wellington in puff pastry with duck pâté, fish filet crusted in spices and herbs and topped with vanilla sauce, or lobster *medaillons* in mango sauce. Flambéed desserts are a specialty, and the Plantation House has one of the most extensive wine lists in town. Plantation House is generally quite crowded, which makes it a bit loud for a truly romantic evening.

See map p. 133. Blvd. Kukulcán, km 10.5, Zona Hotelera, 77500, Cancún, Q. Roo. ☎ *998-883-1433, 998-885-1455.* www.plantationhouse.com.mx. *Reservations recommended. Main courses: $13–$40. AE, MC, V. Open: Daily noon to midnight.*

Pizza Rolandi
$ Ciudad Cancún   ITALIAN

Surprised to find great pizza in Cancún? Don't be — Pizza Rolandi is an institution, and the Rolandi name is synonymous with dining in both Cancún and neighboring Isla Mujeres. At this shaded outdoor sidewalk cafe, you can choose from almost two dozen different wood-oven pizzas and a full selection of spaghetti, calzones, Italian-style chicken and beef, and desserts. A full bar list is available as well. Another Rolandi's Pizza is located in Isla Mujeres and has the same food and prices. Both locations have become standards for dependably good casual fare in Cancún. For a more formal, Italian-dining affair, try the elegant **Casa Rolandi** in Plaza Carocal, Isla Cancún (☎ **988-883-1817**). See Chapter 12 for reviews of both Isla Mujeres restaurants.

See map p. 135. Cobá 12. ☎ 998-884-4047. Fax: 998-884-3994. Reservations not necessary. www.rolandi.com. *Main courses and pizza: $7–$14; pasta $5–$8. AE, MC, V. Open: Daily noon to 11 p.m.*

Rosa Mexicana
$$$ Ciudad Cancún   MEXICAN HAUTE

Rosa Mexicana is a simply stylish bistro and a top choice for downtown dining. Candlelit tables are set indoors and surrounded by colorful *piñatas* and paper streamers and located on a plant-filled patio in back. The menu features "refined" Mexican specialties. Try the *pollo almendro,* which is chicken covered in a cream sauce sprinkled with ground almonds, or the pork baked in a banana leaf with a sauce of oranges, lime, *chile ancho* (smoke-flavored chile pepper), and garlic. The more traditional steak *tampiqueño* is a huge platter that comes with guacamole salad, quesadillas, beans, salad, and rice. Dine to live, romantic Mexican music most nights.

See map p. 135. Claveles 4. ☎ 998-884-6313. Fax: 998-884-2371. Reservations recommended for parties of 6 or more. Main courses: $9–$17; lobster $30. AE, MC, V. Open: Daily 5–11 p.m.

Savio's
$$$ Isla Cancún   ITALIAN

Savio's is a great place to stop for a quick meal or coffee, and it's centrally located in the heart of the Hotel Zone. A stylish bi-level with a black-and-white décor and tile floors, Savio's faces Blvd. Kukulcán through two stories of awning-shaded windows. The bar is always crowded with patrons sipping everything from cappuccino to imported beer. A loyal crowd returns time and again for the large, fresh salads and richly flavored, subtly spiced Italian dishes. Among my favorites are the ravioli stuffed with ricotta and spinach, served in a delicious tomato sauce; and savory wild mushroom and saffron risotto. Live music plays nightly from 7:30 to 10:30 p.m.

See map p. 133. Plaza Caracol. ☎ 998-883-2085 (also fax). Reservations not accepted. Main courses: $9–$30. AE, MC, V. Open: Daily 10 a.m. to midnight.

Stefano's
$$ Ciudad Cancún ITALIAN/PIZZA

Stefano's began primarily as a local restaurant, serving Italian food with a few Mexican accents, and it seems to be a winning combination. Among the menu items are ravioli stuffed with *huitlacoche* (a delicious, mushroom-type fungus that grows on cornstalks); rigatoni in tequila sauce; and seafood with chile peppers. The Stefano special pizza is made with fresh tomato, cheese, and pesto. The ricotta strudel dessert is something out of the ordinary. Stefano's offers lots of different coffees and mixed drinks, plus an expanded wine list. Indoor or outdoor dining, on a small patio, is available.

See map p. 135. Bonampak 177. ☎ ***998-887-9964.*** *Reservations not necessary. Main courses: $7–$17; pizza $6–$16.50. MC, V. Open: Daily 1 p.m. to midnight.*

Fast Facts: Cancún

American Express

The local office is located in Ciudad Cancún at Avenida Tulum 208 (☎ 998-881-4000; or 998-884-6942; www.american express.com/mexico). The office is open Monday to Friday 9 a.m. to 6 p.m. and Saturday 9 a.m. to 1 p.m. Another branch is located in the Hotel Zone, in the La Isla Shopping Center, ☎ 998-885-3905.

Area Code

The telephone area code is **988**.

Baby Sitters

Most of the larger hotels can easily arrange for baby sitters, but many sitters speak limited English. Rates range from $3 to $10 per hour.

Banks, ATMs, and Currency Exchange

Most banks are downtown along Avenida Tulum and are usually open Monday to Friday 9:30 a.m. to 5 p.m., and many now have automatic teller machines for after-hours cash withdrawals. In the Hotel Zone, you can find banks in the Plaza Kukulcán and next to the convention center. Many *casas de cambio* (exchange houses) are in the Hotel Zone, in the plazas, and near the convention center. Avoid changing money at the airport as you arrive, especially at the first exchange booth you see — its rates are less favorable than any in town or others farther inside the airport concourse. In general, the best exchange rates are found at ATMs, casas de cambio, and hotels.

Business Hours

Most downtown offices maintain traditional Mexican hours of operation (9 a.m. to 2 p.m. and 4 to 8 p.m., daily), but shops remain open throughout the day from 10 a.m. to 9 or 10 p.m. Offices tend to close on Saturday and Sunday, but shops are open on Saturday, at least, and increasingly offer limited hours of operation on Sunday. Malls are generally open from 10 a.m. to 10 p.m. or later.

Climate

It's hot but not overwhelmingly humid. The rainy season is May through October. August through October is the hurricane season, which brings erratic weather. November through February is generally sunny but can also be cloudy, windy, somewhat rainy, and even cool, so a sweater and rain protection are handy.

Consular Agents

The **U.S. consular agent** is located in the Playa Caracol 2, 3rd level, rooms 320–323, Boulevard Kukulcán, km 8.5 (☎ 998-883-0272). The office is open Monday to Friday 9 a.m. to 1 p.m. The **Canadian** consulate is located in the Plaza Caracol 2, 3rd level, room 330, Boulevard Kukulcán km 8.5 (☎ 998-883-3360). The office is open from Monday to Friday 9 a.m. to 5 p.m.

Emergencies/Hospitals

To report an emergency, dial ☎ **060,** which is supposed to be similar to 911 emergency service in the United States. For first aid, the **Cruz Roja** (Red Cross; ☎ **065** or 998-884-1616; is open 24 hours a day on Avenida Yaxchilán between avenidas Xcaret and Labná, next to the Telmex building. **Total Assist,** a small, nine-room emergency hospital with English-speaking doctors (Claveles 5, SM 22, at Avenida Tulum; ☎ 998-884-1092; 884-1058 E-mail: totalassist@prodigy.net.mx, is also open 24 hours. American Express, MasterCard, and Visa are accepted. Desk staff may have a limited command of English. Another facility that caters to English-speaking visitors is **Ameri-Med** (Plaza Las Americas, in downtown Cancún, ☎ 998-881-3434) with 24-hour emergency service. An **air ambulance service** is also available by calling ☎ 800-305-9400 (toll-free within Mexico). *Urgencias* means "emergencies."

Information

The **State Tourism Office** (☎ 998-881-9000) is centrally located downtown on the east side of Avenida Pecari 23, next to Banco Bancomer, immediately left of the Ayuntamiento Benito Juárez building, The office is open Monday to Friday 9 a.m. to 5 p.m., and it has maps, brochures, and information on the area's popular sights, including Tulum, Xcaret, Isla Mujeres, and Playa del Carmen. A second tourist information office, the Convention and Visitors Bureau (☎ 998-881-9000), is located on the first floor of the Cancún Convention Center in the Hotel Zone, and is open Monday to Friday 9 a.m. to 5 p.m. Hotels and their rates are listed at each office, as are ferry schedules. For information prior to your arrival in Cancún, visit the Convention Bureau's Web site at www.cancun.info.

Pick up copies of the free monthly *Cancún Tips* or the Cancún Tips booklet, which is published four times a year. Both contain lots of useful information and great maps. The publications are owned by the same people who own the Captain's Cove restaurants, a couple of sightseeing boats, and timeshare hotels, so the information, though good, is not unbiased.

Internet Access

C@ncunet (☎ 998-885-0880), located in a kiosk on the first floor of Plaza Kukulcán (Blvd. Kukulcán km 13), offers Internet access for 20 pesos per 10 minutes or 70 pesos per hour from 10 a.m. to 10 p.m.

Maps

One of the best around is the free American Express map, usually found at the tourist information offices and the local American Express office. *Cancún Tips* (see "Information") also have maps and are generally available through your hotel concierge.

Pharmacy

With locations in both Flamingo Plaza (☎ 998-885-1351) and Kukulkán Plaza (☎ 998-885-0860), **Farmacia Roxanna's** offers delivery service within the Hotel Zone. Plenty of drugstores are in the major shopping malls, open until 10 p.m., in the Hotel Zone. In downtown Cancún, **Farmacia Cancún** is located at Ave. Tulum, ☎ 998-884-1283. You can stock up on Retin-A, Viagra, and many other prescription drugs without a prescription.

Police

To reach the **police** *(seguridad pública),* dial ☎ 998-884-1913 or 998-885-2277.

Post Office

The **main post office** (☎ 998-884-1418) is downtown at the intersection of avenidas Sunyaxchen and Xel-Ha. It's open Monday to Friday 9 a.m. to 4 p.m. and Saturday 9 a.m. to 1 p.m.

Safety

Cancún has very little crime. Tourist areas are generally safe late at night; just use common sense. As at any beach resort, don't take money or valuables to the beach.

Car break-ins are about the only crimes here, although they do happen frequently, especially around the shopping centers in the Hotel Zone.

Swimming on the Caribbean side presents a danger from undertow. Pay attention to the posted flag warnings on the beaches.

Taxes

There's a 10% value-added tax (IVA) on goods and services, and it's generally included in the posted price. Cancún's IVA is 5% lower than most of Mexico due to a special exemption that dates back to its origins as a duty-free port.

Taxis

Taxi prices in Cancún are set by zone, although keeping track of what's in which zone can take some work. Taxi rates within the Hotel Zone are a minimum fare of $5 per ride, making it one of the most expensive taxi areas in Mexico. Rates within the downtown area are between $1.50 and $2. You can also hire taxis by the hour or day for longer trips, when you'd prefer to leave the driving to someone else. Rates run between $12 and $18 per hour with discounts available for full-day rates, but an extra charge applies when the driver doubles as a tour guide. Always settle on a price in advance or check at your hotel, where destinations and prices are generally posted.

Telephone

Avoid the phone booths that have signs in English advising you to call home using a special 800 number — these booths are absolute rip-offs and can cost as much as $20 per minute. The least expensive way to call is by using a Mexican prepaid phone card called Telmex (LADATEL), available at most pharmacies and mini-supermarkets, using the official public phones, Telmex (Lada). Remember, in Mexico, you need to dial 001 prior to a number to reach the United States, and you need to preface long-distance calls within Mexico by dialing 01.

Time Zone

Cancún operates on Central Standard Time, and observes Daylight Savings Time.

Chapter 11

Exploring Cancún

*Y*ou're likely to run out of vacation days before you run out of things to do in Cancún. Snorkeling, jet skiing, jungle tours, and visits to ancient Mayan ruins or modern ecological theme parks are among the most popular diversions in this resort that has a little of everything. Beyond Cancún's renowned beaches are over a dozen malls with name-brand retailers and duty-free shops (featuring European goods with better prices than you can find in the United States), plus a seemingly endless supply of nightclubs to revel in.

In addition to Cancún's own attractions, the resort is a convenient distance from the more Mexican-feeling beach towns in **Isla Mujeres** (see Chapter 12), **Cozumel** (see Chapter 13), and **Playa del Carmen** (see Chapter 14). The **Mayan ruins** at Tulum and Chichén-Itzá are also close by (see Chapter 15). All these diversions are within driving distance for a spectacular day-trip.

So what's worth your time? To help you decide, I devote this chapter to giving you an overview of the best beaches in this mecca of white sand and crystalline waters. I also give you the rundown on the area's popular day-trips and diversions.

Enjoying the Sand and Surf

Face it: If you're in Cancún, you probably decided to come here based on the vision of powdery, white-sand beaches and turquoise waters. If you're in search of a beautiful beach, Cancún may be your nirvana. With the added bonus of the Nichupté Lagoon on the other side of the island, Cancún is packed with ways to make the most of your time in the water.

Combing the beaches

The public beaches located along the stretch of Cancún Island on the calm, Bahía de Mujeres side include **Playa Linda** (Pretty Beach), **Playa Langosta** (Lobster Beach), **Playa Tortuga** (Turtle Beach), and **Playa Caracol** (Snail Beach). Playa Linda (at km 4) has a shuttle service to Isla Mujeres, as well as a few dive shops and snack bars. Playa Langosta (at km 5) is a protected cove near the Hotel Casa Maya that features a tour-boat pier and a watersports concession, plus some shops and restaurants. Next up is Playa Tortuga (at km 7.5), a popular public beach with changing rooms, public restrooms, and restaurants. This bit of sand is frequently overrun with families on weekends. The last beach before the island curves toward the Caribbean is Playa Caracol, which stretches for about a mile and passes the Fiesta Americana and Dreams hotels — a lovely stretch with a few restaurants but no public facilities.

The Caribbean side of Cancún faces the open sea, and it's subject to frequent riptides and strong currents. The beaches here include the regally named **Playa Chac-Mool** (named after the Mayan deity of rain) and **Playa del Rey** (Beach of the King). Playa Chac-Mool (at km 13) has showers, restrooms, and other facilities that make it as popular as Playa Tortuga on weekends. Playa del Rey, the last public beach on the island before Punta Nizac, is an unspoiled treasure. This remarkable stretch of sand ends at the entrance to Club Med.

At most beaches, in addition to swimming, you can rent a sailboard and take lessons, ride a parasail, or partake in a variety of other watersports.

To locate these beaches on a map, please see the "Cancún Orientation Map" in Chapter 10.

Playing in the surf

The big hotels dominate the best stretches of beaches, so you're likely have a fine patch of sand at your hotel. All of Mexico's beaches are public property, so technically, you can use the beach of any hotel by accessing it directly from the sand. *Technically* is the key word here. Although this is the law, the reality is that hotel security guards regularly ask nonguests to relocate. You choose if you want to suffer the potential embarrassment of being asked to leave or, if asked, standing your ground — or beach, as it were.

If you're intent on swimming, be careful on beaches fronting the open Caribbean, where the undertow can be quite strong. By contrast, the waters of **Bahía de Mujeres** at the north end of the island are usually calm and ideal for swimming. Get to know Cancún's water-safety pennant system and make sure to check the flag at any beach or hotel before entering the water.

Here's what each flag means:

- ✔ **White:** Excellent
- ✔ **Green:** Normal conditions (safe)
- ✔ **Yellow:** Changeable, uncertain (use caution)
- ✔ **Black or red:** Unsafe (use the swimming pool instead)

 In the Caribbean, storms can arrive quickly, and conditions can change from safe to unsafe in a matter of minutes, so be alert: If you see dark clouds heading your way, head to shore and wait until the storm passes.

Skiing and surfing

Many beachside hotels offer watersports concessions that include the rental of rubber rafts, kayaks, and snorkeling equipment. Outlets for renting **sailboats, jet skis, windsurfers,** and **water skis** are located on the calm Nichupté Lagoon. Prices vary and are often negotiable, so check around.

A very popular option for getting wet and wild is a **jungle cruise,** offered by several companies. The cruise takes you by Jet Ski or WaveRunner through Cancún's lagoon and mangrove estuaries out into the Caribbean Sea and by a shallow reef. The excursion runs about 2½-hours (you drive your own watercraft) and is priced from $35 to $45, with snorkeling and beverages included. Some of the motorized mini-boats seat you side by side; other crafts seat one person behind the other. The difference? The second person can see the scenery or the back of his or her companion's head, depending on your choice.

The operators and names of boats offering excursions change often. The popular **Aquaworld** (Blvd. Kukulcán, km 15.2; ☎ 998-885-2288; Internet: www.aquaworld.com.mx) calls its trip the Jungle Tour and charges $45 for the 2½-hour excursion, which includes 45 minutes of snorkeling time. The company even gives you a free snorkel, but its watercrafts have the less-desirable seating configuration of one behind the other. Departures are 8:00 a.m., 8:30 a.m., 9:00 a.m., 10:30 a.m., 11:30 a.m., 12 p.m., 1 p.m., 2 p.m., 2:30 p.m., 3:30 p.m., and 4:30 p.m. daily. To find out what's available when you're there, check with a local travel agent or hotel tour desk; you should find a wide range of options. You can also go to the Playa Linda pier either a day ahead or the day of your intended outing and buy your own tickets for trips on the *Nautibus* or to Isla Mujeres (see information later in this chapter). If you go on the day of your trip, arrive at the pier around 8:45 a.m.; most boats leave by 9 or 9:30 a.m.

Exploring the deep blue

Known for its shallow reefs, dazzling colors, and diversity of life, Cancún is one of the best places in the world for beginning **scuba diving.** Punta Nizuc is the northern tip of the **Gran Arrecife Maya (Great Mesoamerican Reef),** the largest reef in the Western Hemisphere and one of the largest in the world. In addition to the sea life present along this reef system, several sunken boats add a variety of dive options. Inland, a series of caverns and wellsprings, known as *cenotes,* are fascinating venues for the more experienced diver. Drift diving is the norm here, with popular dives going to the reefs at **El Garrafón** and the **Cave of the Sleeping Sharks.** For those unfamiliar with the term, *drift diving* occurs when divers drift with the strong currents in the waters and end up at a point different than where they started. The dive boat follows them. In traditional dives, the divers resurface where they began.

Resort courses that teach the basics of diving — enough to make shallow dives and slowly ease your way into this underwater world of unimaginable beauty — are offered in a variety of hotels. Scuba trips run around $64 for two-tank dives at nearby reefs and $100 and up for locations farther out. **Scuba Cancún** (Blvd. Kukulcán, km 5; ☎ **998-849-7508,** 998-849-4736; Internet: www.scubacancun.com.mx), on the lagoon side, offers a four-hour resort course for $84. In addition to calling or visiting, you can make reservations in the evenings from 7:30 to 10:30 p.m. using the preceding phone numbers. Full certification takes four to five days and costs around $368. Scuba Cancún is open from 8:30 a.m. to 6 p.m. and accepts major credit cards.

The largest operator is **Aquaworld,** across from the Meliá Cancún hotel at Blvd. Kukulcán, km 15.2 (☎ **998-885-2288,** 998-848-8300; Internet: www.aquaworld.com.mx). Aquaworld offers resort courses and diving from a manmade, anchored dive platform, Paradise Island. Aquaworld also has the **Sub See Explorer,** a submarine-style boat with picture windows that hang beneath the surface. The boat doesn't actually submerge — it's more like an updated version of the glass-bottom boat concept — but it does provide nondivers with a look at life beneath the sea. This outfit is open from 6:30 a.m. to 10 p.m. and accepts all major credit cards.

Scuba Cancún (☎ **998-849-7808,** 998-849-4736; e-mail: scuba@cancun.com.mx) also offers diving trips to 20 nearby reefs, at 30 feet, and the open ocean at 30 to 60 feet (offered in good weather only). The average dive is around 35 feet. One-tank dives cost $50, and two-tank dives cost $64. Discounts apply if you bring your own equipment. Dives usually start around 10 a.m. and return by 2:15 p.m. Snorkeling trips cost $27 and leave every afternoon after 1:30 p.m. for shallow reefs located about a 20-minute boat ride away.

The Great Mesoamerican Reef also offers exceptional snorkeling opportunities near Cancún, for those who don't want to go too deep. In Puerto Morelos (23 miles south of Cancún; see Chapter 14) this reef hugs the coastline for 9 miles. The closeness of the reef to the shore (about 500 yards) is a natural barrier for the village and keeps the waters calm on the inside of the reef. The depth of the water here is shallow, between 5 to 30 feet, resulting in ideal conditions for snorkeling. The reef here has remained unspoiled due to the stringent environmental regulations implemented by the local community. Only a select few companies are allowed to offer snorkel trips here and must adhere to guidelines that will ensure the ecological preservation of the reef. Among these companies, **Cancún Mermaid** is considered the best — it's a family-run eco-tour company that has been operating in the area since the '70s, known for its highly personalized service. Its tour typically takes snorkelers to two sections of the reef, spending about an hour in each area, however, when conditions allow, the company will have the boat drop off snorkelers and then follow them along with the current — an activity known as *drift snorkeling* — which enables snorkelers to see as much of the reef as possible. The price of the trip is $50 for adults, $35 for children, and includes boat, snorkeling gear, life jackets, a light lunch, bottled water, sodas and beer, plus round-trip transportation to and from Puerto Morelos from Cancún hotels. Departures are Monday through Saturday at 9 a.m. and noon (minimum of four snorkelers required for a trip), and reservations are required; ☎ 998-843-6517, 998-886-4117; Internet: www.cancun mermaid.com.

Reeling in the big one

You can arrange a day of **deep-sea fishing** at one of the numerous piers or travel agencies for around $200 to $360 for four hours, $420 for six hours, and $520 for eight hours for up to four people. Marinas sometimes assist in putting together a group. Charters include a captain, a first mate, bait, gear, and beverages. Rates are lower if you depart from Isla Mujeres or from Cozumel Island, and frankly, the fishing is better closer to these departure points.

Swimming with dolphins

In Cancún, the **Parque Nizuc** (☎ 998-881-3030) marine park offers guests a chance to swim with dolphins and view these wonderful creatures in their own aquarium, Atlántido. It's a fun place for a family to spend the day, with its numerous pools, waterslides, and rides. Another attraction offers the chance to snorkel with manta rays, tropical fish, and tame sharks. Open 10 a.m. to 5:30 p.m., the park is located on the southern end of Cancún at km 25, between the airport and the Hotel Zone. Admission is $27 for adults and $23 for kids.

La Isla Shopping Center (see the "Cancún Orientation Map" in Chapter 10), Blvd. Kukulcán, km 12.5, also has an impressive **Interactive Aquarium** (☎ 998-883-0411, 998-883-0436, or 998-883-0413; Internet: www.aquarium cancun.com) with dolphin swims and the chance to feed a shark while immersed in the water in an acrylic cage. Guides inside the main tank use underwater microphones to point out the sea life, and even answer your questions. Open exhibition tanks enable visitors to touch a variety of marine life, including sea stars and manta rays. The educational dolphin program is $55, while the dolphin swim is $115. The entrance fee to the aquarium is $6 for adults, $4 for children, and it's open from 9 a.m. to 7 p.m., daily.

Another option for close encounters with dolphins is found on Isla Mujeres, where you can swim with dolphins at **Dolphin Discovery** (☎ 998-849-4757; fax: 998-849-4758; Internet: www.dolphindiscovery.

com). There are several options for dolphin interaction, but my choice is the Royal Swim, which includes an educational introduction followed by 30 minutes of swim time. The price is $125, and transportation to Isla Mujeres is an additional $5 for program participants. Reservations are required because capacity is limited each day. Assigned swimming times are 10 a.m., 12 a.m., 2 p.m., and 3:30 p.m., and you must arrive 1½ hours before your scheduled swim time.

Note: Swimming with dolphins has its critics and supporters. You may want to visit the Whale and Dolphins Conservation Society's Web site at www.wdcs.org. For more information about responsible travel in general, check out these two Web sites: Tread Lightly (www.treadlightly.org) and the International Ecotourism Society (www.ecotourism.org).

Exploring on Dry Land

Even by land, Cancún has its share of winning ways to spend the day. Although golf is a latent developer here, more courses are popping up along the coast south of Cancún. Tennis, however, is tops as a hotel amenity, and you can find courts throughout Cancún. Horseback riding and all-terrain vehicle tours are also great choices for land adventures.

The top attractions

Get the best possible view of Cancún atop **La Torre Cancún** (see the "Cancún Orientation Map" in Chapter 10) (☎ **998-849-4848**, 998-889-7777), the rotating scenic tower located at the El Embarcadero park and entertainment complex. One ride will cost you $9, or opt for a day and night pass for $14. It's located at Blvd. Kukulcán, km 4, and is open daily from 9 a.m. to 11 p.m.

To the right side of the entrance to the Cancún Convention Center is the small **Museo Arqueológico de Cancún** (see the "Cancún Orientation Map" in Chapter 10), ☎ **998-883-0305**, a small but interesting museum with relics from archaeological sites around the state. Admission is $3, with no charge for children under 13 (free for all on Sundays and holidays). The museum is open Tuesday to Friday from 9 a.m. to 8 p.m., and Saturday and Sundays from 10 a.m. to 7 p.m.

Another cultural enclave is the **Museo de Arte Popular Mexicano** (☎ **998-849-4848**), located at on the second floor of the El Embarcadero Marina, km 4, Blvd. Kukulcán. It displays a representative collection of masks, regional folkloric costumes, nativity scenes, religious artifacts, musical instruments, Mexican toys, and gourd art, spread over 4,500 feet of exhibition space. Admission is $10, with kids under 12 paying half price. The museum is open daily from 11 a.m. to 11 p.m.

 During the winter tourist season, **bullfights** are held every Wednesday at 3:30 p.m. in Cancún's small bullring **Plaza de Toros** (☎ **998-884-8372**, 998-884-8248), which is located near the northern end of Blvd. Kukulcán opposite the Restaurant Los Almendros (Ave. Bonampak and Sayil). A sport introduced to Mexico by the Spanish viceroys, bullfighting is now as much a part of Mexican culture as tequila. The bullfights usually include four bulls, and the spectacle begins with a folkloric dance exhibition, followed by a performance by the *charros* (Mexico's sombrero-wearing cowboys). You're not likely to see Mexico's best bullfights in Cancún — the real stars are in Mexico City.

Keep in mind that if you go to a bullfight, *you're going to see a bullfight,* so stay away if you're an animal lover or you can't bear the sight of blood. Travel agencies in Cancún sell tickets: $30 for adults, with children admitted free of charge. Seating is by general admission. American Express, MasterCard, and Visa are accepted.

Cancún has its own Mayan ruins, **Ruinas del Rey** (see the "Cancún Orientation Map" in Chapter 10), a small site that's less impressive than the ruins at Tulum or Chichén-Itzá. Mayan fishermen built this small ceremonial center and settlement very early in the history of Mayan culture and then abandoned it. The site was resettled again near the end of the post-classic period, not long before the arrival of the conquistadors. The platforms of numerous small temples are visible amid the banana plants, papayas, and wildflowers. The ruins are about 12 miles from town, at the southern reaches of the Hotel Zone, close to Punta Nizuc. Look for the Hilton Hotel on the left (east) and then the ruins on the right (west). Admission is $4.50 (free on Sundays and holidays); the hours are 8 a.m. to 4:30 p.m. daily.

Keeping active

With plenty of warm-weather activities at your disposal, there's no reason not to be active on your Cancún holiday, so don't forget to pack your tennis shoes!

Teeing off

Although the golf options are limited, the most well-known — and well-used — facility is the 18-hole **Club de Golf Cancún** (see the "Cancún Orientation Map" in Chapter 10) (☎ 998-883-0871; e-mail: poktapok@sybcom.com), also known as the Pok-Ta-Pok Club. Designed by Robert Trent Jones, Sr., it's located on the northern leg of the island. Greens fees run $100 per 18 holes. Clubs rent for $27, shoes run $16, and caddies charge $20 per bag. The club is open daily; American Express, MasterCard, and Visa are accepted. The club also has tennis courts.

The **Melía Cancún** (see the "Where to Stay in Isla Cancún" map in Chapter 10), ☎ 998-881-1100, offers a nine-hole executive course; the fee is $43, and the club is open daily from 7 a.m. to 4:30 p.m. American Express, MasterCard, and Visa are accepted.

The most interesting option is at the **Hilton Cancún Golf & Beach Resort** (see the "Cancún Orientation Map" in Chapter 10), ☎ 998-881-8016; fax: 998-881-8084. Its championship 18-hole, par-72 course was designed around the Ruinas del Rey (Ruins of the King) archeological site. Greens fees for the public are $125 for 18 holes and $99 for 9 holes; Hilton Cancún guests receive a 20% discount off these rates. Greens fees include a golf cart. Golf clubs and shoes are available for rent as well, and the club is open daily from 6 a.m., with closing time varying depending upon the season, and available daylight.

Making time for tennis

Many hotels in Cancún offer excellent **tennis** facilities, and many of the courts are lit for night play. Among the best are the facilities at Le Méridien and the Fiesta Americana Coral Beach hotels.

Guided tours

Need a break from the beach? The following tours give you a great excuse to get off the beach and explore the mainland.

Galloping along on horseback

Rancho Loma Bonita (☎ **998-887-5465,** 998-887-5423; Internet: www.lomabonitamex.com) is Cancún's most popular option for **horseback riding.** Five-hour packages are available for $65. The packages include two hours of riding to caves, *cenotes* (spring-fed, underground caves), lagoons, and Mayan ruins and along the Caribbean coast. After the ride, you have some time for relaxing on the beach. The ranch also offers a four-wheeler ride on the same route as the horseback tour for $55. Ranch Loma Bonita is located about 30 minutes south of Cancún. The prices include transportation to the ranch, riding, soft drinks, and lunch, plus a guide and insurance. Only cash is accepted.

Trailing away through the jungle

Cancún Mermaid (☎ **998-843-6517,** 998-886-4117; Internet: www.cancunmermaid.com), in Cancún, offers all-terrain-vehicle (ATV) jungle tours priced at $49 per person. The ATV tours travel through the jungles of Cancún and emerge on the beaches of the Riviera Maya. The 2½-hour tour includes equipment, instruction, the services of a tour guide, and bottled water; it departs daily at 8 a.m. and 1:30 p.m.

For guided tours of all things aquatic, don't forget to refer to the "Exploring the deep blue" section earlier in this chapter. Outside of Cancún, visitors may take tours to explore nearby Mayan ruins, eco-parks, and even Cozumel's marine life — in a submarine. For more information, refer to the "Going Beyond Cancún: Day-Trips" section at the end of this chapter.

Shopping the Local Stores

Despite the surrounding natural splendor, shopping has become a favored activity in Cancún, and the place is known throughout Mexico for its diverse array of shops and festive malls catering to large numbers of international tourists. Tourists arriving from the United States may find apparel more expensive in Cancún, but the selection here is much broader than in other Mexican resorts.

Numerous duty-free shops offer excellent value on European goods. The largest shop is **UltraFemme** (☎ 998-884-1402, 998-885-0804), specializing in imported cosmetics, perfumes, and fine jewelry and watches. Its downtown-Cancún location on Avenida Tulum, Supermanzana (intersection) 25, offers lower prices than the locations in Plaza Caracol, Kukulcán Plaza, Plaza Mayafair, and Flamingo Plaza.

Handcrafts and other *artesanía* works are more limited and more expensive in Cancún than in other regions of Mexico because they're sold but not produced here. Several **open-air crafts markets** are easily visible on Avenida Tulum in Cancún City and near the convention center in the Hotel Zone. One of the biggest markets is **Coral Negro** (see the "Cancún Orientation Map" in Chapter 10), located at Blvd. Kukulcán, km 9.5 (☎ 998-883-0758; fax: 998-883-0758). It's open daily from 9 a.m. to 10 p.m.

The main venue for shopping in Cancún are the **malls** — not quite as grand as their typical U.S. counterparts, but close. The majority of Cancún's malls are air-conditioned, sleek, and sophisticated, with most located on Avenida Kukulcán between km 7 and km 12. You can find everything from fine crystal and silver to designer clothing and decorative objects, along with numerous restaurants, clubs, and multiplex movie theaters for an afternoon out of the sun. Stores are generally open daily from 10 a.m. to 10 p.m., with clubs and restaurants remaining open much later. Here's a brief rundown on the malls, running from the northern to the southern end of the island — and some of the shops they contain.

The long-standing **Plaza Caracol** (see map p. 119; Blvd. Kukulcán, km 8.5; ☎ 998-883-1038) holds Cartier jewelry, Guess, Waterford Crystal, Señor Frogs clothing, Samsonite luggage, and La Fisheria restaurant. It's just before you reach the convention center as you come in from downtown Cancún.

The entertainment-oriented **Forum by the Sea** (see map on p. 119; Blvd. Kukulcán, km 9; ☎ 998-883-4425) has shops including Tommy Hilfiger, Levi's, Diesel, Swatch, and Harley Davidson, but most people come here for the food and fun. You can choose from Hard Rock Cafe, Coco Bongo, Rainforest Cafe, Sushi-ito, and Santa Fe Beer Factory, plus an extensive food court. It's open 10 a.m. to midnight (bars remain open later).

Planet Hollywood anchors the **Plaza Flamingo** (see map p. 119; Blvd. Kukulcán, km 11; ☎ 998-883-2945), but branches of Bancrecer, Subway, and La Casa del Habano (for Cuban cigars) are located inside.

Maya Fair Plaza/Centro Comercial Maya Fair, frequently called "Mayfair" (Blvd. Kukulcán, km 8.5; ☎ 998-883-2801), is Cancún's oldest mall and features a lively, bricked center with open-air restaurants and bars, including the Outback Steakhouse and Sanborn's Café, as well as stores selling silver, leather, and crafts.

Inside **Plaza Kukulcán** (see map p. 119; Blvd. Kukulcán, km 12; ☎ 998-885-2200; Internet: www.Kukulcanplaza.com) is a large selection of more than 300 shops, restaurants, and entertainment venues. It houses a branch of Banco Serfin; OK Maguey Cantina Grill; a movie theater showing U.S. movies; an Internet-access kiosk; Tikal, a shop with Guatemalan textile clothing; several crafts stores; a liquor store; several bathing-suit specialty stores; record and tape outlets; a leather-goods store (including shoes and sandals); and a store specializing in silver from Taxco. In the food court are a number of U.S. franchise restaurants, including Ruth's Chris Steak House and Houlihan's, plus a specialty-coffee shop. There's also a large indoor garage. The mall is open 10 a.m. to 10 p.m.

The newest and most intriguing mall is the **La Isla Shopping Village** (see map p. 119; Blvd. Kukulcán, km 12.5; ☎ 998-883-5025, 998-883-5725, Internet: www.laislacancun.com.mx), an open-air festival mall that looks like a small village, where walkways lined with shops and restaurants crisscross over little canals. The mall also has a "riverwalk" alongside the Nichupté Lagoon with an interactive aquarium and dolphin-swim facility, as well as the Spacerocker and River Ride Tour — great for kid-friendly fun. Shops include Guess, Diesel, DKNY, Guess, Bulgari, and Ultra Femme. Dining choices include Johnny Rockets, Come and Eat, Häagen Dazs, and the beautiful Mexican restaurant, La Casa de las Margaritas. You also can find a movie theater, a video arcade, and several nightclubs, including Glazz. The mall is across from the Sheraton, on the lagoon side.

Living It Up After Dark

Ready to party? The nightlife in Cancún is as hot as the sun at noon on a cloudless July day, and clubbing is one of the main attractions of this let-loose town. The current hotspots are centralized in **Forum by the Sea** and **La Isla Village,** but it's not hard to find a party anywhere in town. Hotels also compete for your pesos with happy-hour entertainment and special drink prices as they try to entice visitors and guests from other resorts to pay a visit. (Lobby-bar hopping at sunset is one great way to plan next year's vacation.)

Partying at a club

Clubbing in Cancún can go on each night until the sun rises over that incredibly blue sea. Several of the big hotels have nightclubs — sometimes still called discos here — and others entertain in their lobby bars with live music. On weekends, expect to stand in long lines for the top clubs, pay a cover charge of $10 to $20 per person, and spend $5 to $8 on a drink. Some of the higher-priced clubs include an open bar or live entertainment.

A great idea to get you started is the **Bar Leaping Tour** (☎ 998-883-5402). For $49, it takes you by way of the *Froguibus* from bar to club — the list currently includes Señor Frog's, Glazz and Coco Bongo — where you'll bypass any lines and spend about two hours in each place. The price includes entry to the clubs, one welcome drink at each, and transportation by air-conditioned bus, allowing you to get a great sampling of the best of Cancún's nightlife. The tour runs from 8 p.m. to 3:30 a.m., with the meeting point at Come and Eat restaurant in the La Isla Hopping Village. V, MC, and AE are accepted.

What's hot now? As any good clubber knows, popularity can shift like the sands on the beach, but Cancún clubs do seem to have staying power. So take this list as a starting point — extensive research showed me that these were the current hot spots at press time, listed alphabetically:

- ✔ **Bulldog Café** (formerly the opulent disco, Christine), in the Hotel Krystal on the island (☎ **998-848-9800**). With room for over 2,000 revelers, this impressive space has signature laser-light shows, infused oxygen, large video screens and even a VIP Jacuzzi for some truly interesting nocturnal fun. The overall ambience is casual and funky. The music ranges from Hip-Hop to Latino rock, with a heavy emphasis on infectious dance tunes. Bulldog opens at 10 p.m. nightly and stays open until the party winds down. The cover charge is $12 per person or pay $25 for open bar all night long (domestic drinks only).

- ✔ **The City** (see map p. 119; Blvd. Kukulcán, km 9.5; ☎ **998-848-8380,** Internet: www.thecitycancun.com) is currently Cancún's hottest club, featuring progressive electronic music spun by some of the world's top DJs. With visiting DJs from New York, L.A., and Mexico City—Moby even played here—the music is sizzling. You actually need never leave, because The City is a day-and-night club. The City Beach Club opens at 8 a.m., and features a pool with a wave machine for surfing and boogie-boarding, a tower-high waterslide, food and bar service, plus beach cabanas. The Terrace Bar, overlooking the action on Blvd. Kukulcán, serves food and drinks all day long. For a relaxing evening vibe, the Lounge features comfy couches, chill music, and an extensive menu of martinis, snacks and deserts. Open at 10 p.m., the 25,000 sq. ft. nightclub has nine bars, stunning light shows, and several VIP areas. Located in front of Coco Bongo, The City also has a second location in Playa del Carmen.

- ✔ **Coco Bongo** in Forum by the Sea (see map p. 119; Blvd. Kukulcán, km 9.5; ☎ **998-883-5061**; Internet: www.cocobongo.com.mx) continues its reputation as one of the hottest spots in town. This spot's main appeal is that it has no formal dance floor, so you can dance anywhere you can find the space — that includes on the tables, the bar, or even on stage with the live band! Coco Bongo can pack in up to 3,000 people — and regularly does. Despite its capacity, lines are long on weekends and in the high season. The music alternates between Caribbean, salsa, techno, and classics from the 1970s and '80s. Open from 10 p.m.

✔ **Dady'O** (see map p. 119; Blvd. Kulkulcán, km 9.5; ☎ **998-883-3333;** Internet: www.dadyo.com.mx) is a highly favored rave with frequent, long lines. It opens nightly at 10 p.m. and generally charges a cover of $15. **Dady Rock Bar and Grill** (Blvd. Kulkulcán, km 9.5; ☎ **998-883-1626**), the offspring of Dady'O, opens early (6 p.m.) and goes as long as any other nightspot, offering a new twist on entertainment with a combination of live bands and DJ-orchestrated music. It also features an open bar, full meals, a buffet, and dancing.

✔ **Glazz** (at La Isla Shopping Village [see map p. 119; Blvd. Kulkulcán, km 3.5; ☎ **998-849-7588;** Internet: www.laboom.com.mx]) has two sections: One side is a video bar, and the other is a bilevel disco with cranking music. Both sides are air-conditioned. Each night finds a special deal going on: no cover, free bar, ladies' night, bikini contests, and other promos. Popular with 20-somethings, it's open nightly from 10 p.m. to 6 a.m.

✔ **La Boom** (see map p. 119; Blvd. Kulkulcán, km 3.5; ☎ **998-883-1881,** 883-1855) is Cancún's best for chillout, lounge, and house music. There are three main sections, including the China Bistro, which serves Chinese fusion cuisine, if you want to dine before dancing. Glazz Lounge specializes in martinis and chill-out music, while the Club at Glazz ups the beat with house music spun by visiting DJs. The Lounge is open nightly at 6 p.m. nightly, with the Club open Thursdays through Saturdays from 10 p.m. There's no cover in the Lounge, with a varying cover at the Club, depending on who's spinning. Both also offer open bar options starting at $25.

Numerous restaurants, such as **Carlos 'n Charlie's, Planet Hollywood, Hard Rock Cafe, Señor Frog's, TGI Friday's,** and **Iguana Wana,** double as nighttime party spots offering wild-ish fun at much lower prices than the clubs. Check these out:

✔ **Carlos 'n Charlie's** (see map p. 133; Blvd. Kulkulcán, km 5.5; ☎ **998-849-4052;** Internet: www.carlosandcharlies.com) is a reliable place to find both good food and frat-house-type entertainment in the evenings. A dance floor goes along with the live music that starts nightly around 8:30 p.m. A cover charge kicks in if you're not planning to eat. It's open daily 11 to 2 a.m.

✔ **Hard Rock Cafe,** in Plaza Lagunas Mall and Forum by the Sea (☎ **998-881-8120,** 998-883-2024; Internet: www.hardrock.com), entertains with a live band at 10:30 p.m. every night except Wednesday. At other times, you get lively recorded music to munch by. It's open daily 11 to 1 a.m.

✔ **Planet Hollywood** (Flamingo Shopping Center, Blvd. Kulkulcán, km 11; ☎ **998-883-0527;** Internet: www.planethollywood.com) is the still-popular brainchild (and one of the last-remaining) of Sylvester Stallone, Bruce Willis, and Arnold Schwarzenegger. It's both a restaurant and a nighttime music/dance spot with mega-decibel live music. It's open daily 11 to 2 a.m.

✔ **Señor Frog's** (see map p. 133; Blvd. Kukulcán, km 9.5; ☎ 998-883-2188 or 998-883-2189; Internet: www.senorfrogs.com) is another Anderson chain highlight that packs in crowds of those in search of a party. It frequently features live reggae music, karaoke, and even has an indoor waterslide! Open from noon to 3 a.m. daily.

Not into the party scene? The most refined and upscale of all Cancún's nightly gathering spots is the **Lobby Lounge** at the **Ritz-Carlton Hotel** (☎ 998-881-0808). Live dance music and a list of more than 120 premium tequilas for tasting or sipping are the highlights here.

Enjoying a cultural event

Several hotels host **Mexican fiesta nights,** which include a buffet dinner and a folkloric dance show; the price, including dinner, ranges from $35 to $50, but the quality of the performance is likely to be less professional than the show performed at the convention center.

You can also get in the party mood at **Mango Tango** (Blvd. Kukulcán, km 14.2; ☎ 998-885-0303), a lagoon-side restaurant/dinner-show establishment opposite the Ritz-Carlton Hotel. Diners can choose from two seating levels, one nearer the music and the other overlooking the whole production. The music is loud and varied but mainly features Caribbean or salsa. A 45-minute floor show starts nightly at 8:30 p.m. A variety of packages is available — starting at $40 per person — depending on whether you want dinner and the show, open bar and the show, or the show alone. For music and dancing, which starts at 9:30 p.m., you pay a $10 cover charge.

Tourists mingle with locals at the downtown **Parque de las Palapas** for *Noches Caribeñas,* which involves free live tropical music for anyone who wants to listen and dance. Performances begin at 7:30 p.m. on Sunday, and sometimes there are performances on Friday and Saturday.

Going Beyond Cancún: Day-Trips

One of the best ways to spend a vacation day in Cancún is by exploring one the nearby archeological ruins or new ecological theme parks or by sailing away for the day to the quaint, nearby island, Isla Mujeres. Historical and natural treasures unlike any you may have encountered before are within easy driving distance. Cancún is a perfect base for day-trips to these places, which provide a great introduction to Mexico's rich historical past and diverse natural attractions.

The Maya ruins to the south of Cancún at **Tulum** should be your first goal. Then check out the *caleta* (cove) of **Xel-Ha** or take the day-trip to **Xcaret**. See Chapter 15 for more information on the ruins at Tulum and Chapter 14 for more on Xcaret and Xel-Ha.

For day-trips by land, the organized trips are popular and easy to book through any travel agent in town, or you can plan a journey on your own via bus or rental car.

Day-trips to Isla Mujeres

One of the most popular — and, perhaps, best — ways to spend the day is to check out a real Mexican beach town across the narrow channel from Cancún. **Isla Mujeres** (the name means "Island of Women" in Spanish), just 10 miles offshore, is one of the most pleasant day-trips from Cancún. At one end of the island is **El Garrafón National Underwater Park,** which is excellent for snorkeling and diving. At the other end is a captivating village with small shops, restaurants, and hotels, along with **Playa Norte (North Beach),** the island's best beach.

To get from Cancún to Isla Mujeres, you have four options:

✔ The **public ferries** from Puerto Juárez take between 15 and 45 minutes and make frequent trips.

✔ Traveling by **shuttle boat** from Playa Linda or Playa Tortuga is an hour-long ride. The boats offer irregular service.

✔ The **watertaxi** is a more expensive but faster option than the public ferry or a shuttle boat. It's located next to the Xcaret terminal.

✔ Daylong **pleasure-boat trips** to the island leave from the Playa Linda pier.

Pleasure-boat cruises to Isla Mujeres include practically every conceivable type of vessel: modern motor yachts, catamarans, trimarans, and even old-time sloops. More than 25 boats a day take swimmers, sun lovers, snorkelers, and shoppers out into the translucent waters. Some tours include a snorkeling stop at Garrafón, lunch on the beach, and a short time for shopping in downtown Isla Mujeres. Most cruises leave at 9:30 or 10 a.m., last about five or six hours, and include continental breakfast, lunch, and rental of snorkel gear. Others, particularly the sunset and night cruises, go to beaches away from town for pseudo-pirate shows and include a lobster dinner or Mexican buffet. If you want to actually see Isla Mujeres, take a morning cruise or go on your own using the public ferry at Puerto Juárez. Prices for the day cruises run around $45 per person.

The inexpensive Puerto Juárez **public ferries** are just a few miles from downtown Cancún and give you greater flexibility in planning your day. From Isla Cancún or Cancún City, take either a taxi or the Ruta 8 bus (from Avenida Tulum) to Puerto Juárez. Choose the fast ferry (a 15-minute ride) that costs $3.50 per person over the slower one (a 45-minute ride) that costs $2. Departures are every half-hour from 6 to 8:30 a.m. and then every 15 minutes until 8:30 p.m. Upon arrival, the ferry docks in downtown Isla Mujeres near all the shops, restaurants, hotels, and Norte beach. Take a taxi or rent a golf cart to get to Garrafón Park at the other end of the island. You can stay on the island as long as you like (even overnight) and return by ferry, but be sure to check the time of the last returning ferry — the hours are clearly posted.

For more on Isla Mujeres, see Chapter 12.

Scenic boat trips

The **Atlantis Submarine** (☎ 987-872-5671; $81 adults, $48 children ages 4 to 12) provides a front-row seat to the underwater action. Departures vary, depending on weather conditions, and the submarine descends to a depth of 100 feet. Atlantis Submarine departs Monday to Saturday every hour from 8 a.m. until 2 p.m.; the tour lasts about an hour. The submarine departs from Cozumel, so you need to take a ferry to get there or purchase the package that includes round-trip ground and water transportation from your hotel in Cancún ($103 adults, $76 children ages 4 to 12). For more information, see Chapter 13.

You can call any travel agent or see any hotel tour desk to get a wide selection of boat tours to **Isla Contoy**. Prices range from $44 to $65, depending on the length of the trip. Still other boat excursions visit **Isla Contoy**, a **national bird sanctuary** that's well worth the time. However, if you plan to spend time in Isla Mujeres, the Contoy trip is easier and more pleasurable to take from there.

Seeing the archeological sites

Three great archeological sites are within close proximity to Cancún: Tulum, Ruinas del Rey, and Chichén-Itzá. You can arrange day-trips from Cancún through your hotel or through a travel agent in the United States (before you go) or in Mexico.

✔ **Tulum:** Poised on a rocky hill overlooking the transparent, turquoise Caribbean Sea, ancient **Tulum** is a stunning site. Hours are 8 a.m. to 6 p.m. daily in the summer and 7 a.m. until 5 p.m. daily in the winter. Admission is $3.50, with free admission on Sunday. For more information, see Chapter 15.

✔ **Chichén-Itzá:** The fabled pyramids and temples of Chichén-Itzá are the region's best-known ancient monuments. Hours are 8 a.m. to 5 p.m. daily. Admission is $10, free for children under 12, and free for all on Sundays and holidays. For more information, see Chapter 15.

✔ **Ruinas del Rey:** Cancún has some ruins of its own, which are convenient though far less impressive. The hours are 8 a.m. until 4:30 p.m. daily. Admission is $4.50. For more information, see the "Exploring Dry Land" section earlier in this chapter.

Exploring an ecotheme park

The popularity of the Xcaret and Xel-Ha ecoparks has inspired a growing number of entrepreneurs to ride the wave of interest in ecological and adventure theme parks. Be aware that "theme park" more than "ecological" is the operative part of the phrase. The newer parks of Aktun Chen and Tres Ríos are — so far — less commercial and more focused on nature than their predecessors.

Aktun Chen

This nature park, with its large, well-lit caverns and abundant wildlife, is the first time that above-the-ground cave systems in the Yucatán have been open to the public. The main cave contains three rivers and a deep *cenote.*

Traveling to Aktun Chen on your own is easy. From Cancún, go south on Highway 307 (the road to Tulum). Just past the turn-off for Akumal, a sign on the right side of the highway indicates the turn-off for Aktun Chen (at km 107, Cancún-Tulum road). From there, it's a 3-km (nearly 2-mile) drive west along a smooth but unpaved road. Travel time from Cancún is about an hour. For more on Aktun Chen (☎ **998-892-0662;** Internet: www. aktunchen.com), see Chapter 14.

Chikin-Ha

The newest eco adventure in the area is the half-day tour to Chikin-Ha (☎ **984-873-2036;** Internet: www.alltournative.com), also known as the Mayan Canopy Tour. You have the option of hiking or biking through the landscape past a series of three *cenotes* with deep-blue waters. You can stop and swim in each or choose to take a zip-line over the *cenote* and tropical landscape. Departures from Cancún are $87, or $78 for children under 12, and include transportation, guide, equipment, snacks and beverages.

Tres Ríos

Tres Ríos (☎ **998-887-8077**) — meaning three rivers — is the most natural of the area's nature parks. Just 25 minutes south of Cancún on more than 150 acres of land, this park is a true nature reserve that offers guests a beautiful area for kayaking, canoeing, snorkeling, horseback riding, or biking along jungle trails. Essentially, Tres Ríos is just one big natural spot for participating in these activities. Most Cancún travel agencies sell a half-day Kayak Express tour to Tres Ríos. At $45, it includes admission and activities, plus round-trip transportation, lunch, and two nonalcoholic drinks. For more information, see Chapter 14.

Xcaret

Xcaret (pronounced *ish*-car-et), located 50 miles south of Cancún, is a specially built ecological and archaeological theme park and one of the area's most popular tourist attractions. Xcaret has become almost a reason in itself to visit Cancún. With a ton of attractions — most of them participatory — in one location, it's the closest thing to Disneyland in Mexico. In Cancún, signs advertising Xcaret and folks handing out Xcaret leaflets are everywhere. The park has its own bus terminal in Cancún where buses pick up tourists at regular intervals. Plan to spend a full day here; children love it, and the jungle setting and palm-lined beaches are beautiful. Past the entrance booths (built to resemble small Mayan temples) are pathways that meander around bathing coves, the snorkeling lagoon, and the remains of a group of real Mayan temples.

Xcaret may celebrate Mother Nature, but its builders rearranged quite a bit of her handiwork in completing it. If you're looking for a place to escape the commercialism of Cancún, this park may not be it. The park is relatively expensive and may be very crowded, thus diminishing the advertised "natural" experience.

Travel agencies in Cancún offer day-trips to Xcaret that depart at 8 a.m. and offer your choice of a return at 6 p.m., or 9 p.m., after the dinner show Xcaret Spectacular Night. The cost starts at $85 for adults ($45 for children), which includes transportation from Cancún and admission. You can also buy a ticket to the park at the **Xcaret bus terminal** (☎ **998-883-0699**, 998-883-3143, 998-883-0524; Internet: www.xcaretcancun.com), located next to the Fiesta Americana Coral Beach hotel on Cancún Island. Buses leave the terminal at 8:15am and 10:35 a.m. daily. The park is open daily 8:30 a.m. to 9 p.m., and until 10 p.m. in the summer months. For more on Xcaret, see Chapter 14.

Xel-Ha

The sea has carved the Caribbean coast of the Yucatán into hundreds of small *caletas,* or coves. Many *caletas* along the coast remain undiscovered and pristine, but Xel-Ha (shell-*hah*), near Tulum, plays host daily to throngs of snorkelers and scuba divers who come to luxuriate in its warm waters and swim among its brilliant fish. Xel-Ha is a swimmers' paradise with no threat of undertow or pollution. It's a beautiful, completely calm cove that's a perfect place to bring kids for their first snorkeling experience. Experienced snorkelers may be disappointed because the crowds seem to have driven out the living coral and many of the fish here. For more information, see Chapter 14.

Part IV
Traveling Around Isla Mujeres and Cozumel

The 5th Wave
By Rich Tennant

JERRY FAILS TO HEED THE DIVE GUIDE'S REQUEST THAT NO ONE EAT A HEAVY LUNCH BEFORE THE DIVE

Hey- who's gonna know?

In this part . . .

*I*f you're looking for a low-key place that doesn't have the hustle and bustle of Cancún or the boomtown feel of the newer towns along the Riviera Maya (covered in Part V), Isla Mujeres and Cozumel may be right for you.

Although Isla Mujeres is only a few miles off the Cancún mainland, it is nevertheless a world apart. Quiet beaches and casual, open-air restaurants lend the island a relaxed, get-away-from-it-all feel.

Cozumel, while a bit busier than Isla Mujeres, is so laid-back that the name may as well be the Mayan translation for cozy and mellow — you definitely get a tropical-island vibe here. This town is where you come to take the plunge into scuba diving; the offshore reefs are top-notch, and the island has more dive shops than any town on the mainland. If scuba is too challenging, the snorkeling is great as well. As it grows in popularity as a cruise ship port-of-call, Cozumel's days are becoming more lively. When you combine underwater sights, duty-free shopping, and a little low-key nightlife, you have yourself a great "Cozymellow" vacation.

Chapter 12

Isla Mujeres

- -

In This Chapter

▶ Hopping the ferry to Isla Mujeres
▶ Choosing a hotel
▶ Finding the best meals
▶ Having fun and chilling out while you're there

- -

*I*sla Mujeres (Island of Women) is a casual, laid-back refuge from the hyper-commercial action of Cancún, visible across a narrow channel. This island of white-sand beaches is surrounded by turquoise waters and complemented by a town filled with pastel-colored clapboard houses and rustic, open-air seafood restaurants. Just 5 miles long and 2½ miles wide, this fish-shaped island is known as the best value in the Caribbean, assuming that you favor an easy-going vacation pace and prefer simplicity to pretense.

Located just 8 miles northeast of Cancún, "Isla" — as the locals call it — is a quick boat ride away, making it a popular daytime excursion. However, to fully explore the small village of shops and cafes, relax at the broad, tranquil Playa Norte, or snorkel or dive El Garrafón Reef (a national underwater park), you may need more time. Overnight accommodations range from rustic to offbeat chic on this small island where relaxation rules.

Francisco Hernández de Córdoba landed here in 1517 and gave the island its name upon seeing small statues of partially clad females along the shore. These objects are now believed to have been offerings to the Mayan goddess of fertility and the moon, Ixchel. Their presence is an indication that the island was probably sacred to the Maya.

At midday, suntanned visitors hang out in open-air cafes and stroll streets lined with frantic souvenir vendors. Calling out for attention to their bargain-priced wares, the vendors provide a carnival atmosphere to the hours when tour-boat traffic is at its peak. Befitting the size of the island, most of the traffic consists of golf carts, *motos* (also called mopeds), and bicycles. Once the tour boats leave, however, Isla Mujeres reverts back to its more typical, tranquil way of life, where taking a *siesta* in a hammock is a favored pastime.

In recent years, Isla has seen the emergence of several smaller but decidedly upscale places to stay. Anyone wanting the proximity and ease of arrival that Cancún offers — but not the excesses for which Cancún is famous — seriously consider these new options on Isla Mujeres, where a trip to the mainland is less than an hour if you do choose to enjoy its shopping or dining. Isla's budget-priced hotels as well as their more luxury-oriented offerings both offer excellent values — Isla tends to be one of the better bargains among Mexico's resorts. Its location, so close to the excellent air access of Cancún, makes this spot a great choice for travelers wanting an authentic Mexican beach experience at a great price.

Settling into Isla Mujeres

Isla Mujeres is so small, it's easy to get your bearings and find your way around. If you do happen to need a little guidance, it's so comfortably casual that a friendly soul is always around to help you.

The island is about 5 miles long and 2½ miles wide, with the town located at its northern tip. "Downtown" is a compact 4 blocks by 6 blocks, so it's very easy to get around. The **ferry docks** (☎ 998-877-0065) are right at the center of town, within walking distance of most hotels, restaurants, and shops. The street running along the waterfront is Avenida **Rueda Medina,** commonly called the **malecón.** The **market** (Mercado Municipal) is by the post office on **Calle Guerrero,** an inland street at the north edge of town, which, like most streets in the town, is unmarked.

Arriving at Isla Mujeres by ferry

To get to Isla Mujeres, you need to first fly into Cancún's International Airport (CUN). Once inside the terminal, you enter the immigration clearance area where you're asked to show your passport and completed tourist card, called an FMT (see Chapter 9). Once you claim your baggage, you exit the terminal, where taxis or other transportation services are waiting. (See Chapter 9 for details.)

Puerto Juárez (☎ 998-877-0618 for the Isla Mujeres office), just north of Cancún, is the dock where you catch a passenger ferry to Isla Mujeres. This is the least expensive way to travel to Isla. The air-conditioned *Caribbean Express* makes the trip in 20 minutes, has storage space for luggage, and costs about $4, running every hour on the half hour between 6:30 a.m. and 8:30 p.m. Pay at the ticket office — or, if the ferry is about to leave, you can pay onboard.

When you arrive by taxi or bus to Puerto Juárez, be wary of "guides" who offer advice and tell you either that the ferry is cancelled or that it's several hours until the next departure. They offer the services of a private *lancha* (small boat) for about $40 — but it's nothing but a scam. Small boats are available and, on a co-op basis, are priced much cheaper — $15 to $25 for a one-way fare, based on the number of passengers. They take about 50 minutes for the trip over and are not recommended on

Isla Mujeres

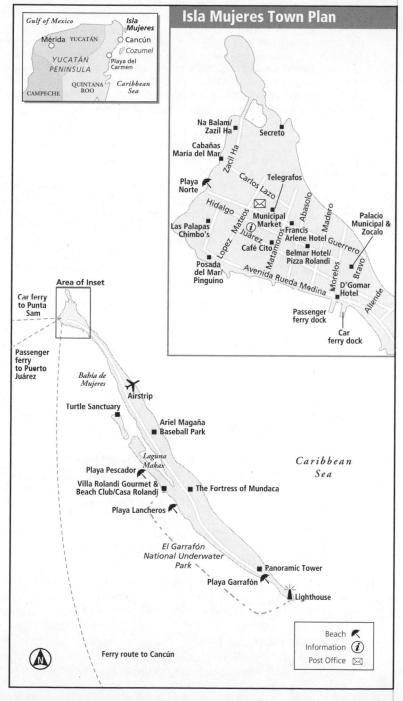

Isla Mujeres Town Plan

Gulf of Mexico

Isla Mujeres

Mérida YUCATÁN

Cancún

YUCATÁN
PENINSULA

Cozumel

Playa del
Carmen

QUINTANA
ROO

CAMPECHE

Caribbean
Sea

Na Balam/
Zazil Ha

Secreto

Cabañas
María del Mar

Zacil Ha

Carlos Lazo

Telegrafos

Playa
Norte

Hidalgo

Abasolo

Municipal
Market

Madero

Palacio
Municipal &
Zocalo

Las Palapas
Chimbo's

Lopez Mateos

Juárez

Francis
Arlene Hotel

Café Cito

Matamoros

Belmar Hotel/
Pizza Rolandi

Guerrero

Bravo

Posada
del Mar/
Pinguino

Avenida Rueda Medina

Morelos

D'Gomar
Hotel

Allende

Area of Inset

Car ferry
to Punta
Sam

Passenger
ferry dock

Car
ferry dock

Passenger
ferry
to Puerto
Juárez

Bahía de
Mujeres

Airstrip

Turtle Sanctuary

Ariel Magaña
Baseball Park

Laguna
Makax

Caribbean
Sea

Playa Pescador

Villa Rolandi Gourmet &
Beach Club/Casa Rolandi

The Fortress of Mundaca

Playa Lancheros

El Garrafón
National Underwater
Park

Panoramic Tower

Playa Garrafón

Lighthouse

Beach

Information

Post Office

N

Ferry route to Cancún

days with rough seas. Check with the ticket office for information — this (clearly visible) office is the only accurate source.

Taxi fares for the trip from Puerto Juarez back to Cancún are now posted by the street where the taxis park, so be sure to check the rate before agreeing to ride. Rates generally run $12 to $15, depending upon your final destination. Moped and bicycle rentals are also readily available as you depart the ferryboat. This small complex also has public bathrooms, luggage storage, a snack bar, and souvenir shops.

Isla Mujeres is so small that a vehicle isn't necessary, but if you're taking one, you have to use the **Punta Sam** port, just beyond Puerto Juárez. The ferry runs the 40-minute trip five or six times daily between 8 a.m. and 8 p.m., year-round except in bad weather. Times are generally as follows: Cancún to Isla at 8 a.m., 11 a.m., 2:45 p.m., 5:30 p.m., and 8:15 p.m., with returns from Isla to Cancún at 6:30 a.m., 9:30 a.m., 12:45 p.m., 4:15 p.m., and 7:15 p.m.; however, check with the tourist office in Cancún to verify this schedule. If you're driving a car, arrive an hour before the ferry departure to register for a place in line and pay the posted fee, which varies depending on the weight and type of vehicle. You can find the only gas pump in Isla at the intersection of Avenida Rueda Medina and Abasolo Street, just northwest of the ferry docks.

Ferries also travel to Isla Mujeres from the **Playa Linda,** known as the Embarcadero pier in Cancún, but they're less frequent and more expensive than those from Puerto Juárez. A **Water Taxi** (☎ 998-886-4270 or 998-886-4847; e-mail: asterix1@prodigy.net.mx) to Isla Mujeres operates from Playa Caracol, between the Fiesta Americana Coral Beach Hotel and the Xcaret terminal on Isla Cancún, with prices about the same as those from Playa Linda and about four times the cost of the public ferries from Puerto Juárez. Scheduled departures are 9 a.m., 11 a.m., and 1 p.m., with returns from Isla Mujeres at noon and 3 p.m. Adult fares are $15; kids ages 3 to 12 are half price, and those under age 3 ride free.

Getting from the ferry dock to your hotel

Ferries arrive at the ferry dock (☎ 998-877-0065) in the center of town. The main road that passes in front of the ferry dock is Avenida Rueda Medina. Most hotels are close by. Tricycle taxis are the least expensive and most fun way to get to your hotel; you and your luggage pile in the open carriage compartment while the driver peddles through the streets. Regular taxis are always lined up in a parking lot to the right of the pier, with their rates posted.

If someone on the ferry offers to arrange a taxi for you, politely decline, unless you'd like some help with your luggage down the short pier — it just means an extra, unnecessary tip for your helper.

Getting around

A popular form of transportation on Isla Mujeres is the electric **golf cart,** available for rent at many hotels for $15 per hour or $45 per day. El Sol

Golf Cart Rental will deliver one to you (☎ 998-877-0791), or you can stop by the office at Avenida Francisco Madero 5 if you're just visiting for the day. The golf carts don't go more than 20 miles per hour, but they're fun. And you don't come to Isla Mujeres to hurry around. They accept MasterCard and Visa, with an added 6% if you pay by credit card.

Many people enjoy touring the island by **"moto,"** the local name for motorized bikes and scooters. Fully automatic versions are available for around $25 per day or $7 per hour. They come with seats for one person, but some are large enough for two. There's only one main road with a couple of offshoots, so you won't get lost. Be aware that the rental price doesn't include insurance, and any injury to yourself or the vehicle comes out of your pocket. **Bicycles** are also available for rent at some hotels for $3 per hour or $7 per day, including a basket and a lock.

If you prefer to use a taxi, rates are about $2.50 for trips within the downtown area, or $4.50 for a trip to the southern end of Isla. You can also rent taxis for about $12 per hour.

Staying in Isla

You can find plenty of hotels in all price ranges on Isla Mujeres. Rates are at their peak during high season, which is the most expensive and most crowded time to go. Those interested in private home rentals or longer-term stays can contact **Mundaca Travel and Real Estate** in Isla Mujeres (☎ 998-877-0025; fax: 998-877-0076; www.mundacatravel.com).

With the exception of a few upscale places to stay along the western shore of the island, Isla's hotel offerings are clustered throughout the downtown area, or along Playa Norte. Although you'll have to walk to the beach from the downtown hotels, remember it's relatively close by, and getting around is both easy and inexpensive.

As far as prices go, I note rack rates (the maximum that a hotel or resort charges for a room) for two people spending one night in a double room. You can usually do better, especially if you're purchasing a package that includes airfare. (See Chapter 5 for tips on avoiding paying rack rates.) Prices quoted here include the 12% room tax.

A kid-friendly icon highlights hotels that are especially good for families.

I note all hotels that have air-conditioning, because this feature is not standard in Isla hotels.

Belmar Hotel
$$ **Downtown**

Situated in the center of Isla's small-town activity, above Pizza Rolandi (consider the restaurant noise), this hotel is run by the same people who serve up those wood-oven pizzas below. (See the "Dining in Isla Mujeres" section later in this chapter for a review.) Each of the simple but stylish rooms comes with two twin or double beds and tile accents. Prices are high for no views, but the rooms are very pleasant. On the other hand, this hotel is one of the few on the island with televisions (that receive U.S. channels) in the room. One large colonial-decorated suite with a whirlpool and a patio is available.

See map p. 167. Av. Hidalgo 110 (between Madero and Abasolo, 3½ blocks from the passenger-ferry pier) ☎ *998-877-0430. Fax: 998-877-0429. E-mail:* hotel.belmar@ mail.caribe.net.mx. *High season $56–$95 double. Low season $28–$45 double. AE, MC, V.*

Cabañas María del Mar
$$ Playa Norte

A good choice for simple accommodations on the beach, the Cabañas María del Mar is located on the popular Playa Norte. The older two-story section behind the reception area and beyond the garden offers nicely out-fitted rooms facing the beach, all with two single or double beds, refrigerators, and balconies strung with hammocks and oceanviews. Eleven single-story *cabañas* closer to the reception and pool are decorated in a rustic Mexican style, and come with a minifridge. The third section, **El Castillo,** is located across the street, built over and beside Buho's restaurant. It contains all "deluxe" rooms with king beds, but some are larger than others; the five rooms on the ground floor all have large patios. Upstairs rooms have small balconies. All have oceanviews and a predominately white décor. Rooms were remodeled in 2004. A small pool is in the garden.

See map p. 167. Av. Arq. Carlos Lazo 1 (on Playa Norte, a half block from the Na Balam hotel). ☎ *800-223-5695 in the U.S., or* ☎ *998-877-0179. Fax: 998-877-0213. High season $109–$123 double. Low season $70–$111 double. MC, V. To get here from the pier, walk left 1 block and then turn right on Matamoros. After 4 blocks, turn left on Lazo, the last street. The hotel is at the end of the block.*

D'Gomar Hotel
$ Downtown

This hotel is known for comfort at reasonable prices. You can hardly beat the value for basic accommodations. Rooms have two double beds, and a private bath. A wall of windows offers great breezes and wonderful views. The higher prices are for rooms with air-conditioning, which is hardly needed with fantastic breezes and ceiling fans. The only drawback is that the hotel has five stories and no elevator. But it's conveniently located kitty-corner (look right) from the ferry pier, with exceptional rooftop views. The name of the hotel is the most visible sign on the "skyline."

See map p. 167. Rueda Medina 150. ☎ *998-877-0541. High season $40 double. Low season $35 double. No credit cards.*

Francis Arlene Hotel
$ **Downtown**

The Magaña family operates this neat little two-story inn built around a small, shady courtyard. This hotel is very popular with families and seniors, and it welcomes many repeat guests. You'll notice the tidy cream-and-white façade of the building from the street. Some of the rooms have oceanviews, and each year they're all remodeled or updated. They're clean and comfortable, with tile floors, all-tile bathrooms, and a very homey feel to them. Each downstairs room has a coffeemaker, refrigerator, and stove; each upstairs room comes with a refrigerator and toaster. Most rooms have either a balcony or a patio. Telephone service is available through the front desk only. Rates are substantially better if quoted in pesos and are reflected as follows. In dollars, they're 15 to 20% higher.

See map p. 167. Guerrero 7 (5½ blocks inland from the ferry pier, between Abasolo and Matamoros). ☎ **998-877-0310** *(also fax) or 998-877-0861. High season $50–$60 double. Low season $40–$50 double (higher prices are for rooms with A/C) MC, V.*

La Casa de los Sueños Resort & Spa Zenter
$$$$$ **Western Coast**

This "house of dreams" is easily Isla Mujeres's most intimate, sophisticated, and relaxing property. Although it was originally built as a private residence, luckily it became an upscale, adults-only B&B in early 1998 (it has since changed ownership), and now caters to guests looking for a rejuvenating experience, with its adjoining "Zenter" offering spa services and yoga classes. Its location on the southern end of the island, adjacent to El Garrafón National Park, also makes it ideal for snorkeling and diving enthusiasts. The captivating design features vivid sherbet-colored walls — think watermelon, mango, and blueberry — and a sculpted architecture. You find a large, open interior courtyard; tropical gardens; a sunken living area (with wireless Internet access); and an infinity pool that melts into the cool Caribbean waters. All rooms have balconies or terraces and face west, offering stunning views of the sunset over the sea, as well as the night lights of Cancún. In addition, the rooms — which have names such as "Serenity," "Passion," and "Love" — also have large, marble bathrooms, Frette bedding, and L'Occitane bath amenities, and are decorated in a serene style that blends Asian simplicity with Mexican details. One master suite ideal for honeymooners has an exceptionally spacious bathroom area, complete with whirlpool and steam room shower, plus other deluxe amenities. Complementary continental breakfast is served in your room, and a restaurant adjacent to their private pier serves healthful, fusion cuisine — it's open to non-guests as well. The Zenter offers a very complete menu of massages and holistic spa treatments, as well as yoga classes, held either outdoors or in a serene indoor space.

Carretera Garrafón s/n. ☎ **998-877-0651** *or 998-877-0369. Fax: 998-877-0708.* www. casadelossuenosresort.com. *E-mail:* direccion@casadelossuenos resort.com. *High season $300–$450. Low season $240–$360. Rates include full continental breakfast. MC, V. No children.*

Na Balam
$$$ Playa Norte

Increasingly, Na Balam is becoming known as a haven for yoga students or those interested in an introspective vacation. This popular, two-story hotel near the end of Playa Norte has comfortable rooms on a quiet, ideally located portion of the beach. Rooms are in three sections, with some facing the beach and others across the street in a garden setting with a swimming pool. All rooms have either a terrace or a balcony, with hammocks. Each spacious suite contains a king-size bed or two queen beds, a seating area, and folk-art decorations. Although other rooms are newer, the older section is well kept, with a bottom-floor patio facing the peaceful, palm-filled, sandy inner yard and Playa Norte. Two extra-private Master suites with pool are ideal for honeymooners, with a new, contemporary décor and outdoor shower. Guests can enjoy complimentary yoga classes, and yoga or Pilates retreats are frequently scheduled. (For more, see the "Exploring your inner self in Isla" sidebar later in this chapter.) The restaurant, **Zazil Ha,** is one of the island's most popular (see the "Dining in Isla Mujeres" section later in this chapter), serving Mexican and Caribbean cuisine, with abundant vegetarian specialties. A beachside bar serves a selection of natural juices and is known as one of the most popular spots for sunset watching during the evenings.

See map p. 167. Zazil Ha 118. ☎ *998-877-0279. Fax: 998-877-0446.* www.nabalam. com. *High season $162–$270. Low season $121–$200 suite. Ask about special weekly and monthly rates. AE, MC, V. Free unguarded parking.*

Posada del Mar
$$ Playa Norte

Simply furnished, quiet, and comfortable, this long-established hotel faces the water and a wide beach 3 blocks north of the ferry pier, and it has one of the few swimming pools on the island. This hotel is probably the best choice in Isla for families, and children younger than age 12 stay free of charge with paying adults. Pets are also welcome. The ample-size rooms are in either a three-story building or one-story bungalow units, and all have patio or balcony, air-conditioning and ceiling fans, plus cable TV and telephone. For the spacious quality of the rooms and the location, this hotel is among the best values on the island and is very popular, though I consistently find the staff to be the least gracious on the island. A wide, seldom-used but appealing stretch of Playa Norte is across the street, where watersports equipment is available for rent. A great, casual *palapa*-style bar and a lovely pool are set on the back lawn along with hammocks. The restaurant **Pinguino** (see the "Dining in Isla Mujeres" section later in this chapter) is by the sidewalk at the front of the property, and also provides room service. From the pier, go left for 4 blocks; the hotel is on the right.

See map p. 167. Av. Rueda Medina 15 A. ☎ *800-544-3005 in the U.S., or 998-877-0044. Fax: 998-877-0266.* www.posadadelmar.com. *High season $67–$77 double. Low season $40–$45 double. Rates include 2 children free in the same room. AE, MC, V.*

Secreto
$$$$$ Playa Norte

This boutique hotel looks like a Hamptons beach house, but it is one of the best B&B values in the Caribbean. What sets Secreto apart — aside from the stunning setting and outstanding value — is the exemplary service. The sophisticated, romantic property has nine air-conditioned suites that overlook a central pool area to the private beach beyond. Located on the northern end of the island, Secreto is within walking distance of town, yet feels removed enough to make for an idyllic, peaceful retreat. The captivating contemporary design features clean, white spaces and sculpted architecture in a Mediterranean style. Tropical gardens surround the pool area, and an outdoor living area offers comfy couches and places to dine. All rooms have private verandas with comfortable seating, ideal for ocean-gazing beyond Halfmoon Beach, and are accented with original artwork. Three suites have king beds, draped in mosquito netting, while the remaining six have two double beds; all rooms are nonsmoking, and have a TV, CD player, and mini-fridge. Although there's no on-site restaurant, the hotel has as arrangement with nearby Rolandi's (see Dining in Isla "Mujeres," later in this chapter) for room service. The hotel has its own boat and divemaster staff for certified scuba training and trips, plus excursions to offshore destinations. Transportation from Cancún airport can be arranged on request, for an additional $50 per van (not per person).

See map p. 167. Sección Rocas, Lote 1. ☎ *877-278-8018 in the U.S., or 998-877-1039.* www.hotelsecreto.com. *High season $183–$250. Low season $167–$230. Rates include daily continental breakfast, plus 1 child younger than age 5 in same room. MC, V.*

Villa Rolandi Gourmet & Beach Club
$$$$$ Western Coast

This hotel is ideal for guests who enjoy Isla's tranquility — but also like being pampered. Villa Rolandi is an exceptional value, with rooms styled in a Mediterranean décor that offer every conceivable amenity, as well as its own small, private beach in a sheltered cove. Each of the 20 oversized suites has an oceanview — across the infinity pool, with its waterfall that flows over to the cove below. Each suite also has a large terrace or balcony with a full-size private whirlpool. (Staff change the water with each guest's arrival.) Floors are made of stone, and ceilings are vaulted. TVs offer satellite music and movies, and rooms all have a sophisticated in-room sound system and are air-conditioned. A recessed seating area extends out to the balcony or terrace. Bathrooms are large and tastefully decorated in deep-hued Tikal marble. The stained-glass shower has dual showerheads, stereo speakers, and jet options, and it even converts into a steam room.

Dining is an integral part of a stay at Villa Rolandi. Its owner is a Swiss-born restaurateur who made a name for himself with his family of Rolandi restaurants on Isla Mujeres and in Cancún (see the following section). It also offers 24-hour room service to guests. This intimate hideaway with highly personalized service is ideal for honeymooners, who receive a complimentary bottle of domestic champagne upon arrival, when notified in advance. Only children older than age 13 are welcome.

See map p. 167. Fracc. Lagunamar SM 7 Mza. 75 L 15 and 16. ☎ *998-877-0700. Fax: 998-877-0100.* www.villarolandi.com. *High season $350-$420 double. Low season $290-$350 double. Rates include round-trip transportation from the dock at Playa Linda in Cancún aboard a private catamaran yacht, Cocoon; daily continental breakfast; and à la carte lunch or dinner in the on-site restaurant. AE, MC, V.*

Dining in Isla Mujeres

Dining in Isla — as most everything else — is a casual affair. The most common options you find are known as **cocinas económicas,** literally meaning an "economic kitchen." Usually aimed at the local population, these spots are great places to find good food at rock-bottom prices, most of which feature regional specialties. But be aware that the standard of hygiene is not what you'll find at more established restaurants, so you're dining at your own risk. The places I include here cater to a more established tourist clientele, so although they're higher priced, they also offer a much better overall dining experience.

Here, even the best restaurants are very casual when it comes to dress. Any man wearing a jacket would be looked at suspiciously. Ladies, however, are frequently seen in dressy resort wear — basically, everything goes, but shorts and T-shirts are typical.

The restaurants I include are arranged alphabetically, with their location and general price category noted. Remember that tips generally run about 15%, and most wait-staff really depend on these for their income, so be generous if the service warrants.

Café Cito
$$ CREPES/ICE CREAM/COFFEE/FRUIT DRINKS

Sabina and Luis Rivera own this cute, Caribbean-blue corner restaurant where you can begin the day with flavorful coffee and a croissant and cream cheese or end it with a hot-fudge sundae. Terrific crêpes are served with yogurt, ice cream, fresh fruit, or chocolate sauces, as well as ham and cheese. The two-page ice-cream menu satisfies most any craving, even one for waffles with ice cream and fruit. The three-course fixed-price dinner starts with soup, includes a main course such as fish or curried shrimp with rice and salad, and is followed by dessert.

See map p. 167. Calle Matamoros 42, corner of Juárez (4 blocks from the pier). ☎ *998-877-1470. Crêpes $2.10-$4.50; breakfast $2.50-$4.50; sandwich $2.80-$3.50. No credit cards. Daily 8 a.m.-2 p.m. During high season also open Fri-Wed 5:30-10:30 or 11:30 p.m., depending on the crowd.*

Casa Rolandi
$$ ITALIAN/SEAFOOD

The gourmet Casa Rolandi restaurant and bar has become the favored fine-dining experience in Isla, with a view overlooking the Caribbean and the most sophisticated menu in the area. It has a colorful main dining area, as well as a more casual, open-air terrace seating for drinks or light snacks. Food is the most notable on the island, although the overall experience falls short, especially with lights that are a bit too bright and music that is a bit too close to what you'd hear on an elevator ride. Along with seafood and northern Italian specialties, the famed wood-burning oven pizzas are a good bet. Careful — the wood-oven baked bread, which arrives looking like a puffer fish, is so divine that you're likely to fill up on it. This restaurant is a great place to enjoy the sunset, and you have a selection of more than 80 premium tequilas.

See map p. 167. On the pier of Villa Rolandi, Lagunamar SM 7. ☎ 998-877-0700. Dinner $8–$35. AE, MC, V.

Las Palapas Chimbo's
$$ SEAFOOD

If you're looking for a beachside *palapa*-covered restaurant where you can wiggle your toes in the sand while relishing fresh seafood, this one is the best of them. Locals recommend it as their favorite on Playa Norte. Try the delicious fried fish (a whole one), which comes with rice, beans, and tortillas. You'll notice a bandstand and dance floor in the middle of the restaurant, and especially the sex-hunk posters all over the ceiling — that is, when you aren't gazing at the beach and the Caribbean. Chimbo's becomes a lively bar and dance club at night, drawing a crowd of drinkers and dancers. (See the "Isla Mujeres after dark" section later in this chapter.)

See map p. 167. Norte Beach (from the pier, walk left to the end of the malecón, and then right onto the Playa Norte; it's about half a block on the right). No phone. Sandwiches and fruit $2.50–$4.50; seafood $6–$9. No credit cards. Daily 8 a.m. to midnight.

Pinguino
$$ MEXICAN/SEAFOOD

The best seats on the waterfront are on the deck of this restaurant/bar, especially in late evening, when islanders and tourists arrive to dance and party. This is the place to feast on lobster — you get a beautifully pre-sented, large, sublimely fresh lobster tail with a choice of butter, garlic, and secret sauces. The grilled seafood platter is spectacular, and fajitas and barbecue ribs are also popular. Breakfasts include fresh fruit, yogurt, and granola, or sizable platters of eggs served with homemade wheat bread. Both free parking and nonsmoking areas are available.

*See map p. 167. In front of the Hotel Posada del Mar (3 blocks west of the ferry pier), Av. Rueda Medina 15. ☎ **998-877-0044**, 998-877-0878. Main courses $4–$7; daily special $7; all-you-can-eat buffets $7. AE, MC, V. Daily 7 a.m.–11 p.m.; bar open to midnight.*

Pizza Rolandi
$$ ITALIAN/SEAFOOD

Practically an institution in Isla, you're bound to dine at least one night at Rolandi's. The plate-sized pizzas or calzones are likely to lure you with exotic ingredients — including lobster, black mushrooms, pineapple, or roquefort cheese, as well as more traditional tomatoes, olives, basil, and salami. A wood-burning oven provides the signature flavor of the pizzas, as well as baked chicken, roast beef, or mixed seafood casserole with lobster. The extensive menu also offers a selection of salads and light appetizers, along with an ample array of pasta dishes, steaks, fish, and scrumptious desserts. The setting is the open courtyard of the Belmar Hotel, with a porch overlooking the action on Hidalgo Street.

*See map p. 167. Av. Hidalgo #10 (3½ blocks inland from the pier, between Madero and Abasolo). ☎ **998-877-0430**. Main courses $3.70–$12.70. AE, MC, V. Daily 11 a.m.–11:30 p.m.*

Zazil Ha
$$ CARIBBEAN/INTERNATIONAL

You can enjoy some of the island's best food at this restaurant while sitting at tables on the sand among palms and gardens. The serene environment is enhanced by the food — terrific pasta with garlic, shrimp in tequila sauce, fajitas, seafood pasta, and delicious molé enchiladas. Caribbean specialties include cracked conch, coconut sailfish, jerk chicken, and stuffed squid. The vegetarian menu is complemented by a selection of fresh juices, and even a special menu is available for those participating in yoga retreats. Between the set hours for meals, you can have all sorts of enticing food, such as vegetable and fruit drinks, tacos and sandwiches, *ceviche,* and terrific nachos. It's likely you'll stake this place out for several meals before you leave.

*See map p. 167. At the Na Balam hotel (at the end of Playa Norte and almost at the end of calle Zazil Ha). ☎ **998-877-0279**. Fax: 998-877-0446. Main courses $8.50–$16. AE, MC, V. Daily 7:30-10:30 a.m., 12:30–6:30 p.m., and 6:30–11 p.m.*

Fun On and Off the Beach in Isla Mujeres

Days in Isla can alternate between adventurous activity and absolute repose. Trips to the Isla Contoy bird sanctuary are popular, as is taking advantage of the excellent diving, fishing, and snorkeling — in 1998, the island's coral coast was made part of Mexico's new Marine National Park. In the evenings, most people find the slow, casual pace one of the island's biggest draws. The cool night breeze is a perfect accompaniment to casual open-air dining and drinking in small street-side restaurants. Most people turn in as early as 9 or 10 p.m., when most businesses close. Those in search of a party, however, can find kindred souls at the bars on Playa Norte, which stay open late.

Isla's best beaches

The most popular beach in town used to be called Playa Cocoteros ("Cocos," for short). Then, in 1988, Hurricane Gilbert destroyed the coconut palms on the beach. Gradually, the name has changed to **Playa Norte,** referring to the long stretch of beach that extends around the northern tip of the island, to your left as you get off the boat. This beach is splendid — a wide stretch of fine white sand and calm, translucent, turquoise-blue water and is definitely where you want to go to rack up serious beach time. Topless sunbathing is permitted, and the row of bordering beach bars adds to the festive atmosphere. You can easily reach the beach on foot from the ferry and from all downtown hotels. You can also rent watersports equipment, beach umbrellas, and lounge chairs. The umbrellas and chairs in front of restaurants usually cost nothing if you use the restaurant as your headquarters for drinks and food. New palms have grown back all over Playa Norte, and it won't be long before it deserves to get its old name back.

Garrafón National Park is known best as a snorkeling area, but a nice stretch of beach is on either side of this park, which now offers food service, diving platforms, and a full range of affiliated services for one admission fee (see the following section). **Playa Lancheros** is on the Caribbean side of Laguna Makax. Local buses go to Lancheros and then turn inland and return to downtown. The beach at Playa Lancheros is nice, but the few restaurants there are high-priced.

Wide Playa Norte is the best swimming beach, with Playa Lancheros second. No lifeguards are on duty on Isla Mujeres, and the system of water-safety flags used in Cancún and Cozumel isn't used here.

Deep blue explorations in Isla

By far the most popular place to snorkel is **Garrafón National Park,** at the southern end of the island, where you can see numerous schools of colorful fish. The well-equipped park has beach chairs, a swimming pool, kayaks, changing rooms, rental lockers, showers, a gift shop, and snack bars. Once a public national underwater park since late 1999, Garrafón has been operated by the same people who manage Xcaret, south of Cancún. Public facilities have been vastly improved, with new attractions and facilities added each year. Activities at the park include snorkeling and "Snuba" (a tankless version of scuba diving, when you descend while breathing through a long air tube), crystal-clear canoes for viewing underwater life, and a zip-line that takes you over the water. The underwater mini-sub **Sea Trek** provides a great view of the submarine landscape while you stay dry, if that's your preference. On land, they have tanning decks, shaded hammocks, a 38-foot climbing tower, and — of course! — a souvenir superstore. Several restaurants and snack bars are available. Admission is $29 for adults and $15 for children. (AE, MC, and V are accepted.) You can also choose an all-inclusive option for $59, which includes food, beverages, locker rental, and snorkeling gear rental. All packages include round-trip transportation (☎ 998-884-9422 or 998-849-4950 in Cancún and 998-877-1100 or 998-877-1108 at the park). The park is open daily 9 a.m. to 5 p.m.

Also good for snorkeling is the **Manchones Reef,** where a bronze cross was installed in 1994. The reef is just offshore and can be reached by boat.

Another excellent location is around the lighthouse (*el faro*) in the **Bahía de Mujeres** at the southern tip of the island, where the water is about 6 feet deep. Boatmen will take you for around $25 per person if you have your own snorkeling equipment, or $30 if you use theirs.

Several dive shops have opened on the island, most offering the same trips. **Bahía Dive Shop,** on Rueda Medina 166, across from the car-ferry dock (☎ 998-877-0340), is a full-service shop with dive equipment for sale or rent, and resort and certification classes. The shop is open daily 10 a.m. to 7 p.m. and accepts Visa and MasterCard only. Another respected dive shop is **Coral Scuba Center** (☎ 998-877-0061 or 998-877-0763), located at Matamoros 13A and Rueda Medina. It offers discounted prices for those who bring their own gear, and it also has rental bungalows available for short-term and long-term stays.

Cuevas de los Tiburones (Caves of the Sleeping Sharks) is Isla's most renowned dive site — but the name is slightly misleading, because shark sightings are rare these days. Two sites where you could traditionally see the sleeping sharks were the Cuevas de Tiburones and **La Punta,** but the sharks have obviously moved on to a more secluded site — after all, would *you* want to have dozens of gawkers watching you snooze? Sharks have no gills and so must constantly move to receive the oxygen they need. (Remember the line in *Annie Hall* equating relationships to sharks: "They must constantly move forward or die"?) The phenomenon here is that the high salinity and lack of carbon monoxide in the caves, combined with strong and steady currents, allow the sharks to receive the oxygen they need without moving. Your chance of actually seeing sleeping sharks is about 1 in 4. The best time to see them, though, is from January to March.

Other dive sites include a wreck 9 kilometers (14½ miles) offshore; Banderas Reef, between Isla Mujeres and Cancún, where there's always a strong current; Tabos Reef on the eastern shore; and Manchones Reef, 1 kilometer (1½ miles) off the southeastern tip of the island, where the water is 15 to 35 feet deep. Another underwater site, "The Cross of the Bay," is close to Manchones Reef. A bronze cross, weighing 1 ton and standing 39 feet high, was placed in the water between Manchones and Isla in 1994, as a memorial to those who have lost their lives at sea. The best season for diving is from June to August, when the water is calm.

To arrange a day of **fishing**, ask at the **Sociedad Cooperativa Turística** (the boatmen's cooperative) located on Avenida Rueda Medina (no phone), next to Mexico Divers and Las Brisas restaurant. You can share the cost with four to six others, and it includes lunch and drinks. Captain Tony Martínez (☎ 998-877-0274) also arranges fishing trips aboard his *lancha, Marinonis,* with advanced reservations recommended. Year-round, you can find bonito, mackerel, kingfish, and amberjack. Sailfish and sharks (hammerhead, bull, nurse, lemon, and tiger) are in good supply in April and May. In winter, larger grouper and jewfish are prevalent. Four hours of fishing close to shore costs around $110; 8 hours farther out goes for $250. The cooperative is open from Monday to Saturday 8 a.m. to 1 p.m. and 5 to 8 p.m., and Sunday 7:30 to 10 a.m. and 6 to 8 p.m.

You can **swim with dolphins** at Dolphin Discovery, located at Treasure Island, on the side of Isla Mujeres that faces Cancún. Swims take place in groups of six people with two dolphins and one trainer. First, swimmers listen to an educational video and spend time in the water with the trainer and the dolphins before enjoying 15 minutes of free swimming time with them. Reservations are recommended, and you must arrive an hour before your assigned swimming time, at 10 a.m., 12 a.m., 2:30 p.m., or 3:30p.m. Make your reservations in Cancún at ☎ 998-849-4757 or ☎ toll free 01-800-713-8862 in Mexico and toll free 800-417-1736 in U.S.(fax: 998-849-4751). Additional information is available at the Web site www.dolphindiscovery.com. Cost is $125 per person, plus $10 if round-trip transportation from Cancún is required.

A very worthwhile outing on the island is to a **Turtle Sanctuary,** dedicated to preserving Caribbean sea turtles and to educating the public about them. As recently as 20 years ago, fishermen converged on the island nightly from May to September waiting for these monster-size turtles to lumber ashore to deposit their Ping-Pong ball-shaped eggs. Totally vulnerable once they begin laying their eggs and exhausted when they have finished, the turtles were easily captured and slaughtered for their highly prized meat, shell, and eggs. Then a concerned fisherman, Gonzalez Cahle Maldonado, began convincing others to spare at least the eggs, which he protected. It was a start. Following his lead, the fishing secretariat founded this **Centro de Investigaciones** ten years ago; both the government and private donations help to support it. Since then, at least 28,000 turtles have been released, and every year local schoolchildren participate in the event, thus planting the notion of protecting the turtles for a new generation of islanders.

Six different species of sea turtles nest on Isla Mujeres. An adult green turtle, the most abundant species, measures 4 to 5 feet in length and can weigh as much as 450 pounds when grown. At the center, visitors walk through the indoor and outdoor turtle pool areas, where the creatures paddle around. The turtles are separated by age, from newly hatched up to 1 year. Besides protecting the turtles that nest on Isla Mujeres of their own accord, the program also captures turtles at sea, brings them to enclosed compounds to mate, and later frees them to nest on Isla Mujeres after they've been tagged. People who come here usually end up staying at least an hour, especially if they opt for the guided tour, which I recommend. The sanctuary is on a piece of land separated from the island by Bahía de Mujeres and Laguna Makax (see map p. 167); you need a taxi to get there. Admission is $3; the shelter is open daily 9 a.m. to 5 p.m. For more information, call ☎ 998-877-0595.

Sightseeing and shopping in Isla

Also at Punta Sur (the southern point of the island, just inland from **Garrafón National Park** (☎ 998-877-1100 or 998-877-1108; www.garrafon.com) and part of the Park, is Isla's newest attraction, the **Panoramic Tower** (see the "Isla Mujeres Map" on p. 167). At 225 feet (50 meters) high, the tower offers visitors a birds'-eye-view of the entire island. The tower holds 20 visitors at a time, and rotates for a ten minutes while you can snap photos or simply enjoy the scenery. Entry fee is $5, a professional photo of you at the tower (touch-ups are included!) is $10, and package prices are available.

Next to this, you'll find **Sculptured Spaces,** an impressive and extensive garden of large sculptures donated to Isla Mujeres by internationally renowned sculptors as part of the 2001First International Sculpture Exhibition. Among Mexican sculptors represented are works by Jose Luis Cuevas and Vlaadimir Cora.

Also nearby is the **Caribbean Village,** with narrow lanes of colorful clapboard buildings that house cafes and shops displaying folkloric art. Plan to have lunch or a snack here at the kiosk and stroll around, before heading on to the lighthouse and Mayan ruins.

Just beyond the lighthouse, at the southern end of the island, are the strikingly beautiful remains of a small **Maya temple,** believed to have been built to pay homage to the moon and fertility goddess, Ixchel. The location, on a lofty bluff overlooking the sea, is worth seeing and makes a great place for photos. It's believed that Maya women traveled here on annual pilgrimages to seek Ixchel's blessings of fertility. If you're at Garrafón National Park and want to walk, it's not too far. Turn right from Garrafón. When you see the lighthouse, turn toward it down the rocky path.

Also at this southern point of the island, and part of the ruins is **Cliff of the Dawn,** the southeastern-most point of Mexico. Open from 7 a.m. to 8 p.m., if you make it there early enough to see the sun rise, you can claim you were the first person in Mexico that day to be touched by the sun!

The Fortress of Mundaca is about 2½ miles in the same direction as Garrafón, about half a mile to the left. (See the "Isla Mujeres" map on p. 167.) The fortress was built by a slave trader who claimed to have been the pirate Mundaca Marecheaga. In the early 19th century, he arrived at Isla Mujeres and proceeded to set up a blissful paradise in a pretty, shady spot, while making money selling slaves to Cuba and Belize. According to island lore, he decided to settle down and build this hacienda after being captivated by the charms of an island girl. However, she reputedly spurned his affections and married another islander, leaving him heart-broken and alone on Isla Mujeres. Admission is $2, and the fortress is open daily from 10 a.m. to 6 p.m.

If you're interested in natural attractions, put a visit to **Isla Contoy** at the top of your list of things to do. This pristine uninhabited island, 19 miles by boat from Isla Mujeres, was set aside as a national wildlife reserve in 1981. The oddly shaped 3.8-mile-long isle is covered in lush vegetation and harbors 70 species of birds, as well as a host of marine and animal life. Bird species that nest on the island include pelicans, brown boo-bies, frigates, egrets, terns, and cormorants. Flocks of flamingos arrive in April. June, July, and August are good months to spot turtles burying their eggs in the sand at night.

Most excursions here troll for fish (which will be your lunch), anchor en route for a snorkeling expedition, and skirt the island at a leisurely pace for close viewing of the birds without disturbing the habitat, and then pull ashore. While the captain prepares lunch, visitors can swim, sun, follow the nature trails, and visit the fine nature museum. For a while, the island was closed to visitors, but it has reopened following an agree-ment that fishermen and those bringing visitors will follow a set of rules for its use and safety. The trip from Isla Mujeres takes about 45 minutes one way, more if the sea is choppy. Because of the tight-knit boatmen's cooperative, prices for this excursion are the same everywhere: $40 for adults and $20 for children. You can buy a ticket at the **Sociedad Cooperativa Turística** located on Avenida Rueda Medina (next to Mexico Divers and Las Brisas restaurant), or at one of several travel agencies, such as **La Isleña,** on Morelos between Medina and Juárez (☎ 998-877-0578). La Isleña is open daily from 7:30 a.m. to 9:30 p.m. and is a good source for tourist information. Contoy trips leave at 8:30 a.m. and return around 4 p.m. Cash is the only accepted form of payment.

Boat captains should respect the cooperative's regulations regarding ecological sensitivity and boat safety, including the availability of life jackets for everyone on board. Snorkeling equipment is usually included in the price, but double-check that before heading out. On the island, you'll find a small government museum with bathroom facilities.

Let me put it simply — you'd never come to Isla for the shopping experi-ence. **Shopping,** as everything else in Isla, is quite a casual affair, with only a few shops of any sophistication. More typically, you're bombarded by shop owners, especially on Hidalgo, selling the whole gamut of tourist kitsch including saltillo rugs, onyx, silver, Guatemalan clothing, blown glassware, masks, folk art, beach paraphernalia, and T-shirts in abun-dance. Prices are lower here than in Cancún or Cozumel, but with the overeager sellers, bargaining is necessary to avoid paying too much.

The one treasure you're likely to take back is a piece of fine jewelry — Isla is known for its excellent, duty-free prices on gemstones and handcrafted

---

Exploring your inner self in Isla

Increasingly, Isla is becoming known as a great place to combine a relaxing beach vacation with various types of yoga practice and instruction. The impetus for this trend began at Na Balam hotel (☎ 998-877-0279; www.nabalam.com), where yoga classes are offered under its large poolside *palapa,* complete with yoga mats and props. The classes, which take place from Monday to Friday beginning at 9 a.m., are free to guests, or $10 per class to visitors. Na Balam is also the site of frequent yoga instruction vacations, featuring respected yoga teachers, and a more extensive practice schedule. Local yoga culture extends down the island to Casa de los Sueños Resort and Zenter (☎ 998-877-0651; www.casadelossuenosresort.com), where yoga classes, as well as chi gong and Pilates, are regularly held.

---

work made to order. You can purchase diamonds, emeralds, sapphires, and rubies as loose stones and then have them mounted while you're off exploring the island. The superbly crafted gold, silver, and gems are available at very competitive prices in the workshops near the central plaza. The stones are also available in the rough. **Rachat & Rome** (☎ 998-877-0331 or 998-877-0299) is the grandest jewelry store, with a broad selection of jewelry at competitive prices. Located at the corner of Morelos and Juárez streets, it's easily the largest store in Isla, open daily 9:30 a.m. to 5 p.m.; it accepts all major credit cards.

Isla Mujeres after dark

Those in a party mood by day's end may want to start out at the beach bar of the **Na Balam** hotel on Playa Norte, which hosts a crowd until around midnight. On Saturday and Sunday, live music plays between 4 and 7 p.m. **Las Palapas Chimbo's** restaurant on the beach becomes a jammin' dance joint with a live band from 9 p.m. until whenever. Farther along the same stretch of beach, **Buho's,** the restaurant/beach bar of the Cabañas María del Mar, has its moments as a popular, low-key hangout, complete with swinging seats! **Pinguino** in the Hotel Posada del Mar offers a convivial late-night hangout, where a band plays nightly during high season from 9 p.m. to midnight. Near Matéos and Hidalgo, **KoKo Nuts** caters to a younger crowd, with alternative music for late-night dancing. The **Om Bar and Chill Lounge,** on Calle Matamoros, serves beer on tap at each table, in a jazzy atmosphere. For a late-night dance club, **Club Nitrox,** on Ave. Guererro, is open Wednesday to Sunday from 9 p.m. to 3 a.m.

Fast Facts: Isla Mujeres

Area Code

The telephone area code is **998**.

Baby Sitters

Baby-sitting services are less common on Isla than in Cancún, and many sitters speak only limited English, but, children are welcome in local restaurants. A recommended service is **Zarina Zina Babysitting Services** (☎ **998-888-0674,** www.zarina zina.com). Generally, rates range from $3 to $8 per hour.

Banks, ATMs, and Currency Exchange

Only one bank is in Isla, HSBC Bank, and it's located directly across from the ferry docks at Av. Rueda Medina (☎ **998-877-0104** or 998-877-0005). It's open from 8:30 a.m. to 6 p.m. Monday through Friday, 9 a.m. to 2 p.m. Saturday. Isla Mujeres has numerous *casas de cambios,* or money exchanges, which you can easily spot along the main streets. Most of the hotels listed here provide this service for their guests, although often at less favorable rates than the commercial enterprises.

Business Hours

Most offices maintain traditional Mexican hours of operation: from 10 a.m. to 2 p.m., and from 4 to 8 p.m. daily, while shops remain open throughout the day. Offices tend to be closed on Saturday and Sunday, while shops will be open on at least Saturday, and increasingly offer limited hours of operation on Sunday.

Emergencies

Police emergency, ☎ 060; **local police,** ☎ 998-877-0458, 877-0082; **Red Cross,** ☎ 998-877-0280.

Hospitals

The **Hospital de la Armada** (Naval Hospital) is on Avenida Rueda Medina at Ojon P. Blanco (☎ **998-877-0001**). It's half a mile south of the town center. It's not generally open to civilians, but they do take you in case of a life-threatening emergency. Otherwise, you're referred to the **Centro de Salud** on Avenida Guerrero, a block before the beginning of the Malecón (☎ **998-877-0117**).

Information

The **City Tourist Office** (☎ **998-877-0767** (also fax) or 998-877-0307) is located on Avenida Rueda Medina, in front of the pier. It's open from Monday to Friday 8 a.m. to 8 p.m. and Saturday 8 a.m. to 2 p.m. Also look for *Islander,* a free publication with history, local information, advertisements, and event listings (if any).

Internet Access

Owned by a lifelong resident of Isla, **Cyber Isla Mujeres.com,** Av. Francisco y Madero 17, between Hidalgo and Juaréz streets (☎ **998-877-0272**), offers Internet access for $1.50 per hour from Monday to Sunday 8 a.m. to 10 p.m and serves complimentary coffee from Veracruz all day.

Maps

Islander, a free publication with history, local information, advertisements, and event listings (if any) also has maps of the island included in it. The City Tourist office, located across from the ferry pier, is the best source of other maps and area information.

Pharmacy

Isla Mujeres Farmacía (☎ 998-877-0178) has the best selection of prescription and over-the-counter medicines. It's located on Calle Benito Juárez, between Morelos and Bravo, across from Rachet & Rome jewelry store.

Post Office

The post office (☎ 998-877-0085), or *correo,* is located on calle Guerrero no. 12, at the corner with López Matéos, near the market. It's open from Monday to Friday 9 a.m. to 4 p.m.

Safety

Isla Mujeres enjoys a very low crime rate. Most crime or encounters with the police are linked to pickpocket crimes, so use common sense and never leave your belongings unattended at the beach.

Taxes

A 10% IVA (value-added) tax is charged on goods and services, and it's generally included in the posted price.

Taxis

Call for a taxi at ☎ 998-877-0066.

Telephone

You can find Ladatel phones accepting coins and prepaid phone cards at the plaza and throughout town. The new **DigaMe** (Ave. Guerrero between Matamoros and Abasolo, ☎ 608-467-4202; info@ digame.com), has mobile phone rentals, private voicemail service, and long-distance phone services available.

Tourist Information

The Isla Mujeres Tourist Information office is located at Av. Rueda Medina 130, across from the Ferry docks (☎ 998-877-0307 or 998-877-0767; fax: 998-877-0307; www.isla-mujeres.net).

Tourist Seasons

Isla Mujeres's tourist season (when hotel rates are higher) is a bit different from that of other places in Mexico. High season runs December through May, a month longer than in Cancún; some hotels raise their rates in August, and some hotels raise their rates beginning in mid-November. Low season is from June to mid-November.

Chapter 13

Cozumel

- -

In This Chapter

▶ Getting around the island

▶ Searching Cozumel for the best hotels and restaurants

▶ Beach-bumming, scuba diving, and other outdoor activities

▶ Shopping for the best duty-free deals

- -

C ozumel was a well-known diving spot before Cancún even existed, and it has ranked for years among the top-five dive destinations in the world. Tall reefs lining the island's southwest coast create towering walls that offer divers a fairytale landscape to explore. For nondivers, Cozumel has the beautiful waters of the Caribbean with all the accompanying watersports and seaside activities. Because the island is also a popular cruise-ship port, you find excellent duty-free shopping here. Cozumel definitely has a get-away-from-it-all feel — roads that don't go very far, lots of mopeds, few buses and trucks, and a certain sense of separation. The island is 12 miles from the mainland, and the name comes from the Maya word *Cuzamil,* meaning "Land of the Swallows."

Getting to Cozumel

Nothing could be simpler than arriving to the island and getting around the place. The airport is small and presents no surprises. The island layout is easy to understand. And if you rent a car, it's not like you have many roads to choose from.

By air

Because of the popularity of package vacations, more international charter flights actually come in and out of the island than regularly scheduled commercial flights. You may want to inquire about buying a ticket from one of the travel packagers, such as Funjet or Apple Vacations, that do most of the chartering. (See Chapter 6 for more information.) Some packagers work with a wide variety of Cozumel's hotels — even some of the smaller independent ones; others allow you to buy a ticket without making it part of a package.

Direct international flights to Cozumel include **AeroMexico** to and from Atlanta, **Continental** to and from Houston and Newark, **US Airways** to and from Charlotte, and **American Airlines** to and from Dallas. **Aerocozumel,** a Mexicana affiliate, has numerous flights to and from Cancún. **Mexicana** flies from Mexico City (other international flights connect through Mexico City).

Knowing what to expect when you arrive

Cozumel's airport is small enough to eliminate any chance for confusion. When you walk into the main building, the lines for immigration are right in front of you. You need proof of citizenship and a picture ID. Showing a passport is always the easiest thing. On the plane, you're given an immigration form to fill out. Most people miss the fact that they have to sign it on the back in two different places. Doing so prevents hold-ups in the line.

When you receive your **Mexican tourist permit (FMT)** put it in a safe place. You're supposed to keep this permit with you at all times — you may be required to show it if you run into any sort of trouble. You also need to turn it in upon departure, or you may be unable to leave without first getting a replacement.

After Immigration, you pass through Customs. They ask you to push a button, which randomly triggers on either a green light or a red light. If it's green, you go right through. If it's red, they may look into your bags. Are you feeling lucky?

Getting from the airport to your hotel

Cozumel's **airport** is immediately inland from the island's only town, San Miguel. If you're picking up a rental car, the counters are along a short hallway to the left of the airport exit. Both **Avis** (☎ 987-872-0099) and **Executive** (☎ 987-872-1308) have staff there. Otherwise, you'll want to buy a ticket for a cab. A counter at the exit reads "**Transportes Terrestres.**" This company provides transportation to all the hotels in air-conditioned Suburbans. To hotels downtown, the fare is $5 per person; to hotels along the north shore, it's $7, and to hotels along the south shore, it's $8 to $12.

By sea

Cozumel is a large island across from Playa del Carmen, 12 miles off the Yucatán coast. Passenger ferries travel to and from Playa del Carmen. See Chapter 14 for more on Playa del Carmen.

Taking the passenger ferry from Playa del Carmen

Barcos México (☎ 987-872-1508 or 987-872-1588) and **Ultramar** (☎ 987-869-2775) operate ferries between Playa and Cozumel. You'll arrive in Cozumel at the municipal dock, one block from the town's main square. The trip takes 30 to 45 minutes, depending on the boat. It costs $9 one

Cozumel Island

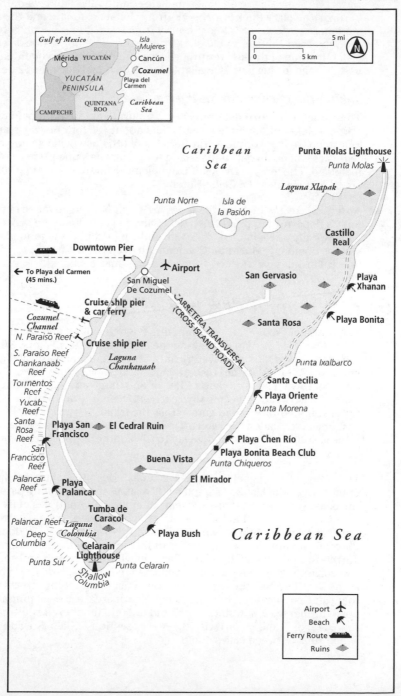

way, and the boats are enclosed and air-conditioned. In Playa del Carmen, the ferry dock is 1½ blocks from the main square and the bus station. Departures are almost hourly from 5 a.m. to midnight. Schedules are subject to change, so check the departure time at the docks, especially the time of the last returning ferry if that's the one you intend to use. Storage for luggage is available at the Cozumel dock for $2 per day.

Taking the car ferry from Puerto Calica

The car ferry to Cozumel from Puerto Calica (5 miles south of Playa del Carmen) takes about an hour and costs about $80 for one-way transport of a standard car. For most travelers it's of little use because you can rent cars when you get to the island for about the same price as on the mainland. The ferry arrives in Cozumel at the International Pier just south of town, near La Ceiba Hotel.

Note: To take a vehicle on the ferry, arrive an hour in advance of the ferry's departure to purchase a ticket and to get in line. The schedule is usually daily at 7 a.m., 1 p.m., 5 p.m. and 9 p.m., but it's a good idea to call the company, **Marítima Chancanaab** (☎ 987-872-0916), to double-check. On Sundays, the last trips are sometimes canceled.

Getting around Cozumel

The island of Cozumel is 45 kilometers (28 miles) long and 18 kilometers (11 miles) wide. A road runs along the along its western shore. Where the road passes along the waterfront of the island's only town, it's known as **Avenida Rafael Melgar.** Outside of town, it has several names: North of town it's called **Santa Pilar** or **San Juan**, south of town it's called **Costera Sur.** It eventually reaches the southern tip of the island (Punta Sur). Another road cuts across the island to the undeveloped east coast. It's called **Carretera Transversal.** When it gets to the ocean, it turns south and goes all the way to the southern tip where it meets the Costera Sur road.

The town of San Miguel is on the west coast. Despite an increase in development over the last 20 years, it's still a small town. Running parallel to the coast (north-south) are *avenidas* numbered in multiples of five — 5, 10, 15, and so on — that increase as you go inland. The main east-west street is **Avenida Juárez,** which starts at the passenger-ferry dock and the main square, and heads east, crossing town and then becoming the Carretera Transversal. It divides San Miguel into northern and southern halves. In the northern half the avenidas are labeled *Norte* (Av. 5 Norte), in the southern half they are labeled *Sur.* Furthermore, the streets (*calles*) that run east and west, parallel to Avenida Juárez, are even numbered north of Juárez (2, 4, 6, and so on) and are odd numbered south of Juárez (1, 3, 5, and so on) with the one exception of Calle Rosado Salas, which runs between calles 1 and 3.

San Miguel de Cozumel

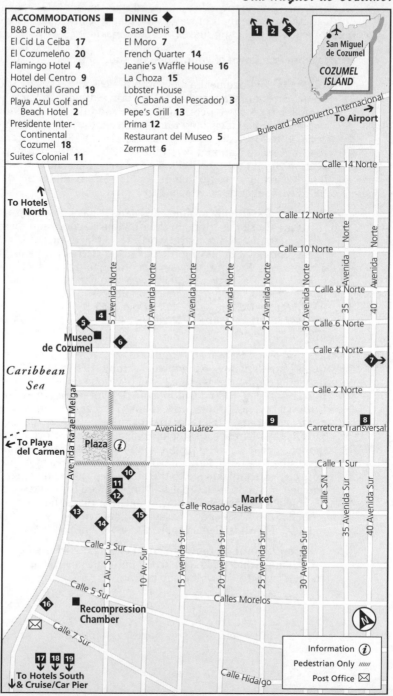

ACCOMMODATIONS ■

B&B Caribo **8**
El Cid La Ceiba **17**
El Cozumeleño **20**
Flamingo Hotel **4**
Hotel del Centro **9**
Occidental Grand **19**
Playa Azul Golf and
  Beach Hotel **2**
Presidente Inter-
  Continental
  Cozumel **18**
Suites Colonial **11**

DINING ◆

Casa Denis **10**
El Moro **7**
French Quarter **14**
Jeanie's Waffle House **16**
La Choza **15**
Lobster House
  (Cabaña del Pescador) **3**
Pepe's Grill **13**
Prima **12**
Restaurant del Museo **5**
Zermatt **6**

San Miguel
de Cozumel

**COZUMEL
ISLAND**

Bulevard Aeropuerto Internacional

To Airport

Calle 14 Norte

↑
**To Hotels
North**

Calle 12 Norte

Calle 10 Norte

Calle 8 Norte

Calle 6 Norte

Calle 4 Norte

**Museo
de Cozumel**

*Caribbean
Sea*

Calle 2 Norte

Carretera Transversal

Avenida Juárez

←**To Playa
del Carmen**

Plaza ⓘ

Calle 1 Sur

Market

Calle Rosado Salas

Calle 3 Sur

Calles Morelos

Calle 5 Sur

**Recompression
Chamber**

Calle 7 Sur

5 Avenida Norte
10 Avenida Norte
15 Avenida Norte
20 Avenida Norte
25 Avenida Norte
30 Avenida Norte
35 Avenida Norte
40 Avenida Norte

Avenida Rafael Melgar

5 Av. Sur
10 Av. Sur
15 Avenida Sur
20 Avenida Sur
25 Avenida Sur
30 Avenida Sur
35 Avenida Sur
40 Avenida Sur
Calle S/N

Calle Hidalgo

17 **18** **19**
↓ ↓ ↓
**To Hotels South
↓& Cruise/Car Pier**

Information ⓘ
Pedestrian Only /////
Post Office ✉

When driving around town, keep in mind that the *avenidas* running north-south have the right of way, and traffic doesn't slow down or stop (except when intersecting Juárez). You often won't see a stop sign.

Here is a brief rundown of your transportation choices in Cozumel:

✔ **Taking taxis:** Cozumel has a wealth of taxis and a strong taxi-driver union. Fares are standardized — so don't attempt to bargain. Sample fares for two people (expect an additional charge for extra passengers) include island tour, $60; from town to southern hotel zone, $5 to $18; from town to northern hotels, $5 to $6; from town to Chankanaab National Park (see the "Visiting the nature parks" section later in this chapter), $7; and in and around town, $3 to $4. It isn't customary to tip taxi drivers in Mexico unless the driver helps with luggage or acts as a tour guide.

✔ **Renting cars:** Driving around the island is easy. The only paved roads are those described in the previous section, and these roads take you to just about all the worthwhile places on the island. There's no point in leaving the pavement unless you're just feeling adventurous. Rental rates vary according to demand. An economy car can go for as little as $30 in low season and for as much as $60 in high season. The local agency numbers are Avis (☎ 987-872-0219); Budget (☎ 987-872-5177); Dollar (☎ 987-872-1196); Executive (☎ 987-872-1308); Hertz (☎ 987-872-5979); and National (☎ 987-872-3263).

✔ **Renting mopeds:** Moped rentals are available all over town and at the big hotels. They cost anywhere from $15 to $30 for 24 hours, depending upon the season. If you decide to use this mode of transport, be careful. Riding a moped made a lot more sense when Cozumel had less traffic; now, thanks to Cozumel's numerous, pushy motorists, it's a risky proposition. Moped accidents easily rank as the highest cause of injury in Cozumel. Before renting a moped, give it a careful inspection to see that all the gizmos are in good shape — horn, light, starter, seat, mirror — and be sure to note any existing damage to the moped on the rental agreement. I've been given mopeds that had unbalanced tires and would wobble above 15 mph, but I was able to replace them with better mopeds with no questions asked. Riding a moped without a helmet outside of town is illegal (subject to a $25 fine).

✔ **Walking around on foot:** The town of San Miguel is small enough for walking, which is helpful when pub crawling. Few places are far enough away to warrant a cab ride.

Fast Facts: Cozumel

Area Code

The telephone area code is **987.**

Banks, ATMs, and Currency Exchange

The island has several banks and *casas de cambio* (currency exchange offices), as well as ATM machines. Most places accept U.S. dollars, but you usually get a better deal paying in pesos.

Business Hours

Most offices maintain traditional Mexican hours of operation (9 a.m. to 2 p.m. and 4 to 8 p.m. daily), but shops remain open throughout the day. Offices tend to close on Saturday and Sunday, but shops are open on Saturday, at least, and increasingly offer limited hours of operation on Sunday.

Climate

From June to November, strong winds and some rain can prevail over the Yucatán. In Cozumel, wind conditions in November and December can make diving dangerous. June to September is the rainy season. Temperature during the day in the summer is 80°F to 90°F; in winter, it's 75°F to 80°F.

Diving

If you intend to dive, bring proof of your diver's certification. Underwater currents can be strong here, and many of the reef drops are quite steep, making them excellent sites for experienced divers but too challenging for novice divers.

Information

The **Municipal Tourism Office** (☎ 987-869-0212) is located on the second floor of the Plaza del Sol commercial building, facing the central plaza, and is open Monday to Friday 9 a.m. to 5 p.m. and Saturday 9 a.m.

to 1 p.m. A handy information booth at the ferry pier is open from 8:30 a.m. to 4 p.m.

Internet Access

Many cybercafes operate in town. Look for any sign that uses the words "Internet" or "cyber." One of the most reliable Internet providers is **Modutel** (Av. Juárez No. 15, at the intersection with Av. 10). Hours are 10 a.m. to 8 p.m.

Police

Dial **060.** Remember that you're unlikely to find an English-speaking operator at the police station.

Post Office

The post office *(correo)* (Av. Rafael Melgar at Calle 7 Sur, at the southern edge of town; ☎ 987-872-0106) is open Monday to Friday 9 a.m. to 4 p.m. and Saturday 9 a.m. to 1 p.m.

Recompression Chamber

Cozumel has four recompression chambers *(cámaras de recompresión)*. **Buceo Médico,** staffed 24 hours, is on Calle 5 Sur, 1 block off Avenida Rafael Melgar between Melgar and Avenida 5 Sur (☎ 987-872-2387, 987-872-1430). Another one is the **Hyperbaric Center of Cozumel** (Calle 4 Norte, between avenidas 5 and 10; ☎ 987-872-3070).

Taxes

A 15% IVA (value-added tax) on goods and services is charged, and it's generally included in the posted price.

Taxis

Fares on the island are fixed with little variation and generally are not open to negotiation. Taxis charge extra for more than two passengers. It isn't customary to tip taxi drivers in Mexico unless the driver helps with luggage or acts as a tour guide. Call ☎ 987-872-0236 for taxi pickup.

Telephone

Avoid the phone booths that have signs in English advising you to call home using a special 800 number — these booths are absolute rip-offs and can cost as much as U.S. $20 per minute. The least expensive way to call is by using a Telmex (LADATEL) prepaid phone card, available at most pharmacies and mini-supers, using the official Telmex (Lada) public phones. Remember, in Mexico, you need to dial 001 prior to a number to reach the United States, and you need to preface long-distance calls within Mexico by dialing 01.

Staying in Cozumel

Almost all of Cozumel's hotels are on the western coast of the island, which faces mainland Mexico. This side is also where the island's only town, San Miguel, is located. This coast is sheltered from the open water and has little surf, which makes it perfect for swimming. The hotels and B&Bs in town tend to be the most economical properties on the island. Staying in town can be both entertaining and convenient, although the hotels in this area tend to be smaller and older. If you choose to stay here, a number of stores, dive shops, travel agencies, restaurants, and nightspots are within easy walking distance. To get to a beach, you need to take a taxi. A few small beaches are nearby for you to enjoy.

But if the most you want to do is hang out around the pool with the occasional dip into the Caribbean, you'll want one of the beach hotels either north or south of town. Most of the beaches on the southern coast are nicer than the ones on the northern coast.

All the northern hotels are lined up in close proximity on the ocean side of the road next to the golf course and a short distance from town and the airport. The hotels to the south of town are closer to the popular Chankanaab National Park and tend to be more spread out. Some are on the inland side of the road, and some are on the ocean side, making for a difference in price. The properties farthest away from town are all-inclusives; the beaches at the southern end of the island tend to be the best.

Finding the place that's right for you

If you're vacationing with your family and want to economize, consider all-inclusive hotels or condo/villa rentals. Both types of lodging allow you to cut costs, but they make for different vacations. If your main goal is to be bone idle and to not work on anything harder than your tan while the kids romp in the pool, then go with an all-inclusive. But if you enjoy striking out on your own and adapting to new surroundings, try a rental.

Choosing to stay at an all-inclusive — if you reserve through one of the large packagers such as Apple Vacations or FunJet (see Chapter 6) — means you pay one lump price for air transport, ground transfers, lodging, food, and drink. You pay only for whatever tours and incidentals you decide to purchase.

A few things to remember about all-inclusive hotels:

- ✔ They operate on narrow profit margins and large volume, so they're usually close to full-capacity in high season. This fact can make it hard to avoid crowds for a little peace and quiet.

- ✔ On the other hand, they have plenty of activities for both adults and kids.

- ✔ They make for an easy vacation in which most things, such as entertainment and food, require a minimum of effort on your part.

- ✔ You tend to be isolated and not get much of a feel for the island or the people.

Renting a condo or an apartment can save you money by avoiding dining out. This way, you also get more privacy. But you'll most likely want to rent a car for trips to the grocery store and for other errands, which is something you need to remember when budgeting. For most first-time visitors to the island, you're probably better off staying at a hotel so that you don't have to get your bearings immediately and you can enjoy getting acquainted with the island at a more relaxing pace.

Checking out Cozumel's best hotels

The prices I quote here are for rack rates (the full rate without discounts) for two people spending one night in a double room. You can usually do better, especially if you're purchasing a package that includes airfare. (See Chapter 6 for tips on avoiding paying rack rates.) Prices quoted here include the 12% room tax. All hotels have air-conditioning unless otherwise indicated.

Because Cozumel is such a big destination for divers, all the large hotels and many small ones offer dive packages. I don't mention this fact in the reviews, but ask about them if you plan to do a lot of diving. All the large waterfront hotels have dive shops on the premises and a pier, so I don't mention these amenities either. But if you prefer staying at a particular hotel while using a different dive operator, no one is going to say anything. Any dive boat can pull up to any hotel pier to pick up customers. Most dive shops don't pick up from the hotels north of town, so it's best to dive with the in-house operator at these hotels.

For info about renting a villa or condo, try **Cozumel Vacation Villas and Condos** *(Av. 10 Sur 124, 77600 Cozumel, Q. Roo;* ☎ ***800-224-5551*** *in the United States, or 987-872-0729;* www.cvvmexico.com*), which offers accommodations by the week.*

B&B Caribo
$ **In town**

The American owner of this B&B goes out of her way to make you feel right at home. The rates are a good deal; they include air-conditioning, breakfast, and several little extras. Six neatly decorated rooms come with cool tile floors, painted furniture, and big bottles of purified drinking water; these units share a guest kitchen. The six apartments (minimum one-week stay) have small kitchens. Most rooms have a double bed and a twin bed. The inn also has a number of common rooms and a rooftop terrace. Breakfasts are good. To find the Caribo from the plaza, walk 6½ blocks inland on Juárez to the smartly painted blue-and-white house on the left.

See map p. 189. Av. Juárez No. 799. ☎ 987-872-3195. www.cozumel.net/bb/ caribo/. *12 units. Rack rates: High season $50 double; $60 apartment; low season $40 double; $50 apartment. Rates include full breakfast. AE, MC, V.*

El Cid La Ceiba
$$$–$$$$ South of town

Located on the beach side of the road, La Ceiba is great for snorkeling and shore diving — a submerged airplane is just offshore. It's a popular hotel with divers as it offers unlimited tanks for shore diving and was voted one of the world's top 15 dive resorts in *Rodale's Scuba Diving* magazine. All rooms have oceanviews, balconies, and two doubles or one king bed. Bathrooms are roomy and well lit, with granite countertops and strong water pressure. Superior rooms are larger than standard and have more furniture. Some suites are available for limited periods and only to guests who make direct reservations, not to groups. The emphasis here is on watersports, particularly scuba diving, and if it's your passion, be sure to ask about the special dive packages when you call for reservations. (Ask for the Frommer's/Dummies' discount.) Diving is available right from the hotel beach. For those post-dive evenings, choose between two restaurants, as well as a bar. Other diversions include a lighted tennis court, a small exercise room with sauna, a whirlpool, and watersports-equipment rentals.

See map p. 189. Costera Sur, km 4.5. ☎ 800-435-3240 in the U.S., or 987-872-0844. Fax: 987-872-0065. www.elcid.com. *98 units. Rack rates: High season $250 double, $533 suite; low season $126 double, $164 suite. AE, DC, DISC, MC, V.*

El Cozumeleño
$$$–$$$$ North of town

This is a popular all-inclusive hotel located not far from town on a pretty part of the north shore. It's a good choice for active sorts who like to get out and do things. One of the hotel's strong points is that its staff coordinates a lot of activities for its guests. For the not-so-active types, the hotel has a large and stunning pool and patio area where you can plop down on a lounger and not move a muscle all day. Rooms are in a nine-story building; half in the old section, half in the new section. Those in the older section are much longer than they are wide and have an awkward furniture arrangement. All rooms are large and have balconies with ocean views. You have a choice of a king-size or two double beds. Beyond the massive pool is a small sand beach and, a little bit to the south are some rocky areas where you can snorkel and spot some fish. This is an all-inclusive property so rates include food and drink. As with other all-inclusives, you get a better deal buying through an agent than going directly to the hotel. *See map p. 189. Carretera Santa Pilar km 4.5* ☎ *800-437-3923 in the U.S. or 987-872-9530. Fax: 987-872-9544.* www.elcozumeleno.com. *252 units. Rack rates: High season $280 double; low season $180–$220 double. AE, MC, V.*

Flamingo Hotel
$ **In town**

A small hotel just off Avenida Rafael Melgar, the Flamingo offers three stories of attractive, comfortable rooms around a small, plant-filled inner courtyard. Highlights include an inviting rooftop terrace and a comfortable bar/coffee bar that serves breakfast. Second- and third-story rooms, which have air-conditioning and TV, cost more. Rooms are large, with two double beds, white-tile floors, medium-size bathrooms, and ceiling fans. A penthouse suite comes with a full kitchen and sleeps up to six. The English-speaking staff is helpful and friendly. To find it, walk three blocks north on Melgar from the plaza and turn right on Calle 6; the hotel is on the left.

See map p. 189. Calle 6 Norte No. 81. ☎ *800-806-1601 in the U.S. or 987-872-1264 (also fax).* www.hotelflamingo.com. *22 units. Rack rates: High season $55–$77 double; low season $36–$45 double. AE, MC, V.*

Hotel del Centro
$ **In town**

Although this surprisingly stylish hotel is five long blocks from the waterfront, it's a bargain if you want a hotel with a pool. The rooms are small but modern, air-conditioned, and clean. They come with two double beds or one king (which costs $10 less). A small courtyard with an oval pool makes for a lovely place to relax. From the plaza, head straight down Juárez; when you get to Ave. 25, it's on your left.

See map p. 189. Av. Juárez 501. ☎ *987-872-5471. Fax: 987-872-0299. E-mail:* hcentro@cozumel.com.mz. *14 units. Rack rates: High season $60–$85 double; low season $45–$60 double. No credit cards.*

Occidental Grand Cozumel
$$$$ **South of town**

This property and its older sister, the Occidental Allegro Cozumel (both all-inclusive), are part of a chain with several hotels across the way, on the mainland, but these enjoy something the others don't: the placid water of Cozumel's protected coast. The older Allegro has a nicer beach and plenty of beach front, but the rooms aren't as large or attractive or comfortable as at the Grand, which is next door. Staying at the Grand allows you access to the Allegro, but not viceversa. Both hotels are in the mold of the village resort—instead of tall modern buildings, groupings of two- or three-story buildings are spread out over the property, with the pool and activities area in the center. A mix of families and couples, North Americans more than Europeans, make up most of the clientele. A quieter pool, which is a little removed from the main activities, enables you to enjoy some relative calm. Either hotel is a good choice for guests who want only to be on the beach, and perhaps do a little diving. Taking a taxi to town from here can be expensive; this hotel, and its sister are at the far southern end of the island. The hotel has three restaurants offering international food served on a buffet, and the two others (one Mexican, one Italian) are open only for dinner. You can also take advantage of a poolside snackbar for lunch. The rates listed below aren't really meaningful because more than 95% of the guests come here as part of a package.

See map p. 189. Carretera Costera Sur km 17 ☎ *800-858-2258 in the U.S. and Canada, or 987-872-9730. Fax: 987-872-9745.* www.occidentalhotels.com. *255 units. Rack rates: High season $290–$333 double; low season $240–$260 double. Rates include all food, beverages, and nonmotorized watersports equipment. AE, MC, V.*

Playa Azul Golf and Beach Hotel
$$$$ North of town

This quiet hotel is perhaps the most relaxing of the island's beachfront properties. It has a small beach with shade *palapas* (thatched roofs) that is one of the best on this side of the island. Service is attentive and personal. Almost all the rooms come with balconies and views of the ocean. The rooms in the original section are all suites — large suites with very large bathrooms painted in cool white and decorated with a taste for simplicity (no televisions). The new wing mostly has standard rooms that are comfortable and large and decorated with light tropical colors and furniture. All rooms come with either a king bed or two double beds; suites also offer two convertible single sofas in the separate living-room area. There's also a restaurant, two bars, a small pool, and a nearby golf course that guests can access. On the beach is a watersports-equipment rental pavilion, and a game room with pool table, TV, and videos is located above the lobby. This is an especially good hotel for golfers because guests receive unlimited golf privileges and don't pay greens fees.

See map p. 189. Carretera San Juan, km 4. ☎ *987-872-0199 or 987-872-0043. Fax: 987-872-0110.* www.playa-azul.com. *50 units. Free parking. Rack rates: High season $185 double, $220–$300 suite; low season $130 double, $160–$260 suite. AE, MC, V.*

Presidente InterContinental Cozumel
$$$$$ South of town

This hotel is Cozumel's finest in terms of location, quality of beachfront, on-site amenities, and service. Palatial in scale and modern in style, the Presidente spreads across a long stretch of coast with only distant hotels for neighbors. Rooms come in four categories — superior, deluxe, deluxe oceanfront, and deluxe beachfront — distributed among four buildings (two to five stories tall). Superior rooms come with a view of the garden; deluxe rooms come with a view of the ocean. Most deluxe and superior rooms are spacious with large, well-lit bathrooms. Deluxe oceanfront rooms (on the second floor) and beachfront rooms (at ground level, with direct access to the beach) are even larger and have spacious balconies or patios. Most rooms come with a choice of one king bed or two double beds and are furnished with an understated, modern taste. A long stretch of sandy beach dotted with palapas and palm trees fronts the entire hotel, as does a large pool, wading pool, and a dive shop/watersports-equipment rental booth. The hotel has two restaurants and a bar, plus 24-hour room service. A special in-room dining option with a serenading trio is available for beachfront rooms. Two lighted tennis courts, a fully equipped gym, and a moped-rental service for getting around the island are also on-site. A children's activities center makes this hotel a good choice for families.

See map p. 189. Costera Sur, km 6. ☎ **800-327-0200** *in the U.S., or 987-872-9500. Fax: 987-872-9528.* www.cozumel.intercontinental.com. *253 units. Free parking. Rack rates: High season $385–$730 double; low season $275–$675 double. Discounts and packages available. AE, DC, MC, V.*

Suites Colonial
$ **In town**

Around the corner from the main square, on a pedestrian-only street, you'll find this pleasant four-story hotel. Standard rooms, called "studios," are large and have large bathrooms and attractive red-tile floors, but could be better lit. They come with air-conditioning, a small fridge, and one double and one twin bed. The suites come with air-conditioning, too, and hold two double beds, a kitchenette, and a sitting and dining area. The hotel supplies free coffee and sweet bread in the morning. Note that the phone number listed also takes reservations for another hotel, Casa Mexicana (not reviewed in this book), so when you call, specify the Colonial.

See map p. 189. Av. 5 Sur 9. ☎ **987-872-9080.** *Fax: 987-872-9073.* www.casamexicana cozumel.com. *28 units. Rack rates: High season $65 studio, $75 suite; low season $50 studio, $58–$68 suite. Rates include continental breakfast. AE, MC, V.*

Dining in Cozumel

For such a small town on such a small island, Cozumel offers a wide variety of restaurants where you can choose from extensive menus. As in most Mexican beach resorts, even the finest restaurants are casual when it comes to dress. Men seldom wear jackets, although women are occasionally seen in dressier resort wear.

Taxi drivers may attempt to take you to restaurants that pay them commissions. They may tell you the restaurant you want to go to is closed or that the quality has declined. Taxi drivers aren't the only ones who do this. I strongly suspect that cruise ship staff steer their passengers toward certain restaurants because I always see them eating at the same places.

Tips run about 15%, and most wait-staff really depend on these tips for their income, so be generous if the service warrants. Please see Chapter 18 for more information on Mexican cuisine.

If you're in the mood for just a little bread or pastry to go with your coffee, try **Zermatt** (☎ 987-872-1384), a terrific little bakery on Avenida 5, at Calle 4 Norte (see the "San Miguel de Cozumel Map" on p. 189).

Casa Denis
$ **In town** YUCATECAN/MEXICAN

This yellow wooden house, one of the few remaining houses built in the old island style, is a great homestyle Mexican restaurant. Small tables are scattered outside on the pedestrian-only street. A few tables are in back, on the shady patio. You can make a light meal from empanadas filled with potatoes, cheese, or fish, or, try one of the Yucatecan specialties such as *pollo pibil, panuchos,* or *tacos de cochinita pibil.*

See map p. 189. Calle 1 Sur 267 (just off the main plaza). ☎ *987-872-0067. Reservations not accepted. Breakfast $3–$5; main courses $7–$11. No credit cards. Open: Mon–Sat 7 a.m.–11 p.m.; Sun 5–11 p.m.*

El Moro
$$ **In town** SEAFOOD/REGIONAL

El Moro is an out-of-the-way place, which has been around for a long time and has always been popular with the locals, who come for the food, the service, and the prices — but not the décor, which is orange, orange, orange, and Formica. Get there by taxi, which will only cost a couple of bucks. Portions are generous. Any of the shrimp dishes use the real jumbo variety when available. For something different, try the *Pollo Ticuleño,* a specialty from the town of Ticul, a layered dish of tomato sauce, mashed potatoes, crispy baked corn tortilla, and fried chicken breast, topped with shredded cheese and green peas. Other specialties include enchiladas and seafood prepared many ways, plus grilled steaks and sandwiches.

See map p. 189. 75 BIS Norte (between calles 2 and 4). ☎ *987-872-3029. Reservations not accepted. Main courses: $5–$15. MC, V. Open: Fri–Wed 1–11 p.m.*

French Quarter
$$$ **In town** LOUISIANA/SOUTHERN

In a pleasant upstairs open-air setting, the French Quarter serves Southern and Creole classics. The jambalaya and étouffée are delicious. The menu also lists such specialties as blackened fish, and the owner goes to great lengths to get the freshest lump crabmeat, which usually appears in one form or another as a daily special. The filet mignon with red-onion marmalade is a real charmer. The restaurant has an air-conditioned dining room and a bar area downstairs. The French Quarter is on Av. 5, one and a half blocks south of the town square.

See map p. 189. Av. 5 Sur 18. ☎ *987-872-6321. Reservations recommended in high season. Main courses $10–$27. AE, MC, V. Open: Daily 5–10 p.m.*

Jeanie's Waffle House
$ **In town   BREAKFAST/DESSERTS**

The specialty here is crisp, light waffles served in a variety of ways, including waffles *ranchero* with eggs and salsa, waffles Benedict with eggs and hollandaise sauce, and waffles with whipped cream and chocolate. Hash browns, homemade breads, and great coffee are other reasons to drop in for breakfast, which is served until 3 p.m.

See map p. 189. Av. Rafael Melgar between calles 5 and 7 Sur. ☎ *987-872-4145. Reservations not accepted. Breakfast: $4–$7. No credit cards. Open: Mon–Sat 6 a.m.–9 p.m.; Sun 6 a.m. to noon.*

La Choza
$$ **In town   YUCATECAN/MEXICAN**

Local residents consider this one of the best Mexican restaurants in town. Platters of poblano chiles stuffed with shrimp, *mole poblano,* and *pollo en relleno negro* (chicken stuffed with a preparation of scorched chilies) are among the specialties. The table sauces and guacamole are great, and the daily specials are a good bet. This open-air restaurant has well-spaced tables under a tall thatched roof. From the ferry pier, walk two blocks inland on Juárez, turn right on Av. 10, and walk another two blocks. The restaurant is on the corner.

See map p. 189. Rosado Salas 198 (at Av. 10 Sur). ☎ *987-872-0958. Reservations not accepted. Breakfast $4; main courses $9–$15. AE, MC, V. Open: Daily 7:30 a.m.–11 p.m.*

Lobster House (Cabaña del Pescador)
$$$$ **North of town   LOBSTER**

The thought I often have when I eat a prepared lobster dish is that the cook could simply have boiled the lobster to better effect. The owner of this restaurant seems to agree. The only item on the menu is lobster boiled with a hint of spices and served with melted butter, accompanied by sides of rice, vegetables, and bread. The weight of the lobster tail you select determines the price, with side dishes included. The glow of candles and soft lights amidst dark woodwork creates intimate spaces in the cozy dining rooms, which are bordered by gardens, fountains, and a small duck pond. The owner, Fernando, will even send you next door to his brother's excellent Mexican seafood restaurant, El Guacamayo, if you must have something other than lobster.

See map p. 189. Carretera Santa Pilar, km 4 (across from Playa Azul Hotel). No phone. Reservations not accepted. Main courses: $19–$30, lobsters sold by weight. No credit cards. Open: Daily 6–10:30 p.m.

Pepe's Grill
$$$ In town STEAKS/SEAFOOD

The chefs at Pepe's were the first on the island (and up and down the mainland coast) to popularize grilled food. They seem fascinated with fire; what they don't grill in the kitchen, they flambé at your table. The most popular items are the prime rib, filet mignon, and lobster. For something out of the ordinary, try the shrimp Bahamas, which is shrimp flambéed with a little banana and pineapple in a curry sauce with a hint of white wine. Pepe's is a second-story restaurant with one large air-conditioned dining room under a massive beamed ceiling. The lighting is soft, and a guitar trio plays background music. Large windows look out over the town's harbor. The children's menu offers breaded shrimp and broiled chicken. For dessert, Pepe's offers a few more flaming specialties: bananas Foster, crêpes suzette, and café Maya (coffee, vanilla ice cream, and three liquors).

See map p. 189. Av. Rafael Melgar at Calle Rosado Salas. ☎ *987-872-0213. Reservations recommended. Main courses: $18–$35; children's menu $7. AE, MC, V. Open: Daily 5–11:30 p.m.*

Prima
$$ In town NORTHERN ITALIAN

Everything at this popular dinner hangout is fresh — the pastas, vegetables, and seafood. Owner Albert Domínguez grows most of the vegetables in his local hydroponic garden. The menu changes daily and specializes in northern Italian seafood dishes. It may include shrimp scampi, fettuccine with pesto, or lobster and crab ravioli with cream sauce. The fettuccine Alfredo is wonderful, the salads are crisp, and the steaks are USDA choice. Pizzas are cooked in a wood-burning oven. Desserts include Key lime pie and tiramisu. Dining is upstairs on the breezy terrace.

See map p. 189. Calle Rosado Salas No. 109A (corner with Av. 5) ☎ *987-872-4242. Reservations recommended. Pizzas: $6–$14; pastas $8–$12; seafood $10–$20; steaks $15–$20. AE, MC, V. Open: Daily 5–11 p.m.*

Restaurant del Museo
$ In town AMERICAN/MEXICAN

The most pleasant place in San Miguel to have breakfast or lunch (weather permitting) is at this rooftop cafe above the island's museum. It offers a serene view of the water, removed from the traffic noise below and sheltered from the sun above. The tables and chairs are comfortable and the food reliable. Your choices are limited to the mainstays of American and Mexican breakfast and lunch dishes such as eggs and bacon, huevos à la mexicana, sandwiches, enchiladas, and guacamole — all well prepared with a slight Mexican accent. It's three blocks north of the ferry pier. *See map p. 189. Av. Rafael Melgar (corner of Calle 6).* ☎ *987-872-0838. Breakfast $4–$5; lunch main courses $5–$9. No credit cards. Open: Daily 7 a.m.–2 p.m.*

Having Fun on the Beach and in the Water

For **diving and snorkeling,** you have plenty of dive shops to choose from, including those recommended in this section. For **island tours, ruins tours** on and off the island, **glass-bottom boat tours, fiesta nights, fishing,** and other activities, go to a travel agency such as **InterMar Cozumel Viajes,** Calle 2 Norte 101-B, between avenidas 5 and 10 (☎ 987-872-1535; fax: 987-872-0895; e-mail: cozumel@travel2mexico.com). It's not far from the main plaza.

One of the advantages of vacationing in Cozumel is that you can indulge in a true island experience and still be just a short hop from mainland Mexico and some of its remarkable sites. **Playa del Carmen** on the mainland is a convenient 45-minute ferry ride away. Travel agencies on the island can set you up with a tour to see the major ruins on the mainland, such as **Tulum** or **Chichén-Itzá,** or one of the nature parks such as **Xel-Ha** and **Xcaret** (check out Chapter 14).

Cozumel also has its own ruins, but they can't compare with the major sites on the mainland. Some believe that during pre-Hispanic times, each Mayan woman traveled the 12 miles by boat to the island at least once in her life to worship the goddess of fertility, Ixchel. More than 40 sites containing shrines remain around the island today, and archaeologists still uncover the small dolls that were customarily offered in the fertility ceremony.

Scoring quality beach time

Although most of Cozumel's shoreline is rocky, the island has some nice beaches. The beaches here have advantages over the mainland because the island's western shore is protected — you get the optimum combination of placid water without the seaweed that you find in the sheltered areas along the mainland. On the unprotected eastern shore, the water is rougher and not suitable for swimming; however, if you only want to catch some rays and avoid the crowds, you're likely to have some of the eastern shore's small beaches and coves all to yourself. This side of the island sees few people except on Sundays, when the locals have picnics here.

One of the most popular attractions is the **Chankanaab National Park,** which is about 5 miles south of town. It has a great beach with beach chairs and a beautiful small inland lagoon. It's a great place if you don't mind crowds, which usually arrive late in the morning from the cruise ships. This is why it's best to get there early. Admission to the park is

$10, and it's open from 8 a.m. to 5 p.m. daily. Taxis charge $9 for up to four people for the ride. For more details see the upcoming section "Visiting the nature parks."

Along both the east and the west coasts are signs advertising this or that beach club. A "beach club" in Cozumel usually means a *palapa* (thatched roof) hut open to the public serving soft drinks, beer, and fried fish. In the last five years or so they've become more elaborate. Some beach clubs now rent water gear, have pools and locker rooms, and even offer motorized watersports, such as banana boats and para-sailing. The two biggest of these are **Mr. Sancho's** (☎ 987-879-0021; www. mrsanchos.com) and **Playa Mia** (☎ 987-872-9030; www.playamia.com). These do lots of business with the cruise ship passengers and can be crowded on days when several cruise ships dock on the island. Quieter versions of beach clubs are **Nachi Cocom** (no phone), **Playa San Francisco** (no phone), and **Playa Palancar** (no phone). These three beach clubs are south of Chankanaab Park, and don't get all the cruise ship crowds that the two closer ones do. They are easily visible from the road. Each offers a swimming pool with beach furniture, a restaurant, and snorkel rental. The quality of the beaches is excellent. Admission for Mr. Sancho's is free; Playa Mia ranges from $12 for the basic package to $42 for the most all-inclusive package, with a couple of half packages in between. Nachi Cocom is $10; the other two cost around $5.

Beach clubs in the original, more basic, style include **Paradise Cafe** on the southern tip of the island across from Punta Sur Nature Park and **Playa Bonita, Chen Rio,** and **Punta Morena** on the eastern side.

At the very tip of the island, you can find a very lonely beach at the **Punta Sur Ecological Reserve.** This place charges $10 and has activities you may enjoy; for more details see the upcoming section "Visiting the nature parks."

Going deep: Scuba diving

Cozumel is the *numero uno* dive destination in the Western Hemisphere. Don't forget to bring your dive card and dive log. The dive shops on the island rent scuba gear, but they won't take you out on the boat until they see some documentation. If you have a medical condition, bring a letter signed by a doctor stating that you're cleared to dive. A two-tank, morning dive costs around $60; some shops are now offering an additional one-tank, afternoon dive for $10 for folks who took the morning dives. A lot of divers save money by buying a hotel and dive package with or without air transportation and food. These packages usually include two dives a day with the standard day off at the end.

 Diving in Cozumel is drift diving, which can be a little disconcerting for novices. The current that sweeps along Cozumel's reefs, pulling nutrients into them and making them as large as they are, also dictates how you dive here. The problem is that it pulls at different speeds at different depths and in different places. When it's pulling strong, it can quickly scatter a dive group, which is why you need a dive master experienced with the local conditions who can pick the best place for diving, given the current conditions.

Fortunately, Cozumel has a lot of reefs to choose from. Here are just a few:

- ✔ **Palancar Reef:** Famous for its caves and canyons, plentiful fish, and a wide variety of sea coral

- ✔ **Santa Rosa Wall:** Monstrous reef famous for its depth, sea life, coral, and sponges

- ✔ **San Francisco Reef:** Features a shallower drop-off wall than many reefs and fascinating sea life

- ✔ **Yucab Reef:** Highlights include beautiful coral

Finding a dive shop in town is easy: At least 50 operators are on the island. Two that I can recommend are the following: Bill Horn's **Aqua Safari,** on Avenida Rafael Melgar at Calle 5 (☎ 987-872-0101; fax: 987-872-0661; www.aquasafari.com), which is a PADI five-star instructor center. I also recommend **Dive House,** on the main plaza (☎ 987-872-1953; fax: 987-872-0368), which offers PADI, NAUI, and SSI instruction.

 Underwater Yucatán offers two twists on diving — *cenote* diving and snorkeling. On the mainland, the peninsula's underground *cenotes* (say-*noh*-tehs), or sinkholes, which were sacred to the Maya, lead to a vast system of underground caverns. Here, the gently flowing water is so clear that divers appear to be floating on air through the *cenotes* and caves that look just like those on dry land, complete with stalactites and stalagmites.

The experienced cave divers of **Yucatech Expeditions** (☎ 987-872-5659 (also fax); e-mail: yucatech@cozumel.czm.com.mx) offer a trip five times a week. *Cenotes* are 30 to 45 minutes from Playa del Carmen, and a dive in each *cenote* lasts around 45 minutes. (Divers usually do two or three.) Dives are within the daylight zone, about 130 feet into the caverns and no more than 60 feet deep. Company owner Germán Yañez Mendoza inspects diving credentials carefully, and divers must meet his list of requirements before cave diving is permitted. He also offers the equivalent of a resort course in cave diving and a full cave-diving course. For information and prices, call or drop by the office at Avenida 15 No. 144, between Calle 1 Sur and Rosado Salas. Several other *cenote* dive operators on the mainland are closer to the *cenotes*, especially in Akumal and near Tulum.

Enjoying snorkeling

Anyone who can swim can snorkel. Rental of the snorkel (breathing tube), goggles, and flippers should cost only about $5 to $10 for half a day, and you can probably have a good time snorkeling in front of the hotel. But what's more fun is to take a trip to snorkel Paradise Reef and a couple of other good locations. When contracting for a snorkel tour, stay away from the companies that cater to the cruise ships. Those tours are crowded and not very fun. For a good snorkeling tour, you can contact Victor Casanova (☎ 987-872-1028; e-mail: wildcatcozumel@hotmail.com). He speaks English, owns a couple of boats and does a good 5-hour tour. He takes his time and doesn't rush through the trip. Another operator that specializes in snorkeling trips is the **Kuzamil Snorkeling Center** (☎ 987-872-4637 or 987-872-0539). It's located at the far end of town at Av. 50. bis 565 Int. 1, between 5 Sur and Hidalgo, Colonia Adolfo López Matéos. It's better to make arrangements over the phone or through a local travel agency rather than visiting the office. A full-day snorkel trip costs $65 per person; $50 for children younger than 12. Half-day trips are $40 for adults and $30 for children. The price includes the boat, the guide, a buffet lunch, and snorkel equipment.

Visiting the nature parks

Chankanaab National Park is the pride of many island residents. Chankanaab means "little sea," which refers to a beautiful land-locked pool connected to the sea through an underground tunnel — a sort of miniature ocean. Snorkeling in this natural aquarium is not permitted, but the park has a lovely beach for sunbathing and good snorkeling just a few yards off shore. Arrive early to stake out a chair and palapa before the cruise-ship crowd arrives. Likewise, the snorkeling is best before noon. You can also watch a sea lion show for $5 per person; it uses rescued sea lions that had been captured illegally. Tickets are available through any travel agency in town. And don't miss the scarlet macaws, beautiful birds that were confiscated from captors and are part of a reproduction-and-release program. The park has bathrooms, lockers, a gift shop, several snack huts, a restaurant, and a palapa for renting snorkeling gear.

Surrounding the lagoon is a botanical garden with shady paths and 351 species of tropical and subtropical plants from 22 countries, as well as 451 species from Cozumel. Several Maya structures have been re-created within the gardens to give visitors an idea of Maya life in a jungle setting. The park has a small natural history museum as well. Admission to the park costs $10. Hours are 8 a.m. to 5 p.m. daily. Taxis are always available.

Punta Sur Ecological Reserve (admission $10) is a large area encompassing the southern tip of the island, including the large Columbia Lagoon. The only practical way of going there is to rent a car or scooter; there is no taxi stand, and, usually, few people. This area is an ecological reserve, not a park, so don't expect much infrastructure. The reserve has an information center, several observation towers, and a snack bar. In addition, guides point out things of interest about the habitat on the four boat rides per day around the Colombia Lagoon (bring bug spray). Punta Sur has some interesting snorkeling (bring your own gear) and lovely beaches kept as natural as possible. Regular hours are 9 a.m. to 5 p.m. A special program (☎ 987-872-2940 for info) allows visitors to observe turtle nests in season, and you can participate as a volunteer in the evenings during the nesting season.

Cruising the seas

Travel agencies and hotels can arrange boat trips, a popular pastime on Cozumel. Your options include evening cruises, cocktail cruises, glass-bottom boats, and more. Do inquire whether the trip will be filled with cruise-ship passengers, because trips that cater to the cruise-ship crowds can be packed. Tour operators are usually pretty open about this subject, but you may want to double-check. Departures before 10 a.m. are a good bet if you prefer smaller crowds.

One rather novel boat trip is a ride in a submarine, offered by **Atlantis Submarines** (☎ 987-872-5671). The sub can hold 48 people. It operates almost 3 kilometers (2 miles) south of town in front of the Casa del Mar hotel and costs $81 per adult; $42 for kids. Call ahead or inquire at one of the travel agencies in town. This submarine ride is a far superior experience to the **Sub See Explorer** offered by **Aqua World,** which is really a glorified glass-bottom boat. To inquire into any of these cruises go to a travel agency such as **InterMar Cozumel Viajes** (Calle 2 Norte, No. 101-B, between avenidas 5 and 10; ☎ 987-872-1535; fax: 987-872-0895; e-mail: intermar@cozumel.com.mx). The agency isn't far from the main plaza.

Catching the big one

The best months for fishing offshore Cozumel are from April to September, when the catch includes blue and white marlin, sailfish, tarpon, swordfish, *dorado,* wahoo, tuna, and red snapper. Fishing excursions costs $450 for six people for the whole day, or $80 to $85 per person for four people for a half day. One travel agency that specializes in fishing (deep-sea and fly-fishing) is **Aquarius Travel Fishing** (Calle 3 Sur No. 2, between Avenida Rafael Melgar and Avenida 5; ☎ 987-872-1092; e-mail: gabdiaz@yahoo.com).

Swimming with dolphins

Dolphin Discovery offers visitors the experience of swimming with dolphins with several different programs. It's located inside the **Chankanaab National Park.** You'll need to make reservations well in advance. Contact Dolphin Discovery (☎ 998-849-4757 in Cancún; www.dolphindiscovery.com) for information and reservations. But, if you're already in Cozumel, you can try by calling ☎ 987-872-9702. The most extensive encounter with the dolphins is the dolphin swim, which costs $119 and features close interaction with these beautiful swimmers. You can combine your swim with the other activities that the park offers. See above for details.

Keeping Your Feet on Dry Land

If you want some time off from all the strenuous sunbathing and paddling around the pool, Cozumel offers a number of activities to interest you. Some local Maya ruins make for a short, pleasant outing, or you can do a day-trip to one of the major Maya sites on the mainland. Several companies offer bus tours to places like Chichén Itzá or Tulum. Or how about a round of golf? Or perhaps some shopping. The following sections offer a few ideas to keep you busy.

Hitting the links

Cozumel has a new 18-hole course designed by Jack Nicklaus. It's at the **Cozumel Country Club** (☎ 987-872-9570), just north of San Miguel. Greens fees are $149, including tax. You can reserve tee times three days in advance. A few hotels have special memberships with discounts for guests and advance tee times, especially Hotel Playa Azul and El Cid La Ceiba (both hotels are reviewed in the "Checking out Cozumel's best hotels" section earlier in this chapter).

Seeing the sites

Companies offer a couple of tours of the island, but to be frank, the best part of Cozumel isn't on land; it's what's in the water. If you're starting to look like a prune from all the time in the water or you simply want to try something different, travel agencies can book you on a group tour of the island for around $40. Prices vary a bit depending on whether the tour includes lunch and a stop for snorkeling and swimming at Chankanaab Park. If you're only interested in Chankanaab, go by yourself and save money. Taxi drivers charge $60 for four-hour tours of the island, which most people would consider only mildly amusing depending on the personality of the taxi driver.

Exploring Maya ruins on Cozumel

One of the most popular island excursions is to **San Gervasio** (100 B.C.– A.D. 1600). Follow the paved transversal road. You see the well-marked turn-off about halfway between town and the eastern coast. Stop at the entrance gate and pay the $1 road-use fee. Go straight ahead over the pothole-laden road to the ruins (about 3 kilometers or 2 miles farther) and pay the $5 fee to enter; still and video camera permits cost $5 each. A small tourist center at the entrance sells cold drinks and snacks.

"Jungle" tours a dubious choice

One ranch south of town contracts with the local travel agencies to offer visitors a four-hour horseback tour of the island's interior jungle during which you see some very minor ruins and are told a few things about the fauna of the island. Even in the best of times, this ride can't be called spectacular. Most of the terrain is flat, and the jungle is more scrublike than the term *jungle* indicates. The same can be said for some "jungle Jeep tours" and "jungle ATV tours." If you're interested in any of these ho-hum trips, look up the folks at the InterMar Cozumel Viajes travel agency. (See the listing under the "Cruising the seas" section, earlier in this chapter.)

When it comes to Cozumel's Maya remains, getting there is most of the fun — do it for the mystique and for the trip, not for the size or scale of the ruins. The buildings, though preserved, are crudely made and would not be much of an attraction if they were not the island's principal ruins. More significant than beautiful, this site was once an important ceremonial center where the Maya gathered, coming even from the mainland. The important deity was Ixchel, the goddess of weaving, women, childbirth, pilgrims, the moon, and medicine. Ixchel was the wife of Itzamná, the sun god, and as such, preeminent among all Maya gods.

Tour guides charge $10 for a tour for one to six people. A better option is to find a copy of the green booklet *San Gervasio,* sold at local checkout counters or bookstores, and tour the site on your own. Seeing it takes 30 minutes. Taxi drivers offer a tour to the ruins for about $25; the driver will wait for you outside the ruins.

Day-tripping off to the mainland

Going to the nearby seaside village of **Playa del Carmen** and the **Xcaret** nature park on your own is as easy as a quick ferry ride from Cozumel. (For more details on Playa del Carmen and Xcaret, see Chapter 14.) Cozumel travel agencies offer an Xcaret tour that includes the ferry fee, transportation to the park, and the park admission fee for $100 for adults, $60 for children. Given what the package includes, this price is reasonable.

Travel agencies can also arrange day-trips to the fascinating ruins of **Chichén-Itzá** either by air or by bus. The ruins of **Tulum,** overlooking the Caribbean, and **Cobá,** in a dense jungle setting, are closer to Cozumel, so they cost less to visit. Trips to Cobá and Tulum begin at 8 a.m. and return around 6 p.m. For more information on these sites, check out Chapter 15.

Looking at the island's natural history

In town, fronting the water, is a small museum, **Museo de la Isla de Cozumel,** (see the "San Miguel de Cozumel Map" on p. 189) on Avenida Rafael Melgar between calles 4 and 6 Norte (☎ 987-872-1475). It's more than just a nice place to spend a rainy hour. The first floor of the museum has an excellent exhibit displaying endangered species in the area, the origin of the island, and its present-day topography and plant and animal life, including an explanation of coral formation. The second-floor galleries feature the history of the town, artifacts from the island's pre-Hispanic sites, and colonial-era relics like cannons, swords, and ship paraphernalia. The museum is open daily from 9 a.m. to 6 p.m. Admission is $3; guided tours in English are free. A rooftop restaurant serves breakfast and lunch.

Shopping in Cozumel

If you like shopping for silver jewelry, you can spend a great deal of time examining the wares of all the jewelers along Melgar who cater to cruise-ship shoppers. Numerous duty-free stores sell items such as perfumes and designer wares. If you're interested in Mexican folk art, a number of stores now display a wide variety of interesting pieces. Check out the following shops, all of which are on Avenida Melgar (with the exception of Sante Fe): **Los Cinco Soles** (☎ 987-872-2040); **Indigo** (☎ 987-872-1076); and **Viva Mexico** (☎ 987-872-5466). Some import/ export stores can be found in the new Punta Langosta Shopping Center in the southern part of town in front of the Punta Langosta Pier.

Enjoying Cozumel's Nightlife

Most of the music and dance venues are in two areas: one is just north of the main plaza on Rafael Melgar, and includes the **Hard Rock Cafe** (☎ 987-872-5271); the other is in the Punta Langosta shopping center, in front of the pier of the same name, not far from Hotel Plaza Las Glorias. Here you'll find **Carlos 'n' Charlie's** (☎ 987-869-1646) and **Señor Frog's** (☎ 987-869-1651). At the corner of Rosado Salas and Av. 5 sur (across from Prima) is a new nightclub called **La Pura Vida** (☎ 987-878-7831) that offers live salsa music (from a good Cuban band) Wednesday to Sunday with no cover and no minimum. It also offers free salsa dance lessons early in the evening. On Sunday evenings the place to be is the main square, which usually has a free concert and lots of people strolling about and visiting with friends. People sit in outdoor cafes enjoying the cool night breezes until the restaurants close.

Part V
Exploring the Yucatán

SHELLING ON MEXICO'S YUCATÁN COAST

© RICHTENNANT

"Oooo! Back up Robert. There must be a half dozen Lightening Whelks here."

In this part . . .

*I*f you want to leave the hustle and bustle of Cancún behind, you've come to the right place. Chapter 14 covers the stretch of coastline called the Riviera Maya, named for the yin-and-yang combination of luxurious modern resorts and ancient Maya ruins found throughout the region. From funky beach towns like Playa del Carmen to ecotheme parks like Tres Ríos to the get-away-from-it-all cabañas at Tulum, the Riviera Maya is where you can take a deep breath and absorb the essence of warm-weather Mexico.

This neck of the Yucatán Peninsula is also home to some of Mexico's most spectacular ruins, where pyramids, statues, and mysterious carvings provide tantalizing clues to ancient civilizations. In Chapter 15, we introduce you to the most impressive and easily accessible of these sites.

Chapter 14

Playa del Carmen and the Riviera Maya

. . . .

In This Chapter

▶ Chilling out in funky Playa del Carmen
▶ Searching out the best snorkeling and scuba diving
▶ Beach-bumming along the coast
▶ Enjoying the area's many eco-parks

. . . .

The Riviera Maya is a stretch of the Yucatán's Caribbean coast from just south of Cancún to the town of Tulum. It's a beautiful coastline that harbors a mix of "eco-parks," small resort towns, and all-inclusive resorts. A reef system protects this coast and offers many snorkeling and diving opportunities. Where gaps appear in the reef, you find good beaches — mainly at Playa del Carmen (the major town on the coast), Xpu-ha, and Tulum. The action of the surf washes away silt and seagrass and erodes rocks, leaving a sandy bottom. Where the reef is prominent, you can expect good snorkeling just offshore with lots of fish and other sea creatures. And this increasingly popular stretch of coastline bustles with development; every month it seems another new resort has opened somewhere along the coast.

Exploring the Riviera Maya Region

The Riviera Maya is an easy region to navigate. A single highway connects all the towns of the coast. From Cancún to Playa del Carmen it's a four-lane divided road, and from Playa to Tulum it's a wide, two-lane road with good shoulders. Although bus service is plentiful, I prefer to rent a car and set my own schedule. (For more on seeing the region by rental car, see the "The Riviera Maya" section later in this chapter.) Here's a brief rundown of the best towns and attractions:

✔ **Playa del Carmen:** Playa (as locals call it) is a small town on one of the best stretches of beach. It's perfect for enjoying the simple (and perhaps the best) pleasures of a seaside vacation — taking in the sun and the sea air while working your toes into soft, white sand; cooling down with a swim in clear blue water; and strolling leisurely and aimlessly down the beach while listening to the wash of waves and feeling the light touch of tropical breezes on your skin.

✔ **Puerto Morelos:** So far, this town located 30 minutes south of Cancún has remained a sleepy little village with a few small hotels and rental houses. Locals refer to it as "Muerto Morelos" (Dead Morelos) during the off-season for the lack of activity. It's a short distance from the bustle of Cancún and Playa del Carmen and can be considered a convenient escape from the crowds, perfect for a relaxed vacation of lying about the beach and reading a book (with perhaps the occasional foray into a watersport or two). The coast is sandy and well protected by an offshore reef, which means good snorkeling and diving nearby, but some seagrass on the beach and in the water.

✔ **Tres Ríos:** A few miles before you get to Playa, you see signs for this eco-park. This natural reserve has 150 acres where you can ride horseback, paddle a canoe or kayak, bike along jungle trails, or just hang out at the beach. This eco-park is the least developed of the three on this coast.

✔ **Xcaret:** Just south of Playa del Carmen is this large eco-park that draws people, mostly families from Cancún, Cozumel, and all points along this coast. Highlights include floating through an underground river (not for everybody), nightly shows, and lots of seaside activities.

✔ **Xpu-ha:** You won't find anything to see here but a long, wide stretch of perfect sandy beach. You can elect to stay here or stay elsewhere and make a day-trip out of it.

✔ **Akumal:** This small, modern, and ecologically oriented community is built on the shores of two beautiful bays — Akumal and Half-Moon Bay. This community has been around long enough that it feels more relaxed than other places on the coast that are booming, such as Playa and Tulum. A lot of families vacation here.

✔ **Xel-ha:** A large, well-protected lagoon is the centerpiece for this lovely eco-park. It attracts crowds of snorkelers who come to view the fish in the calm, clear waters. The park also offers dolphin swims and a small grouping of ruins.

✔ **Tulum:** The town of Tulum (82 miles from Cancún and close by the ruins of the same name) has a hotel district of about 30 *palapa* (thatched roof) hotels, stretching down a beautiful beach. The town itself has a half-dozen restaurants, a bank, and three cybercafes A few years ago, Tulum was mainly a destination for backpacker types, but with some of the most beautiful beaches on this coast and many improvements in hotel amenities, it's attracting a greater variety of visitors. Construction is booming, both in the town and along the coast. But you can enjoy the beach here in relative solitude and quiet (unless your hotel is busy building additional rooms). Of course, the flip side of peace and quiet is that Tulum doesn't have the variety of restaurants that Playa and Cancún do.

The Riviera Maya Region

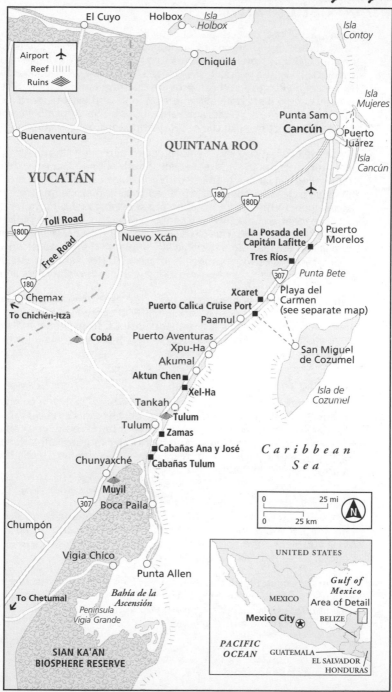

Playa del Carmen

Playa started out attracting a lot of ex-hippie types who weren't interested in the mass tourism of Cancún. Many settled into the village building small, simple hotels and shops to supply the needs of like-minded travelers. Over the years, it has changed, and though no longer having the feel of a village, it still can provide that rare combination of simplicity (you can go just about anywhere on foot) and variety (with its many one-of-a-kind hotels, restaurants, and shops). This appealing combination sets it apart from all the other destinations on this coast.

If solitude is what you're seeking, go elsewhere. Playa now draws crowds of visitors with its lively street scene. South of town is a large development called Playacar, complete with golf course and a dozen large, all-inclusive hotels. Farther south is a cruise-ship pier. People from both places come to the town's beaches and shopping areas. Playa has a casual feel. The local architecture has adopted elements of native building — rustic clapboard walls, thatched roofs, lots of tropical foliage, irregular shapes and angles, and a ramshackle, unplanned look. All these features reflect its toned-down approach to tourism. In the last few years, though, slicker architecture has appeared along with chain restaurants and stores.

A strong European influence has made topless sunbathing (nominally against the law in Mexico) a nonchalantly accepted practice anywhere there's a beach. The beach grows and shrinks, from broad and sandy to narrow with occasional rocks, depending on the currents and wind. Even on a bad-weather day, it's a beauty.

Settling into Playa

Playa is one of those places that's easy to enjoy. Once you've reached the end of the chain of taxis, airplanes, buses, and rental cars that it took to bring you here, and you're finally in your hotel room, you can simply switch to autopilot. Nothing could be simpler or more effortless than settling into this town and enjoying what it has to offer. Here's the skinny on how to arrive in Playa.

Getting from the Cancún airport to Playa

For getting through customs and such at the Cancún airport, see Chapter 9. If you're **driving,** follow the signs as you exit the airport. It feeds you right on to Hwy. 307 (head south, or you're going to end up in Cancún). The ride takes about 40 minutes.

As you approach Playa, the highway divides, and two extra lanes are added in each direction. Stay in the left lane; you're able to make a left turn at either of two traffic lights. If you don't stay left, you have to keep going until you find a turn-around.

Playa del Carmen

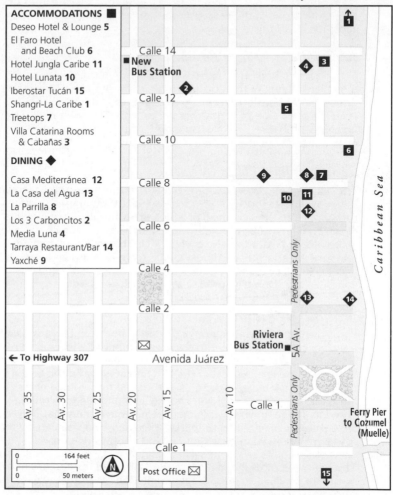

ACCOMMODATIONS ■

Deseo Hotel & Lounge **5**
El Faro Hotel
    and Beach Club **6**
Hotel Jungla Caribe **11**
Hotel Lunata **10**
Iberostar Tucán **15**
Shangri-La Caribe **1**
Treetops **7**
Villa Catarina Rooms
    & Cabañas **3**

DINING ◆

Casa Mediterránea **12**
La Casa del Agua **13**
La Parrilla **8**
Los 3 Carboncitos **2**
Media Luna **4**
Tarraya Restaurant/Bar **14**
Yaxché **9**

■ New
Bus Station

Calle 14
Calle 12
Calle 10
Calle 8
Calle 6
Calle 4
Calle 2

Riviera
Bus Station■

⊠

← To Highway 307   Avenida Juárez

Av. 35   Av. 30   Av. 25   Av. 20   Av. 15   Av. 10   Calle 1

Calle 1

5A Av.

Pedestrians Only

Caribbean Sea

Ferry Pier
to Cozumel
(Muelle)

0 ——— 164 feet
0 ——— 50 meters

Post Office ⊠

Calle 1

The first traffic light is Avenida Constituyentes, which you want to take for destinations in northern Playa. The second is Avenida Juárez, the artery that connects the highway to the town's main square and ferry pier.

A company called **Autobuses Riviera** offers **bus** service from the Cancún airport about 12 times a day. Cost is $8 one-way. **Taxi** fares from the Cancún airport are high — about $70 one-way. Playa has two **bus** stations. Buses coming from Cancún and places along the coast, such as Tulum, arrive at the Riviera station, at the corner of Juárez and Avenida 5, by the town square. Buses coming from destinations in the interior of the peninsula arrive at the new ADO station, on Avenida 20 between 12th and 14th streets.

Taking the ferry from Cozumel

A much less common route to Playa is through the Cozumel airport and then transferring to the Cozumel ferry. (See Chapter 13 for schedules, prices, and other details.) The passenger-ferry dock in Playa is 1½ blocks from the main square and within walking distance of hotels. **Tricycle taxis** meet the ferry and can transport your luggage to any central hotel or to a taxi if your destination is farther away.

Getting around Playa

The main street, **Avenida Juárez,** leads to the *zócalo* (town square) from Highway 307. As it does so, it crosses several numbered avenues that run parallel to the beach, all of which are multiples of 5. Avenida 5 is closest to the beach; it's closed to traffic from the zócalo to Calle 6 (and some blocks beyond, in the evening). On this avenue are many hotels, restaurants, and shops. Almost all the town is north and west of the zócalo. South of the ferry pier is the Playacar development, with a golf course, a small airstrip, private residences, and large resort hotels.

Staying in Playa

For grown-ups, staying in one of the small hotels in Playa is usually more fun than staying in one of the growing number of all-inclusive resorts along this coast. Don't hesitate to stay in a place that's not on the beach. Town life here is a big part of the fun, and staying on the beach in Playa has its disadvantages — the noise produced by a couple of the beachside bars, for one thing. And if you choose accommodations off of the beach, you don't have to worry about not being able to find that perfect strip of sand. Beaches are public property in Mexico, and you can lay out your towel anywhere you like without anyone bothering you.

The following rates listed include the 12% hotel tax and assume double occupancy. High-season rates generally don't include the week between Christmas and New Year's, when rates go still higher.

Deseo Hotel + Lounge
$$$ **Playa del Carmen**

This is the hippest, coolest place in town these days. It's all about making the scene, and the lounge plays the central role, serving all the functions of lobby, restaurant, bar, and pool area. It is a raised open-air platform with bar, pool, and self-serve kitchen. You'll find large daybeds for sunning or for enjoying an evening drink when the bar is in full swing. The clientele is predominantly 25- to 45-year-olds, and the music is contemporary. The rooms face two sides of the lounge. They are comfortable, original, and striking. Unlike the usual plush hotel room, they try to get you to go out and socialize; there's no TV, no minibar, and no cushy armchair to tempt you to vegetate. Their simplicity gives them an almost oriental feel, heightened by nice touches such as sliding doors of wood and frosted glass. The mattresses, however, are thick and luxurious. All rooms have king beds. From the bottom of each bed, a little drawer slides out with a night kit containing three things: incense, earplugs, and condoms.

Av. 5 (at Calle 12). ☎ *984-879-3620. Fax: 984-879-3621.* www.hoteldeseo.com. *15 units. Rack rates: High season $190–$220 double, $255 suite; low season $180–$200 double, $240 suite. AE, MC, V.*

El Faro Hotel and Beach Club
$$$$ **Playa del Carmen**

The hotel fronts 75 meters of sandy beach in the middle of Playa del Carmen. Its grounds are graced by tall palms and manicured gardens. A stunning pool (heated in winter) has islands of palms inside and is bordered by cushioned lounges and a *palapa* bar. The rooms, most of which are in two-story buildings with white-and-cream stucco exteriors, have clay-tile floors, ceiling fans, and marble bathrooms. They hold one king, one queen, or two double beds. Most have a large balcony or terrace. Rates vary according to the dominant view — garden, sea, or beachfront — the size of the room, and the time of year. Some new suites and a spa were added to the hotel this year. The rates below are for all of the year except December, when they run 50% higher.

See map p. 215. Calle 10 Norte. ☎ *888-243-7413 from the U.S., or 984-873-0970. Fax: 984-873-0968.* www.hotelelfaro.com. *34 units. Limited free guarded parking. Rack rates: $200–$250 double; $275 and up for suites. Rates include full breakfast. AE, MC, V.*

Hotel Jungla Caribe
$$ **Playa del Carmen**

Located right in the heart of the Avenida 5 action, "La Jungla" is an imaginative place, with a highly stylized look that mixes neoclassical with Robinson Crusoe. Its character is perfectly in keeping with the quirkiness of the town. Owner Rolf Albrecht envisioned space and comfort for guests, so all but eight of the standard rooms are large, with gray-and-black marble floors, the occasional Roman column, and large bathrooms. Fifteen of the rooms are suites. Catwalks connect the "tower" section of suites to the hotel. There's an attractive pool in the courtyard beneath a giant *Ramón* tree. Eight small rooms lack air-conditioning and are priced lower than the rates listed here.

See map p. 215. Av. 5 Norte at Calle 8. ☎ *984-873-0650 (also fax).* www.jungla caribe.com. *25 units. Rack rates: High season $80 double, $100–$115 suite; low season $45 double, $60–$70 suite. AE, MC, V.*

Hotel Lunata
$$ **Playa del Carmen**

The Lunata offers a combination of location, comfort, attractiveness, and price that no other hotel in this category can beat. It's built in hacienda style, with cut stone and wrought iron, and decorated in contemporary Mexican colors. The rooms show a lot of polish, with good air-conditioning and nicely finished bathrooms. They also come with a TV, a small fridge, and a safe. The majority of rooms are deluxe, which are medium to large and come with a king or two doubles. A complimentary continental breakfast is served in the garden, and the third-story terrace makes a nice place to hang out. This hotel is right on Avenida 5; if you like to go to bed early, think of staying elsewhere.

See map p. 215. Av. 5 (between calles 6 and 8) ☎ *984-873-0884. Fax: 984-873-1240.* www.lunata.com. *10 units. Free guarded parking. Rack rates: $50–$80 double, $70–$120 deluxe and jr. suite. Rates include continental breakfast. AE, MC, V.*

Iberostar Tucán
$$$ **Playa del Carmen**

This all-inclusive hotel is a member of a large chain of resorts based in Spain. The Tucán is actually just one half of the resort; the other half is called Iberostar Quetzal. They're exactly the same, so don't be confused by the different names when talking to travel agents or packagers. The cheapest rates are to be had through a vacation packager or travel agent rather than booking the hotel yourself. In fact, most guests stay here as part of a package that combines airfare and ground transportation. Families make up the majority of the guests, and Iberostar makes sure to have plenty for children to do, including evening shows and a day-time kids club. The food is reliable. The hotel has three restaurants: a main buffet restaurant and two restaurants (Mexican and Italian) open only for dinner. It also has four pools: a large general pool, an activities pool, kids pool, and an adults-only pool with swim-up bar.

See map p. 215. Lote Hotelero 2, Fracc. Playcar. ☎ *888-923-2722 in the U.S., or 984-877-2000.* www.iberostar.com. *350 units. Rack rates: High season $330 double; low season $230 double. Rates include all food and beverages, and water-sports-equipment rental. AE, MC, V.*

Shangri-La Caribe
$$$–$$$$ **Playa del Carmen**

This hotel — a loose grouping of cabanas on one of the best beaches in Playa — is hard to beat for sheer fun and leisure. And it's far enough from the center of town to be quiet yet convenient. The older, south side of the hotel (the "Caribe" section) consists of one- and two-story cabanas. The north ("Playa") side is a few larger buildings, holding 4 to 6 rooms.

A preference for one or the other section is a matter of taste; the units in both are similar in amenities, privacy, and price. The real difference in price depends on the proximity to the water — beachfront, oceanview, or garden view. Garden view is the best bargain, being only a few steps farther from the water. Many garden-view rooms (mostly in a third section called "Pueblo") have air-conditioning, which adds $6 to the price. All rooms have a patio or porch complete with hammock. Most come with two double beds, but a few have a king bed. Windows are screened, and ceiling fans circulate the breeze. Book well in advance during high season.

See map p. 215. Calle 38 and the beach. ☎ 800-538-6802 in the U.S. or Canada, or 984-873-0611. Fax: 984-873-0500. www.shangrilacaribe.net. *107 units. Free guarded parking. Rack rates: High season $180 gardenview, $220 oceanview double, $270 beachfront double; low season $130 gardenview $170 oceanview double, $210 beachfront double. Rates include breakfast and dinner. Book well in advance during high season. AE, MC, V.*

Treetops

$ Playa del Carmen

Treetops not only offers a good price, but good location, too: half a block from the beach, half a block from Avenida 5, which is just enough distance to filter out the noise. The rooms at Treetops encircle a pool, a small *cenote*, and patch of preserved jungle that shades the hotel and lends the proper tropical feel. Rooms are large and comfortable and have air-conditioning, fans, refrigerators, and either balconies or patios. Some of the upper rooms, especially the central suite, have the feel of a treehouse. Two other suites are large, with fully loaded kitchenettes and work well for groups of four.

See map p. 215. Calle 8 s/n. ☎ 984-873-0351 (also fax). www.treetopshotel.com. *17 units. Rack rates: High season $50–$85 double, $125–$150 suite; low season $35–$65 double, $100–$125 suite. MC, V.*

Villa Catarina Rooms and Cabañas

$ Playa del Carmen

Hammocks stretch out in front of each of the stylishly rustic rooms and *cabañas* at this property nestled in a grove of palms and fruit trees, just a block from the beach. Each of the clean, well-furnished rooms has one or two double beds on wooden bases with carpet or wood floors. Some rooms have a small loft for reading and relaxing; others have *palapa* roofs or terraces. Furnishings and Mexican folk-art decorations add a great touch that's uncommon for hotels in this price range. Bathrooms are detailed with colorful tiles, and some of the larger rooms have sitting areas. Good cross-ventilation through well-screened windows keeps the rooms relatively cool. Complimentary coffee is available every morning.

See map p. 215. Calle Privada Norte between av. 12 and 14. ☎ 984-873-2098. Fax: 984-873-2097. 14 units. High season $65–$85 double; low season $45–$60 double. MC, V.

Dining in Playa

Restaurants in Playa constantly open and close. None of the following restaurants accept reservations — which isn't a problem, because you rarely have trouble getting a table. If you want to try some local food I can recommend a taco restaurant, **Los 3 Carboncitos,** on Calle 12 between avenidas 10 and 15.

La Casa del Agua

$$-$$$ **Playa del Carmen   EUROPEAN/MEXICAN**

This new arrival to Playa offers some of the best of both Old and New Worlds. What I tried was delicious — chicken in a wonderfully scented sauce of fine herbs accompanied by fettuccine, and a well-made tortilla soup listed as *sopa mexicana.* A number of cool and light dishes are appetizing for lunch or an afternoon meal; for example, an avocado stuffed with shrimp and flavored with a subtle horseradish sauce on a bed of alfalfa sprouts and julienned carrots — a good mix of tastes and textures. The dining area is upstairs under a large and airy *palapa* roof.

See map p. 215. Av. 5 at Calle 2. ☎ *984-803-0232. Main courses: $9–$15. AE, MC, V. Open: Daily 2 p.m. to midnight.*

Casa Mediterránea

$$ **Playa del Carmen   ITALIAN**

Tucked away on a quiet little patio off Quinta Avenida, this small, homey restaurant serves excellent food. Maurizio Gabrielli and Giovanna Furian are usually there to attend the customers and make recommendations. They came to Mexico to enjoy the simple life, and this inclination shows in the restaurant's welcoming, unhurried atmosphere. The menu is mostly northern Italian, with several dishes from other parts of Italy. Daily specials are offered, too. Pastas (except penne and spaghetti) are made in-house, and none is precooked. Try fish and shrimp ravioli or penne alla Veneta. Several wines, mostly Italian, make a perfect accompaniment. The salads are good and carefully prepared—dig in without hesitation.

Av. 5, between calles 6 and 8. ☎ *984-876-3926. Reservations recommended in high season. Main courses: $8–$15. No credit cards. Open: Daily 1–11 p.m.*

La Parrilla

$$ **Playa del Carmen   MEXICAN/GRILL**

One of the most popular restaurants in town, this place has an open dining area where the aroma of grilling fajitas permeates the air. The chicken fajitas make for a larger serving. Grilled lobster is also on the menu. The cooks do a good job with Mexican standards, such as tortilla soup, enchiladas, and quesadillas. Mariachis show up around 8 p.m.; if you want to avoid them and dine in relative tranquillity, get a table on the upper terrace in back.

See map p. 215. Av. 5 at Calle 8. ☎ *984-873-0687. Reservations not accepted. Main courses: $8–22. AE, MC, V. Open: Daily noon to 1 a.m.*

Media Luna
$$ **Playa del Carmen   VEGETARIAN/SEAFOOD**

The owner-chef here has come up with an outstanding, eclectic menu that favors grilled seafood, sautés, and pasta dishes with inventive combinations of ingredients. Everything I had was quite fresh and prepared beautifully, taking inspiration from various culinary traditions — Italian, Mexican, and Japanese. Keep an eye on the daily specials. The open-air restaurant also makes sandwiches and salads, black bean quesadillas, and crêpes. The décor is primitive-tropical chic.

See map p. 215. Av. 5, between calles 12 and 14. ☎ *984-873-0526. Main courses: $8–$15; sandwich with a salad $5–$7; breakfast $4–$6. No credit cards. Open: Daily 8 a.m.–11:30 p.m.*

Tarraya Restaurant/Bar
$ **Playa del Carmen   SEAFOOD/BREAKFAST**

"The restaurant that was born with the town," proclaims the sign outside of this establishment. This restaurant is also the one locals recommend as the best for seafood. It's right on the beach, and the water practically laps at the foundations. Because the owners are fishermen, the fish is so fresh that it's practically still wiggling. The place doesn't look like much, but the cooks know their trade and can prepare your fish in several ways. If you haven't tried the Yucatecan specialty *tik-n-xic* fish (prepared in a native style of barbecue), this restaurant is a good place to do so. Tarraya is on the beach across from the basketball court. It's also open for breakfast with a set menu that includes hot cakes, French toast, and eggs any style.

See map p. 215. Calle 2 Norte at the beach. ☎ *984-873-2040. Main courses: $4–$9; whole fish $8 per kilo; breakfast is $2.50–$5. No credit cards. Open: Daily 7 a.m.–9 p.m.*

Yaxché
$$–$$$ **Playa del Carmen   MAYA/YUCATECAN**

The menu here makes use of many native foods and spices to produce a style of cooking different from what you usually get when ordering Yucatecan food. You find such things as a cream of *chaya* (a native leafy vegetable) or xcatic chile stuffed with cochinita. I also like the classic fruit salad, done Mexican style with lime juice and dried powdered chile. The menu is varied and includes a lot of seafood dishes. The ones I had were fresh and well prepared.

See map p. 215. Calle 8 between Av. 5 and 10. ☎ *984-873-2502. Main courses: $9–$25. AE, MC, V. Open: Daily noon to midnight.*

Having fun on and off the beach

Time spent in Playa can be as active or as relaxing as you want it to be. You can easily arrange a trip to see the ruins or spend the day at Xcaret. And, as is the case with just about anywhere on this coast, you can always line up a snorkel or scuba trip, which leaves the evening free for strolling about Playa and taking in the town's amusing street scene.

Getting quality beach time

Playa is Spanish for beach and in this town, life *is* a playa. Stroll down the beach to find your favorite spot. I like swimming at the beach that's between the Porto Real and the Shangri-La Caribe hotels. It's broad and flat. Playa has "beach clubs" where, for a small fee, you can get a variety of amenities, including beach furniture, shade, and bar service. They're a good deal if you plan on spending the day at the beach.

Diving and snorkeling

Tank-Ha Dive Center (☎ 984-873-0302; fax: 984-873-1355; www.tankha.com) offers dive trips to sites nearby. The owner, Alberto Leonard, came to Playa by way of Madrid. He can set you up for a dive offshore, or, if you're up for it, he arranges excursions to the *cenotes* down the coast. Snorkeling trips cost around $30 and include soft drinks and equipment. Two-tank dive trips are $55; resort courses with SSI and PADI instructors cost $75. If you're traveling down the coast on this same trip, it's probably best to hold off on the *cenote* diving until then. (See the section on Akumal, later in this chapter.)

Teeing off and playing tennis

If golf is your bag, an 18-hole championship **golf course** (☎ 984-873-0624), designed by Robert Von Hagge, is adjacent to the Continental Plaza Playacar. Greens fees are $160 (includes cart) in the morning, and $120 after 2 p.m. Caddies cost $20, club rental costs $20, and the price includes tax. The club also has two **tennis** courts. Two **tennis** courts are also available at the club at a rate of $10 per hour.

Day-tripping to Maya ruins and nature parks

One of the most popular bus tours from Playa is a day-trip to **Chichén-Itzá.** (See Chapter 15 for information on the ruins and the surrounding area.) The trip usually includes a couple of stops, including one for lunch and perhaps a swim. You usually get to the ruins shortly after noon and return about 5 or 6 p.m. In many cases, you can reserve a tour through your hotel, if not, you can do so at any of the local travel agencies.

You can also go to Chichén-Itzá by rental car. Choosing this approach lets you enjoy a morning at the beach before driving to the ruins in the heat of the afternoon. (Be sure to rent a car with air-conditioning.) Check into a hotel and perhaps go see the evening sound-and-light show and then get up early and see the ruins in the morning. When you do it this way, you avoid most of the bus tours, which arrive in the afternoon, and you see the ruins in the coolness of the morning. Driving to Chichén is fairly easy; the ruins are 2½ hours from Playa. For more details, see Chapter 15.

Another popular bus tour combines a half day at Tulum (described in Chapter 15) with a half day at the eco-park Xel-Ha (described later in this chapter) for swimming and snorkeling. This itinerary makes for a convenient, no-hassle trip with a nice combination of activities — you work up a sweat at the ruins and then cool off in the lagoon at Xel-ha. (Don't do it the other way.)

The other most popular trip is to **Xcaret** (see the section on Xcaret, later in this chapter). If you want to set your own schedule, take a taxi there and back rather than buy admission and transportation as a package. However, some tours include dropping you back in Playa for lunch and taking you back to the park for the afternoon and evening. You can also take tours to **Cozumel,** but these trips are disappointing. You see exactly what the cruise-ship passengers see — lots of duty-free, souvenir, and jewelry shops. You're better off going by yourself on the ferry and spending at least a couple of nights there (see Chapter 13).

For information or to sign up for a tour, you can contact any travel agency in Playa. A reputable one, with smaller tours is Turquoise Reef Tours (☎ 984-879-3456). It's on Calle 16 between Av. 5 and the beach. One of the large bus tour outfits is Caribbean Coast Travel (☎ 984-873-1689). It's located at Av. 10 Norte 211, B-6.

Going shopping

Playa del Carmen offers lots of **shopping** choices. Most of the stores are along its popular Avenida 5, or just off to one side or the other. On this pedestrian-only street, you can find dozens of trendy shops selling imported batik (Balinese-style) clothing, Guatemalan clothing, premium tequilas, Cuban cigars, masks, pottery, hammocks, and a few T-shirts. Throw in a couple of tattoo parlors, and you complete the mix.

Living la vida loca: Playa's nightlife

It seems like everyone in Playa is out on Avenida 5 or on the square until 10 or 11 p.m. Pleasant strolls, meals and drinks at street-side cafes, and visiting shops fill the early hours of the evening. Then music starts up at a few locations on the avenue. **Apasionado** (☎ 984-803-1101), at the corner of Calle 14, has live jazz Wednesday to Saturday. For salsa, go to **Mambo Café** (☎ 984-803-2656) on Calle 6 around the corner from Avenida 5. Down by the ferry dock is a **Señor Frog's** (☎ 987-873-0930), with its patented mix of thumping dance music, gelatin shots, and frat-house antics; it's on the beach at Calle 4. And, of course, there's the perennial favorite beachside bar in Playa at the **Blue Parrot** (☎ 987-873-0083), on the beach around the corner from Calle 12.

Fast Facts: Playa del Carmen

Area Code

The telephone area code for Playa del Carmen and Tulum is **984**.

Banks, ATMs, and Currency Exchange

Playa has several banks with automated teller machines, along with several money-exchange houses. Many of these offices are close to the pier and along Avenida 5 at Calle 8. Outside of Playa, Tulum, and Puerto Morelos there are few ATMs. It's a good idea to keep a cash reserve, if you're staying elsewhere.

Business Hours

Most offices maintain traditional Mexican hours of operation (10 a.m. to 2 p.m. and from 4 p.m. to 8 p.m. daily), but shops remain open throughout the day. Offices tend to close on Saturday and Sunday. Shops are usually open on Saturday but still generally respect the tradition of closing on Sunday. During peak season, many shops remain open until 9 or even 10 p.m.

Internet Access

Playa now has many Internet providers with high speed connections. They are everywhere. Just keep a lookout for signs with the words "Internet" or "cyber."

Doctor

For serious medical attention, go to Hospital Hospiten in Cancún (☎ 998-881-3700). In Playa, Dr. Jorge Mercado is a capable general practitioner who speaks English. His office is at the corner of 10 Av. and Av. Constituyentes (☎ 984-873-3908).

Pharmacy

The **Farmacia del Carmen** (☎ 987-873-2330), on Avenida Juárez between avenidas 5 and 10, is open 24 hours.

Post Office

The post office is on Avenida Juárez, 3 blocks north of the plaza on the right after the Hotel Playa del Carmen and the launderette.

Taxes

A 15% IVA (value-added tax) is taxed on goods and services, and it's generally included in the posted price.

Telephone

Avoid the phone booths that have signs in English advising you to call home using a special 800 number — these booths are absolute rip-offs and can cost as much as $20 US per minute. The least expensive way to call is by using a Telmex (LADATEL) prepaid phone card, available at most pharmacies and mini-supers, using the official Telmex (Lada) public phones. Remember, in Mexico, you need to dial 001 prior to a number to reach the United States, and you need to preface long-distance calls within Mexico by dialing 01.

The Riviera Maya

The largest towns on this coast from north to south are Puerto Morelos, Playa del Carmen (covered in the previous section), Puerto Aventuras, Akumal, and Tulum. The ecoparks are Tres Rios, Xcaret, Xel-ha, and Aktun Chen. Highway 307, runs the length of the Riviera Maya. From Cancún to Playa del Carmen (51 kilometers; 32 miles), it's a four-lane divided highway with speed limits up to 110 kmph (68 mph). A couple of traffic lights and several reduced-speed zones around the major turnoffs also appear. From Playa to Tulum (80km; 50 miles), the road becomes a smooth two-lane highway with wide shoulders. Speed limits are the same, but with more spots that require you to reduce your speed. It takes around 1½ hours to drive from the Cancún airport to Tulum. Lots of buses travel this stretch of highway, but I prefer renting a car because many buses only stop in the larger towns, or they leave you a half mile from the beach you're trying to get to. A car gives you more flexibility. Beyond Tulum is a large natural preserve called the Sian Ka'an, and from there all the way to Belize the coast is predominantly mangrove with only a few poor-quality beaches.

It's always a good idea when traveling this coast to have plenty of cash in pesos. Aside from Playa del Carmen, you don't find a lot of banks or cash machines, and in the smaller towns and resorts and gas stations, you often can't pay with a credit card. In Puerto Morelos, there is only one cash machine in the town, which is out of service on occasion, and another on the Highway at the turnoff junction. After Playa del Carmen, the next cash machines are in Tulum. One more thing to note: Sometimes power failures occur on this coast, and they can last a whole day; during one of these failures, you can't get cash or gasoline.

Puerto Morelos and environs

For the most part, development has bypassed Puerto Morelos; not even the opening of four luxury spa resorts in the general vicinity has altered the sleepy character of the town. Offshore is a prominent reef, which has been declared a national park for its protection. Because of the reef, the beaches in Puerto Morelos have a lot of seagrass. But the water is as clear and calm as anywhere along the coast and offers good snorkeling, diving, and kayaking. If you want to get away from the crowds, you'll find this a cozy spot. And if you run through your reading material too quickly, visit the large English-language bookstore on the main square, which is open during high season. Puerto Morelos is also the terminus for the car ferry to Cozumel.

Getting there

Drive south from Cancún on Highway 307. At the km 31 marker is a traffic light for the turnoff to Puerto Morelos. It's well marked. The town is 2 kilometers (1¼ miles) from the highway. Many buses going either from the Cancún bus station or the airport to Playa del Carmen stop in Puerto Morelos. A taxi ride costs about $50. Puerto Morelos used to be the terminus for a car ferry for Cozumel Island. Now, the ferries use a dock south of Playa called Puerto Calica. (See the earlier chapter on Cozumel.)

Getting around

Puerto Morelos is so small that you can get around most of the town on foot, but you need a car to visit nearby attractions and beaches. Or you can hire a local taxi, which you can usually find around the main square.

For trips farther away, you can take a bus. The best way to catch a bus is to take a taxi to the highway, where the bus stop is.

Staying in and around Puerto Morelos

Lodging in Puerto Morelos tends to be simple, except for the four nearby luxury spa resorts. These resorts target a well-heeled crowd, offering spa treatments, privacy, and personal service, all in a Caribbean setting. Rack rates for the least expensive rooms run $300 to $600 a night, but in the off-season, you may score a discount. I review the least expensive of the four — **Ceiba del Mar** — in this section.

Of the other three, **Paraiso de la Bonita** (☎ 800-327-0200; www.paraiso delabonitaresort.com) has the largest and most impressive spa, which specializes in French Thalassotherapy (seawater-based spa treatments). The rooms here are lovely and look out to a great stretch of beach. **Maroma** (☎ 866-454-9351; www.maromahotel.com) has an even prettier beach, beautiful gardens, and a cozier feel. The rooms are tasteful and luxurious, though not as stunning as those at Paraiso de la Bonita; however, the common areas, especially the beachside restaurant and bar, are more welcoming. **Ikal del Mar** (☎888-230-7330; www.ikaldelmar.com) is smaller and still more private than Maroma. Accommodations are in large individual *palapas* tucked away in the jungle and connected by illuminated paths. The beach is rocky and not as good for swimming as the beaches at Paraiso and Maroma, but all three resorts have impressive outdoor pools. If someone were to give me a gift certificate (please make it out to David Baird) to any of these resorts, I'd choose Maroma, for its beauty, atmosphere, and beach.

Amar Inn
$ **Puerto Morelos**

Simple, rustic rooms on the beach, in a home-style setting, make this small inn a good place for those wanting a quiet seaside retreat. The cordial hostess, Ana Luisa Aguilar, is the daughter of Luis Aguilar, a Mexican singer and movie star of the 1940s and '50s. She keeps busy promoting environmental and equitable-development causes. She can arrange snorkeling and fishing trips and jungle tours for guests with small operators. The inn boasts three cabañas in back, opposite the main house, and five upstairs rooms with views of the beach. The best is a third-story room with a great view of the ocean. The cabañas get less of a cross-breeze than the rooms in the main house but still have plenty of ventilation. They are large and come with kitchenettes. Rooms in the main building are medium to large. Bedding choices include one or two doubles, one king, or five twin beds. A full Mexican breakfast is served in the garden.

Av. Javier Rojo Gómez, at Lázaro Cárdenas. ☎ *998-871-0026. E-mail:* amar_inn @hotmail.com. *Rack rates: High season $55–65 double; low season $45–$55 double. Rates include full breakfast. No credit cards.*

Ceiba del Mar
$$$$ Puerto Morelos

This resort consists of eight three-story buildings, each with a rooftop terrace with Jacuzzi. The carefully tended white sand beach with thatched shade umbrellas is inviting, as is a seaside pool with Jacuzzi, bar, and a native-style steambath (*temascal*). The spa is quite complete and offers a long menu of treatments. The air-conditioned rooms are large, with either two doubles or one king-size bed, and have a terrace or balcony, and CD player, TV/VCR, and minibar. The large, well-appointed bathrooms have shower/tub combinations, marble countertops, and makeup mirrors. Suites are very large, with two bedrooms, two or three full bathrooms, and separate entryways. Emphasis is on personal service; for example, each morning, you get coffee and juice delivered to your room through a closed pass-through.

Av. Niños Héroes s/n, ☎ *877-545-6221 from the U.S. or 998-873-8060. Fax: 998-872-8061.* www.ceibadelmar.com. *Rack rates: High season $380–$420 deluxe, $450 and up for suites; low season $360–$400 deluxe, $420 and up for suites. Rates include continental breakfast, ground transfer. AE, MC, V.*

Casita del Mar
$ Puerto Morelos

An attractive hotel on the beach, Casita del Mar offers pleasant rooms and good prices. Rooms come with either two full beds or one king, mostly with soft mattresses. The standard units are medium size and well furnished. Oceanview rooms are larger, with larger bathrooms; three have tubs. A pretty terrace overlooks the beach.

Calle Roberto Frías SMZA 2, MZA 14, Lote 6. ☎ *998-871-0301. Rack rates: High season $70–$85 double; low season $55–$65 double. MC, V.*

Hotel Ojo de Agua
$ Puerto Morelos

What I like best about this hotel is that it offers the convenience and service of a higher-priced hotel, including a good dive shop and watersports-equipment rental service. Two three-story buildings stand on the beach at a right angle to each other. The simply furnished rooms have balconies or terraces; most have a view of the ocean. Standard rooms have one double bed. Deluxe rooms are large and have two doubles. Studios have a double and a twin and a small kitchenette but no air-conditioning (the rest of the rooms do have A/C). Some rooms come with TV and phone. A highly respected instructor heads the dive shop. If you've wanted to try windsurfing, this is the place: The American who rents the boards takes his time with customers and is quite helpful.

Supermanzana 2, lote 16 ☎ *998-871-0027 or 998-871-0507. Fax: 998-871-0202.* www.ojo-de-agua.com. *36 units. Rack rates: High season $45–$55 double, $60 studio; low season $30–$40 double, $50 studio. Weekly and monthly rates available. AE, MC, V.*

La Posada del Capitán Lafitte
$$$ South of Puerto Morelos

A large sign on the left side of Hwy. 307, eight miles south of Puerto Morelos, points you in the direction of La Posada del Capitán Lafitte. This lovely seaside retreat sits on a solitary stretch of sandy beach. Here, you can enjoy being isolated while still having all the amenities of a relaxing vacation. The one- and two-story white stucco bungalows, which hold one to four rooms each, stretch along a powdery white beach. They're smallish but comfortable, with tile floors, small, tiled bathrooms, either two double beds or one king-size bed, and an oceanfront porch. Twenty-nine bungalows have air-conditioning; the rest have fans. The hotel offers transportation to and from the Cancún airport for $50 per person (minimum of two passengers). Your room price includes both breakfast and dinner, plus there's a poolside grill and bar. Amenities include a medium-size pool, dive shop, watersports equipment, and a TV/game room.

Carretera Cancún-Tulum (Hwy. 307) km 62. ☎ *800-538-6802 in the U.S. and Canada, or 984-873-0214.* www.mexicoholiday.com. *62 units. Free guarded parking. Rack rates: High season $210–$240 double; low season $150–$170 double. Rates include breakfast and dinner. MC, V.*

Dining in and around Puerto Morelos

This town isn't known for its fine dining. It's fairly small, and there has been a remarkable turnover rate among its restaurants. The one enduring restaurant, **Los Pelícanos,** offers seafood that's overpriced for a town such as this, and it gets most of its customers from people just passing through. Most of the other restaurants have set up around the town's main square or just around the corner. One of these is **Caffe del Puerto** — good for salads, sandwiches, and grilled daily specials. There's also **Hola Asia,** which works off a simple menu of Asian dishes. The most expensive place in town is **John Grey's,** which is a couple of blocks north of the plaza and about 3 blocks inland. It's open for dinner except on Sundays. The owner is a former chef for the Ritz Carlton, and I've enjoyed his cooking.

Enjoying the great outdoors

Besides stretching out on the beach or by the pool and reading a favorite book, the main activities are snorkeling, diving, and kayaking. You can line up these things by asking at one of the local hotels, or you can visit the local dive shop **Mystic Divers** (☎ **998-871-0634** (also fax); www.mysticdiving.com). It's well recommended, not only for diving but for fishing trips, too. The owner, Victor Reyes, speaks English and takes small groups. He is a PADI and NAUI instructor and gives his customers a lot of personal attention. The shop is open all year. A two-tank dive costs $45. The reef directly offshore is very shallow and is protected by law. Snorkelers are required to wear a life vest to prevent them from damaging the reef.

Activities on dry land include jungle tours such as the one offered by a local resident Goyo Morgan, which includes a swim in a *cenote* (sinkhole) and a visit to a local ranch ($40 for a half-day tour). Also in the area are a couple of roadside amusements. One is a zoological park specializing in crocodiles called **Croco Cun** (☎ **998-884-4782**). It's on the east side of Hwy. 307 a couple of miles north of the Puerto Morelos turnoff. It's an interactive zoo with crocodiles in all stages of development, as well as animals of nearly all the species that range, crawl, or slither around the Yucatán. A visit to the new reptile house is fascinating, though it may make you think twice about venturing into the jungle. The rattlesnakes and boa constrictors are particularly intimidating, and the tarantulas are downright enormous. The guided tour lasts 1½ hours. Children enjoy the guides' enthusiasm and are entranced by the spider monkeys and wild pigs. Wear plenty of bug repellent. The restaurant sells refreshments. Croco Cun is open daily 8:30 a.m. to 5:30 p.m. As with other attractions of this sort along the coast, entrance fees are high: $15 adult, $9 children 6 to 12, free for children under 6.

Tres Ríos

About midway between Puerto Morelos and Playa del Carmen is **Tres Ríos** (☎ **998-887-8077** in Cancún; www.tres-rios.com), an eco-adventure park similar to Xcaret and Xel-ha. It's actually a nature reserve on more than 150 acres of land. Admission is $34 for adults and $20 for children ages 5 to 11, which includes canoe trips; the use of bikes, kayaks, and snorkeling equipment; and the use of hammocks and beach chairs after you tire yourself out. It does not include food, scuba diving, horseback riding, and extended guided tours through the preserve and its estuary. It's definitely less commercial than the other eco-theme parks and is essentially just a great natural area for participating in these activities. An array of inclusive packages exists that include food and drink and tours. Prices run from $61 to $116 for adults and $36 to $58 for children. Make reservations. Tres Ríos also has bathroom facilities, showers, and a convenience store; however, the facilities are much less sophisticated than the area's other, more developed eco-theme parks. The park is open daily 9 a.m. to 5 p.m.

After Tres Ríos, you come to Playa del Carmen. The town is big enough that I cover it in the first section of this chapter.

Xcaret

Ten kilometers (6½ miles) south of Playa del Carmen (and 80 kilometers (50 miles) south of Cancún) is the turnoff to Xcaret (pronounced ish-car-*et*), an "eco-archaeological" theme park that many call Mexico's answer to Disneyland, with all that the label implies. Attractions are varied and numerous, kids love it, and the jungle setting and palm-lined beaches are beautiful. But this "natural" park is highly engineered, down to the Mayan temple-style ticket booths. Admission and food prices are high, and crowds can be plentiful.

Pathways meander around bathing coves, the snorkeling lagoon, and the remains of a group of real Mayan temples. You have access to swimming beaches; limestone tunnels to snorkel through; a wild-bird breeding aviary; a *charro* (Mexican cowboy) exhibition; horseback riding; scuba diving; a botanical garden and nursery; a sea turtle nursery that releases the turtles after their first year; a pavilion showcasing regional butterflies; and a tropical aquarium, where visitors can touch underwater creatures such as manta rays, starfish, and octopi. One of the park's most popular attractions is the "Dolphinarium," where visitors (on a first-come, first-served basis) can swim with the dolphins for an extra charge of $85 to $115.

Another attraction is the Seawalker, a type of special suit and helmet with an air hose. You can walk on the ocean floor or examine a coral reef in a small bay, without having to be constantly going back up for air, as you would if you were snorkeling. It's great for nondivers.

The park is famous for its evening spectacle that is a celebration of the Mexican nation. It is some show, with a large cast and lots of props. It starts with the Maya and an interpretation of how they may have played the pre-Hispanic game/ritual known as *pok-ta-pok,* and then to another version of a ball game still practiced in western Mexico. From there it moves on to the arrival of the Spanish and eventually to the forging of the new nation, its customs, its dress and its music and dance.

The visitor center has lockers, first-aid assistance, and a gift shop. Visitors aren't allowed to bring in food or drinks, so you're limited to the rather high-priced restaurants on-site. No personal radios are allowed, and you must remove all suntan lotion if you swim in the lagoon to avoid poisoning the lagoon habitat.

Xcaret is open Monday to Saturday 8:30 a.m. to 8 p.m. and Sunday 8:30 a.m. to 5:30 p.m. The admission price is $49 per adult, $25 for children 5 to 12.

Up close and personal with the dolphins

Traveling south from Xcaret, you see the turn-off for Puerto Aventuras 26 kilometers (16 miles) down the road. This marina community has a few restaurants and hotels and a lot of condos. The buildings are mostly modern glass constructions, which makes Puerto Aventuras look like a mini-Cancún. Here you can go swimming with dolphins. Make reservations with **Dolphin Discovery** (☎ **984-883-0779;** www.dolphin discovery.com) and grab a bite to eat. Since this is also the largest marina in the vicinity, you can also go on a fishing trip. **Captain Rick's Sportfishing Center** (☎ **984-873-5195;** www.fishyucatan.com) is a professional outfit.

This entitles you to use the facilities, boats, life jackets, and lounge chairs. Other attractions cost extra, such as snorkeling tour ($39), horseback riding ($30), and scuba diving ($55 for certified divers; $75 for a resort course). Locker rental is $2/day, snorkel equipment $10/day. Some equipment (such as beach chairs) may be scarce, so bring a beach towel and, if you have it, your own snorkeling gear. For more information, call ☎ 998-883-3143 or visit www.xcaret.net.

Xpu-Ha

Thirty kilometers (18½ miles) south of Xcaret is the beautiful beach of Xpu-Ha. If you want quality beach time, this is the place. Xpu-Ha is a wide bay lined by a broad, beautiful sandy beach. At each end of the bay is an all-inclusive resort (**Xpu-Ha Palace** and **Robinson Club**), and in the middle is another, the **Hotel Copacabana.** But the beach is long and wide enough that it usually feels empty — except on weekends, when people from up and down the coast come for the day. To get to the beach, turn off when you see the Copacabana and take either the road that goes along the south side of the hotel or the next road after that. (The latter is labeled X-6.) Construction work is always changing the signs and road around, so I can't provide specific directions. But no one can close off access, because some restaurants and small hotels are on the beach.

If Xpu-Ha sounds like your idea of the perfect home base for a Riviera Maya vacation, then consider staying at either of these all-inclusives. The **Hotel Copacabana** (☎ 800-562-0197 in the U.S.; www.hotelcopacabana.com) is owned and operated by an Acapulco-based outfit. The design of the hotel preserves much of the native flora, with large parts of the central area up on stilts. The rooms are in three-story buildings. The hotel has a lovely pool and, of course, you have the beach beyond it. The **Xpu-Ha Palace** (☎ 866-385-0256 in the U.S.; no local number; www.xpuha-palace.com) is built on the site of a failed eco-park. The area is lovely. Rooms are in *palapa*-style bungalows. This resort has a lot of things for kids to do, and staying here involves a good amount of walking, because the hotel is fairly spread out. You can make reservations at either of these hotels through travel agents or packagers. The **Robinson Club** is marketed mainly to Germans, and you run the risk of being an outcast unless you speak German, so I don't recommend it.

The other option is to stay at one of the small, basic hotels on this beach. Rooms are quite simple: two twin or full beds, private bathroom, cement floors, and perhaps a ceiling fan. Most are rented on a first-come, first-served basis. Rates vary from $20 to $50 a night, depending upon how busy they are. The nicest establishment is **Villas del Caribe Xpu-Ha** (☎ 984-873-2194), which lets you make a reservation. Rates run $35 to $50 for a double; no credit cards accepted. Another option is to stay in nearby Akumal (see the next section) and drive the short distance to the beach.

Akumal

Akumal is a small, ecologically oriented community built on the shores of two beautiful bays. This community has been around long enough that it feels more relaxed than the booming places on the coast, such as Playa and Tulum. It's popular with families who can rent a condo or a villa for a week and save money by doing their own cooking. Akumal's location makes it a perfect base camp for organizing expeditions for snorkeling, diving, beach-combing, or visiting the ruins. Otherwise, you may enjoy just stopping here for a few hours to take a dip and have a bite at one of the restaurants.

Getting there and getting around

Continue south on Highway 307 from Xpu-Ha for only 3 kilometers (2 miles). You'll come to the turnoff that is marked with a sign that reads Playa Akumal. (Don't be confused by other turnoffs marked Villas Akumal or Akumal Aventuras or Akumal Beach Resort.) Less than 1 kilometer (½ mile) down the road is a white arch. Just beyond the arch is Akumal Bay; the road to the left of the arch takes you to shallow, rocky Half Moon Bay, lined with two- and three-story villas, and eventually to Yalku Lagoon, a small, perfectly placid lagoon, good for swimming.

Navigating Akumal is simple. At the white arch, you find a couple of convenience stores (including the Super Chomak, where you can buy groceries) and a good place to take your laundry. Passing through the arch, you come to Akumal Bay. To the right is the Club Akumal Caribe Hotel. If you go left and keep to the left, you arrive at Half Moon Bay after crossing some *monster* speed bumps. (Nobody speeds in this town.) The same road, after running the distance of the bay, ends at Yalku Lagoon.

Staying in Akumal

You can rent most of the condos and villas in Akumal for a week at a time. Here are a few agencies specializing in rentals: **Info-Mexico** (☎ 866-849-9984 in the U.S.; www.info-akumal.com), **Akumal Vacations** (☎ 800-448-7137 in the U.S. www.akumalvacations.com), and **Caribbean Fantasy** (☎ 800-523-6618 in the U.S. www.caribbfan.com). You can also find a few hotels, which are a more flexible option because you can rent by the day.

Club Akumal Caribe/Hotel Villas Maya Club
$$–$$$ **Akumal**

The hotel rooms and garden bungalows of this hotel, set along the pristine and tranquil Akumal Bay, are both large and comfortable. The 40 Villas Maya bungalows are simply furnished and come with kitchenettes. The 21 rooms in the three-story beachfront hotel are more elaborately furnished. They come with refrigerators and a king or two queen beds. Both the bungalows and the rooms have air-conditioning, tile floors, and good-size bathrooms, but neither have phones or TVs. A large pool on the grounds, a children's activities program (during high season), two restaurants, and a bar round out the facilities. This hotel also leases villas and condos, such as the **Villas Flamingo** on Half Moon Bay. The villas have two or three bedrooms and large living, dining, and kitchen areas, as well as a lovely furnished patio just steps from the beach.

Carretera Cancún-Tulum (Hwy. 307) km 104. ☎ *800-351-1622 in the U.S., 800-343-1440 in Canada, or 915-584-3552 for reservations; 987-875-9012 direct.* www.hotel akumalcaribe.com. *70 units. Free parking. Rack rates: High season $120 bungalow, $145 hotel room, $165–$425 villa/condo; low season $70 bungalow, $85 hotel room; $80–$240 villa/condo. Ask for low-season special packages. AE, MC, V. Cash only at the restaurants.*

Vista del Mar Hotel and Condos
$$ Half Moon Bay

This beachfront property is a great place to stay for several reasons. It offers hotel rooms at good prices and large, fully equipped condos that you don't have to rent by the week. The lovely, well-tended beach in front of the hotel has chairs and umbrellas. An on-site dive shop has an experienced staff. Hotel rooms contain a queen bed or a double and a twin. The 12 condos are large, and though they lack air-conditioning, they have ceiling fans and good cross-ventilation. They consist of a kitchen, a living area with TV, and two or three bedrooms and one or two bathrooms. All have balconies or terraces facing the sea and are equipped with hammocks. Several rooms come with whirlpool tubs.

Half Moon Bay. ☎ *877-425-8625 in the U.S. Fax: 505-988-3882 in the U.S.* www. akumalinfo.com. *27 units. Free parking. Rack rates: High season $90 double; $190–$290 condo. Low season $56 double; $95–$170 condo. MC, V.*

Dining in Akumal

Akumal has about ten places to eat and a good grocery store (**Super Chomak**) by the archway. The **Turtle Bay Café and Bakery,** near the Akumal Dive Shop, is good for breakfast or a light lunch. A good dining spot for lunch or dinner is **La Buena Vida,** on Half Moon Bay.

Enjoying the great outdoors

On Akumal Bay are two dive shops with PADI-certified instructors. The older is the **Akumal Dive Shop** (☎ 984-875-9032; www.akumal.com), one of the oldest and best dive shops on the coast. Offshore, you can visit almost 30 dive sites (from 9 to 24m or 30 to 80 feet deep). The shop also specializes in *cenote* diving at some of the less-visited sites. Both Akumal Dive Shop and **Akumal Dive Adventures** (☎ 984-875-9157), the dive shop at the Vista del Mar hotel on Half Moon Bay, offer resort courses as well as complete certification.

A bit beyond Akumal is the turnoff for **Aktun Chen** cavern (☎ 998-892-0662 or 998-850-4190; www.aktunchen.com), a type of eco-park. This park, consisting of a spectacular 5,000-year-old grotto and an abundance of wildlife, marks the first time that above-the-ground cave systems in the Yucatán have been open to the public. The name means "cave with an underground river inside." The main cave containing three rivers is more than 600 yards long with a magnificent vault. Discreet illumination and easy walking paths make visiting the caves more comfortable, without appearing to alter the caves too much from their natural state. The caves contain large chambers with thousands of stalactites, stalagmites, and sculpted rock formations, along with a 40-foot-deep *cenote* with clear blue water.

Aktun Chen was once underwater itself, and you can see fossilized shells and fish embedded in the limestone as you walk along the paths. Caves are an integral part of this region's geography and geology, and knowledgeable guides lead you through the site while providing explanations and offering mini history lessons on the Maya's association with these caves. Tours have no set times — guides are available to take you when you arrive — and groups are kept to a maximum of 20 people. The tour takes about an hour and requires a good amount of walking. The footing is generally good.

Nature trails surround the caves throughout the 988-acre park, where spotting deer, spider monkeys, iguanas, and wild turkeys is common. A small, informal restaurant, gift shop, and zoo with specimens of the local fauna are also on-site.

You can easily travel to Aktun Chen on your own. On Highway 307 (the road to Tulum), just past the turnoff for Akumal, a sign on the right side of the highway indicates the turnoff for Aktun Chen (at km 107, Cancún–Tulum road). From there, it's a 3- to 5-kilometer (2- to 3-mile) drive west along a smooth but unpaved road. The park is open daily from 9 a.m. to 5 p.m. Admission is $17 for adults, $9 for children.

Xel-Ha

Thirteen kilometers (8 miles) south of Akumal is a nature park called **Xel-Ha** (☎ 998-884-9422 in Cancún, 984-873-3588 in Playa, or 984-875-6000 at the park; www.xelha.com.mx). The centerpiece of Xel-Ha (shell-*hah*) is a large, beautiful lagoon where freshwater and saltwater meet. You can swim, float, and snorkel in beautifully clear water surrounded by jungle. A small train takes guests upriver to a drop-off point. There, you can store all your clothes and gear in a locked sack that is taken down to the locker rooms in the main part of the building. The water moves calmly toward the sea, and you can float along with it. Snorkeling here offers a higher comfort level than the open sea — no waves and currents to pull you about, but there's plenty of marine life to view, including rays.

Inside the park, you can rent snorkeling equipment and an underwater camera. Platforms allow nonsnorkelers to view the fish. Another way to view fish is to use the park's "snuba" gear — a contraption that allows you to breathe air through 6m (20-ft.) tubes connected to scuba tanks floating on the surface. It frees you of the cumbersome tank while allowing you to stay down without having to hold your breath. Rental costs $42 for approximately an hour. Like snuba but more elaborate is "sea-trek," a device consisting of an elaborate plastic helmet with air hoses. It allows you to walk around on the bottom breathing normally and perhaps participate in feeding the park's stingrays. Another attraction is swimming with dolphins. A 1-hour swim costs $115; a 15-minute program costs $40. Make reservations (☎ **998-887-6840**) at least 24 hours in advance for one of the four daily sessions.

Other attractions include a plant nursery, an apiary for the local, stingless Mayan bees, and a lovely path through the tropical forest bordering the lagoon. Xel-Ha is open daily from 8:30 a.m. to 5 p.m. Parking is free. Admission: For the basic package, adults are $29 on weekdays, $22 on weekends; children age 5 to 11 are $18 on weekdays, $11 on weekends; children under 5 enter free. Admission includes use of inner tubes, life vest, and shuttle train to the river, and the use of changing rooms and showers. An all-inclusive option includes snorkeling equipment rental, locker rental, towels, food, and beverages. Adults are $56 all week long and children $38. The park has five restaurants, two ice cream shops, and a store. It accepts American Express, MasterCard, and Visa, and has an ATM.

If you're driving, just south of the Xel-Ha, turn off on the west side of the highway, don't miss the ruins of **ancient Xel-Ha.** You're likely to be the only one there as you walk over limestone rocks and through the tangle of trees, vines, and palms. There's a huge, deep, dark *cenote* to one side, a temple palace with tumbled-down columns, a jaguar group, and a conserved temple group. A *palapa* shelter on one pyramid guards a partially preserved mural. Admission is $2.50.

Xel-Ha is also close to the ruins at **Tulum** (see Chapter 15) and makes a good place for a dip after you finish climbing the Mayan ruins. The best time to visit both sites is during the weekend when fewer people attend the park or the ruins.

On the way to Tulum

Only a couple of kilometers past Xel-ha, you see a sign on your right advertising **Hidden Worlds Cenotes** center (☎ **984-877-8535**; www.hiddenworlds.com.mx), which offers an excellent opportunity to snorkel or dive in a couple of nearby caverns. The caverns are part of a vast network that makes up a single underground river system. The water is crystalline (and a bit cold) and the rock formations impressive. These caverns were filmed for the IMAX production *Journey into Amazing Caves.* If you've been considering snorkeling or diving in a *cenote* to see what it's like, this spot is the perfect place to do so. The site is close to a good dive shop. Snorkel tours cost $40 and take you to two different caverns. The main form of transportation is "jungle mobile," with a guide who throws in tidbits of information and lore about the jungle plant life that you see. Some walking is involved, so take shoes or sandals.

After you pass Hidden Worlds, the next couple of turnoffs to the left lead to Soliman and Tankah bays. On Punta Soliman Bay is a good beach restaurant called **Oscar y Lalo's,** where you can rent kayaks and snorkel equipment and paddle out to the reefs for some snorkeling. Approximately 3 kilometers (2 miles) farther is the turnoff for Tankah. Pull in here, and you come to a *cenote* by a lovely bay. The bay is good for snorkeling. The *palapa* restaurant next to the *cenote* serves grilled food. A couple of small hotels are on this bay. The most interesting is **Casa Cenote** (☎ 998-874-5170; www.casacenote.com). It has an underground river that surfaces at a *cenote* in the back of the property then goes underground and bubbles up into the sea just a few feet offshore. Casa Cenote has seven rooms, all on the beach. The double rate, including breakfast and dinner at the restaurant, is $168. The owner, an American, provides kayaks and snorkeling gear and can arrange dives, fishing trips, and sailing charters.

Tulum

About 15 kilometers (10 miles) south of Xel-ha is the walled Maya city of Tulum, a large post-Classic site overlooking the Caribbean in a dramatic setting. (See Chapter 15 for a description.) You also find the small town of present-day Tulum and on the coast a long stretch of beautiful beach dotted with small cabaña hotels. The only electricity here is what's generated by each hotel. Tulum is a good choice if you like to splash around in the water and lie on the beach far away from the resort scene. The town has a half-dozen restaurants, three cybercafes, a bank, and three cash machines.

Getting there and getting around

The town of Tulum (130 kilometers or 81miles from Cancún) lies directly on the highway a little beyond the entrance to the ruins. But before you get to the town, you come to a highway intersection with a traffic light. The road to the left leads to the Hotel Zone.

Don't expect much when you arrive in Tulum. It's a small town and basically consists of what fronts the highway and about two locks on either side of the road. To get to the hotels on the beach, turn east at the highway intersection that's located just as you enter the town. (To the west is the highway to Cobá, see Chapter 15.) Go 3 kilometers (2 miles), and you'll run into a "T" junction. The best cabaña hotels are to the right. The pavement quickly turns into sand, and on both sides of the road, you start seeing cabañas. If you were to stay on this road, you would eventually enter the **Sian Ka'an Biosphere Reserve.** The road can make for slow going during the rainy season, July through October.

Staying in Tulum

You can stay either on the beach at one of the cabaña hotels in the Hotel Zone, or in town. The seven or eight hotels in town are cheaper than all but the most basic of beach accommodations, but they aren't as much fun. They offer basic lodging for $20 to $50 a night. I really like staying in the cabaña hotels. You have more than 20 to choose from, and they run the gamut from minimal lodging requirements to refined luxury.

 Most of the cheap cabañas are on the coast closest to the ruins. Several travelers have had their possessions stolen at some of the cheapest places.

 ### Cabañas Ana y José
$$–$$$ **Punta Allen Peninsula**

These cabañas offer a tranquil escape that feels worlds away from the rest of civilization and provide sufficient creature comforts to make for a relaxing stay. The beach in front of the hotel is pure white sand. The rock-walled cabañas closest to the water (called "oceanfront") are a little larger than the others and come with two double beds. I also like the attractive second-floor "vista al mar" rooms, which have tall *palapa* roofs. The standard rooms are much like the others but don't face the sea. The hotel has one suite. The cabañas have 24-hour electricity for lights and ceiling fans but no TV. All rooms have tile or wood floors, one or two double beds, and patios or balconies. The hotel, located 4 miles from the Tulum ruins, can have a rental car waiting for you at the Cancún airport. Reservations are a must in high season, and around Christmas and the New Year, the rates are a little higher than normal high-season prices.

Carretera Punta Allen km 7. ☎ *987-887-5470. Fax: 987-887-5469.* www.anayjose. com. *15 units. Free parking. Rack rates: High season $100–$140 double; low season $90–$130 double. AE, MC, V.*

Cabañas Tulum
$ **Punta Allen Peninsula**

Next door to Ana y José's is a row of bungalows facing the same beautiful ocean and beach. This place offers basic accommodations. Rooms are simple yet attractive and large, though poorly lit. The large bathrooms are tiled. All rooms have two double beds (most with new mattresses), screens on the windows, a table, one electric light, and a porch facing the beach. Electricity is available from 7 to 11 a.m. and 6 to 11 p.m. Billiard and Ping-Pong tables provide entertainment. The cabañas are often full between December 15 and Easter, and in July and August.

Carretera Punta Allen km 7. ☎ *984-879-7395. Fax: 984-871-2092.* www.hotelstulum. com. *32 units. $60–$80 double. No credit cards.*

Zamas
$$ **Punta Allen Peninsula**

The owners of these cabañas, a couple from San Francisco, have made their rustic getaway most enjoyable by concentrating on the essentials: comfort, privacy, and good food. The cabañas are simple, attractive, well situated for catching the breeze, and not too close together. Most rooms are in individual structures; the suites and oversized rooms are in modest two-story buildings. For the money, I like the six individual garden *pala-pas*, which are attractive and comfortable, with either two double beds or a double and a twin. Two small beachside cabañas with one double bed go for a little less. The most expensive rooms are the upstairs oceanview units, which enjoy a large terrace and lots of sea breezes. I like these especially. They come with a king- and a queen-size bed or a double and a queen-size bed. The restaurant serves the freshest seafood — I've seen the owner actually flag down passing fishermen to buy their catch. A white-sand beach stretches between large rocky areas. The hotel's restaurant has great food.

Carr. Punta Allen, km 5. ☎ *415-387-9806 in the U.S.* www.zamas.com. *20 units. Rack rates: High season $110–$145 oceanview double, $80–$105 double; low season $80–$110 oceanview double, $50–$80 double. No credit cards.*

Dining in Tulum

A few restaurants in the town of Tulum have reasonable prices and good food. **Charlie's** (☎ 987-871-2136), my favorite for Mexican food, and **Don Cafeto's** (☎ 987-871-2207) are two safe bets. Both places are on the main street. There's a good, authentic-Italian restaurant called **Il Giardino di Toni e Simone** (☎ 044-987-804-1316, a cellphone; closed Wed) one block off the highway. Look for a large building-supply store called ROCA — the restaurant is on the opposite side of the road one block away. A couple of roadside places that grill chicken and serve it with rice and beans are also in town. Two good hotel restaurants are on the coast — the one at **Zamas** (great seafood) and the one at **Cabañas Ana y José**. (See the previous section for information on both these places.)

Enjoying the great outdoors

In the Tulum area, the main thing to do is to visit the **Tulum ruins.** Staying here gives you the advantage of seeing them early in the morning before it gets hot and before the large tour buses (and attendant crowds) arrive. If you have a car, you can also visit the nearby ruins of **Cobá.** For more on these two ruins sites, see Chapter 15.

You can arrange an interesting day-trip to visit the mammoth **Sian Ka'an Biopreserve.** You're guaranteed to see several species of wildlife and learn some interesting things about the plant life in the area. Most tours include a boat ride around the park's large lagoon and perhaps through one of the canals that connect it to small lakes. In Tulum, contact **Sian Ka'an Tours** (☎ 984-871-2363; e-mail: siankaan_tours@hotmail.com); the tour office is on the east side of the road, one block south of the highway intersection. This outfit offers a general-interest day tour and a sunset tour.

Chapter 15

A Taste of the Maya: Nearby Ruins

. . . .

In This Chapter
▶ Choosing which ruins to visit
▶ Getting there and back
▶ Exploring the ruins
▶ Understanding the ancient Maya

. . . .

From top to bottom and from coast to coast, the Yucatán is littered with the ruined cities and settlements of the ancient Maya. At its peak, the area must have been super-populated, for even today it seems that you can hardly trek out into the forest without tripping over some yet undiscovered site.

Of course, most of these smaller ruins aren't of interest to the casual observer because they're mere mounds of earth and stone overgrown by forest; they tell you nothing about the past. It's only with excavation and reconstruction that you can get an idea of what this ancient civilization was all about, and, even then, seeing these cities reconstructed generally begs more questions than it answers. But they're fascinating sights with dramatic architecture, and exotic surroundings. If you can tear yourself away for a day from the comforts of beach life, you may enjoy a visit to one or more of these places.

 All of the Yucatán is *"tierra caliente"* (the hotlands), so be prepared. Take sun protection and remember that you'll be walking and perhaps climbing at these sites, so you need comfortable shoes or sandals and a bottle of water. And try to see the sights as early in the day as possible. At Cobá, you need mosquito repellent.

Deciding Which Ruins to Visit

From Cancún or anywhere else along the Caribbean coast, four major ruins are within easy reach and worth visiting. Each is remarkably different from the others, offering a lot of variety. But don't try to see more than one or two; leave the rest for another trip. You can easily overdo the ruins, and they're best appreciated when viewed with fresh eyes.

✔ **Chichén Itzá:** No, it doesn't rhyme with "chicken pizza;" the accents are on the last syllables (chee *chin* eat-*zah*). Without a doubt, this complex is the marquee ruins site of the Yucatán. You can marvel at many things here, but the most famous sights are the much-photographed pyramid known as **El Castillo;** the mysterious and ancient-looking **sacrificial** *cenote* (say-*noh*-teh), a natural well or sinkhole found only in the Yucatán), which is 180 feet across and 60 feet down to the water; and the great **ballcourt** adorned with graphic depictions of players literally losing their heads. Chichén Itzá is in the heart of the Yucatán, two hours by car from Cancún. Many day tours by bus leave from Cancún, Playa del Carmen, and most of the big resorts. Or you can rent your own car and stay overnight in the area.

✔ **Tulum:** Built later than Chichén Itzá and on a much smaller scale, these ruins represent the only major coastal ruins in this part of the Yucatán. The setting is gorgeous: Picture a stylish Maya pyramid crowning a tall cliff jutting out over the turquoise waters of the Caribbean, and you've got the idea. Below this pyramid is a pretty little beach, so take your swimsuit. To me, the buildings in Tulum are less grand than those of the other three sites, but the other three don't have the Caribbean setting. Tulum is 1½ hours south of Cancún.

✔ **Cobá:** Older than Chichén Itzá and much larger than Tulum, Cobá was the dominant city of the eastern Yucatán before A.D. 1000. The site is large and spread out. Two lakes border the ruins, and the tropical forest grows thickly between the different temple groups. Rising high above the forest canopy are tall, steep classic Mayan pyramids. Of the four sites, this one is the least reconstructed, and so disappoints those who expect another Chichén Itzá. Appreciating it requires a greater exercise of the imagination. Cobá is a little more than a half-hour inland from Tulum.

✔ **Ek Balam:** Off the beaten track (but not for long) are these impressive ruins where some startling recent discoveries are making waves in the archaeological world. See Ek Balam now before it becomes a major attraction. Highlights include a ceremonial doorway representing the gaping mouth of the Maya underworld god, Itzamná. The site also has the tallest pyramid in the upper Yucatán. Not hard to get to, Ek Balam is off the same toll highway leading to Chichén Itzá — one exit earlier and about 14 kilometers (about 8½ miles) north.

 Tourism in the Yucatán follows a weekly cycle, and from Friday to Sunday is when most are traveling back and forth. This fact makes weekends the best time for visiting the ruins. Also, it's obviously much more comfortable to view the ruins in the cool of the morning rather than in the afternoon.

The Yucatán Peninsula's Major Ruins

Chichén Itzá

Many people coming to the Yucatán for the first time will feel the need to see these ruins, if only so as not to have to explain to their friends and neighbors how it was that they traveled this far without seeing them. Although it's true that Chichén Itzá is plenty hyped, it does live up to its reputation. But if ruins aren't your cup of tea and the beach is, have the courage of your convictions and be ready to tell people who ask that it's none of their business what you did on your vacation. I do this as a matter of principle.

If you plan to see these ruins, the question to ask yourself is whether you want to overnight here. The advantage is that you can catch the sound-and-light show at night and then see the ruins in the early morning when it's cooler and before most of the tour buses arrive. The drawback is that you need to rent a car or take regular bus service.

Getting there

Chichén Itzá is on the old main Highway 180 in the interior of the peninsula. To get there by car, you can take the modern *autopista* (toll highway) and take the exit for Chichén Itzá and the village of Pisté. It's clearly marked. The toll is expensive ($20) but much faster than the free Highway 180, which takes you through a lot of tiny villages and over their not-so-tiny speed bumps. Once you exit the toll road, you will be on a connecting road that joins with the old highway at the village of Pisté.

Any number of bus tours depart from Cancún and Playa del Carmen. These tours usually stop a few times for lunch, a snack, or a swim. You usually arrive at the ruins around noon or shortly thereafter, and you're back in Cancún or Playa del Carmen by nightfall. Regular bus service is trickier and more frequent from Cancún than from Playa del Carmen.

Where to stay

The expensive hotels in Chichén all occupy beautiful grounds, are close to the ruins, and have good food. All have toll-free reservations numbers, which I recommend. Some of these hotels do a lot of business with tour operators — they can be empty one day and full the next. The inexpensive hotels are in the village of Pisté, 2 kilometers (1¼ mile) away.

Hacienda Chichén
$$$ At the ruins

The smallest and most private of the hotels at the ruins is also the quietest and the least likely to have bus tour groups. This was the hacienda that served as the headquarters for the Carnegie Institute's excavations in 1923. Several bungalows, built to house the staff, have been modernized and are now the guest rooms. Each is simply and comfortably furnished (with a dehumidifier and ceiling fan in addition to air-conditioning) and is a short distance from the others. Each bungalow has a private porch from which you can enjoy the beautiful grounds. Standard rooms come with two twin or two double beds. Suites are larger and have larger bathrooms and double or queen beds. The main building was part of the original hacienda and holds the restaurant, which offers dining on the terrace by the pool or inside in air-conditioning.

Zona Arqueológica. ☎ *800-624-8451 in the U.S or 985-851-0045.* www.yucatãn adventure.com.mx. *28 units. Free guarded parking. Rack rates: $150 double; $165 suite. AE, DC, MC, V.*

Hotel Dolores Alba
$ Old Highway east of the ruins

This little motel is perfect if you come by car. It's a bargain for what you get: two pools (one is an "ecological" pool with a stone bottom and nonchlorinated water), *palapas* (thatched roofs) and hammocks around

Chichén Itzá Ruins

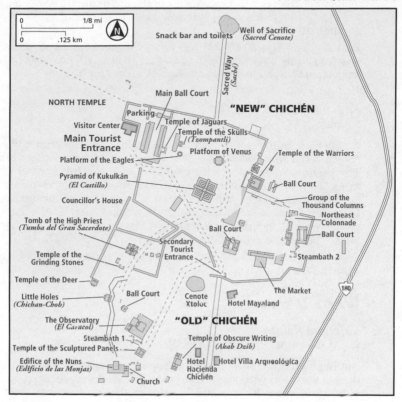

the place, and large, comfortable, air-conditioned rooms. The restaurant serves good meals at moderate prices. You also get free transportation to the ruins and the Caves of Balankanché during visiting hours, though you will have to take a taxi back. The hotel is on the highway 2½ kilometers (1½ miles) east of the ruins.

Carretera Mérida–Cancún. km 122 ☎ *985-858-1555.* www.doloresalba.com. *40 units. Free parking. Rack rates: $40 double. No credit cards.*

Hotel Mayaland
$$$$ At the ruins

The main doorway frames El Caracol (the observatory) in a stunning view — that's how close this hotel is to the ruins. If a drawback exists, it's that the hotel books large bus tours, but this isn't so bad because the hotel is on a large piece of property that uses space liberally. The main building is long and three stories high. The rooms are large, with comfortable beds and large tiled bathrooms. Bungalows, scattered about the rest of the grounds, are built native style, with thatched roofs and stucco walls; they're a good deal larger than the rooms. The grounds, including three pools, are gorgeous, with huge trees and lush foliage — the hotel has had 75 years to get them that way.

Zona Arqueológica. ☎ *800-235-4079 in the U.S., or 985-851-0127. 97 units. Free guarded parking. Rack rates: High season $162 double, $227 bungalow, $262 suite; low season $110 double, $160 bungalow, $220 suite. AE, MC, V.*

Pirámide Inn
$ Pisté

A mile west from the ruins, in the village of Pisté, this hotel has simple rooms, most with two double beds (a few with three twins or one king). The bathrooms are nice, with counter space and tub/shower combinations. The air-conditioning is quiet and effective. Hot water comes on between 5 and 10 a.m. and 5 and 10 p.m. A well-kept pool and a *temascal* (a native form of steambath) occupy a small part of the landscaped grounds, which include the remains of a Maya wall. Try to get a room in the back. The hotel is right on the highway.

Calle 15 No. 30. ☎ *985-851-0115. Fax: 985-851-0114.* www.piramideinn.com. *44 units. $47 double. MC, V.*

Where to dine

Cafetería Ruinas
$ At the ruins INTERNATIONAL

Although this cafeteria has the monopoly on food at the ruins, it actually does a good job with such basic meals as enchiladas, pizza, and baked chicken. It even offers some Yucatecan dishes. Eggs and burgers are cooked to order, and the coffee is good. You can also get fruit smoothies and vegetarian dishes. Sit outside at the tables farthest from the crowd, and relax.

In the visitor center. ☎ *985-851-0111. Reservations not accepted. Breakfast: $4; sandwiches $4–$5; main courses $4–$8. AE, MC, V. Open: Daily 9 a.m.–6 p.m.*

Fiesta
$ Pisté YUCATECAN/MEXICAN

Although relatively inexpensive, the food here is dependable and good. You can dine inside or out, but make a point of going for supper or early lunch when the tour buses are gone. The buffet is quite complete, and the menu has many Yucatecan classics. Fiesta is on the west end of town.

Highway 180 in Pisté. ☎ *985-851-0038. Reservations not accepted. Main courses $4–$6; buffet $8.50 (served from 12:30–5 p.m.). No credit cards. Open: Daily 7 a.m.–9 p.m.*

Exploring Chichén Itzá

When you think of a Maya pyramid, chances are that it's the main pyramid at Chichén Itzá that springs to mind. It's called **El Castillo** and it's dedicated to the feathered serpent god Kukulkán. No doubt you have seen pictures of it everywhere — in guidebooks, on posters, and on Web sites. The funny thing is that El Castillo shouldn't be the poster child for Maya architecture. It doesn't look like most Maya pyramids, and experts know for certain that the god Kukulkán was not originally worshipped in the Maya heartland but came here from Central Mexico (where he was known as Quetzalcoatl). Also, many architectural features of this city are strikingly similar to the Toltec city of Tula, in Central Mexico.

The burning question about Chichén Itzá (Chichén, for short) is, "Who really ran the show here?" Experts know that they called themselves the "Itzá," and the name of the city means "Well of the Itzá." It's pretty certain that the ones following orders here — the laborers, peasants, and artisans — were native Maya. The head honchos were perhaps either invading Toltecs who later intermarried with the Maya, or the Putún Maya, a merchant people from the Gulf coast who were receptive to foreign influences and more cosmopolitan than their Yucatán neighbors. Or maybe it was a combination of both. More digging at the site is necessary to answer this question, and that event doesn't look likely anytime soon.

Chichén Itzá occupies 6.5 square kilometers (4 sq. miles), and it takes most of a day to see all the ruins. Hours for the site are 8 a.m. to 5 p.m. daily. Service areas are open 8 a.m. to 10 p.m. Admission is $11, free for children under 12. A video camera permit costs $4. Parking is extra. Chichén Itzá's **sound-and-light** show is worth seeing and is included in the cost of admission. For more information, see the "More cool things to see and do" section later in this section.

Toltec tall tales

Based on an intriguing myth from Central Mexico, some scholars argue that the Toltecs founded Chichén. The short version goes like this: The god Quetzalcoatl (Feathered Serpent) was tricked by his brother, the god Tezcatlipoca (Smoking Mirror), and shamed into leaving. He fled to the Gulf coast of Mexico and there ascended into the east toward Venus, the morning star. According to these scholars, this myth represents a shorthand account of a Toltec religious civil war fought between the followers of these two gods. The losers, under the leadership of a priest-king, who naturally assumed the name of Quetzalcoatl, were pushed east to the Gulf of Mexico and from there moved to the Yucatán where they managed to build a new city at Chichén Itzá and reestablish the cult of the feathered serpent.

The large, modern visitor center, at the main entrance where you pay the admission charge, is beside the parking lot and consists of a museum, an auditorium, a restaurant, a bookstore, and bathrooms. You can see the site on your own or with a licensed guide who speaks English or Spanish. Guides usually wait at the entrance and charge around $40 for one to six people. Although the guides frown on it, there's nothing wrong with approaching a group of people who speak the same language and asking whether they want to share a guide. Be wary of the history-spouting guides — some of it is just plain out-of-date — but the architectural details they point out are enlightening. Chichén Itzá has two parts: the northern (new) zone, which shows distinct Toltec influence, and the southern (old) zone, with mostly Puuc architecture.

El Castillo pyramid

Once you pass the entrance gates, **El Castillo pyramid** will be in front of you. At 23 meters (75 feet) tall, the pyramid is a giant numbers game tied to the old Pre-Columbian calendars: Four stairways have 91 steps each, which adds up to 364; when you add the top platform where they meet, the total is 365, the number of days in a year. On each side of these stairways are 9 terraces, making a total of 18 per side, which is the number of months in their solar calendar. Each face has 52 panels, equaling the 52 years that represented the magical cycle for all pre-Hispanic civilizations. This time period is how long it would take for the solar and the religious calendars to coincide.

Consider the pyramid's mysterious alignment. It's positioned so that twice a year, on the **spring** and **fall equinoxes** (March 21 and September 21), the corner edges of the pyramid cast shadows on the sides of the north stairway; these shadows resemble the geometric patterns on the body of a snake such as the diamondback. At the bottom of each side of the north stairway is a serpent's head carved in stone, so the shadow effect was probably intentional. As the sun rises, the shadows, representing the body of the snake, move slowly downward, making the "serpent" appear to descend into the ground. To be honest, watching the shadow effects is more of an intellectual curiosity than a dramatic sight, especially for those raised on the high-excitement Indiana Jones movies. I don't think it's worth fighting the crowds that come to witness it. In truth, experts don't know what the pyramid may have looked like originally, because all the surfaces of this pyramid, including the stairways, were covered with a thick coat of smooth stucco and painted bright colors, perhaps in patterns.

El Castillo was an enlargement of an earlier pyramid. The Maya frequently did this kind of thing. Archeologists have carved a narrow stairway into the pyramid at the western edge of the north staircase. It leads inside to the temple of the original structure, to a sacrificial altar-throne — a red jaguar encrusted with jade. The stairway is open from 11 a.m. to 3 p.m.; the inside is cramped, humid, and uncomfortable. A visit as close to the opening time as possible is best. Photos of the jaguar figure are forbidden.

Juego de Pelota (the main ball court)

Among all the peoples of pre-Columbian Mexico, there existed a popular game that was part ritual, part sport. Historians only know of it as "the ball game" or "pok-ta-pok" in Mayan. Ball courts have been found as far north as New Mexico and as far south as Honduras and everywhere in between. The **main court** at Chichén is one of at least nine in this city and is much larger and better preserved than any ball court found elsewhere. You find it immediately northwest of El Castillo. Carved on both walls of the ball court are scenes showing Maya figures dressed as ball players and decked out in heavy protective padding. The carved scene also shows a headless player kneeling with blood shooting from his neck; another player holding the head looks on.

Players on two teams tried to knock a hard rubber ball through one of the two stone rings placed high on either wall, using only their elbows, knees, and hips (no hands). According to legend, the losing players paid for defeat with their lives. However, some experts say the victors were the only appropriate sacrifices for the gods. One can only guess what the incentive for winning may be in that case. Either way, the game must have been riveting, heightened by the wonderful acoustics of the ball court.

Other highlights of Chichén Itzá

Temples are at both ends of the ball court. The **North Temple** has sculptured pillars and more sculptures inside, as well as badly ruined murals. The acoustics of the ball court are so good that from the North Temple, a person speaking can be heard clearly at the opposite end, about 136 meters (450 feet) away.

Follow the dirt road (actually an ancient *sacbé*, or causeway) that heads north from the Platform of Venus; after 5 minutes, you come to *Cenote de los Sacrificios* **(Sacrificial Cenote),** the great natural well that may have given Chichén Itzá its name. This well was used for ceremonial purposes, not for drinking water — according to legend, sacrificial victims were drowned in this pool to honor the rain god Chaac. Research done early in the 20th century uncovered bones of both children and adults in the well.

Edward Thompson, who was the American consul in Mérida, purchased the ruins of Chichén early in the 20th century and explored the *cenote* with dredges and divers. His explorations exposed a fortune in gold and jade. Most of the riches wound up in Harvard's Peabody Museum of Archaeology and Ethnology — a matter that continues to be of concern to Mexican archeologists. Excavations in the 1960s unearthed more treasure, and studies of the recovered objects detail offerings from throughout the Yucatán and even farther away.

Due east of El Castillo is the *Templo de los Guerreros* **(Temple of the Warriors),** named for the carvings of warriors marching along its walls. It's also called the Group of the Thousand Columns for the rows of broken pillars that flank it. During the recent restoration, hundreds more of the columns were rescued from the rubble and put in place, setting off the temple more magnificently than ever. A figure of Chaac-Mool sits at the top of the temple, surrounded by impressive columns carved to look like enormous feathered serpents. South of the temple was a square building that archaeologists called the **Market** (*mercado*); a colonnade surrounds its central court. Beyond the temple and the market in the jungle are mounds of rubble, parts of which are being reconstructed.

Construction of the *El Caracol* **(the Observatory),** a complex building with a circular tower, was carried out over centuries; the additions and modifications reflected the Maya's careful observation of celestial movements and their need for increasingly exact measurements. Through slits in the tower's walls, astronomers could observe the cardinal directions and the approach of the all-important spring and autumn equinoxes, as well as the summer solstice. The temple's name, which means "snail shell," comes from a spiral staircase within the structure.

On the east side of El Caracol, a path leads north into the bush to the **Cenote Xtoloc,** a natural limestone well that provided the city's daily water supply. If you see any lizards sunning there, they may well be *xtoloc,* the lizard for which this *cenote* is named.

More cool things to see and do

From cave visits to laser shows, Chichén and the surrounding area hold even more interest for travelers.

✔ **"Head" on over to** *Tzompantli* **(the Temple of the Skulls).** To the right of the ball court is the Temple of the Skulls, an obvious borrowing from the post-Classic cities of central Mexico. Notice the rows of skulls carved into the stone platform. When a sacrificial victim's head was cut off, it was impaled on a pole and displayed in a tidy row with others. Also carved into the stone are pictures of eagles tearing hearts from human victims. The word *Tzompantli* is not Mayan but comes from Central Mexico. Reconstruction using scattered fragments may add a level to this platform and change the look of this structure by the time you visit.

✔ **Stay for the evening sound-and-light show.** The kind of severe geometry characteristic of Maya architecture really lends itself to this kind of spectacle; besides, you already paid for the show when you bought you ticket. The show, held at 7 or 8 p.m. depending on the season, is in Spanish, but headsets are available for rent ($4.50) in several languages so that you can enjoy the dramatic narrative.

✔ **Visit** *Chichén Viejo* **(Old Chichén).** For a look at more of Chichén's oldest buildings, constructed well before the time of Toltec influence, follow signs from the Edifice of the Nuns southwest into the bush to Old Chichén, about 1 kilometer (½ mile) away. Be prepared for this trek with long trousers, insect repellent, and a local guide. The attractions here are the *Templo de los Inscripciones Iniciales*

(Temple of the First Inscriptions), with the oldest inscriptions discovered at Chichén; and the restored *Templo de los Dinteles* (Temple of the Lintels), a fine Puuc building.

🖛 Explore the cave of Balankanché. You see signs for this cave about 5½ kilometers (3½ miles) from Chichén Itzá on the old highway to Cancún. The entire excursion takes about a half hour, but the walk inside is hot and humid. The highlight is a round chamber with a central column the size of a large tree trunk. You come up the same way you go down. The cave became a hideaway during the War of the Castes. You can still see traces of carving and incense burning, as well as an underground stream that served as the sanctuary's water supply. Outside, take time to meander through the botanical gardens, where most of the plants and trees are labeled with their common and scientific names. The caves are open daily. Admission is $6, free for children 6 to 12. Children younger than age 6 are not admitted. Use of a video camera costs $4 (free if you've already bought a video permit in Chichén the same day). Tours in English are at 11 a.m., 1 p.m., and 3 p.m.; and, in Spanish, at 9 a.m., noon, 2 p.m., and 4 p.m. Double-check these hours at the main entrance to the Chichén ruins.

🖛 Check out Cenotes Dzitnup and Sammulá. The Cenote Dzitnup (also known as Cenote Xkekén) is along the same Highway 180 as Balankanché, about 20 miles further toward Cancún. It's worth a side trip, especially if you have time for a dip. Watch for the signs. When you get there, you descend a short flight of rather perilous stone steps, and at the bottom, inside a beautiful cavern, is a natural pool of water so clear and blue that it seems plucked from a dream. If you decide to swim, be sure that you don't have creams or other chemicals on your skin — they damage the habitat of the small fish and other organisms living there. Also, no alcohol, food, or smoking is allowed in the cavern. Admission is $2. The *cenote* is open daily 7 a.m. to 7 p.m. About 100 yards down the road on the opposite side is another recently discovered *cenote*, Sammulá, where you can also swim. Admission is $2.

Fast Facts: Chichén Itzá

Area Code

The telephone area code for Chichén and the neighboring village of Pisté is **985**.

Banks, ATMs, and Currency Exchange

You can find ATMs and banks in the nearby town of Valladolid, which you pass on your way to Chichén if you take the old Highway 180.

Medical

You can find a small first-aid station in the visitor center at the ruins.

Taxes

A 15% IVA (value-added tax) on goods and services is usually included in the posted price.

Tulum: Fortress City

Tulum was a Mayan fortress-city built over the most rugged part of the coast. In looking at the layout and scope of the city, it becomes clear that the builders of this citadel were interested in two things uppermost: trade and defense. And they picked the perfect spot for their city. It is a beautiful site facing out over the Caribbean. On the city's other three sides they constructed stout walls with watchtowers and fortified areas. The stonework used to build the ceremonial centers is of poorer quality than in other sites such as Chichén or Cobá, as if the temples were constructed in haste.

 Tulum is also the name of the laid-back town adjacent to the ruins, where you find beautiful and mostly isolated beaches, as well as a string of interesting hotels. For more on Tulum the town, see Chapter 14.

The city's origins date from the ninth century, which was the end of the Classic period and the beginning of Maya civilization's decline. The large cities to the south were abandoned, and smaller city-states rose to fill the void. Tulum was one of these city-states. Its original name was "Zama," meaning dawn, a good name because it obviously faces east toward the rising sun. It came to prominence in the 13th century as a seaport, controlling maritime commerce along this section of the coast, and remained inhabited well after the arrival of the Spanish. The primary god here was the diving god, depicted on several buildings as an upside-down figure above doorways. Seen at the Palace at Sayil and Cobá, this curious, almost comical figure is also known as the bee god.

The most imposing building in Tulum is a large stone structure above the cliff called the **Castillo** (castle). Actually a temple as well as a fortress, it was once covered with stucco and painted. In front of the Castillo are several unrestored palace-like buildings with partial remains of the old stucco covering. On the **beach** below, where the Maya once came ashore, visitors swim and sunbathe, combining a visit to the ruins with a dip in the Caribbean.

The **Temple of the Frescoes,** directly in front of the Castillo, contains interesting 13th-century wall paintings, though entry is no longer permitted. Distinctly Maya, they represent the rain god Chaac and Ixchel, the goddess of weaving, women, the moon, and medicine. On the cornice of this temple is a relief of the head of the rain god. If you pause a slight distance from the building, you see the eyes, nose, mouth, and chin. Notice the remains of the red-painted stucco — at one time, all the buildings at Tulum were painted bright red.

Much of what historians know of Tulum at the time of the Spanish Conquest comes from the writings of Diego de Landa, third bishop of the Yucatán. He wrote that Tulum was a small city inhabited by about 600 people who lived in platform dwellings along a street and who supervised the trade from Honduras to the Yucatán. Although it was a walled city,

Tulum Ruins

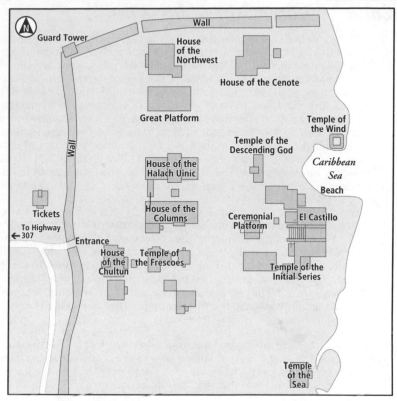

most of the inhabitants probably lived outside the walls, leaving the interior for the residences of governors and priests and ceremonial structures. Tulum survived about 70 years after the Conquest, when it was finally abandoned. Because of the great number of visitors this site receives, you can no longer to climb the ruins and are asked to remain behind roped-off areas to view them.

The ruins are open to visitors from 7 a.m. to 5 p.m. in the winter and from 8 a.m. to 6 p.m. in the summer. If you can, go early before the crowds start showing up around 9:30 a.m. The entrance to the ruins is about a 5-minute walk from the archaeological site. You find artisans' stands, a bookstore, a museum, a restaurant, several large bathrooms, and a ticket booth. After walking through the center, visitors pay the admission fee to the ruins ($4), another fee ($1.50) if you choose to ride an open-air shuttle to the ruins, and, if you're driving, another fee ($3) to park. A video camera permit costs $4. Licensed guides have a stand next to the path to the ruins and charge $20 for a 45-minute tour in English, French, or Spanish for up to four persons. They can point out many architectural details that you may otherwise miss.

Cobá ("Water Stirred by Wind")

The Maya built many intriguing cities in the Yucatán, but few grander than Cobá ("water stirred by wind"). Much of the 67 square kilometer (42 square mile) site, on the shores of two lakes, is unexcavated. A 96-kilometer (60-mile) long *sacbé* (a pre-Hispanic raised road or causeway) through the jungle — remains of which are still visible — linked Cobá to Yaxuná, once a large, important Maya center 48 kilometers (30 miles) south of Chichén-Itzá. It's the Maya's longest known *sacbé*, and at least 50 shorter ones lead from here. Cobá flourished from A.D. 632 (the oldest carved date found here) until after the founding of Chichén-Itzá, around 800. Then Cobá slowly faded in importance and population until it was finally abandoned. Scholars believe Cobá was an important trade link between the Yucatán Caribbean coast and inland cities.

You can line up a bus tour to Cobá from Cancún or Playa del Carmen. (See Chapters 11 and 14 for details.) If you're driving, follow Highway 307 down the coast to Tulum. After you pass the entrance to those ruins but before you enter the town, you see a highway intersection with a traffic light. Turn right and follow this road for 40 minutes to reach the ruins. Always be on your guard for the ever-present speed bumps known as *topes*. They sometimes appear without warning. A couple of small restaurants are in the town, with another one in the Hotel Villa Arqueológica.

 Once at the site, keep your bearings — getting lost on the maze of dirt roads in the jungle is easy, and *be sure* to bring bug spray. Branching off from every labeled path are unofficial narrow paths into the jungle, used by locals as shortcuts through the ruins.

The **Grupo Cobá** boasts a large, impressive pyramid, *La Iglesia* **(Temple of the Church),** which you can find if you take the path bearing right after the entrance. Walking to it, notice the unexcavated mounds on the left. Although the urge to climb the temple is great, the view is better from El Castillo in the Nohoch Mul group farther back.

From here, return to the main path and turn right. You pass a sign pointing right to the ruined *juego de pelota* (ball court), but the path is obscure.

Continuing straight ahead on this path for 5 to 10 minutes, you come to a fork in the road. To the left and right are jungle-covered, unexcavated pyramids, and at one point, you see a raised portion crossing the pathway, which is the visible **remains of the** *sacbé* to Yaxuná. Throughout the area, stelae (the free standing sculpted stone columns that the Maya were so fond of making) stand by pathways or lie forlornly in the jungle underbrush. Although protected by crude thatched roofs, most are too weatherworn for the observer to discern the figures.

The left fork leads to the **Nohoch Mul Group,** which contains **El Castillo.** With the exception of Structure 2 in Calakmul, this pyramid is the tallest

Cobá Ruins

in the Yucatán (rising even higher than the great El Castillo at Chichén-Itzá and the Pyramid of the Magician at Uxmal). So far, visitors are still permitted to climb to the top. From this magnificent lofty perch, you can see unexcavated jungle-covered pyramidal structures poking up through the forest all around.

The right fork (more or less straight on) goes to the **Conjunto Las Pinturas.** Here, the main attraction is the **Pyramid of the Painted Lintel,** a small structure with traces of its original bright colors above the door. You can climb up to get a close look. Although maps of Cobá show ruins around two lakes, only two groups of ruins have truly been excavated.

Admission is $4, free for children younger than age 12. Parking is $1. A video camera permit costs $4. The site is open daily 8 a.m. to 5 p.m., sometimes longer.

Ek Balam ("Dark Jaguar")

More than any of the better-known sites, Ek Balam excites a sense of mystery and awe at the scale of Maya civilization and the utter ruin to which it came. No tour buses serve these ruins yet, but travel agencies in Cancún and Playa can get you on a smaller tour in a van. These tours are held sporadically, so you have to depend somewhat on luck.

If you're driving, take the new *autopista* (toll highway) from Cancún as if you were going to Chichén. Exit the highway at the intersection of Highway 295. The sign reads "Valladolid Tizimín." Turn right (north) as if you're headed for Tizimín. In 8 miles, you'll see a clearly marked, newly-constructed turn-off to the right leading straight to the ruins, which are 8 miles from the highway.

Built between 100 B.C. and A.D. 1200, the smaller buildings are architecturally unique — especially the large, perfectly restored **Caracol.** Flanked by two smaller pyramids, the imposing central pyramid is 157m (517 ft.) long and 61m (200 ft.) wide. At more than 30m (100 ft.) high, it is easily taller than the highest pyramids in Chichén Itzá and Uxmal. On the left side of the main stairway, archaeologists have uncovered a large ceremonial doorway of perfectly preserved stucco work. It is an astonishingly elaborate representation of the gaping mouth of the underworld god. Around it are several beautifully detailed human figures. Excavation inside revealed a long chamber filled with Mayan hieroglyphic writing. From the style, it appears that the scribes probably came from Guatemala. So far this chamber is closed to the public. From this script, an epigrapher, Alfonso Lacadena, has found the name of one of the principle kings of the city — Ukit Kan Le'k.

He is still working on deciphering the full meaning of the text. If you climb to the top of the pyramid, in the middle distance you can see untouched ruins looming to the north. To the southeast, you can spot the tallest structures at **Cobá,** 48 kilometers (30 miles) away. Also plainly visible are the **raised causeways** of the Maya — the sacbé appear as raised lines in the forest vegetation.

The entrance fee is $3, plus $4 for each video camera. The site is open daily 8 a.m. to 5 p.m.

Part VI
The Part of Tens

The 5th Wave   By Rich Tennant

"Well, if you're not drinking Tequila with your breakfast burrito, then why is your cereal bowl rimmed in salt."

In this part . . .

These three chapters are the *For Dummies* top ten lists, which cover in brief paragraphs the best, worst, and lesser-known charms of a Mexican vacation. We give you the ten best ways to avoid looking like a gringo. We also explain the most common myths and misconceptions about Mexico. For example, if you think all Mexican food is fiery hot, keep reading. And, speaking of Mexican food, we share our top-ten picks for the most deliciously Mexican dishes in this region.

Chapter 16

Ten Ways to Avoid Looking Like a Gringo

*H*ow savvy of a traveler are you? If you follow the seasoned advice, "When in Rome . . .", you'll want to know a bit more about the customs and culture of Mexico before heading south of the border. This chapter offers tips and insights designed to clue you in to a few of the nuances of the Mexican way of life. Before you know it, you'll look a little more like a local.

Wake Up and Ask for the Coffee . . . Correctly

 In Mexico, whenever you ask for cream for your coffee, you're served milk, or occasionally, evaporated milk, but never "cream," which is of a very heavy consistency in Mexico — you'd have to spoon it into your coffee. Simply request, *"Leche para el café, por favor"* (Milk for the coffee, please).

Practice Your Check Etiquette

In Mexico, it's considered rude for a waiter to bring your check before you've asked for it — after all, he wouldn't want to appear to be unwelcoming or to be rushing you. Always remember to ask, *"La cuenta, por favor"* (Check, please) when you're ready to leave.

Be on the Lookout for the Bus

Use care in crossing the streets, especially in view of public buses, which seem to regularly race one another in an attempt to reach more potential passengers. Their speed, combined with their sheer size, result in several fatalities each year. You'd rather be alive than right, right?

Go to the Pharmacy for Advice

When feeling under the weather, most Mexicans visit their local pharmacist before checking with a doctor — these professionals are used to dispensing advice, and the recommended remedy, even if it's a prescription medication back home. Pharmacies in Mexico generally don't require prescriptions (except in the case of more tightly controlled substances), so visitors routinely stock up on items such as Rogaine, Viagra, Retin-A, and birth control pills because of their accessibility and relatively low prices.

Beware the Jewelry Scams

In Mexico, the difference between silver jewelry and silver-*colored* jewelry is a big one. When buying jewelry or other items made of silver, first look for the ".925" stamp, an alleged measure of the silver content of the piece. However, even if a stamp is visible, be aware that most of the silver-colored jewelry sold by strolling beach vendors is actually made from *alpaca,* a lesser quality metal with a heavy copper content. Established stores are your best bets for quality silver purchases.

In the Yucatán, you may also run into vendors trying to pass off plastic for Black Coral — a popular jewelry item in these parts. Black Coral is an endangered and protected species — you cannot even take it into the United States without a certificate of origin to establish that it was harvested from an area where Black Coral is being "raised" for specific harvest purposes. Furthermore, authentic Black Coral is extremely expensive. So if the item you want is too cheap to be true coral, it's probably plastic. And if you didn't buy it from a certified jeweler who deals with proper Black Coral harvesters, you're promoting the extinction of a rare kind of coral that took millions of years to create.

Know the Truth about the "Flower Girls"

At night, strolling and dining couples are invariably approached by children selling individual roses for the "nice couple" or *"la señorita"* (the young lady). The sharpest vendors hand you the rose, and once you take it, ask for anywhere between 10 and 20 pesos ($1 to $2) in exchange.

If you don't feel like buying the rose, don't take it to begin with; after it's in your hands, it's too late. These children are generally "managed" by adult operators, known as *Marías*. If you truly feel sorry for them or want to help the children, bring them toys or clothes on your next trip. Buying flowers from them simply assures their continued place on the streets — and the money mostly goes to their "manager."

Say Hello Like a Local

Despite the "macho" image of Mexico's men, when it comes to exchanging greetings, there's little reserve — in Mexico, everybody greets each other effusively. Men friends commonly share a big bear hug punctuated by a slap or two on the back. Men kiss women on the cheek once. Women kiss each other on the cheek once as well. Long-time friends hug and hold both hands for several seconds. Friends and acquaintances — and even people who have just met — exchange kisses and hugs when saying good-bye as well.

Distinguish between a Catcall and a Compliment

In Mexico, light-skinned, light-haired people are referred to as *güero* or *güera,* so if you're blonde and female, be prepared for lots of "güera, güerita" as you walk by. Understand that it's intended more as a compliment — though at times it may sound as if it's a sleazy catcall.

Recognize the Sign of the Cross

Confirming the deeply ingrained Catholic background of the Mexican culture, people often cross themselves as they walk or ride in front of a church as a sign of devotion, or cemetery, as a sign of respect.

Mind the Macho Manner

 Mexicans love to party and mingle, but Mexican men are known for being very jealous and protective of their women. Whenever you're at a nightclub, make sure that you check that the Mexican beauty you strike up a conversation with is not there with a boyfriend, husband, or other male companion. In large groups, your best bet is to start up a conversation with the guys in the group and let them introduce you to the girls.

Chapter 17

Ten (or So) Top Myths and Misconceptions about Mexico

● ●

In This Chapter

▶ Getting the geography straight

▶ Dissecting the stereotypical preconceptions

▶ Solving food and drink misconceptions

● ●

*I*f you've never visited Mexico, you may have some preconceptions about what you're likely to find here. Perhaps you think that the geography — apart from the beaches — is an arid landscape with a uniformly hot climate. Or you may think that you should drink tequila only as a shot — doused with lime and salt.

This chapter explains some of the most common misconceptions about this vast country and its rich culture. Read on — and the next time someone starts talking about how you can't drink the water in Mexico, you can set them straight!

Don't Drink the Water

In the past, visitors often returned home from Mexico with stomach ill-nesses (a condition known in Mexico as *turista* and colloquially in the United States as "Montezuma's revenge"), but this type of vacation sou-venir is a rarity today. Massive investments in an improved infrastruc-ture and a general increase in standards of cleanliness and hygiene have practically wiped out the problem. However, you can easily play it safe and drink bottled water. In addition, ice served in tourist establishments is purified. For more on how to prevent turista, see Chapter 9.

Mexicans Who Don't Speak English Are Hard of Hearing

At least it *appears* that many visitors buy into this statement. Some travelers seem to believe that a native Spanish speaker will somehow get over his or her inability to understand English if the English-speaking individual talks *even louder.* Many Mexicans understand at least some English, especially those in popular tourist areas.

Try this tip — and I guarantee it will work: Instead of panicking and starting to yell in order to get your point across, ask nicely for help, and an English-speaking local will come to assist you. (Better yet, try a few of the handy Spanish phrases listed in Chapter 1 to start a conversation.)

Another thing to keep in mind: Should you voice any negative comments about Mexico or Mexicans, don't assume that no one around you can understand your comments — you may find yourself in an embarrassing situation.

Mexico Is the Land of Sombreros and Siestas

The common image of a Mexican napping under his sombrero exists in some minds, but this stereotype is mostly made of myth. Today, Mexico is a mix of contemporary business professionals and traditional agrarian populations. The afternoon break — from 2 to 4 p.m. — is still a wonderful tradition, but rather than being a time for siesta, it's the time when families come together for their main meal of the day. The more familiar you become with Mexico, the more you find that the people are overwhelmingly hard-working, hospitable, and honest.

All Mexican Food Is Spicy

Not all Mexican food is spicy — although Mexican food does include some of the most intriguingly flavored foods I've ever enjoyed. Although spicy sauces are likely to be in the vicinity of the food you're served, the truth is that many delicious Mexican dishes don't include chile peppers among their ingredients. (See Chapter 18 for a list of some of my favorite regional dishes.) Another common condiment you're likely to find are *limones,* the small, green citrus fruit with a taste similar to a lemon. Squeezing a slice into a soup, or on fresh fish, is a common practice — and provides a great complement to the chiles.

Mexico Has No Drinking or Drug Laws

When on vacation, many travelers tend to let loose — and some tend to overindulge. Because of the welcoming and casual nature of Mexico, many visitors believe that the sale of alcoholic beverages — or illegal drugs — is unregulated. This belief is simply not true. The legal drinking age in Mexico is 18, and technically, you're not allowed to drink openly in public. However, if you're not acting intoxicated, you can generally enjoy a beer or even a cocktail while you stroll around town.

As with most things in Mexico, it's not so much what you do but how you do it. Although you can drink on public beaches, you can't be inebriated in public, so once again, beware of how much you drink and how well you can handle your alcohol intake. White-clad police patrolling Mexico's beaches are a common sight.

 With regard to drugs, let me get straight to the point: They're illegal, and carrying even a small amount of marijuana or cocaine can earn you a very unpleasant trip to jail. So keep your trip free of undesired encounters with the law and don't carry, buy, or use any kind of drugs. Remember that Mexican law states that you're guilty until proven innocent.

A Jeep Rental Is Really $10 a Day

One of the most common lures a timeshare salesperson uses is the "Rent a Jeep for $10 per day" enticement. Sure, it's true that the Jeep is only $10, but only after you spend up to half a day listening to an often high-pressured sales pitch. You decide — what's your vacation time really worth? And always remember: *If it looks too good to be true. . . .*

If in Trouble, Pay a Mordida

The concept of paying off someone for a favor or to overlook a transgression is as clichéd as the image of the sleeping Mexican under his sombrero. Although the idea of paying a *mordida* (translated literally as "little bite") may have been rooted in truth for a long time, in Mexico's new political era, an active campaign is underway to keep dishonesty to a minimum and to clean house of corrupt public servants. Many old-school traffic cops will still take a bribe when offered; however, officers belonging to the new generation of federal policemen are tested for honesty, and the penalties for corrupt behavior are severe — as are the penalties for those civilians inducing corruption by offering bribes to police officers. My suggestion is don't offer a "tip" or mordida to ease your way out of trouble; the best course of action is to simply act politely and see what the problem is.

You Can Go Everywhere Wearing Just Your Swimsuit

You may be in a seaside resort, but keep in mind that it's also a home and place of business for many Mexicans. Wearing swim trunks or a *pareo* (sarong) skirt wrapped around your bikini while you're on your way to the beach is fine, but I recommend that you put on a shirt or a sundress when you plan to explore the town or when you take a tour that involves riding around in a bus. You can still go casual, but Mexicans frown upon tourists who can't tell the difference between beach and town — especially true when it comes to going into any church wearing inappropriate clothing.

 If you want to blend in, just take a few minutes to see what the locals wear around town. Usually, walking shorts and T-shirts are fine everywhere. One more thing: Topless sunbathing is neither customary nor legal in Mexico — so avoid problems with the law and keep your top on. One exception is in Playa del Carmen, where topless tanning is common.

Mexico Is a Desert, and It's Hot Everywhere

It's not true that Mexico is arid year-round: The geography of Mexico includes pine forests, and occasional snowfalls hit some of the country's higher elevations. Although the Yucatán beach resorts covered in this book do enjoy sultry climates, bringing along a sweater or light jacket for cool evenings is always wise, especially during winter months.

Chapter 18

Ten Most Delicious Yucatecan Dishes

. . . .

In This Chapter

▶ Discovering the region's most notable specialties and sauces

▶ Indulging in uniquely Mexican beverages

. . . .

Some like it hot . . . and then there's Mexican food! But true Mexican cuisine is noted more for its unique way of combining flavors — sweet and hot, chocolate and chiles — than for its fire appeal.

This chapter explains some of the most flavorful and traditional Mexican dishes popular in the Yucatán region that you're likely to see on a menu here — go ahead and be adventurous! Let your taste buds have a vacation from the foods you know and explore the favored flavors of Mexico.

Pescado Tikik-Chik

You're in a Mexican beach resort, so you're almost certain to indulge in the fresh fish and seafood. One of the most traditional and tasty ways to prepare fish is to grill it after it's marinated in a flavorful sauce. The name of this preparation — and the spices in the sauce — vary by region. Along the Yucatán coast, the Mexican-Caribbean variation of this fish is called *tikik-chik* or *tikin-chik* and is prepared by marinating the fish in a sauce of Worcestershire, lime juice, sour-orange juice, mild red-pepper paste, and *achiote* — annatto seed paste. The fish is then sandwiched between two tikin palm fronds and cooked slowly over a wood fire. Yum!

Pibil

Pibil is a thick, rich sauce used to prepare either pork or chicken. The traditional cooking method calls for the meat to be first marinated in this sauce made from *achiote* (annatto seed paste) plus a mixture of bitter orange juice, onions, tomatoes, habanero peppers, and the herb *epazote.* The meat is then wrapped in banana leaves and cooked in an underground pit, called a *pib.*

Cochinita Pibil is shredded pork in *pibil* sauce, traditionally served in tacos (corn tortillas). Typical garnishes include *Xnipec* (minced purple onions and habanero peppers in sour orange juice) or pickled onions (a milder version of *Xnipec,* prepared without habanero peppers).

Tamales

Tamales served in the Yucatán area are quite different from the ones typically found in the United States, which tend to be compact and greasy. Here, these tasty bundles of corn dough are cooked in several different ways, but all of them are wrapped in banana leaves, rather than the corn husks that are used in the central and northern regions of Mexico. They come with a variety of fillings, but usually include pork or chicken.

One popular variety is the *Vaporcitos* (translated as "little steamed ones"), steamed tamales filled with either chicken or corn in a red sauce made with annatto seed paste, tomatoes, oregano, onions, and garlic. Other tamales are baked rather than steamed; these types are called *chachaquas.* A popular variation is the *Tamal Pibipollo,* which is a huge chicken-filled tamale wrapped in banana leaves and cooked in an underground pit *(pib).* These tamales look charred due to their method of cooking, but when you open the leaves (which you don't eat), you cut into a fluffy, cake-like tamale filled with juicy chicken. The bean-filled version of this pit-baked tamale is called *Tamal de Espelóns* (espelóns are tiny black beans). *Colados* are tamales where the dough is cooked by simmering it in chicken broth and then wrapped in banana leaves and steamed.

Panuchos

The Yucatán's favorite snack, the *panucho,* is a must to try when you visit these lands. Panuchos are pan-fried corn tortillas, which puff up and are then slit and filled with refried beans and shredded pork or chicken. The tortilla is then topped with lettuce and accompanied by pickled onions.

Salbutes

One of the most traditional dishes in Yucatecan cuisine, *salbutes* are usually served as a snack or appetizer. A Mayan version of an enchilada, they're made from a corn tortilla dipped in a pumpkin seed puree, which is stuffed with hard-boiled eggs, topped with more puree, and served warm with a mild tomato sauce.

Huevos Motuleños

Mexican food lovers and connoisseurs would frown if I said that *huevos motuleños* are the Yucatán's version of the traditional Mexican *huevos rancheros*. Instead, I'll say that, though they share the same basic principles of assembly, *motuleños* are in a class of their own. This layered dish consists of refried beans spread on a plate topped by a pan-fried corn tortilla, topped by a fried egg, followed by a lightly spiced tomato sauce, another fried tortilla, and then more sauce. The whole creation is finished off with chopped ham, peas, and fried plantain slices.

Ceviche

Ceviche is one of Mexico's more traditional ways to enjoy fish and seafood. Ceviche is usually made of fish, but it may also be made from other seafood, including shrimp, octopus, crab, and even conch (the last is a Cancún specialty). The fresh fish — or seafood — is marinated in lime and vinegar and mixed with chopped tomatoes, onions, and — depending on the region — cucumbers and carrots. Note that the lime and vinegar effectively "cook" the fish or seafood.

Puchero

The traditional Sunday dish in the Yucatán, *puchero* is a tasty three-meat (chicken, pork, and beef) stew with mashed vegetables and cooked plantains. People in the Yucatán say that Sundays aren't complete unless they have puchero.

Liquados

Not quite a meal, yet more than a beverage, *liquados* are blended drinks of fresh fruit, ice, and either water or milk. Popular flavors include mango, banana, pineapple, or watermelon. You can also make up your own combination of tropical fruit flavors. They're delicious, especially in the sultry heat.

Café de Olla

The popularity and tradition of drinking coffee is nothing new to Mexico, so to experience a taste of the past, try the traditional Mexican version called *café de olla*. The espresso-strength coffee is prepared in an earthenware pot and spiced with cinnamon, cloves, and raw brown sugar. It's certain to wake you up!

Appendix

Quick Concierge

Abbreviations

Common address abbreviations include *Apdo.* (post office box), *Av.* or *Ave.* (*avenida;* avenue), *Blvd. (boulevard), c/* (*calle;* street), *Calz.* (*calzada;* boulevard), *Dept.* (apartments), and *s/n* (*sin numero* or without a number).

The "C" on faucets stands for *caliente* (hot), and "F" stands for *fría* (cold). "PB" *(planta baja)* means ground floor, and most buildings count the next floor up as the first floor (1).

American Express

All major resort destinations have local American Express representatives. For a detailed list of all representatives, visit the AmEx Web site at www.american express.com/mexico. For credit card and traveler's checks information, call ☎ **800-504-0400** toll-free inside Mexico. The office that services the destinations covered in this guide is located in Cancún (Av. Tulum 408; ☎ 998-884-6942).

ATMs

Automated teller machines are widely available in the major resort towns, although you find fewer in smaller destinations. They're a great option to get cash at an excellent exchange rate. To find the closest ATM, visit these Web sites for the most popular networks: Plus (www.visa.com/pd/atm) and Cirrus (www.mastercard.com/atm). See Chapter 5 for further details.

Business Hours

In general, businesses in resort destinations are open daily between 9 a.m. and 8 p.m.; although many close between 2 and 4 p.m. Smaller businesses also tend to close on Sundays. The larger resort destinations have extended business hours — many shops stay open until 9 or 10 p.m. Bank hours are Monday to Friday 8:30 or 9 a.m. to anywhere between 3 and 7 p.m. Increasingly, banks are offering Saturday hours in at least one branch.

Credit Cards

Most stores, restaurants, and hotels accept credit cards. However, smaller destinations along the Riviera Maya, such as Tulum, where telephone lines aren't always available to process the authorization for the charge, may not be so credit-card friendly. The same goes for smaller, family-run shops and restaurants. You can withdraw cash from your credit card at most ATMs, but make sure that you know your PIN and you've cleared the card for foreign withdrawals with your bank. For credit-card emergencies, call the following numbers: **American Express** ☎ 001-880-221-7282, **MasterCard** ☎ 001-880-307-7309, and **Visa** ☎ 001-880-336-8472. These numbers connect you to the U.S. toll-free numbers to report lost or stolen credit cards; however, the call is not toll-free from Mexico.

Currency

The currency in Mexico is the Mexican peso. Paper currency comes in denominations of 20, 50, 100, 200, and 500 pesos.

Coins come in denominations of 1, 2, 5, 10, 20 pesos, and 50 centavos (100 centavos equal 1 peso). The currency-exchange rate is about 11 pesos to one U.S. dollar.

Customs

All travelers to Mexico are required to present proof of citizenship, such as a valid passport, an original birth certificate with a raised seal, or naturalization papers, and also need to have a Mexican tourist card (FMT), which is free of charge and can be attained through travel agencies and airlines and at all boarder-crossing points going into Mexico. For more information, see Chapter 6.

Doctors/Dentists

Every embassy and consulate can recommend local doctors and dentists with good training and modern equipment; some of the doctors and dentists even speak English. See the list of embassies and consulates under the "Embassies/Consulates," section later in this appendix. Hotels with a large foreign clientele can often recommend English-speaking doctors as well.

Drug Laws

To be blunt, don't use or possess illegal drugs in Mexico. Mexican officials have no tolerance for drug users, and jail is their solution. If you go to jail, you have very little hope of getting out until the sentence (usually a long one) is completed or heavy fines or bribes are paid. Remember, in Mexico, the legal system assumes that you're guilty until proven innocent. (*Note:* It isn't uncommon to be befriended by a fellow user, only to be turned in by that "friend," who then collects a bounty.) Bring prescription drugs in their original containers. If possible, pack a copy of the original prescription with the generic name of the drug. U.S. Customs officials are also on the lookout for diet drugs that are sold in Mexico but are illegal in the United

States. Possession of these drugs may land you in a U.S. jail. If you buy antibiotics over the counter (which you can do in Mexico) — say, for a sinus infection — and still have some left, you probably won't be hassled by U.S. Customs.

Electricity

The electrical system in Mexico is 110 volts AC (60 cycles), as it is in the United States and Canada, but in reality, it may cycle more slowly and overheat your appliances. To compensate, select a medium or low speed for hair dryers. Many older hotels still have electrical outlets for flat, two-prong plugs; you'll need an adapter for any modern electrical apparatus that has three prongs or an enlarged end on one of the two prongs. Many first-class and deluxe hotels have the three-holed outlets (*trifásicos* in Spanish). Hotels that don't have these outlets may have adapters to loan, but to be sure, carry your own.

Embassies/Consulates

Embassies and consulates can provide valuable lists of doctors and lawyers, as well as regulations concerning marriages in Mexico. Contrary to popular belief, your embassy cannot get you out of a Mexican jail, provide postal or banking services, or fly you home when you run out of money. However, consular officers can provide you with advice on most matters and problems. Most countries have a representative embassy in Mexico City, and many have consular offices or representatives in the provinces.

The embassy of the **United States** is in Mexico City (Paseo de la Reforma 305; ☎ 55-5209-9100). Its hours are Monday to Friday 8:30 a.m. to 5:30 p.m. You can visit the embassy's Web site at www.usembassy-mexico.gov for a list of street addresses for the U.S. consulates inside Mexico. U.S. consular agencies are

in Cancún (☎ 998-883-0272) and in
Cozumel (☎ 987-872-4574).

The embassy of **Australia** is in Mexico City
at Rubén Darío 55, Polanco (☎ **55-1101-
2200;** fax: 55-5531-9552). It's open Monday
to Friday 9 a.m. to 1 p.m.

The Embassy of **Canada** is also in Mexico
City (Schiller 529, in Polanco; ☎ **55-5724-
7900**). It's open Monday through Friday
9 a.m. to 1 p.m. and 2 to 5 p.m. (At other
times, the name of an officer on duty is
posted on the embassy door.) Visit the Web
site at www.canada.org.mx for a complete list of the addresses of the consular
agencies in Mexico. In Cancún, the
Canadian Consulate is at Plaza Caracol 3rd
floor, (☎ 998-883-3360; e-mail: cancun@
canada.org.mx). It's open Monday
through Friday 9 a.m to 5 p.m.

The embassy of **New Zealand** in Mexico
City is at José Luis Lagrange 103, 10th
floor, Col. Los Morales Polanco (☎ **55-
5283-9460;** fax: 5-5283-9460; e-mail:
kiwimexico@compuserve.com.mx).

The Embassy of the **United Kingdom** is at
Río Lerma 71, Col. Cuauhtemoc (☎ **55-
5207-2089,** 55-5242-8500) in Mexico City.
The embassy's Web site, which you can
visit at www.embajadabritanica.
com.mx, has an updated list of honorary
consuls in Mexico. Honorary British consuls are in Acapulco (☎ 744-484-1735),
Cancún (☎ 998-881-0100), and Huatulco
(☎ 958-587-1742).

The Embassy of **Ireland** is located in Mexico
City on Blvd. Cerrada Avila Camacho 76,
3rd floor, Col. Lomas de Chapultepec
(☎ **55-5520-5803**).

The embassy of **South Africa** is also in
Mexico City on Andres Bello, 109th floor,
Col. Polanco (☎ **55-5282-9260**).

Emergencies

In case of emergency, always contact your
embassy or consulate. For police emergencies, you must dial ☎ **060,** which will
connect you to the local police department. Remember that in most cases, the
person answering the phone doesn't speak
English. The 24-hour tourist help line from
Mexico City is ☎ **800-903-9200** or 55-5250-
0151. A tourist legal assistance office
(Procuraduría del Turista) is located in
Mexico City (☎ 55-5625-8153, 55-5625-
8154). Although the phones are frequently
busy, they do offer 24-hour service, and an
English-speaking person is always available.

Health

No special immunizations are required. As
is often true when traveling anywhere in
the world, intestinal problems are the most
common afflictions experienced by travelers. Drink only bottled water and stay
away from uncooked foods, especially
fruits and vegetables. Antibiotics and
antidiarrheal medications are readily available in all drugstores.

Hotlines

The **Mexico Hotline** (☎ 800-44-MEXICO)
is an excellent source for general information; you can request brochures on the
country and get answers to the most commonly asked questions. While in Mexico,
contact the 24-hour tourist help line,
Infotur (☎ 800-903-9200), for information
regarding hotels, restaurants, attractions,
hospitals with English-speaking staff, and
so on.

Information

The best source of information is the
tourist help line **Infotur** (☎ 800-903-9200);
however, it's important that you have a
general idea of the information you're
requesting — the approximate name of the
hotel or restaurant, the name or subject

matter of the museum, and so on. You can also find telephone-number information inside Mexico by dialing ☎ 040; however, it's very common to find that the telephone numbers are not listed under the known name of the establishment. A reminder: Very few information operators speak English.

Internet Access

In large cities and resort areas, most 4- and 5-star hotels now offer business centers or cafes with Internet access. You can also find cybercafes in most other destinations — even in remote spots, Internet access is common now — it's often their best way of communicating with the outside world. If you plan to check your e-mail while in Mexico, one of the easiest ways is to register for a Web-based e-mail address, such as those from Hotmail or Yahoo!.

Language

The official language in Mexico is Spanish, but you'll find that a fair number of Mexicans who live and work in resort areas speak some English. Mexicans are very patient when it comes to foreigners trying to speak Spanish. See Chapter 2 for commonly used terms in Spanish.

Legal Aid

Should you require legal assistance while in Mexico, see "Embassies/Consulates" and "Emergencies," earlier in this appendix.

Liquor Laws

The legal drinking age in Mexico is 18; however, it's extremely rare that anyone is asked for identification or denied purchase. Grocery stores sell everything from beer and wine to national and imported liquors. You can buy liquor 24 hours a day, but during major elections and a few official holidays, dry laws often are enacted as

long as 24 hours beforehand. The laws apply to foreign tourists as well as local residents, even though it's not uncommon to find a few hotels and nightclubs that manage to obtain special permits to sell alcohol. Mexican authorities are beginning to target drunk drivers more aggressively. It's a good idea to drive defensively.

Drinking in the street is not legal, but many tourists do it. Use your better judgment and try to avoid carrying on while sporting beer bottles and cans — you're not only exposing yourself to the eyes of the authorities, but most Mexicans consider public intoxication tacky behavior.

Mail

Postage for a postcard or letter is 59¢, and the item may arrive at its destination anywhere between one to six weeks after you send it. A registered letter costs $1.90. Sending a package can be quite expensive — the Mexican postal service charges $8 per kilo (2.20 pounds) — and unreliable; it takes between two and six weeks, if it arrives at all. Packages are frequently lost within the Mexican postal system, although the situation has improved in recent years. Federal Express, DHL, UPS, or other reputable, international-mail services are the best options.

Newspapers/Magazines

A national English-language newspaper no longer exists in Mexico, however newspaper kiosks in larger Mexican cities carry a selection of English-language newspapers (a day old) as well as magazines. Most resort towns have their own local publications in English, which provide helpful hints and fun reading tailored to visitors. In Cancún, you can find a wealth of information in *Cancún Tips,* a monthly publication in two formats: a small guide, and a larger, glossy magazine.

Pharmacies

Farmacias will sell you just about anything you want, with or without a prescription. Most pharmacies are open Monday to Saturday 8 a.m. to 8 p.m. Generally, one or two 24-hour pharmacies are located in the major resort areas. Pharmacies take turns staying open during off-hours, so if you're in a smaller town and you need to buy medicine after normal hours, ask for the *farmacia de turno* (pharmacist on duty).

Police

It's quite common to find that the majority of police forces in tourist areas are very protective of international visitors. Several cities, including Cancún, have gone so far as to set up a special corps of English-speaking tourist police to assist with directions, guidance, and more. In case of a police emergency, dial ☎ 060 to contact the local police department, keeping in mind that, unless you're dealing with tourist police, the force is unlikely to speak English.

Restrooms

Public restrooms are usually more of an adventure than a service — you can never tell whether they'll be clean or if toilet paper will be available. Public restrooms usually charge anywhere between 2 and 5 pesos (20 to 50¢), which gives you access and a few squares of toilet paper.

Safety

Most resort areas in Mexico are very safe; however, it's better to be prepared than sorry. A few points to keep in mind: Before you leave home, prepare for the theft or loss of your travel documents by making two photocopies of them. Keep each copy and the original documents in separate places. Lock your passport and valuables in the hotel safety-deposit box. Keep credit-card company phone numbers and the numbers of traveler's checks somewhere other than your purse or wallet. Don't dress or behave in a conspicuous manner. When visiting crowded places, be aware of your wallet or purse at all times. Leave your best jewelry at home — who wants jewelry tan lines anyway?

Taxes

Most of Mexico has a 15% value-added tax (IVA) on goods and services, and it's supposed to be included in the posted price. This tax is 10% in Cancún and Cozumel, as they're considered "port zones" and qualify for a reduction of duties. Mexico charges all visitors an entry tax of $15, which is usually included in the price of your plane ticket. Mexico also imposes an exit tax of around $18 on every foreigner leaving the country, which again, is usually included in the price of airline tickets.

Telephone/Fax

After a recent countrywide system change, all telephone numbers in Mexico are now seven digits plus a three-digit area code, except for Mexico City, Guadalajara, and Monterrey, where local calls require that you dial the last eight digits of the published phone number. Many fax numbers are also regular telephone numbers — you have to ask whoever answers your call for the fax tone. *("Me da tono de fax, por favor.")* **Cellphones** are very popular for small businesses in resort areas and smaller communities. To dial a cell number inside the same area code, dial 044 and then the number — depending on the area, you may need to dial the last seven digits or the seven digits plus the three-digit area code. To dial a cellphone from anywhere else in Mexico, first dial 01 and then the ten-digit number, including the area code.

To dial any number inside Mexico from the United States, just dial 011-52 plus the ten-digit number.

The country code for Mexico is 52. To call home from Mexico, dial 00 plus the country code you're calling and then the area code and phone number. To call the United States and Canada, you need to dial 001 plus the area code and the number. The country code for the United Kingdom is 44; the country code for New Zealand is 64, and the country code for Australia 61. You can reach an **AT&T** operator at ☎ 01-800-288-2872, **MCI** at ☎ 01-800-021-8000, **Sprint** at ☎ 001-800-877-8000, and **British Telecom** (BT) at ☎ 01-800-123-0244. Mexican pay phones may sometimes require a coin deposit.

To call operator assistance for calls inside Mexico, dial 020; for operator assistance for international calls, dial 090. Both numbers provide assistance for person-to-person and collect calls.

Time Zone

Mexico's Yucatán peninsula falls within **Central Standard Time.** Also, Mexico currently observes Daylight Savings Time.

Tipping

Most service employees in Mexico count on tips for the majority of their income — especially true for bellboys and waiters. Bellboys should receive the equivalent of 50¢ to $1 U.S. per bag; waiters generally receive 10% to 20%, depending on the level of service. In Mexico, it's not customary to tip taxi drivers, unless you hire them by the hour, or they provide guide or other special services. Don't use U.S. coins to tip.

Water

Most hotels have decanters or bottles of purified water in the rooms, and the better hotels have purified water from regular taps or special taps marked *agua purificada.* Some hotels charge for in-room bottled water. Virtually any hotel, restaurant, or bar will bring you purified water if you specifically request it, but they usually charge you. Bottled, purified water is sold widely at drugstores and grocery stores. Some popular brands are Santa María, Ciel, and Bonafont. Evian and other imported brands are also widely available.

Toll-Free Numbers and Web Sites

Airlines Serving Cancún Airport

Aeromexico
☎ 800-237-6639 in U.S.
☎ 01-800-0214010 in Mexico
www.aeromexico.com

Alaska Airlines
☎ 800-252-7522
www.alaskaair.com

American Airlines
☎ 800-433-7300
www.aa.com

American Trans Air
☎ 800-225-2995
www.ata.com

British Airways
☎ 800-247-9297
☎ 0345-222-111 or 0845-77-333-77 in Britain
www.british-airways.com

Continental Airlines
☎ 800-525-0280
www.continental.com

Delta Air Lines
☎ 800-221-1212
www.delta.com

Mexicana
☎ 800-531-7921 in U.S.
☎ 01800-502-2000 in Mexico
www.mexicana.com

Northwest Airlines
☎ 800-225-2525
www.nwa.com

United Airlines
☎ 800-241-6522
www.united.com

US Airways
☎ 800-428-4322
www.usairways.com

Major Car-Rental Agencies

Advantage
☎ 800-777-5500
www.advantagerentacar.com

Alamo
☎ 800-327-9633
www.goalamo.com

Auto Europe
☎ 800-223-5555
www.autoeurope.com

Avis
☎ 800-331-1212 in Continental U.S.
☎ 800-TRY-AVIS in Canada
www.avis.com

Budget
☎ 800-527-0700
www.budget.com

Dollar
☎ 800-800-4000
www.dollar.com

Enterprise
☎ 800-325-8007
www.enterprise.com

Hertz
☎ 800-654-3131
www.hertz.com

National
☎ 800-CAR-RENT
www.nationalcar.com

Payless
☎ 800-PAYLESS
www.paylesscarrental.com

Thrifty
☎ 800-367-2277
www.thrifty.com

Major Local Hotel and Motel Chains

Best Western International
☎ 800-528-1234
www.bestwestern.com

Camino Real
☎ 800-722-6466
www.caminoreal.com

Days Inn
☎ 800-325-2525
www.daysinn.com

Dreams Resorts
☎ 866-237-3267
www.dreamsresorts.com

Fiesta Americana
☎ 800-FIESTA-1
www.fiestaamericana.com

Hilton Hotels
☎ 800-HILTONS
www.hilton.com

Holiday Inn
☎ 800-HOLIDAY
www.holiday-inn.com

Hyatt Hotels and Resorts
☎ 800-228-9000
www.hyatt.com

Inter-Continental Hotels and Resorts
☎ 888-567-8725
www.interconti.com

Le Méridien Hotel
☎ 800-543-4300
www.lemeridien-hotels.com

Marriott Hotels (and JW Marriott)
☎ 800-228-9290
www.marriott.com

Omni
☎ 800-THEOMNI
www.omnihotels.com

Quinta Real
☎ 888-561-2817
www.quintareal.com

Ritz-Carlton Hotel
☎ 800-241-3333
www.ritzcarlton.com

Sheraton Hotels and Resorts
☎ 800-325-3535
www.sheraton.com

Westin Hotels and Resorts
☎ 800-937-8461
www.westin.com

Where to Get More Information

The following tourist boards and embassies provide valuable information regarding traveling in Mexico, including information on entry requirements and customs allowances.

The **Mexico Tourism Board** (www.visitmexico.com) has offices in several major North American cities, in addition to the main office in Mexico City (☎ 55-5203-1103). The toll-free information number is ☎ **800-44-MEXICO** in the United States and Canada. U.S. offices are in Chicago (300 N. Michigan, 4th Floor, Chicago, IL, 60601; ☎ 312-228-0517); Houston (4507 San Jacinto, Suite 308, Houston, TX, 77074; ☎ 713-772-2581, ext.105); Los Angeles, CA (2401 W. 6th St., Los Angeles, CA, 90057; ☎ 310-282-9112; fax: 310-282-9116); Miami, FL (1200 NW 78th St., Miami, FL, 33126; ☎ 305-718-4095), and New York, NY (375 Park Ave., Suite 1905, New York, NY, 10021; ☎ 212-308-2110). In addition, the Mexican Embassy Tourism Delegate is in Washington, D.C. (1911 Pennsylvania Ave., Washington, DC 20005; ☎ 202-728-1750). Locations in Canada include Montreal (1 Place Ville-Marie, Suite 1931, Montreal, QUEB, H3B 2C3; ☎ 514-871-1052); Toronto (2 Floor St. W., Suite 1502, Toronto, ON, M4W 3E2; ☎ 416-925-0704); and Vancouver (999 W. Hastings, Suite 1110, Vancouver, BC, V6C 2W2; ☎ 604-669-2845). The Mexican Embassy office is at 1500-45 O'Connor St., Ottawa, ON, K1P 1A4 (☎ 613-233-8988; fax: 613-235-9123).

The **U.S. State Department** and the Overseas Citizens Services division (☎ 202-647-5225) offer a consular information sheet on Mexico that contains a compilation of safety, medical, driving, and general travel information gleaned from reports by official U.S. State Department offices in Mexico. In addition to calling, you can request the consular information sheet by fax at ☎ 202-647-3000. The State Department is also on the Internet: Check out http://travel.state.gov/mexico.html for the consular information sheet on Mexico; http://travel.state.gov/travel_warnings.html for other consular information sheets and travel warnings; and http://travel.state.gov/tips_mexico.html for the State Department's *Tips for Travelers to Mexico.*

For a **24-hour Tourist Help Line,** dial ☎ 800-903-9200 toll-free inside Mexico, and you can get information from English-speaking operators as to where to go for medical assistance and other types of assistance. It's also a great source for general tourism information. You can always find helpful operators who will try to get the information that you need. To call this office from the United States, dial ☎ 800-482-9832.

Health information

The **Centers for Disease Control** Hotline (www.cdc.gov/travel) is an excellent source for medical information for travelers to Mexico and elsewhere. The main Centers for Disease Control (CDC) Web site (www.cdc.gov/) provides detailed information on health issues for specific countries; otherwise, you can call the CDC directly at ☎ 800-311-3435 or 404-639-3534. For travelers to Mexico and Central America, the number with recorded messages about specific health issues related to this region is ☎ 877-FYI-TRIP. The toll-free fax number for requesting information is ☎ 888-232-3299.

Embassies and consulates provide valuable lists of doctors and lawyers, as well as regulations concerning travel in Mexico (see "Embassies and Consulates," earlier in this appendix).

Local sources of information

Local **tourist information offices** offer all kinds of information to travelers, including brochures, maps, and destination-specific magazines and posters. If you want them to mail information to you, allow four to six weeks for it to reach you. Try these offices:

- ✔ **Cancún Convention and Visitors Bureau** (Blvd. Kukulkan km. 9, Zona Hotelera, Cancún, Quintana Roo, Mexico 77500; ☎ 998-884-6531; Internet: www.cancun.info).

- ✔ **Isla Mujeres Tourism Office** (Av. Rueda Medina 130, Isla Mujeres, Quintano Roo, Mexico, C.P. 77400) across from the main pier between Immigration and Customs; ☎ 998-877-0767; e-mail: infoisla@prodigy.net.mx).

Mexico on the Web

Following is a list of several Web sites where you can find updated information about Mexico's most popular beach resorts. But keep in mind that most of the companies that these Web sites recommend received this lofty status by paying some sort of advertising fee.

The **Mexico Tourism Promotion Council** developed another official site www.visitmexico.com) with more current information on the different destinations in Mexico. The site features sections for travelers divided by region; a good search engine usually takes you to the information you're looking for.

For low-impact travel planning, visit the **Eco Travels in Mexico** section of the award-winning Web site www.planeta.com. You can find up-to-date information on reliable eco-tour operators in Mexico. This site, updated monthly, is also an excellent source for banks and telephone services.

The electronic version of **Connect Magazine** (www.mexconnect.com) is the ideal site to begin a more in-depth, online exploration about when and where to visit Mexico. The site offers an index where you can find everything from out-of-the-way adventures to Mexico's history to recommended accommodations.

Cancún South (www.cancunsouth.com) is a great site for independent travelers looking to explore the Riviera Maya. The site is easy to navigate and offers a wealth of information specific to the area.

Cozumel.net (www.cozumel.net) provides detailed information about the island's life. In my opinion, this site has the most reliable information about Cozumel — it even lists ferry schedules in the "About Cozumel" section.

Other Internet travel resources

Following is a selection of Web sites that can help you with the important stuff related to your Yucatán vacation — figuring out where to get cash, how to ask for a cold beer, how to find really great deals, and so on.

At **Foreign Languages for Travelers** (www.travlang.com), you can learn basic terms in more than 70 languages and click on any underlined phrase to hear what it sounds like. *Note:* Free audio software and speakers are required.

Intellicast (www.intellicast.com) has weather forecasts for all 50 United States and cities around the world. *Note:* Temperatures are in Celsius for many international destinations.

The **Universal Currency Converter** (ww.xe.net/ucc/) lets you see what your dollar or pound is worth in more than 100 other countries.

With **Visa ATM Locator** (www.visa.com) or **MasterCard ATM Locator** (www.mastercard.com), you can find ATMs in hundreds of cities in the United States and around the world.

Travel Secrets (www.travelsecrets.com) is one of the best travel sites around. The site offers advice and tips on how to find the lowest prices for airlines, hotels, and cruises, and it also provides a listing of links for airfare deals, airlines, booking engines, discount travel, resources, hotels, and travel magazines.

Index

SINESS, CAREERS & PERSONAL FINANCE

7645-5307-0   0-7645-5331-3 *†

Also available:

- Accounting For Dummies †
  0-7645-5314-3
- Business Plans Kit For Dummies †
  0-7645-5365-8
- Cover Letters For Dummies
  0-7645-5224-4
- Frugal Living For Dummies
  0-7645-5403-4
- Leadership For Dummies
  0-7645-5176-0
- Managing For Dummies
  0-7645-1771-6

- Marketing For Dummies
  0-7645-5600-2
- Personal Finance For Dummies *
  0-7645-2590-5
- Project Management
  For Dummies
  0-7645-5283-X
- Resumes For Dummies †
  0-7645-5471-9
- Selling For Dummies
  0-7645-5363-1
- Small Business Kit For Dummies *†
  0-7645-5093-4

ME & BUSINESS COMPUTER BASICS

7645-4074-2   0-7645-3758-X

Also available:

- ACT! 6 For Dummies
  0-7645-2645-6
- iLife '04 All-in-One Desk Reference
  For Dummies
  0-7645-7347-0
- iPAQ For Dummies
  0-7645-6769-1
- Mac OS X Panther Timesaving
  Techniques For Dummies
  0-7645-5812-9
- Macs For Dummies
  0-7645-5656-8
- Microsoft Money 2004 For Dummies
  0-7645-4195-1

- Office 2003 All-in-One Desk
  Reference For Dummies
  0-7645-3883-7
- Outlook 2003 For Dummies
  0-7645-3759-8
- PCs For Dummies
  0-7645-4074-2
- TiVo For Dummies
  0-7645-6923-6
- Upgrading and Fixing PCs
  For Dummies
  0-7645-1665-5
- Windows XP Timesaving
  Techniques For Dummies
  0-7645-3748-2

OD, HOME, GARDEN, HOBBIES, MUSIC & PETS

7645-5295-3   0-7645-5232-5

Also available:

- Bass Guitar For Dummies
  0-7645-2487-9
- Diabetes Cookbook For Dummies
  0-7645-5230-9
- Gardening For Dummies *
  0-7645-5130-2
- Guitar For Dummies
  0-7645-5106-X
- Holiday Decorating For Dummies
  0-7645-2570-0
- Home Improvement All-In-One
  For Dummies
  0-7645-5680-0

- Knitting For Dummies
  0-7645-5395-X
- Piano For Dummies
  0-7645-5105-1
- Puppies For Dummies
  0-7645-5255-4
- Scrapbooking For Dummies
  0-7645-7208-3
- Senior Dogs For Dummies
  0-7645-5818-8
- Singing For Dummies
  0-7645-2475-5
- 30-Minute Meals For Dummies
  0-7645-2589-1

ERNET & DIGITAL MEDIA

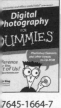

7645-1664-7   0-7645-6924-4

Also available:

- 2005 Online Shopping Directory
  For Dummies
  0-7645-7495-7
- CD & DVD Recording For Dummies
  0-7645-5956-7
- eBay For Dummies
  0-7645-5654-1
- Fighting Spam For Dummies
  0-7645-5965-6
- Genealogy Online For Dummies
  0-7645-5964-8
- Google For Dummies
  0-7645-4420-9

- Home Recording For Musicians
  For Dummies
  0-7645-1634-5
- The Internet For Dummies
  0-7645-4173-0
- iPod & iTunes For Dummies
  0-7645-7772-7
- Preventing Identity Theft
  For Dummies
  0-7645-7336-5
- Pro Tools All-in-One Desk
  Reference For Dummies
  0-7645-5714-9
- Roxio Easy Media Creator
  For Dummies
  0-7645-7131-1

parate Canadian edition also available
parate U.K. edition also available

able wherever books are sold. For more information or to order direct: U.S. customers
www.dummies.com or call 1-877-762-2974.
customers visit www.wileyeurope.com or call 0800 243407. Canadian customers visit
v.wiley.ca or call 1-800-567-4797.

SPORTS, FITNESS, PARENTING, RELIGION & SPIRITUALITY

0-7645-5146-9

0-7645-5418-2

Also available:
- Adoption For Dummies
  0-7645-5488-3
- Basketball For Dummies
  0-7645-5248-1
- The Bible For Dummies
  0-7645-5296-1
- Buddhism For Dummies
  0-7645-5359-3
- Catholicism For Dummies
  0-7645-5391-7
- Hockey For Dummies
  0-7645-5228-7

- Judaism For Dummies
  0-7645-5299-6
- Martial Arts For Dummies
  0-7645-5358-5
- Pilates For Dummies
  0-7645-5397-6
- Religion For Dummies
  0-7645-5264-3
- Teaching Kids to Read
  For Dummies
  0-7645-4043-2
- Weight Training For Dummies
  0-7645-5168-X
- Yoga For Dummies
  0-7645-5117-5

TRAVEL

0-7645-5438-7

0-7645-5453-0

Also available:
- Alaska For Dummies
  0-7645-1761-9
- Arizona For Dummies
  0-7645-6938-4
- Cancún and the Yucatán
  For Dummies
  0-7645-2437-2
- Cruise Vacations For Dummies
  0-7645-6941-4
- Europe For Dummies
  0-7645-5456-5
- Ireland For Dummies
  0-7645-5455-7

- Las Vegas For Dummies
  0-7645-5448-4
- London For Dummies
  0-7645-4277-X
- New York City For Dummies
  0-7645-6945-7
- Paris For Dummies
  0-7645-5494-8
- RV Vacations For Dummies
  0-7645-5443-3
- Walt Disney World & Orlando
  For Dummies
  0-7645-6943-0

GRAPHICS, DESIGN & WEB DEVELOPMENT

0-7645-4345-8

0-7645-5589-8

Also available:
- Adobe Acrobat 6 PDF
  For Dummies
  0-7645-3760-1
- Building a Web Site For Dummies
  0-7645-7144-3
- Dreamweaver MX 2004
  For Dummies
  0-7645-4342-3
- FrontPage 2003 For Dummies
  0-7645-3882-9
- HTML 4 For Dummies
  0-7645-1995-6
- Illustrator CS For Dummies
  0-7645-4084-X

- Macromedia Flash MX 2004
  For Dummies
  0-7645-4358-X
- Photoshop 7 All-in-One Desk
  Reference For Dummies
  0-7645-1667-1
- Photoshop CS Timesaving
  Techniques For Dummies
  0-7645-6782-9
- PHP 5 For Dummies
  0-7645-4166-8
- PowerPoint 2003 For Dummies
  0-7645-3908-6
- QuarkXPress 6 For Dummies
  0-7645-2593-X

NETWORKING, SECURITY, PROGRAMMING & DATABASES

0-7645-6852-3

0-7645-5784-X

Also available:
- A+ Certification For Dummies
  0-7645-4187-0
- Access 2003 All-in-One Desk
  Reference For Dummies
  0-7645-3988-4
- Beginning Programming
  For Dummies
  0-7645-4997-9
- C For Dummies
  0-7645-7068-4
- Firewalls For Dummies
  0-7645-4048-3
- Home Networking For Dummies
  0-7645-42796

- Network Security For Dummie
  0-7645-1679-5
- Networking For Dummies
  0-7645-1677-9
- TCP/IP For Dummies
  0-7645-1760-0
- VBA For Dummies
  0-7645-3989-2
- Wireless All In-One Desk Refer
  For Dummies
  0-7645-7496-5
- Wireless Home Networking
  For Dummies
  0-7645-3910-8